SEEKERS
OF TOMORROW

*Masters of Modern
Science Fiction*

by

SAM MOSKOWITZ

HYPERION PRESS, INC.
WESTPORT, CONNECTICUT

809.3
M911a

Library of Congress Cataloging in Publication Data

Moskowitz, Samuel.
 Seekers of tomorrow.

 Reprint of the ed. published by World Pub. Co.,
Cleveland.
  1. Science fiction—History and criticism.
I. Title.
₍PN3448.S45M66 1973₎ 809'.3876 73-15073
ISBN 0-88355-129-2
ISBN 0-88355-158-6 (pbk.)

Published in 1966
by The World Publishing Company, Cleveland, Ohio.
Copyright 1966, 1964, 1963, 1962, 1961 by Sam Moskowitz.
Reprinted by permission of the copyright owner.

Hyperion reprint edition 1974

Library of Congress Catalogue Number 73-15073

ISBN 0-88355-129-2 (cloth ed.)
ISBN 0-88355-158-6 (paper ed.)

Printed in the United States of America

CONTENTS

Contents

To

Christine

who

understood

INTRODUCTION

No one pretends that science fiction is the tail that wags the dog in the United States. No one pretends that science fiction is in the forefront in trend-setting, but facts require no pretense—or defense. It is no longer uncommon to visit a bookstore with a large paperback section and to see as many as one hundred science-fiction titles on display. The majority of these titles are reprints from science-fiction magazines and clothbound books, and they run the gamut of the range and history of the literature. But predominantly the books are those written by the "modern" science-fiction writers of the past few years.

Science-fiction titles are a regular part of hard-cover book publishing. Significantly, an increasing number of "mainstream" authors are discovering that it is an effective way of presenting certain themes, particularly social criticism. The realization has dawned that Aldous Huxley in *Brave*

1

New World and George Orwell in *1984* had made no mistake in adopting a science-fiction framework any more than had Jonathan Swift in *Gulliver's Travels*. Pierre Boulle, French author of *The Bridge Over the River Kwai,* reverses the positions of man and apes on a distant planet around the star Betelgeuse to expose the weaknesses of man's behavior in *Planet of the Apes;* William Burroughs, fresh from the sensationalism of *Naked Lunch,* takes his lurid satirical observations into space in *Nova Express;* Anthony Burgess, exhilarated by favorable response to *A Clockwork Orange,* moves into the future in *The Wanting Seed* to warn of the social impact of the population explosion. Should there be doubt that these writers adopt the genre because they read modern science fiction, Burgess gives evidence to the point when he attaches the names Heinlein and Asimov to characters in his story.

Among the "angry" talented young stars on the literary horizon, ample evidence is present of fascination with science fiction. Kingsley Amis, highly regarded for such "comic" novels as *Lucky Jim,* gave a series of lectures on science fiction at Princeton University during 1958 and 1959 and collected and expanded these talks into *New Maps of Hell: A Survey of Science Fiction* (Harcourt, Brace & World, 1960), concluding that "at least a dozen current practitioners seem to me to have attained the status of the sound minor writer whose example brings into existence the figure of real standing." He has also edited a series of science-fiction anthologies (with Robert Conquest) underscoring his point. Colin Wilson, who caused a literary stir with *The Outsider,* displays high regard for science fiction. He very much likes the work of Robert A. Heinlein, of whom he states in his book *The Strength to Dream* (1962): "Among living writers of science fiction, he has the most consistently high quality and, together with Weinbaum, is the writer whose work most deserves to be considered as literature." His most laudatory view of science fiction itself is expressed in the lines: "Again one becomes aware that science fiction seems to have escaped the general sense of defeat, the cult of 'the little man' that pervades so much modern writing."

One peculiarity of modern science fiction is that the same stories possess appeal for the teenage student and the literary intellectual. Of the former, the late Max Herzberg, nationally known educator and chairman of the Selection Committee of the Teen Age Book Club, writing in *Scholastic Teacher* for October 8, 1952, pointedly stated: "Teachers who continue to regard all science fiction as trash will do well to look into some of it and test their judgment against the claim of one devotee, for instance, that Robert Heinlein has done work comparable to that of John Erskine." He then announced selections for the Teen Age Book Club by A. E. van Vogt and Edmond Hamilton as well as Heinlein, and recommended that, in addition, teachers sample Ray Bradbury, Murray Leinster, and Clark Ashton Smith.

The influence of science fiction is widespread. The comic books, spearheaded by Superman, abound with its concepts. The current vogue for monster magazines, inaugurated by James Warren and Forrest J. Ackerman's FAMOUS MONSTERS OF FILMLAND, owes as much to the science-fiction magazines as it does to the motion pictures their contents reflect. Even a large number of children's toys and games have evolved from popular elements of the science-fiction story.

The men and women who weave the fabric that forms the tapestry of modern science fiction should therefore be of more than casual interest to the thinking members of our society. The waves created by the notions they have dropped into the communal pool of world ideas have traveled to the four corners of the earth. Their influence may not be profound but it is slowly being recognized, even in the academic world, as undeniably significant. Term papers on science fiction are becoming increasingly numerous; a science-fiction library has been established in a temperature-controlled vault at Harvard College; a specialized space-fiction collection was begun at the university library in Syracuse, N. Y.; a credit course in science fiction has been inaugurated at Colgate University under the direction of Mark Hillegas; a scholarly biannual, EXTRAPOLATION: A SCIENCE-FICTION NEWSLETTER, is being published by the Department of English, The College of Wooster, edited by Thomas D. Clareson. Fundamentally, though, the academic world, like the literary world, possesses no more than the most superficial and elementary information concerning the authors who are the movers of today's science-fiction advance.

This book is an effort to fill that void. Chronologically it follows the author's *Explorers of the Infinite: Shapers of Science Fiction* (World, 1963), a synoptic history of science fiction to 1940. This volume is a webwork history of science fiction from then to 1965, told through the lives, works, and influences of more than a score of its most outstanding practitioners of the past twenty-five years.

Each of the authors treated here was selected for his demonstrable contribution toward building the pattern of today's science fiction. It must be recognized that many of these men (and one woman) are still very much engaged in developing their careers. It is not possible, without historical hindsight, to wrap up an opinion about them with finality, yet their status as leaders can be justified by reference to their accomplishments to date.

Two of the choices perhaps require brief explanation; they carried science fiction into new areas of mass entertainment. Mort Weisinger was not selected for his contributions as an author, but for his role in transferring the ideas of science fiction to the comic magazines, foremost of which is *Superman,* which he edits. Robert Bloch, while a skillful and highly original writer of science fiction, has been included to indicate the debt that the motion picture and television world owes to science fiction in its handling of suspense.

The dominant status of the other authors in shaping the direction of modern science fiction can scarcely be challenged. Yet there is another group of writers whose contributions cannot be ignored. Those are the craftsmen who have written at least one major story so outstanding that it has already become a recognized science-fiction classic. Specific mention is made in the final chapter of this book of such notables. Brief reference is also made to authors who obviously rank high, but who are just entering the summer of their careers.

This volume, therefore, while the most comprehensive dissertation yet published on modern science fiction and the authors who create it, is essentially selective. With the exception of Ray Bradbury, on whose career several monographs have been published, the material in this book represents the most complete biographical and critical treatment the several authors discussed have ever received. For all but two, it is the only serious appraisal in depth yet attempted.

Fundamentally, all material in this book is the result of basic research. Since all but one of the authors were alive at the time of writing, biographical material was obtained, in a majority of the cases, directly from the individual by interviews and correspondence, and supplemented by material from relatives, friends, and other secondary sources.

The entire published science-fiction output of every science-fiction writer discussed in this book (the average career spans more than twenty-five years) was read, or rather reread. With very few exceptions, all the books, periodicals, letters, clippings, and other related material referred to in the text of this book are owned by the writer and on file in his library. As a prelude to writing this book, every science-fiction magazine containing original material ever published in the English language was collected (as well as hundreds in foreign languages), and thousands of the key books, bulletins, newspaper clippings, and related items were assembled. Quite literally, it took thirty years of reading and collecting to make the writing of this book possible.

In the earlier volume, *Explorers of the Infinite,* which covered the first three hundred years of the history of science fiction, each major figure more or less cleanly represented an era or facet of the field. The authors covered in this second volume wrote mainly in the twenty-five year period between 1940 and 1965. Their works, in many cases, appeared contemporaneously. Therefore, this part of the history is a webwork, a reworking of the same period over and over again from the point of reference of each author, until the pattern of the era emerges.

In the process, the roles of all the major editors, particularly that of the tremendously influential John W. Campbell, Jr., are exposed in historical bas-relief. The part played by the science-fiction fan movement in shaping modern science fiction is acknowledged. The contributions of general fiction and specialized magazines to the development of the genre are revealed.

The first part of the book is devoted to six "bridge" authors, men who helped lay the foundation for modern science fiction and whose works spanned both the early and late periods of development.

A second group, Eric Frank Russell, L. Sprague de Camp, and Lester del Rey, represent the precursors of the "moderns," pioneering techniques of storytelling.

With one exception, Clifford D. Simak, the heavy guns of the movement did not get their start until 1939; exemplifying modern science fiction in its purest form are Robert A. Heinlein, A. E. van Vogt, Theodore Sturgeon, Isaac Asimov, Fritz Leiber, as well as Simak.

A third group is characterized by the infusion of the fantasy element, since C. L. Moore, Henry Kuttner, and Robert Bloch were nurtured by WEIRD TALES and later turned to science fiction.

The final group includes three authors who developed independently of the main movement and achieved success on their own terms: Ray Bradbury, Arthur C. Clarke, and Philip José Farmer.

These twenty-one are the masters of modern science fiction. They represent just one step in the history of science fiction, but a major one. What form science fiction may take in the future has not yet crystallized. Perhaps its internationalization will see the rise of major writers in many nations. Predicting that trend, on the basis of present evidence, falls more in the province of science fiction itself than in literary surmise.

It is a particular source of satisfaction to the author that the definition of science fiction given in *Explorers of the Infinite* is beginning to gain circulation and acceptance. Gratifying were statements by reviewers such as August W. Derleth in THE (Madison, Wisconsin) CAPITAL TIMES, June, 27, 1963, who said it was "perhaps the most satisfactory definition ever set down on paper." The definition is repeated here:

> Science fiction is a branch of fantasy identifiable by the fact that it eases the "willing suspension of disbelief" on the part of its readers by utilizing an atmosphere of scientific credibility for its imaginative speculations in physical science, space, time, social science, and philosophy.

A note of appreciation is due Norman Lobsenz and Cele Lalli, editors of AMAZING STORIES, who published as special features much of the material that appears in this book. A real affection is expressed for Jerome Fried, who conceived this history as a two-volume project and took a personal interest in seeing that it was considered. Most especially, recognition must be given to Wallace Exman, who saw the potentials of this volume within the context of the new direction The World Publishing Company was taking, and carried it through.

SAM MOSKOWITZ
Newark, N. J.
June, 1965

1

EDWARD E. SMITH, Ph.D

The hypothesis of an expanding universe was first formulated in 1912, when Vesto Melvin Slipher applied what is today known as the Doppler-Fizeau effect to the Andromeda nebula, establishing that it was one of only a few not receding into space. Despite this, the imagination of the science-fiction world stagnated within the confines of our solar system until 1928, when Edward E. Smith's *The Skylark of Space* lifted mental horizons to the inspiring wonder of the galaxy.

Why the awakening had to await the coming of Smith is difficult to say. It should have occurred when Camille Flammarion, the famed French astronomer and author, popularized the theories of worlds around other stars in the nineteenth century. It seemed to have arrived in 1904 when Jean Delaire's heroes outraced light on their way to the far places in *Around a Distant Star* (John Zony, London), or when, the following year, the Rev. W. S. Harris merchandised *Life in a Thousand Worlds* (G. Holzapfel, Cleona, Pennsylvania) into a best-seller by subscription.

It is possible that because Delaire and Harris were primarily intent upon expounding religious ideas their spotlight on the devil blinded men to a new approach to reverence. When *The Skylark of Space*, which began as a three-part serial in the August, 1928, AMAZING STORIES, reached its final installment, publisher Hugo Gernsback said: ". . . We are certain you will agree with us that it is one of the outstanding scientifiction stories of the decade; an interplanetarian story that will not be eclipsed soon. It will be referred to by all scientifiction fans for years to come. It will be read and reread."

Eighteen-year-old John W. Campbell, Jr., on summer vacation preparatory to entering Massachusetts Institute of Technology, would haunt the newsstands relentlessly, impatient at the wait between installments. Because of the impact that story would have on him and others like him, science fiction would never again be the same.

What were the elements that have caused writers as well as readers to cherish *The Skylark of Space* as the seedling of cosmic literature destined to burgeon limitlessly in awesome concepts? It was not that it stood alone. That same month of August, Edmond Hamilton began a two-part novel on an extra-solar-system scale, *Crashing Suns,* in WEIRD TALES. Earlier that year, invasion and counterinvasion had crisscrossed the vastness between earth and the system of Sirius in J. Slchossel's *The Second Swarm* (AMAZING STORIES QUARTERLY, Spring, 1928).

Perhaps it was the description of an atomic explosion perilously close to prophecy. More likely it was the suspenseful presentation of scientific dilemmas solved by miracle men with bus bars and test tubes. Unquestionably, the marvel of distances and places which strained comprehension, unrolled in an enthralling odyssey, contributed.

Certainly it could not have been the plot line, involving

cloak-and-dagger manipulations for scientific secrets or the "corny" kidnapping of Dorothy Vaneman, the betrothed of the almost superhuman scientist Richard Seaton, by the villainous Dr. Marc "Blackie" DuQuesne. Surely the stilted love scenes and the use of ephemeral slang in the dialogue detracted more than they added.

Yet, despite the superficial Victorianisms of the plot, most likely it was the combination of these very elements with the superscience concepts that gave *The Skylark of Space* titanic stature in science fiction's hall of fame. The events described were happening to people, some of them stereotypes, others superhuman; but what happened in the novel was more than an attempt at prediction, it was a *story.* Characters *reacted* to mind-staggering situations.

Not all the characters were cardboard. No more remarkable villain has been depicted in the annals of science fiction than DuQuesne. He steals the show. Physically powerful, mentally a genius, distinctly amoral, he is the ultimate pragmatist: murder without compunction for an *end,* but do not lift a finger for mere sadistic satisfaction nor permit a promise of pleasure to distract you from your purpose.

Despite the fact that Smith had a Ph.D. after his name and his character Seaton was prone to semitechnical monologues with jarring frequency, such hard-to-accept notions as speed many times that of light and the manipulation of matter by the power of the mind were strongly challenged in the "Discussion" department of subsequent issues of AMAZING STORIES. These criticisms failed to alter the fact that apotheosis to the Olympus of science fiction was immediately in prospect for the author.

This soon-to-be saint of the starways, the second youngest of five children, was born to Fred J. Smith, an ex-whaler working at shipping on the Great Lakes, and Caroline Mills Smith on May 2, 1890, in Sheboygan, Wisconsin. Both parents were of British extraction and staunch Presbyterians. They christened the boy Edward Elmer, and the same year moved to Spokane, Washington, where the father became a contractor in carpentry and cabinet work. A poor business-man, after many lean times he settled on a homestead of 160 acres on the Pend d'Oreille River in northern Idaho, raising baking potatoes for the dining cars of The Great Northern Railroad.

The youthful E. E. Smith logged in the winter, swamped brush, felled trees, worked in sawmills, did stretches as a lumberjack, and floated lumber down the river. His gram-mer school education was in the Spokane schools and he began high school at Priest River, five miles from home, where he was regarded as an outsider by the other children and had to pulverize every other boy in the school pugilisti-cally to achieve minimal toleration, let alone friendship.

There might have been no education beyond that had the father been less of an emotional disciplinarian. The break came at the age of 18 in a near-violent disagreement over the fine points of fertilizing a potato field with a load of manure. Young E. E. stormed off to Spokane for a brief stint as a conductor on a horse-drawn streetcar.

There had been great closeness and affection between E. E., his two brothers, and his two sisters. His older broth-er, Daniel, soon teamed up with him to haul asphalt for a street-paving job. The profits from this enterprise, together with contributions from his older sister Rachel, were used to send him to prep school at the University of Idaho.

After the first year, he decided he wanted to be a civil engineer. At the age of 19, he helped run a railroad line north from Belton, Montana, into Canada, but seven months of life in the wilderness changed his mind about civil engi-neering. He went to work in a mine to get enough money to re-enter school. One night he awoke in his room on the fourth floor of a boarding house to find that his bed was afire. In a single convulsive leap he was out through the window, sash and all. He broke five ribs and a leg, but the worst damage was to his wrist, which couldn't be used for a year and hurt for ten years more. Manual labor was now out of the question and home he came.

The resourceful brother, Daniel, soon afterward emerged from a Saturday-night-to-Monday-morning poker game with the pot, $310.50 in winnings. "You," he said, gesturing at E. E., "with your gimpy wing can't earn much. Take this money and go back to college." Not only sister Rachel, but sister Mary Elizabeth, as well, sent money to help him through.

Their confidence was justified. Majoring in chemical engineering, he secured a junior year scholarship for the highest scholastic rating. The schedule called for 160 credits to graduate and he got "A" in all 160 credits. Before graduation, he had taken a civil service examination for junior chemist in Washington, D.C., and had been offered the position. He had no money, so Daniel, who was now working as a railroad clerk, collected $150 in five minutes from his fellow employees for the fare.

There was one piece of unfinished business to take care of before he left. During his senior year, roommate Allan MacDougall had shown him pictures of a sister, Jeanne Craig MacDougall, back in Boise, Idaho. Bowled over, E. E. started a correspondence with her. He went to Washington, D.C., via Boise, where he met Jeanne for the first time. He discovered that a contributing reason for the superlative photos of her was that Jeanne worked as a photographer's model. They were engaged within 10 minutes of their meeting.

Working for the U.S. Bureau of Standards in Washington, D.C., Smith helped establish tolerances on the weight of commercially sold butter. He established standards for oysters in New England in a laboratory on the prow of a ship at the price of perpetual seasickness. By the fall of 1915 he had saved enough money to marry and bring his wife to Washington, D.C. It appeared, though, that his ambition of obtaining a doctorate would have to be sacrificed to the responsibility of supporting a family. But Jeanne went to work as a stenographer to help out, and in 1919 he got his Ph.D. from George Washington University.

Smith's writing career started at a men's smoker in 1915. It was a hot, humid night and a discussion ensued with a former classmate of his, Carl D. Garby, Ph.D., who now lived across the hall from him, on what the temperature was in outer space. Others present contributed their ideas on the subject. That night, Carl told his wife, Lee Hawkins Garby, about the conversation. She thought the idea was intriguing and urged Smith to write a story based on it. He was dubious bacause he felt a story had to have love interest and he doubted his ability to handle that part of the plot. She suggested a collaboration in which Smith handled the science and action and the love element could be left to her.

It wasn't necessary to twist Smith's arm too hard to get him to agree. A regular reader of ARGOSY, he was particularly fond of that magazine's science fiction. In book form, he cherished everything published of H. G. Wells, Jules Verne, H. Rider Haggard, Edgar Allan Poe, and Edgar Rice Burroughs. Beyond that, his reading enthusiasms included poetry, philosophy, ancient and medieval history, and all of English literature.

The two worked at the novel industriously through 1915 and 1916, finishing about one-third of it. Then interest waned, and the work was put aside.

At the end of the war Smith became chief chemist for F. W. Stock & Sons, Hillsdale, Michigan, a position he was to occupy until 1936. His specialty was the infant field of doughnut mixes, the formulation of which is regarded as a specialized art by cereal chemists.

One evening late in 1919, bored with baby sitting while Jeanne was out to a movie, he took up the unfinished novel and continued where it had been left off. He kept Garby informed about his progress, but wrote the remainder of the story himself, *including* the love interest. In the spring of 1920, the completed story began to make the rounds of the publishers.

The consistency of rejections was ego-shattering. The

only encouragement he received in eight years of submissions was a three-page letter from Bob Davis, editor of ARGOSY, in 1922. Davis liked the story immensely, but felt it was just too "far out" to be accepted by his readership.

"Every" book publisher in the country had a look at the manuscript and turned it down. Whenever a new magazine appeared, Smith hopefully sent it out. Finally, one day he picked up the April, 1927, AMAZING STORIES at a newsstand, read a few pages on the spot of the first story, *The Plague of the Living Dead,* by A. Hyatt Verrill, dashed home, got the manuscript, and mailed it out.

Editor T. O'Conor Sloane replied with high enthusiasm and a low offer of $75 for the 90,000-word novel. Smith accepted (though he had spent more than that on postage through the years), but by the time the novel appeared, AMAZING STORIES had examined its conscience and a check arrived for $125. He split the sum with Mrs. Garby and *The Skylark of Space* was published as a collaboration.

The first installment had not been on sale a month when Sloane wrote asking for a sequel. Mrs. Garby wasn't interested in participating further, so Smith started on his own. The sequel, *Skylark Three,* was in every sense a continuation of the first novel. As science fiction it was also a better novel. The story was unified and the pace sustained. Most important, Smith showed that, whatever his weaknesses at dialogue and love interest his ability to develop suspenseful action grippingly on a cosmic scale was limited only by the scope of his imagination. He was probably the only writer alive who could weave a thousand words of scientific explanation into a battle scene and not slow the pace for an instant.

Skylark Three, upon its appearance in the August, September, and October, 1930, issues of AMAZING STORIES, did more than even its predecessor to change the paraphernalia of science fiction. Tremendous battles of conflicting forces with an assortment of offensive rays and defensive force screens were popularized by the new novel. Spaceships miles in length and a fabulous array of bizarre aliens which justified the novel's subtitle: "The tale of the galactic cruise which ushered in universal civilization," became standard science-fiction fare. Science-fiction writers would never again be bound to their solar system.

Smith had sold all rights to *The Skylark of Space* but he released only magazine privileges for its sequel. AMAZING STORIES voluntarily paid him ¾ of a cent a word for that second story, ¼ of a cent more per word than they had paid any author up to that time.

The Skylark stories had been carried as far as Smith planned, and he now proceeded on what he thought would be a new series. *The Spacehounds of IPC* began in the July, 1931, issue of AMAZING STORIES, before the letter column had ceased ringing the praises of *Skylark Three*. It was an exciting, imaginative story depicting space battles, stupendous scientific discovery, and ingeniously conceived alien intelligences, every bit as good and as well-sustained as *Skylark Three*. It even predicted the ion drive for space ships decades before Herman Oberth proposed it in RADIO ELECTRONICS magazine in the early fifties. Nevertheless, letters tempered praise with protest because Smith had stayed within the confines of our solar system in the development of the story. Editor Sloane sided with the readers and made a point of suggesting that Smith make the setting of his next story far out in the Milky Way.

Smith was angered at Sloane, not only for the reprimand but for unauthorized changes in the published story, so when Harry Bates, editor of Clayton's ASTOUNDING STORIES, dangled the carrot of 2 cents a word on acceptance for first look at his next story, he agreed. A sequel to *The Spacehounds of IPC* was now impossible, since the new story must be offered to a competing magazine. Instead, Smith wrote *Triplanetary,* a novel of the unified worlds of Earth, Mars, and Venus attacked by an amphibian menace from a distant star. Though much of the action appeared to advance the plot but little, Smith's writing had improved over even *The Spacehounds of IPC* and he had once again ventured out into the far places, so the story was great fun. Scientifically, it introduced the notion of the "inertialess" drive to attain speeds faster than light, which while not provable, cannot be disproved and therefore is considered the best device over proposed to conquer the light-speed limit.

The problem here turned out to be with the market. By the time Smith submitted *Triplanetary* to ASTOUNDING STORIES, that magazine had become a bimonthly and was paying on publication instead of acceptance. An announcement that the story was forthcoming appeared in their January, 1933, issue, and the cover illustration of the March, 1933, number (the last under the Clayton chain's ownership) was taken from a situation in *Triplanetary*. But the company was being disbanded so the manuscript was returned to Smith.

Still not talking to AMAZING STORIES, he decided to give WONDER STORIES a look at *Triplanetary*. To his humiliation, he not only received a rejection, but the editor, Charles D. Hornig, later *bragged* about it in an article titled *Stories We Reject*—in the science fiction fan magazine FANTASY MAGAZINE (December, 1934-January 1935). Now there was no alternative but to submit *Triplanetary* to AMAZING, by whom it was accepted and published in four parts beginning with the January, 1934, number; but Smith's rates were ignominiously dropped to a half-cent a word.

Further to embitter his cup of hemlock, shortly after the sale to AMAZING, Smith received a letter from F. Orlin Tremaine, new editor of ASTOUNDING STORIES, which had been bought and revived by Street & Smith Publications in the interim, offering a cent a word for *Triplanetary*. When Tremaine learned that it was already scheduled for AMAZING STORIES, he suggested a third story in the Skylark series.

All winter of 1933-34, Smith worked away on *The Skylark of Valeron*. With each succeeding chapter, the concepts grew increasingly grandiose. In over his head, the story out of his control, Smith collected his first draft, typed on an assorted mass of pink, blue, and white sheets of paper, and sent it to Tremaine with a distraught note explaining that he couldn't handle the theme and would welcome any suggestions.

Tremaine wrote to say that he had only one suggestion: that Smith cash the enclosed check for $850.

What happened then makes one of the most remarkable chapters in the history of science-fiction magazine publishing. Tremaine, a crack editorial hand, veteran of top posts at SMART SET, TRUE STORY, and the Clayton pulp chain, had been building a dramatic and exciting new team of authors. The Smith name was just what he needed. The full-page editorial in the June, 1934, ASTOUNDING STORIES was titled "The Skylark." "For six long years, readers of science fiction have talked about the 'Skylark' stories," it began. "They have been called the greatest science fiction ever written. There were two, you remember, both pointing toward a culminating story which never appeared. . . . *The Skylark of Valeron* starts in the August issue of ASTOUNDING STORIES!"

Not only did the editorial cover a full page, but there was another three-quarter-page announcement of the virtues of *The Skylark of Valeron* in the same issue. The following month, he announced that a new type style would increase wordage by 25,000 so readers would get the "Skylark" in addition to everything else. He exhorted each reader to introduce one new friend to ASTOUNDING. "We have kept faith with you," he told the readers, "now you keep faith with us."

They did. The circulation of ASTOUNDING STORIES leaped 10,000 with the first installment of *The Skylark of Valeron* (which ran in no less than seven parts) and the magazine showed a profit for the first time in its history. Before the novel was finished, both competitors, AMAZING and WONDER, were financially on the ropes. Within a year, the two of them were skipping issues. Eventually they had to sell out.

As much as he accomplished for himself, Tremaine accomplished even more for Smith. Great as had been Smith's reputation after *Skylark Three,* it was incomparably greater now.

But Smith was unable to take immediate advantage of the situation. Personal problems interfered with his writing. Though he was one of the few doughnut mix specialists in America (running a $5,000,000 annual doughnut mix business) he found after years of effort there was a low ceiling on his salary. He shifted to Dawn Doughnut, Jackson, Michigan, in January, 1936, on a salary plus share-of-the-profit arrangement. To get his new firm out of the red, he worked 18 hours a day, seven days a week, for almost a year, even designing new machinery to implement his plans. Once the company was over the hump, he sat down and wrote an 80-page outline for a 400,000-word novel divided into four segments: *Galactic Patrol, The Grey Lensman, Second Stage Lensman,* and *Children of the Lens.* He actually wrote the last chapter of *Children of the Lens* after completing the rough draft of *Galactic Patrol.* This outline was submitted to Tremaine, who told him to go ahead; he would buy the entire package.

Galactic Patrol (ASTOUNDING STORIES, September, 1937, to February, 1938) shares with Olaf Stapledon's *The Star Maker* (published earlier in 1937) the distinction of popularizing the "community of worlds" or galactic empire backdrop in science fiction. Edmond Hamilton had presented the idea eight years earlier, but Smith and Stapledon appear to have brought its potentialities into focus.

The Galactic Patrol is an interstellar police force organized to combat the piracy and lawlessness threatening the structure of galactic civilization. Behind the scenes, dimly seen, are prime movers. The Arisians, whose spores, projected through the galaxy, caused life to form in their image on many worlds, manipulate events for good. The Eddorians, creatures from another space continuum, in their lust for power are the cause of most ills. Good and evil are sharply defined and the battle is joined.

While the allegory seems obvious, the device of the prime mover shows up in a slightly more sophisticated form in a number of A. E. van Vogt's novels, including *Slan, The Weapon Shops,* and *World of A.* The idea of a prime mover is implied in references to a Second Foundation in Isaac Asimov's stories. These are but two of many authors who demonstrate that Smith has been influential on several levels, shaping not only the background but the plot structure of modern science fiction.

Kimball Kinnison is the hero of the novels that would become known as the "Lensman" series. The lensmen are a group of men and women from many worlds, trained to mental and physical attainment so high as to mark them as the beginning of a superior race. Ultimately, through selective mating, they will achieve a point of development where they can replace the Arisians as guardians of the galaxy. The lens itself is a communication device worn on the wrist of a lensman, so attuned to the personality of the wearer that it is virtually artificially alive. If worn by anyone but its owner it proves deadly.

The Grey Lensman is probably best of the series, with *Galactic Patrol* running it a close second. When Fantasy Press decided to publish all of Smith's works in hard covers, he rewrote *Triplanetary,* adding six chapters in the process, to make it part of the series. Several of the new chapters, each of which is a complete story in itself, are quite as good as anything Smith ever did, but the interpolation of Arisian and Eddorian influences into the body of the original *Triplanetary* removes much of the zest from the work.

Writing *Triplanetary* into the series made necessary a bridge novel, *The First Lensman,* to link it with *Galactic Patrol. The First Lensman* was published in hardcover by Fantasy Press in 1950, never appearing in magazine form. It deals vividly with the events that required the organization of a Galactic Patrol and the training experiences of the first lensman.

It was partially because serialization of *The Grey Lens-*

man in ASTOUNDING SCIENCE-FICTION began in October, 1939, that Edward E. Smith, was invited to be guest of honor at the Second World Science Fiction Convention, held in Chicago September 1 and 2, 1940. Few of his audience listening to him deliver a speech on "What Does This Convention Mean?" in the style of the most active and rabid science-fiction fan, realized that Smith was in trouble. Because of the war, any company selling products containing sugar and flour needed no formulation specialist, least of all one who received a percentage of the profits. Smith found himself out of a job. He tried to do some writing, but couldn't seem to concentrate. Meanwhile, he lived on his savings.

Then suddenly there was a special appeal. F. Orlin Tremaine, who had left Street & Smith in 1938, was back editing a new science-fiction magazine titled COMET. There were nearly a dozen competitors, most of them better financed. He was finding the going rough. Could Smith help him?

Smith readily agreed to do a series of novelettes constructed around the character Neal Cloud, a professional blaster of atomic vortices from power plants out of control, an extrapolation of the business of dynamiting blazing oil wells. *The Vortex Blaster,* first of the series, proved too little too late. It appeared in the July, 1941, issue of COMET, the magazine's last. Circumstances would not collaborate in a repeat performance of the previous Tremaine-Smith success.

Politically, Smith's move had been ill-advised. ASTOUNDING SCIENCE-FICTION was the leading market and John W. Campbell, Jr., its editor, was not happy about Smith's move, particularly since Tremaine was reportedly aiming to replace ASTOUNDING in its position of leadership among science-fiction magazines. Campbell began to pay more attention to building up strong newcomers; the old-timers would have to take their chances.

Two other stories in "The Vortex Blaster" series, *Storm Cloud on Deka* and *The Vortex Blaster Makes War* appeared in ASTONISHING STORIES in 1942. In 1960, the first three stories together with additional new material were combined into a book called *The Vortex Blasters*. Two separate editions, one by Fantasy Press and one by Gnome Press, were published, but after a promising title story, the whole proved undistinguished.

Unable to find work immediately after Pearl Harbor, Smith applied to the army. At 51, he was overage, but they put him to work at the Kingsbury, Indiana, Ordnance Plant, working on explosives and shells. He was fired in 1944 for his refusal to pass shells he regarded as below standard. This phase of his life is described in complete detail in Chapter 5, "1941," of the book version of *Triplanetary*. He finished out the last year of the war as a metallurgist for Allis-Chalmers.

In 1945, he reentered the doughnut mix business with J. W. Allen, Chicago, remaining there until his retirement in 1957. Settled in his new job at the end of World War II, Smith began work on the final novel in his series, *The Children of the Lens*. It was a scarcely camouflaged secret that traits of Smith's own three children, Roderick, Verna Jean, and Clarissa, would appear in the physical and mental characteristics of the novel's protagonists. But, in truth, "Doc" Smith was a father image to thousands of the science-fiction readers and he regarded them with a benign paternalism that implied he regarded them all as his "children."

Therefore, when the son of a well-to-do Boston family, Thomas P. Hadley, decided to take a flyer at book publishing and asked for *The Skylark of Space*, it is doubtful if Smith even bothered to ask for terms. Hadley knew nothing about book publishing or marketing, but he managed to get a seven-line notice of the book with the correct price and full address on the bottom of page 110 of the August, 1946, ASTOUNDING SCIENCE-FICTION. A limited edition of 1,000 copies at $3 each sold out completely by mail order from that single mention!

Inundated with orders, Hadley didn't even begin to know

how to go about handling them. In desperation he appealed to Lloyd Arthur Eshbach, a former science-fiction author who had some familiarity with publishing procedures. Eshbach bailed him out and the book went into an elaborate illustrated second printing which cost almost as much per copy to print as it sold for. Years later the book would see still a third printing under the auspices of F. F. F. Publishers, Brooklyn, but in the meantime Eshbach threw up his hands at Hadley's economics and withdrew.

Borrowing Hadley's list of *The Skylark of Space* purchasers, he formed his own publishing company, Fantasy Press, leading off with Smith's *The Spacehounds of IPC* and eventually printing all ten remaining novels Smith had then written, among other titles. So popular were the Smith books that at one point Fantasy Press took the six volumes in the Lensman series, titled them *The History of Civilization,* bound them uniformly in half morocco, boxed them, and sold the set for $30.

The spate of book publishing firms specializing exclusively in fantasy that sprang up after World War II may be attributed in no small measure to the success of the Smith titles. Scores of pulp-magazine classics were immortalized in hard covers under the imprint of such firms as Shasta Publishers, The Fantasy Publishing Co., Inc., Gnome Press, The Avalon Co., and New Era Publishers, in addition to Arkham House, which had been established by August Derleth before the war. Most of them perished when the big trade publishers began to schedule science fiction seriously in the early 1950's.

The excitement accompanying revision of novels for book publication, plus the implied prestige of hard covers, distracted Smith's attention from the fact that *Children of the Lens,* which began in the November, 1947, ASTOUNDING SCIENCE FICTION, was being presented with something less than the customary fanfare. It was the first Smith novel that rated less than two covers in that magazine. The advance notice was a masterpiece of casualness: "The November cover will be a Rogers cover—he's working on it now. It's for . . . something called . . . uhumm . . . oh, yes! 'Children of the Lens' by an author we haven't heard from since he stopped making edible powders for doughnuts and started making the more active kind about December, 1941.

"Doc Smith is back."

The novel failed to have any special impact. It didn't matter. Smith was too busy working on his books to notice and remained so for the next ten years revising his novels for book publication. When Fantasy Press, virtually with its dying gasp, passed on *The Vortex Blaster* like a literary baton to be distributed under the Gnome imprint, all of Smith's magazine serials but one, *The Galaxy Primes,* had found their way between boards.

While Smith's books, the past ten years, had sold comfortingly well, they had been reviewed with a great deal of condescension as period pieces. This bothered Smith, who now was determined to prove that he could emulate the current vogue. Campbell at ASTOUNDING SCIENCE FICTION was then partial to stories with a strong element of what he termed psi phenomena: stories of teleportation, telekinesis, telepathy, levitation, and extrasensory perception. Smith built *The Galaxy Primes* around those elements with a dash of naughtiness and considerable "way out" dialogue to prove he was no back number. It didn't set well with Campbell, who rejected it, but it was serialized in three installments beginning in the March, 1959, AMAZING STORIES. Smith settled back for the reaction. It proved considerably less than enthusiastic.

Popularity frequently carries obligations. A fan named E. Everett Evans had been among Smith's most ardent boosters. In his fifties, Evans determined to become a writer and succeeded. Among his published works were two very Smithlike novels aimed at teenagers, *Man of Many Minds* (1953) and *Alien Minds* (1955), both published by Fantasy Press. Evans died of a heart condition with the first draft of another novel, *Masters of Space,* on his desk. To help Evans' widow sell it, Smith did a complete revision and polishing job and the story ran as a collaboration in IF (November, 1961-January, 1962). Dealing with the pooling of minds telepathically as a means of invading and destroying a planet, the story failed to come off.

Smith then experimented with a detective novel, but it interested no one.

A rapprochement with Campbell resulted in the plotting of a new novel, for which *Subspace Survivor,* a novelette appearing in the July, 1960, ASTOUNDING SCIENCE FICTION was a prelude. The major story and sequel, *Subspace Explorers,* was another attempt on the part of Smith to write what he felt was wanted in modern science-fiction. Campbell didn't agree with him in the result and the effort was eventually published as an original book by Canaveral Press, publishers of Edgar Rice Burroughs hard-cover editions (1965).

It was time for Smith to review. Here he was 73, retired and living in a trailer in Florida. What was he trying to prove?

The Skylark of Space in 1928 had given the science-fiction world the stars.

Galactic Patrol in 1937 had unified those stars into a community.

Each time he had dared to be himself and the result had altered the direction of a literature.

What he had been doing the past few years was attempting to conform to a literary vogue instituted by someone else, in the process imitating writing methods popularized by someone else, rewriting a story conceived by someone else, and patterning a plot to suit someone else.

At the 21st World Science Fiction Convention in Washington, D.C. (birthplace of *The Skylark of Space* nearly a half-century earlier), September 1, 1963, First Fandom presented its Hall-of-Fame Award to Edward E. Smith for his pivotal contributions to science fiction. From the floor, John

W. Campbell honored him with the statement: "Smith made the last big breakthrough in science fiction; we're still waiting for someone else to make another." Almost too overcome with emotion to speak, Smith, whose eyes were almost blinded by cataracts, accepted the award.

Inevitably, someone asked the question: "What's your next story, Doc?"

Smith's hand trembled slightly, but the answer was sharp and clear. "The title of my next story," he said, "is *Skylark DuQuesne!*"

August 31, 1965, Edward E. Smith died of a heart attack.

Two weeks earlier, the October, 1965 IF had appeared, completing serialization of *Skylark Duquesne* begun in its July issue. In it Blackie Duquesne proposes marriage and finds a soul mate.

It was as though *Skylark Duquesne* was his last literary will and testament. E. E. Smith had finally done right by the noblest villain of them all.

2

JOHN W. CAMPBELL

AND NOW CAMPBELL!" That was the title, set in thick 36-point type, of an editorial in the October, 1934, ASTOUNDING STORIES.

In December we bring you a great booklength novel by an author you have asked us to get for *Astounding Stories.* John W. Campbell, Jr., comes to us with a story of vast conceptions, *The Mightiest Machine.* . . . He has been called one of the two greatest science fiction authors. We have obtained stories from both (E.E.) Smith and Campbell. . . . Don't miss this story. It's Campbell at his best. Diametrically opposed to Smith's theories but a worthy opponent.

The editorial voice behind the "pitch" was that of F. Orlin Tremaine. Procuring Campbell for his magazine was almost like driving the last nail in the coffins of his competitors. One year earlier ASTOUNDING STORIES had been revived by Street & Smith as the third science-fiction monthly in a field of three. Now it was the unquestioned leader in quality and circulation.

Campbell was a true giant in popularity among those authors who had grown out of the science-fiction magazines. *The Mightiest Machine,* which began in the December, 1934, ASTOUNDING STORIES and ran for five issues, epitomized the type of story that had created his following. Mighty spaceships move at speeds faster than light from star system to star system, warping themselves through another dimension at the whim of Aarn Munro, a mental and physical superman, descendant of earthmen raised on the surface of the planet Jupiter. He custom-contrives universe-shaking energy weapons to combat alien fleets in universe-wide battles. Like Edward E. Smith, Campbell was undeniably a literary Houdini in the mind-staggering art, convincingly manipulating stupendous forces on a cosmic scale.

Time was running out on macrocosmic spectaculars like *The Mightiest Machine;* changes were occurring in plotting and writing science fiction that were to make the story a period piece before it was completed; yet its impact was so profound on a youthful Englishman, Arthur C. Clarke, that nearly twenty years later he would use a race similar to the devillike villains, the Teff-hellani, in his greatest critical success, *Childhood's End.* At the other literary extreme, Richard S. Shaver (or Raymond A. Palmer, who actually wrote most of the stories carrying the Shaver name) would adapt Campbell's premise that this evil race once lived in vast caverns under Mu and was driven away in a prehistoric Ragnorok, as the basis of the Shaver "Mystery."

Notwithstanding, Campbell's major contribution in both storytelling and influence was yet to come. More than is true of most writers, his early life and background shaped the direction he would take in specific plot ideas as well as in method.

John Wood Campbell, Jr., was born in a two-family frame house at 16 Tracey Ave., Newark, New Jersey, on June 8, 1910. The street bordered the then fashionable

Clinton Hill section. His father, John W. Campbell, Sr., an electrical engineer, had come to Newark one year earlier. Having secured a position with New Jersey Bell Telephone, whose headquarters were in Newark, the elder Campbell returned to Napoleon, Ohio, to marry Dorothy Strahern, whose family tree made her eligible for the Daughters of the American Revolution.

He took his wife back to Newark, a break in family tradition, since the Campbells were influential society in Napoleon. They had come to Napoleon from Rochester, Vermont, where members of the family had been in the state legislature. Campbell's father had been a Congressman for that district, a Master in Chancery, and a Judge of Equity.

After seven years in Newark, the family moved to Maplewood, a suburb of Newark, where John, Jr., attended public school. Precociously intellectual, interested in everything around him, young John had virtually no friends. At home, his relationship with his parents was emotionally difficult. His father carried impersonality and theoretical objectivity in family matters to the brink of fetish. He almost never used the pronoun "I." All statements were in the third person: "It is necessary," "One must," "It appears that," "One should." Not only was he an authoritarian in his own home but a self-righteous disciplinarian as well, who put obedience high on the list of filial duties. Affection was not in his makeup, and if he felt any for the boy he managed to repress it.

The mother's changeability baffled and frustrated the youngster. Self-centered, flighty, moody, she was unpredictable from moment to moment. While she was not deliberately cruel, her gestures of warmth appeared to him so transitory and contrived as to be quickly discounted. His mother had a twin sister who was literally identical. So close were they in appearance that no one, let alone John, could tell them apart. The sisters were in psychological conflict because John's mother had married first, and he found himself used as an innocent pawn by his mother who fawned over him at great length as a subtle taunt to her twin.

The result was that John's aunt treated him with such abruptness that he was convinced she thoroughly hated him. This created a bizarre situation. The boy would come running into the house to impart something breathlessly to a woman he thought was his mother. He would be jarred by a curt rebuff from her twin. Every time his aunt visited the home, this situation posed itself until it became a continuing and insoluble nightmare. Was the woman standing in front of him friend or "foe?"

His only "friend" was a sister, Laura, born in 1917. The two got along well, but the seven-year gap in their ages made her always too young to be much of an ally. So loneliness directed his alert and curious mind into everything. He blew up the basement with his chemistry experiments. Manually dexterous, he repaired bicycles for other kids. For their parents he revitalized electrical appliances. He read omnivorously, particularly myths, legends, folklore, and anthropology. He discovered Edgar Rice Burroughs' Tarzan and John Carter of Mars at the age of 7½. At 8 he was perusing Jeans, Eddington, and astronomy texts.

At 14 he was packed off to Blair Academy, an exclusive boys' school in Blairstown, New Jersey. He succeeded in making only a few friends there, none of them instructors, whose "errors" he corrected in class. Sports did not attract him, though he developed a good game of tennis and a mild interest in intramural football.

Despite four years at Blair, he never obtained a diploma. He was strong in physics and Spanish, but his marks ran the gamut in other subjects.

One of the few times he and his father saw eye to eye was when the latter suggested that he be enrolled at the Massachusetts Institute of Technology in 1928. Perhaps his reasonableness in this was partly motivated by John's ingenuity. At 15, in order to circumvent directives, he had become so facile in the use of logic that the father found himself hard-pressed to justify himself, his ideas, or his behavior.

In still another respect, a disciplinary peculiarity of his father had a direct bearing in sharpening his embryonic writing skills. The older Campbell frequently checked the boy's homework, and if he didn't approve of a phrase he would demand it be rewritten. To save revision time, John made a game of rewording the phrase in the same line. The result was increased dexterity and economy in the use of words.

Though he did not mingle much socially with the other students at MIT, John became very close with his roommate Rosario Honore Trembley, who had a sense of fun and humor the teen-age Campbell found compatible. That, however, was as far as he cared to go in conforming. In class, Campbell was up to his old trick of straightening out instructors. In one instance, this penchant made him a friend. He challenged, before the students, a statement by Professor Blanchard, his chemistry instructor, regarding the "impossibility" of amalgamating iron. Campbell brought in an experimental arrangement and performed the "impossible" in the classroom. Instead of being angry, the professor was delighted and began to take a personal interest in Campbell, expressing sincere disappointment when his "prodigy" did not go on to make chemistry his life's work.

John had instinctively gravitated toward science fiction. He bought ARGOSY fairly regularly and WEIRD TALES whenever he was certain it contained science fiction. He spotted the first issue of AMAZING STORIES when it appeared in April, 1926, and became a regular customer. When science-fiction authors' imaginations showed signs of breaking out of the confines of the solar system, Campbell was enthralled. Smith's *The Skylark of Space* established a lifelong admiration for that author and an immediate desire to emulate.

Stemming from his awareness that science-fiction authors frequently made obvious scientific errors, his first writing attempt, a short story called *Invaders from the Infinite*, was aimed at correcting one of the more widespread misconceptions: that there would be a problem in heating an interplanetary ship in space. The story, sent to AMAZING STORIES, was accepted. Elated, Campbell pounded out a longer story, *When the Atoms Failed,* and that, too, was accepted. His enthusiasm waned, however, as the months passed and neither story appeared. Home on vacation in the summer of 1929, Campbell decided to visit T. O'Conor Sloane, the editor who had been in correspondence with him, and straighten out the matter.

Now six-foot-one, with hawklike features, he presented a formidable appearance as he was ushered into Sloane's editorial offices at 381 Fourth Avenue, New York. Sloane had a flowing, long white beard. At the age of 80 he had finally been given the title of "Editor," following the passing of the magazine from the ownership of its founder, Hugo Gernsback, to that of The E. P. Co., Inc.

Despite his appearance, the old man was anything but a stuffed shirt. Kindly, almost genial, he made the embryonic author at home and then owned up to the fact that the manuscript of *Invaders from the Infinite* had been lost. Every corner of the office had been searched but it couldn't be found.

Did the author, perhaps, have a carbon?

He did not?

Well, his career would have to be launched with *When the Atoms Failed,* to be scheduled soon. In retrospect, Campbell always felt that the lost story would have more aptly been cast as an article and it was better lost.

Sloane more than made up for the disappointment by carrying an illustration for *When the Atoms Failed* on the cover of the issue in which it appeared and beginning the blurb of the story: "Our new author, who is a student at the Massachusetts Institute of Technology, shows marvelous ability at combining science with romance, evolving a piece of fiction of real scientific and literary value."

The story did contain original ideas. First, though the idea of thinking brains in robots had been used frequently before, the concept of a stationary supercalculator, like today's Univac, had not appeared in the magazines. Scientists in science fiction, never sissies, previously disdained to use even an adding machine in whipping together mathematical concepts destined to change the very shape of the cosmos. Not so Steven Waterson, Campbell's hero, who, improving on the Integraph, an electrical machine capable of calculus in use at MIT in 1930, built himself a pre-space-age electronic "brain" to aid in his problems.

Secondly, it delved into the greater power to be derived from material energy—the actual destruction of matter—as opposed to atomic energy. This knowledge enables Steven Waterson to defeat a group of invading Martians, force the nations of the earth to scrap all their weapons, and set himself up as "president" of the planet. The issue in which Campbell's first published story, *When the Atoms Failed,* appeared was dated January, 1930.

By one of those coincidences that seem destined to gird the faith of doubting astrologers, just then a new magazine of science fiction appeared on the newsstands. The first issue of ASTOUNDING STORIES OF SUPER SCIENCE, too, was dated January, 1930, and this was the magazine that Campbell was to make his literary monument.

A sequel to *When the Atoms Failed, The Metal Horde,* appeared in the April, 1930, AMAZING STORIES. This attemped to show what would happen if calculators were refined to the point where they could reason. Scientist Steven Waterson, in the course of the story, defeats and destroys a thinking machine, (originating on a planet of the star Sirius,) that has traveled through space for 1600 years accompanied by a brood of obedient mechanicals intent upon setting up a world of machines on Earth.

Elements of J. Slchossel's *The Second Swarm* (AMAZING STORIES QUARTERLY, Spring, 1928) are apparent in this story and in *The Voice of the Void,* his next appearance, in the Summer, 1930, AMAZING STORIES QUARTERLY. This novelette tells of a ten-billion-year-old civilization on Earth, confronted by the final cooling of the sun, which utilizes "phase velocity" as a means of going faster than light and escaping to another system. Campbell explained it this way:

> Phase velocity is due to a wave traveling along the wave chain. A man can go faster than the train he is riding on by walking toward the engine, but practically speaking he cannot reach the station before the train. Similarly, the phase velocity cannot reach the station before the light or X-rays do. But for countless ages the light has poured forth from the sun, and a message sent down that long train would be able to go many, many trillions of miles at a speed far greater than that of light.

Utilizing this principle, earth ships, in an attempt to colonize plants around the star Betelguese, fight a series of battles with sentient force-creatures in that system. Though mindless, the force creatures adapt to a series of ever-more-potent weapons and give the earth men quite a tussle before they are exterminated.

Few of the students at MIT during that period seemed to be interested in science fiction, but Campbell did secure the friendship of Norbert Weiner, professor of mathematics who is today hailed as the godfather of "thinking machines." Weiner helped the young author with the scientific background of some of those early stories and may have been the inspiration of the "thinking machine" ideas.

The names (Arcot, Wade, and Morey) of a group of characters in *Piracy Preferred* (AMAZING STORIES, June, 1930) provided the label for a major series that was to catapult Campbell to the top rank among science-fiction writers. In the world of 2126, a super criminal, Wade, with the technology to make his high-speed rocket ship invisible, uses a gas that will penetrate metal and temporarily paralyze all who come in contact with it, for his antisocial activities. He puckishly leaves stock certificates for Piracy, Inc., in the amount of the money he steals.

A team of young geniuses—Richard Arcot, a physicist; William Morey, mathematician and son of the president of Transcontinental Airways—in company with John Fuller, a design engineer, chase the pirate into an orbital trap around the earth. The culprit is permitted to join the group instead of being punished. The sympathetic handling of the "evildoer" may have been a holdover from E. E. Smith's creation of the popular "villain" DuQuesne in *The Skylark of Space.*

The group, in a ship powered by a new discovery which causes all molecules to move in the same direction and uses the power derived from the heat so created, takes off for the planet Venus in *Solarite* (AMAZING STORIES, November, 1930). There they find two warring races and side with one against the other, employing Wade's invisibility device and paralyzing gas in the process. When the enemy fathoms the secret of invisibility and uses it against them, pellets of radium paint are employed to locate them, whereupon they are finished off with a molecular-motion weapon.

AMAZING STORIES QUARTERLY was an 8½ by 11 pulp production, almost ¾ of an inch thick, featuring 130,000 words of text and plenty of illustrations for 50 cents. This magazine would sometimes run three complete novels in a single issue and publication in it was a mark of prestige. *The Black Star Passes,* which received the cover of the Fall, 1930, edition, focused attention on Campbell and launched him on his first high wave of popularity, which was to challenge that of E. E. Smith, whose *Skylark Three* was running concurrently in the monthly AMAZING STORIES.

In *The Black Star Passes,* an ancient race of hydrogen-breathing creatures living on a planet circling a vagrant dead star sweeps close to our solar system and decides to transfer to a fresh planet, Earth. In thousands of words of thrilling action (and many thousand dull words of scientific gobbldy-gook) they are defeated by the team of Arcot, Wade, Morey, and Fuller and retire to their retreating star. However, the battle has instilled them with new spirit and they are determined that the next star they pass they will conquer.

The *Islands of Space* in AMAZING STORIES QUARTERLY for Spring, 1931, was Campbell's first full-length novel and he let out all the stops. Exceeding the speed of light by bending the curvature of space, Arcot, Wade, and Morey in their good ship *Ancient Mariner* tour a succession of worlds, finding new wonders and challenges on each. Finally, lost in an infinity of light, they seek to find a race that can guide them, and in the process they help decide a war on a world ten-million light years away from earth.

The novel that followed, *Invaders from the Infinite* (AMAZING STORIES QUARTERLY, Spring-Summer, 1932), represented the apex of approval for Campbell's super-science stories. This time, a tremendous ship manned by canines that have risen high on the evolutionary ladder lands on Earth to seek help against a universal menace. In the *ne plus ultra* of intergalactic ships, *Thought,* Arcot, Wade, and Morey search the far-flung star clusters for an answer to the danger, finally discovering it after as pyrotechnic a series of space battles as has ever appeared in science fiction. Especially gripping is one episode illustrating the power of suggestion on the course of a battle, when emotions are magnified and projected by a special device.

Campbell's preoccupation with writing might have had something to do with his standing at MIT for in 1931 he was asked to leave. He had flunked out in German.

While at MIT he had met Dona Stuart, a young girl attending a Latin school in Waltham. He married her in the summer of 1931, after leaving school.

Despite their differences, his father helped maintain him while he majored in physics for one year at Duke University and received his degree in science. Writing now became a welcome source of income as well as an avocation.

Trying to support a wife and himself while finishing college during the depths of the worst depression in the history of the United States, Campbell decided to try other markets. He sold *The Derelicts of Ganymede* to WONDER STORIES, where it appeared in January, 1932. The story is a satiric slap at the questionable ability of a business tycoon to come out on top if he lets a young man start on even keel.

This was followed by *The Electronic Siege* (WONDER

STORIES, April, 1932), featuring Captain Don Barclay, a physically powerful and mentally extraordinary Jovian prototype of Aarn Munro, who breaks up an illicit medical experimental station on a planetoid. He brought Don Barclay back again in *Space Rays* (WONDER STORIES, December, 1932) to aid in the capture of a space pirate. Hugo Gernsback, the publisher, was moved to write a special editorial instead of the customary blurb for this story. Titled "Reasonableness in Science Fiction," it offered the opinion that Campbell was obviously writing a science-fiction burlesque: "If he has left out any colored rays, or any magical rays that could not immediately perform certain miraculous wonders, we are not aware of this shortcoming in this story. . . . We were tempted to rename the story 'Ray! Ray!' but thought better of it."

The truth was that Campbell wasn't burlesquing anybody. This was the way he always wrote. The combination of the left-handed compliment and the fact that WONDER STORIES, in financial difficulties, was paying very slowly soured him on that market.

Average rates for AMAZING STORIES and WONDER STORIES in 1932 was ½ cent a word on publication. AMAZING STORIES paid promptly on publication, but its editor, now heading for 90 years of age, tended to take the long view. One year after acceptance was a breakneck race into publication for him and instances where five years intervened were not unknown. WONDER STORIES published quickly, but frequently paid a good time after publication. In these circumstances, Campbell was obliged to find a job.

He tried selling Fords for a short period. Then he switched to exhaust fans for homes and stores in the summer. As a salesman, he found that his imagination was an asset. For example, he sold four 30-inch fans to a chain restaurant by suggesting that all the windows be open when they were in use so the establishment could carry the slogan: "Always a breeze."

At the approach of winter he took to promoting gas

heaters. The Boston utility company had a much lower rate for those who also used gas for heating. Campbell was able to show a restaurant chain that by converting their heating units to gas, they would pay for their cooking gas at lower rates and save $2,500 a year. It worked! Three other companies signed up for the change-over and he was out of a job. It would take his small company *years* to install all the business he had obtained, so they wouldn't be needing any salesmen for a while. So, as was to happen to E. E. Smith when the war years came, Campbell found himself looking for work despite—or perhaps because of—his efficiency.

Subtly, though, a change was taking place in Campbell's thinking and writing. It was first evidenced in the introductory passages of *The Black Star Passes,* where an atmosphere of hopelessness and sympathy was engendered for the great people of a dying planet now thousands of years on the decline. It began to take form in *The Last Evolution* (AMAZING STORIES, August, 1932), in which the courageous battle of thinking machines to save their creators from a cosmic menace, climaxing in the evolution of the mechanisms into energy consciousnesses of pure thought, raises them to an allegorical heaven. Our machines will be our friends to the last, inevitably outlive us, progress beyond us, and possibly even go to their just reward, Campbell suggests.

The Last Evolution marks the point of transition in Campbell's writing career, the change to stress on mood and writing technique from the superscientific action characteristic of past Campbell stories. Campbell credited his reading of *The Red Gods Call* by C. E. Scoggins for the change.

Temporarily living in Wilson, North Carolina, he set out to write a story in which mood and characterization would predominate and science would play a secondary role. He had in mind a story that would "sing," that would figuratively serve as a symphonic mood piece in words set to a science-fiction theme. This was the story; *Twilight.*

Seven million years from today, it is the twilight of man.

A mighty civilization served by faithful automatic machinery continues to function: "When Earth is cold, and the Sun has died out, those machines will go on. When Earth begins to creak and break, those perfect, ceaseless machines will try to repair her—." No drive, no progress lies in the dwindling human race. Only stagnation. The man from our day, visiting this future, programs machines to work on the creation of a mechanism with built-in curiosity. The story suggests, as did *The Last Evolution,* that even if man goes, the machines can build their own civilization.

Despite Campbell's popularity, every magazine of early 1933 rejected the story and it went back into his files. Then, in late 1933, F. Orlin Tremaine assumed editorship of ASTOUNDING STORIES and began a drive for leadership in the field.

A high point in his dramatic bid was securing the third story in E. E. Smith's "Skylark" series, *The Skylark of Valeron.* The logical next step was to obtain Campbell, the leading contender for Smith's popularity. Tremaine wrote to Campbell, asking if he had a superscience story along the lines that had established his popularity. In 1933 Campbell had sold *The Mightiest Machine* to Sloane at AMAZING. Over a year had passed and Sloane had not published this story, nor had he yet scheduled another Campbell novel, *Mother World.* Campbell got Sloane to return the story and submitted it to Tremaine, who purchased it immediately.

Heartened, Campbell dusted off *Twilight* and sent it in. Tremaine went quietly mad about it and couldn't get it into print fast enough.

Twilight, rushed into the November, 1934, issue, a month before *The Mightiest Machine,* could not be published under Campbell's own name for two reasons. First, most obviously it would destroy the build-up in progress for *The Mightiest Machine.* Secondly, it was so different in approach that it would disorient the readers accustomed to a certain style of story from Campbell. The problem was solved with a pen name, Don A. Stuart, derived from the maiden name of Campbell's wife, Dona Stuart.

"A new writer," Tremaine blurbed, "a profoundly different and beautiful treatment of an always fascinating idea—*Twilight* by Don A. Stuart. A story of the far, faint future, of the fabulous cities and machines of man—and of his slow decline into eternal sleep."

H. G. Wells' *Time Machine* possessed, in its description of the decadent civilization of the Eloi, certain elements of *Twilight*. The concept of automatic, near-perfect cities, functioning long after man has forgotten how to repair them, was superbly delineated in *The Machine Stops* (1928) by E. M. Forster. Similarly, the lonely, magnificent, nearly eternal, but deserted cities of Bronson Beta are described movingly by Edwin Balmer and Philip Wylie in *After Worlds Collide* (BLUE BOOK, 1933). Yet mood had never been the primary purpose in the presentations of the civilizations and cities of these other authors. Nor had anyone so completely attempted to canonize the machine. Over and over again, Campbell's message remained clear: The machine is *not* the enemy and ruination of man; it is his friend and protector.

Don A. Stuart bid fair to eclipse Campbell in popularity as a result of this single story, *Twilight*. Its appearance was to alter the pattern of science-fiction writing. Warner Van Lorne's immensely popular *Strange City* (ASTOUNDING STORIES, December, 1935) and *World of Purple Light* (ASTOUNDING STORIES, December, 1936) were unquestionably inspired by it. Arthur C. Clarke, in both *Rescue Party* (ASTOUNDING SCIENCE-FICTION, May, 1946) and *Against the Fall of Night* (STARTLING STORIES, November, 1948), displays his debt to *Twilight*. Lester del Rey's inspiration for intelligent dogs in *The Faithful* may derive from a brief section in *Twilight*.

Stuart appeared again with *Atomic Power* in the December, 1934, ASTOUNDING STORIES, a story in which men prevent the structure of our solar system from being blown up by atomcrackers in the macrocosmos. The lead story of the issue was the first installment of *The Mightiest Machine,* and a third story by Campbell in the same issue, *The Irrelevant,* resulted in months of debate in the readers' column, since he presented a theoretical evasion of the law of conservation of energy. This was published under the pseudonym Karl van Kampen, the name of a Dutch great-grandfather on his father's side.

Blindness (ASTOUNDING STORIES, March, 1935), as Stuart, was a poignant sketch of a scientist who loses his sight in space to bring the world the blessings of atomic energy, only to learn that inadvertently another discovery of his provides a cheaper power source. He dies embittered because the world does not want his atomic energy.

One of the most remarkable and underrated performances under the Stuart name was *The Escape* (ASTOUNDING STORIES, May, 1935), written as the result of an argument with a would-be writer as to whether or not it was possible to write a successful love story in the framework of science fiction. A girl who runs off with a boy she loves to escape marrying the selection of the Genetics Board is finally captured and brought back and psychologically reconditioned to "love" the "right" man. This remains one of the finest love stories science fiction has yet produced.

With *The Mightiest Machine* receiving reader accolades, Campbell thought sequels were in order. He wrote three, continuing the adventures of Aarn Munro and his companions. The first, a 15,000-word novelette, *The Incredible Planet,* utilized the well-worn device of losing his characters in space thus enabling them to stumble upon a world whose inhabitants have remained in suspended animation for 400 billion years; a second sequel, *The Interstellar Search,* finds the earthmen aiding a planet whose sun is about to become a nova; and in the final story, *The Infinite Atom,* they arrive home in time to block an invasion by creatures whose previous visit to earth gave rise to the centaur legends.

Tremaine rejected all three. He felt that the day of the superscience epic was past and insisted that Campbell stick strictly to Stuart-style stories. Another augury was the mild response to *Mother World,* a story of the revolt of the oppressed working groups against their fiendish masters, with the planet as the prize, serialized at last in the January, February, and March, 1935, issues of AMAZING STORIES as *The Contest of the Plants.* The three sequels to *The Mightiest Machine* eventually were published as a Fantasy Press book, *The Incredible Planet,* in 1949.

Campbell was forced to give full emphasis to Don A. Stuart in a series which he called "The Teachers," but which never was so labeled, beginning in the February, 1935, ASTOUNDING STORIES with *The Machine.* In this story, a thinking machine that has provided every comfort for men leaves the planet for their own good, forcing them to forage for themselves. This story inspired Jack Williamson's *With Folding Hands* and its sequel *". . . And Searching Mind,"* concerning robots that overprotect man from every possible injury or error, and from himself.

The Invaders (ASTOUNDING STORIES, June, 1935), a sequel to *The Machine,* describes a mankind reverted to savagery, easily enslaved by the Tharoo, a race from another world.

Rebellion (ASTOUNDING STORIES, August, 1935) finds the human race, through selective breeding, becomes more intelligent than the Tharoo, driving the invaders back off the planet.

The foregoing were not primarily mood stories, but they were adult fare—the predecessors of an entirely new type of science fiction.

In *Night,* a sequel to *Twilight,* published in the October, 1935, ASTOUNDING STORIES, Campbell stirringly returned to the mood story. A man of today moves into the inconceivably distant future, when not only the sun but the stars themselves are literally burnt out. At his presence, machines from Neptune move to serve him, but he recognizes them for what they are: "This, I saw, was the last radiation of the heat of life from an already-dead body—the feel of life and warmth, imitation of life by a corpse," for man and all but the last dregs of universal energy are gone.

"You still wonder that we let man die out?" asked the machine. "It was best. In another brief million years he would have lost his high estate. It was best." Campbell had matured. A civilization of machines, he now understands, is but parody, movement without consciousness. It is not and can never be "the last evolution."

Campbell returned to his home state of New Jersey, in 1935, working at a variety of jobs: the research department of Mack Truck in New Brunswick; Hoboken Pioneer Instruments; and finally Carleton Ellis, Montclair, in 1936, setting up residence at Orange, New Jersey, to be near his work. Carleton Ellis, namesake and founder of the firm, had more chemical patents than any man in the world and was a consultant on the subject. He is credited with making the first paint remover that worked. Campbell was able to tolerate only six months of writing and editing textbooks and technical literature for Ellis, but nevertheless the position gave him discipline in editing and publishing that would soon prove invaluable.

Out of work, Campbell accepted the assignment of writing a monthly article on astronomy for Tremaine, plus an occasional Stuart story. These activities barely kept food on the table. Campbell's most successful story in 1936 was *Frictional Losses* (ASTOUNDING STORIES, July, 1936), under the Stuart byline, in which a method of eliminating friction proves the ultimate weapon against invaders from outer space.

WONDER STORIES had been sold by Gernsback to Standard Magazines and now appeared as THRILLING WONDER STORIES. Campbell arranged with the editor, Mort Weisinger, for a series of stories under his own name, built

around the characters of Penton and Blake, two fugitives
from Earth. The best of the group was the first, *Brain
Stealers of Mars* (THRILLING WONDER STORIES, December,
1936), concerning Martians capable of converting themselves into an exact replica of any object or person. They
provide a knotty problem for the visitors from Earth. This
story and those that followed had the light note of humor
and the wacky alien creatures which Stanley G. Weinbaum
had recently made so popular.

Closest in quality to *Night* and *Twilight* proved to be *For-
getfulness* (ASTOUNDING STORIES, June, 1937), in which
earthmen landing on a distant planet assume that a race is
decadent because it has deserted the automatic cities and
mighty power devices that man, in his current state of progress, associates with civilization.

Influential as well as entertaining was his novelette of the
Sarn, *Out of Night* (ASTOUNDING STORIES, October, 1937).
A matriarchial society of aliens who have conquered the
earth and have ruled it for 4,000 years are challenged by
Aesir, a black, amorphous mass vaguely in the shape of man,
ostensibly personifying humanity's unified yearnings past and
present. This device was picked up by Robert A. Heinlein
in *Sixth Column*, where it helps to route the Asiatic
conquerors.

Cloak of Aesir, a sequel, demonstrated the use of psychology in driving the "people" of the Sarn from their domination of Earth, and terminated the short series in ASTOUNDING
SCIENCE-FICTION for March, 1939.

Tremaine's duties had been expanded to cover editorial
directorship of TOP-NOTCH, BILL BARNES, ROMANCE RANGE,
CLUES, and a number of other Street & Smith periodicals.
To assist him, he hired an editor for each of the magazines.
Campbell's availability, his skill as a writer, and his intensive
if limited editorial experience with Carleton Ellis put him in
line for the position with ASTOUNDING. He was put on the
payroll of Street & Smith in September, 1937. Inevitably his
writing, except for special occasions, had to cease.

F. Orlin Tremaine left Street & Smith in May, 1938, as the result of internal pólitics. Campbell was completely on his own, and there would be less time than ever.

Few authors ever made their literary exit more magnificently than did Campbell.

From the memories of his childhood he drew the most fearsome agony of the past: the doubts the fears, the shock, and the frustration of repeatedly discovering that the woman who looked so much like his mother was not who she seemed. Who goes there? Friend or foe? He had attempted the theme once before, employing a light touch, in *Brain Stealers of Mars.* This time he was serious. *Who Goes There?* (ASTOUNDING SCIENCE-FICTION, August, 1938) deals with an alien thing from outer space that enters the camp of an Antarctic research party and blends alternately into the forms of the various men and dogs in the camp. The job is to find and kill the chimera before, in the guise of some human being or animal, it gets back to civilization.

An impressive display of writing talent, *Who Goes There?* is in one sense one of the most thrilling detective stories ever written. The suspense and tension mount with each paragraph and are sustained to the last. Reading this story inspired A. E. van Vogt to turn to science fiction with *Vault of the Beast,* a direct take-off on the idea. In Europe, Eric Frank Russell picked up the notion in *Spiro,* one of his most effective stories. RKO, altering the story considerably, produced it as a profitable horror picture called *The Thing* (1951).

A few more Stuart stories would sporadically appear. *The Elder Gods* (UNKNOWN, October, 1939), a swiftly paced sword-and-sorcery tale, was written as a last-minute fill-in when a cover story by Arthur J. Burks proved unsatisfactory. Together with *The Moon Is Hell,* a short novel of stark realism drawing a parallel between the survival problems of Antarctic and moon explorers, it made its appearance as a Fantasy Press book in 1951.

Fifteen years after he had quit writing for a living, Campbell still displayed excellent technique in *The Idealists,* a novelette written expressly for the hard-cover anthology *9 Tales of Space and Time,* edited by Raymond J. Healy for Henry Holt in 1954. Scientists aren't always "good guys," was the point he made, and a high degree of technical development does not necessarily carry with it maturity in dealing with different cultures.

But for all practical purposes, Campbell's writing career ended at the age of 28 with *Who Goes There?* As one of the first of the modern science-fiction writers, he had a profound influence on the field. As editor of the leading, best-paying magazine, he taught, coerced, and cajoled his type of story. As a result, for the more than a quarter-century since he ceased writing, older readers have been haunted by half-remembered echoes in the plot structure of hundreds of stories and in the lines of scores of writers. It is not strange if sometimes readers shake the hypnotic wonder of the wheeling cosmos from their minds and demand: "Who goes there?"

3

MURRAY LEINSTER

The whole thing began when the clock on the Metropolitan Tower began to run backwards." That was the opening sentence of *The Runaway Skyscraper* in the February 22, 1919, issue of ARGOSY, and with those words Murray Leinster began his science-fiction writing career. Already a veteran with two years of steady magazine sales behind him, young Leinster had sold ARGOSY a series of Happy Village stories and was fed up with predigested pabulum. There would be no more in that series for a while, he wrote editor Matthew White, Jr., since he was working on a story opening with the lines, "The whole thing began when the clock on the Metropolitan Tower began to run backwards."

"By return mail," recalls Leinster, "I got a letter telling me to let him see it when I finished. So I had to write it or admit I was lying."

At the time the story was written, the tower of the home

office of the Metropolitan Life Insurance Company was one of the tallest and most distinctive skyscrapers in New York topped by a clock that was a city landmark. Readers of ARGOSY were enthralled to read of the building's remarkable journey in time back to a period hundreds of years before white men appeared on this continent. Some two thousand workers in the skyscraper thus find themselves confronted with the task of obtaining enough food to eat and suitable fuel to run the building's mammoth generators. Little help can be expected from the few thoroughly "shaken" Indians that have witnessed this strange occurrence. The scientific "explanation," that the skyscraper has sunk back in time instead of down into a pool of water created by a spring beneath it, taxed one's credulity only slightly less than the unimpaired functioning of the entire elevator, telephone, and cooking systems of the building, even though outside sources of power were hundreds of years away. Leinster's characters poked around a bit, but since the author couldn't quite seem to figure out the solution of the sustenance problem, he had the hero reestablish the equilibrium of the structure in its own time by pouring soapsuds into the subsurface water. The building reappears at exactly the same moment it left, and no one believes the tale its occupants tell.

An ARGOSY readership that was still completing Garret Smith's novel that whisked them into the future of *After a Million Years* and had accepted the revival of Aztec gods in the modern world as offered by Francis Stevens in *Citadel of Fear* only months earlier was not inclined to quibble over "details." They greeted Murray Leinster's effort with enthusiasm and one of the most fabulous writing careers in science-fiction history was launched. Forty-three years later, in 1962, Murray Leinster was voted one of the six favorite *modern* writers of science fiction; more of his stories had been anthologized than any living science-fiction writer's, including classics as *First Contact, The Strange Case of John Kingman, Symbiosis, A Logic Named Joe,* and *The Lonely Planet.*

Other writers who started and achieved fame in the same

period as Leinster—Ray Cummings, Garret Smith, Victor Rousseau, Francis Stevens, Homer Eon Flint, Austin Hall, J. U. Giesy—are dead and their work lives only in the nostalgic memories of a dwindling group of old-time readers. But their contemporary, Murray Leinster, is very much alive; his novelette *Exploration Team* received the Hugo* as the best story in its class in 1956, and in 1960 his novel *Pirates of Ersatz* was nominated for the best novel of the year.

William Fitzgerald Jenkins was born in Norfolk, Virginia, in 1896. His alter ego, Murray Leinster, would not come into being until Jenkins had passed his twenty-first birthday. His family tree has roots deep in colonial times; an ancestor eight generations back, was governor of North Carolina. Another of his roots lay in Leinster County, ireland, inhabited by a people proud in the knowledge that the kings of Leinster were the last of that country to give up their independence.

His education terminated abruptly after only three months of the eighth grade, never to be resumed. Young Jenkins' burning ambition was to be a scientist, and inquiry into the nature of things prompted him to buy materials to build a glider, which he successfully flew at Sandstorm Hill, Cape Henry, Virginia, in 1909, winning a prize from FLY, the first aeronautical magazine, for his achievement.

The same year, at the age of 13, he placed an essay about Robert E. Lee in the VIRGINIAN PILOT, making that his first published work. Technically, it was also his first "paid" authorship, for an old Confederate veteran sent him five dollars upon reading it. To earn a living, he worked as an office boy, writing at night. Every day for a year he wrote 1,000 words and tore it up. At the age of 17 he began to place fillers and epigrams with SMART SET, the NEW YORKER of pre-World War I days. Such fragments did not constitute a living ($5 for 12 epigrams) so Will Jenkins set his sights

---

* The "Hugo" is the science fiction world's synonym for the "Oscar," a cast metal space ship awarded annually at the World Science Fiction Convention, to the fields outstanding contributors.

on the pulps, which were replacing the dime-novel as the reading matter of American youth. The editors of SMART SET, George Jean Nathan and H. L. Mencken who included one epigram in a book and paid a five-cent beer for royalties, perfectly straight-faced, suggested that he use a pen name for ARGOSY or ALL-STORY so as not to hurt his reputation in the "big time." Jenkins thought this was Grade-A advice and together with a friend, Wynham Martyn, concocted Murray Leinster out of his family lineage.

He had moved to Newark, New Jersey, to work as a bookkeeper for the Prudential Insurance Company, and that city later served as the locale of a number of his stories, most notably *The Incredible Invasion.* Clicking regularly at Munsey and other publishing houses, Leinster resigned his post with Prudential on his twenty-first birthday and, apart from a stint in the Office of War Information during World War II, has never held a salaried position since.

In 1919, Street & Smith, watching the prosperity of Munsey's ARGOSY and ALL-STORY magazines, with their heavy emphasis on science-fiction, fantasy, supernatural, and off-trail stories, decided to bring out a magazine whose fiction would stress those elements. They called it THRILL BOOK and put it under the editorship of Eugene Clancy and Harold Hersey. Before the first issue appeared, dated March 1, 1919, the editors found that new fantasies were difficult to obtain, so they dropped the notion of an all-fantasy periodical and filled out the greater part of the magazine with straight adventure and mystery stories.

Hersey had read Leinster's *The Runaway Skyscraper* in ARGOSY a few weeks earlier and was also familiar with the Will Jenkins stories in SMART SET. He urged the young writer to try his hand at science fiction for THRILL BOOK. Three stories resulted. The first, *A Thousand Degrees Below Zero,* in the July 15, 1919, number, involved an inventor who succeeds in building a machine which will draw all heat from objects toward which it is directed, resulting in death for living things and brittle disintegration for inanimate objects. A vigorous bout with the United States government ends in the inventor's defeat, but this story pattern, with a variety of inventions, was to remain a Leinster standard for the next twenty-five years.

A sequel, *The Silver Menace,* appeared in two installments, in the September 1 and September 15, 1919, numbers of THRILL BOOK. This time the world is threatened by a swiftly multiplying life-form that virtually turns the seas to glimmering jelly.

The final issue of THRILL BOOK, October 15, 1919, carried Leinster's third story, *Juju,* a straightforward adventure novelette set in an African locale. What makes this story worth mentioning is that by this time the value of the "Murray Leinster" name rated the cover illustration of the magazine.

Jean Henri Fabre's books on insects inspired Leinster to write *The Mad Planet,* the first of a trilogy which, if not his finest contribution to science fiction, is among his best. A secondary purpose of the author was to confound those literary critics who claimed that stories with little or no dialogue could not retain a modern reader's interest. *The Mad Planet* was a sensation when it appeared in ARGOSY for June 12, 1920. Depicting a world of the far distant future, where climatic conditions have made it possible for insects and plants to grow to gigantic proportions and mankind is reduced to a primitive, hunted state, *The Mad Planet* held readers in thrall. Burl, a primitive genius, slowly begins to lead man back out of savagery. *The Mad Planet* struck a chord of universal appeal.

The sequel, *Red Dust,* in ARGOSY for April 2, 1921, is an even better story than the original. Burl's adventures and explorations thrillingly expand the scope of man's knowledge and hopes. Each time these two stories have been reprinted —in AMAZING STORIES in 1926; in TALES OF WONDER in 1939; and in FANTASTIC NOVELS, 1948-49—a new generation of readers has endorsed Leinster's artistry.

Finally, twenty-two years after the appearance of the first story, Leinster completed the trilogy with *Nightmare Planet* in the June, 1953, issue of SCIENCE-FICTION PLUS. It was an older, more philosophical, more thoughtful Leinster writing in this story, but the magic of the first two was still there.

With the locale changed to another planet for scientific reasons, the three appeared in hard covers as *The Forgotten Planet,* a book of such appeal that it is unlikely to become a forgotten classic.

From 1923 on, one of the pillars of fantasy in the United States was WEIRD TALES, a magazine which developed such favorites as H. P. Lovecraft, Robert E. Howard, Clark Ashton Smith, Henry S. Whitehead, C. L. Moore, and many others during its lifetime. Leinster's initial contribution to this magazine, *The Oldest Story in the World,* was done more as a favor to editor Farnsworth Wright than for monetary reward. A tale of greed and torture in Old India, it was the favorite story in the August, 1925, issue in which it appeared, receiving such wildly enthusiastic salutes from fellow writers Seabury Quinn and Frank Belknap Long as "equal to Kipling."

A three-part novel, *The Strange People,* about a group of foreigners held in bondage in a New England valley because of an artificially induced skin condition that resembled leprosy, beginning in the March, 1928, issue of WEIRD TALES, scored very high with the readers and kept the name of Murray Leinster before the readers in the fantasy field at a time when most of his efforts were concentrated elsewhere.

In 1929, Leinster submitted a novelette entitled *Darkness on Fifth Avenue* to DETECTIVE FICTION WEEKLY, along with sketches of three sequels. Howard Bloomfield, the editor, returned the story and recommended a try at ARGOSY, noting that though it might qualify as a detective yarn on a technicality, its suggested sequels could make no similar claim. The editors of that magazine gave the cover of the November 30, 1929, issue to this story of a detective who, using nothing but common sense, hunts down and defeats a brilliant scientific criminal who has built a device which will absorb all light from any area in which he desires to function. This carefully wrought story deserved the bouquets it received from its readers.

The sequel, *The City of the Blind,* went into print in the December 28, 1929 issue. This time the evil genius extends the radius of his machine so it will keep New York in perpetual impenetrable darkness until it pays ransom and delivers up or destroys the men who are fighting against him. A side effect of the process of drawing light from the atmosphere is the generation of heat. This heat, over so large an area, rises, permitting cooler currents to sweep in beneath and resulting in tremendous storms that accompany the blackness.

This second attempt is overcome, and the storm-creating effect becomes the focus of the third story in the series, *The Storm That Had to Be Stopped* in ARGOSY for March 1, 1930. Winds of many times hurricane force devastate New York State and the arch-criminal demands power and money to stop them. U. S. tanks and science foil this plot, only to fall into a fourth and final situation in *The Man Who Put Out the Sun,* in ARGOSY for June 14, 1930. In this one, the Heaviside layer is impregnated with an electrical field which renders the air no longer transparent to the sun's rays. If the problem is not quickly solved, the world will freeze to death. In the corniest action of the group of stories, the errant scientist is destroyed and all's right with the world.

In most of Leinster's stories, the basic theme is that of man battling against nature. *The Runaway Skyscraper* finds men desperately striving to wrest subsistence from the wilderness. *The Mad Planet* and *Red Dust* play weak and ignorant men against savage and powerful insect life. Even though a man technically has created the problem in *Darkness on Fifth Avenue,* the emphasis is never on the villain (who does not appear in any of the four stories until the final pages of the last one), but always on the battle of men against the

physical manifestations of the mad scientist's actions. In
Darkness on Fifth Avenue the battle of men against darkness
is almost allegorical and much of the story's appeal lies in
the link between darkness and evil. *The City of the Blind*
underscores both man's helplessness and his ingenuity in
combating and overcoming a condition of perpetual darkness;
The Storm That Had to Be Stopped chronicles the effort
against wind, rain, and darkness; *The Man Who Put Out the
Sun* pictures man fighting against killing cold.

A majority of Leinster's stories emphasize that it is the
battle, not the ultimate victory, that is important. Man
courageously, sometimes magnificently, fights a mindless, im-
placable creature, phenomenon, or condition. Even if some
man has caused the situation, he is rarely the fundamental
antagonist.

This principle reappears in many of the more recent
Leinsters, specifically *Sand Doom* (ASTOUNDING SCIENCE
FICTION, December, 1955) where man is confronted by
death from frightful heat and shifting sand; *Exploration Team*
(ASTOUNDING SCIENCE FICTION, March, 1956), in which a
new planetary colony is almost destroyed, then ingeniously
works to stay alive against the viciousness of alien beasts;
Critical Difference (ASTOUNDING SCIENCE FICTION, July,
1956) depicting the struggle to keep an entire planet from
freezing over after its sun's heat output has fallen off; *The
Swamp Was Upside Down* (ASTOUNDING SCIENCE FICTION,
September, 1956), in which men on a watery planet exert
desperate efforts to prevent the sea from overwhelming them
and to keep their land from sliding into the ocean.

Another group of stories, known as the "Medic" series,
including *Ribbon in the Sky, The Mutant Weapon,* and *The
Grandfathers' War* are chronicles of medicine against otherworldly disease.

Basically, Will Jenkins, writing as Murray Leinster, does
not concede that there can be a struggle of man against
himself. He recognizes man against nature and he will permit the *appearance* of man battling against man but disallows

the Freudian concept of man against himself. He believes
that psychosomatic ills can exist, but (as in *Ribbon in the
Sky* in ASTOUNDING SCIENCE FICTION for June, 1957, where
people in isolated cities who believe they will become ill if
they come in contact with inhabitants of other communities
do become ill because they believe they will) he indicates
that the cure of this condition is physical action, not psychiatric treatment.

Perhaps an explanation of this attitude may be found in
Leinster's religious faith. Born into an Episcopalian family,
he married a Catholic girl with the understanding that their
children would be raised as Catholics. To understand his four
daughters better and answer their questions intelligently,
Leinster began to study the Catholic religion. The more he
learned the more certain he became that these were beliefs
with which he could live in harmony, because they represented his attitudes even as a youth.

Like many converts, he is, if anything, a more enthusiastic
and outspoken supporter of his faith than most born into it.
Yet, no evidence of proselytizing appears in his works. That
Catholicism has on occasion expressed reservations concerning psychiatry and that Murray Leinster's stories express a
similar attitude doubtless results from the fact that Leinster
thinks that way, not that he is pushing religious belief. His
is a philosophical dislike of Freudian psychology. There is
little probing for motivation. Things happen and man re-
sponds to events. In science fiction, where what happens is
frequently more important than why it happens or to whom
it happens, this tendency has easily been overlooked.

Tanks, a well-constructed short story which appeared in
the very first issue of ASTOUNDING STORIES, January, 1930,
presents a crucial incident in a war between East and West.
The story is noteworthy for the importance it sets on tank
warfare. It also indicates the value of helicopters in a battle
area. But no reason is given for the war to which the reader
is a spectator. While it is evident that wars are planned by
men and men have motivations, for all practical purposes

Leinster handles warfare as though it were an act of *nature*.

The Fifth Dimension Catapult (ASTOUNDING STORIES, January, 1931) is a takeoff on the well-worn theme of another world existing in the fourth dimension. Leinster makes the interesting point that since the fourth dimension is *time,* only our past or future may be found there, so to find another world we must explore a *fifth* dimension. This story, closely allied to the scientific romances so popular in the old ARGOSY, made good enough reading to justify sequel, *The Fifth Dimension Tube* (ASTOUNDING STORIES, January, 1933), in which that other world is more thoroughly explored and the fight is joined against the jungles which are gradually destroying the cities of the intelligent race of that dimension.

One of the few stories in which Leinster takes any pains to bring his villain into focus is the four-part novel, *Murder Madness,* which ran serially in ASTOUNDING STORIES beginning in May, 1930. A man known as The Master gains control over a large part of South America by introducing into the water supply a drug which regularly needs an antidote to prevent people from going berserk and killing one another. The populace becomes dependent upon the antidote for their sanity, just as diabetics depend on insulin to maintain a normal life. The Master is eventually introduced to the readers as a rather kindly old man whose ultimate purpose is to use his dictatorial powers for the good of mankind.

Heroes are something else again, and Leinster will frequently have two or more in a single story. He is also inclined to attach a nationality to his heroes, so we find in the "Darkness" series the Irish detective Hines and the accented German scientist Schaaf. In *The Power Planet* (AMAZING STORIES, June, 1931), a prophetic space story of a disk-shaped station in space (not an earth satellite), whose function is to convert the sun's heat into power which it then transmits to Earth, the heroes are a German (Ferdel) who commands the station and will not surrender it to a war rocket from Earth and a Russian Jew (Skeptsky) who sacrifices his life to blow up the threatening vessel.

In *Morale* (ASTOUNDING STORIES, December, 1931), a ship beaches itself on the New Jersey shore during wartime. It blows up and releases a tank many times larger than a house which wreaks havoc in the countryside with the purpose of diverting thousands of troops away from the front to combat it. The monster tank is eventually destroyed by its own supporting bombing planes through a trick played on its crew. The story is of interest primarily because it suggests LSTs for landing tanks, and air support for land armor.

Far more prophetic was *Invasion* (ASTOUNDING STORIES, March, 1933), in which the countries of the world are divided into two factions, the United Nations (no less!) and the Com-Pubs (communists). The Russians, who have been leading in space exploration, build a spaceship which is detoured so that it will appear to be a visitor from Mars. This first lures the air fleets of the United Nations to investigate, then traps them between two spheres of force so that the communists can conquer the world at will. Though not a particularly outstanding story, it was nevertheless a chilling projection of future political conditions.

The Racketeer Ray (AMAZING STORIES, February, 1932) belongs with the *Darkness* series. An electromagnetic beam, so powerful that it can draw anything of metal and even siphon off electrical current, gets into the hands of gangsters and is used for criminal purposes. When the gangsters are eventually tracked down, one of them, learning that the machine's range is infinite, turns it on the moon overhead and disappears into space clinging to the apparatus rather than spend his life in prison.

Bombing from a height of eight miles through the use of an infra-red ray camera is a projection that Leinster made first in *Morale* and then again in *Politics* (AMAZING STORIES, June, 1932), in which political chicanery almost causes the sinking of the fleet and the surrender of the United States.

Pocket battleships such as Germany used in World War II are introduced, and the aircraft carrier and air power are given some recognition, though it is a battleship with automatic range finders that eventually wins the day.

Leinster's motif of a scientific invention used by gangsters for criminal purposes is repeated in *The Sleep Gas,* a long novelette in ARGOSY for January 16, 1932. With most writers, a device such as this would bring on simple hack work, but the care with which this story is plotted and the realism with which it is told, combined with a very evident and intimate knowledge of New York City, make this story of the use of a sleep gas for criminal purposes outstanding. Leinster's interest in science has been sustained throughout his writing career and he has always had a home laboratory. As a result, even when he was improvising his science out of blue sky, it was usually convincing.

A powerful foundation for convincing science fiction was derived from Leinster's very real interest in science. At his summer home, "Ardudwy," in Gloucester, Virginia, which he acquired in 1921 and has lived in ever since, he tinkered incessantly in his own laboratory. Strange things, with useful applications, came out of that laboratory. Before World War II he had set up a way of isolating radioactive isotopes utilizing equipment costing but $10. He developed a method of reproducing photographs between wet newspapers on a wooden bench. There were scores of other innovations, but most remarkable was Jenkins Systems, a method for making moving pictures without sets, in which live actors walk into sets made up of projected backgrounds. It is currently being used by CBS and is under license to Fairchild Instruments, New York, which maintains a demonstration studio which can be rented by anyone desiring to make use of the method.

The Earth Shaker, an exciting and very readable three-part novel beginning in ARGOSY for April 15, 1933, adopts another Leinster formula that originated as far back as *A Thousand Degrees Below Zero* in THRILL BOOK. A scientist discovers a means of manufacturing earthquakes through the use of ultrasonic waves and begins to shake down city after city in an attempt to establish himself as dictator, but he is finally tracked down.

Back in the 1930's, ARGOSY was a leader in pulp magazines and regular contributors were generally of superior writing ability, on a level halfway between the pulp and the slick magazines. Murray Leinster, under his own name Will Jenkins, was already appearing in SATURDAY EVENING POST, COLLIER'S, LIBERTY, AMERICAN, and other mass-readership magazines of the period. He was in every sense a cut above the markets in which his science fiction appeared. His short story, *A Very Nice Family,* won a $1,000 first prize in LIBERTY at that time and was subsequently reprinted some twenty-five times. Hard-cover book and motion picture sales were also accumulating. Up to 1965, of over 1,300 stories, one-third would be sold to the big-time slicks and a dozen would become pictures.

However, guaranteed assignments from science-fiction magazines were generally filled, even at the relatively low rates that market paid, because they took care of periods when Leinster had nothing else on the fire and because he had always remained an avid fan.

When F. Orlin Tremaine assumed editorship of ASTOUNDING STORIES in 1933, he inaugurated a policy of "thought variants," stories with daring new ideas, to make a bid for leadership in the field. An old friend of Leinster, he approached him for stories under the Leinster name. Of all authors in the field, Leinster seemed a poor choice, for while strong on gadgets he appeared limited in plot variations. At that very moment he was putting the final touches on a short novel for ARGOSY, *War of the Purple Gas*, in which New Asia was again conquering the United States, this time with a device that disintegrated metals. It seemed unlikely that new ideas could be ground from such grain.

His first contribution to Tremaine, *Beyond the Sphinx's Cave,* in the November, 1933, ASTOUNDING STORIES, tells of the discovery of the mythological creatures of Greece in caves beneath that country. It suggests that radioactive mutation of human beings is one of the answers to their existence; the Gorgon's head becomes an artistically wrought projector of a paralysis ray.

This was merely a test run. The story that followed, *Sideways in Time* (ASTOUNDING STORIES, June, 1934), introduces an idea on time travel which had never previously been used. It suggests that the past, future, and present travel not in a straight line, but like a curving river, a concept similar to J. W. Dunne's theories. Not only are events of the actual past, present, and future blended, but also time tracks that never actually happened. As the result of a fault in time, segments of all of these elements superimpose simultaneously, creating a world where Roman Legions still march, the South has won the Civil War, Chinese have settled America, prehistoric monsters roam mindlessly, and Indians raid towns, all in one kaleidoscopic melange. The unfortunate thing was that Leinster took only 20,000 words instead of 100,000 to expound his hypothesis. The result was an outline more than a story, from which other authors reaped the benefits.

Sideways in Time proved no one-shot success. Altering his old formula of letting a remarkable invention fall into the hands of a criminal so as to let the emphasis rest on extrapolation rather than on detection, Leinster's *The Mole Pirate* in the November, 1934, ASTOUNDING STORIES easily ranks among the half-dozen best science-fiction stories he has produced. The seldom-used concept of a machine whose atomic structure can be altered so that it can serve as an underground ship, passing wraithlike through all solid substances, offered fascinating and highly dramatic sequences in an immensely satisfying conjecture.

Proxima Centauri, which ran only a few months later, was as remarkable an effort. Readers of the March, 1935, ASTOUNDING STORIES were treated to one of the earliest stories of an interstellar spaceship that is a world in itself, as well as one presenting a civilization of intelligent carnivorous plants, logically thought out and with intimations of their psychology and motivations.

Leinster was not letting his ASTOUNDING efforts distract him from ARGOSY. *The Rollers* in the December 29, 1934, issue of that magazine was a dramatic story of a man who creates supertornadoes by temporarily nullifying gravity in limited regions. *The Morrison Monument* in the August 10, 1935, issue was intended to be the time travel story to end all time travel stories, pointing out that time machines might remain permanently fixed, indestructibly present in the same spot for the entire duration of their journey into time, to be viewed by generation after generation of humans. *The Extra-Intelligence* in the November 30, 1935, issue was one of Leinster's weaker efforts, however, dealing with the revival of the dead and the efforts of a disembodied superintelligence to take over at the time the feat is accomplished.

Much more successful was *The Fourth Dimensional Demonstrator,* one of the funniest stories ever to appear in science fiction. A machine is built which, by moving back in time, will bring into being a replica of an object placed upon it. First used for duplicating valuables, it accidentally copies fiancees and police officers. This frolic is an example of better science fiction humor.

Leinster's last science-fiction effort in the thirties was a novel, *The Incredible Invasion,* a tale more of the variety that he had popularized in ARGOSY, telling of invaders from another dimension who paralyze the entire city of Newark, New Jersey, and loot it until they are stopped. Beginning in ASTOUNDING STORIES for August, 1936, and running for six installments, it belongs in the category of "good fun."

The slant in science fiction began to change. Technical knowledge was downgraded. An entirely new approach was taken, with the stress more heavily on the sociological and psychological impact of future changes than on the scientific advances themselves. Many of the old-time favorites were unable to adjust and were replaced by bright new stars, such as Robert A. Heinlein, L. Sprague de Camp, A. E. van Vogt, Lester del Rey, Theodore Sturgeon, Isaac Asimov, and L. Ron Hubbard. Leinster, identified with an outdated era, did not seem to belong.

Then, in 1942, several short stories by Murray Leinster appeared in ASTOUNDING SCIENCE-FICTION. Those in the "know" passed these off as fillers made possible by the wartime shortage of writers. Then, Murray Leinster lowered the boom with *First Contact*. A novelette appearing in AS-TOUNDING SCIENCE-FICTION for May, 1945, it approached from an entirely new angle the idea of earthmen meeting aliens of high technological status. An intersteller Earth ship meets another ship of comparably advanced design in the great vastness between star systems. The crew does not dare ignore the contact, for the alien ship may trail the Earth ship back to Earth, and there is no way to be sure if it constitutes a menace to mankind. The alien ship is in a similar dilemma. The situation is eventually resolved by an exchange of ships so that both groups can benefit from new knowledge without revealing their locations.

This aspect of the problems of meeting another intelligent race had never previously been examined or evaluated. Every top writer in the field stood at attention and saluted. Anthology appearances began to multiply and the story was quickly accepted as one of the great classics of modern science fiction. An entire anthology titled *Contact,* leading off with Leinster's story, was edited for Paperback Library by Noel Keyes (pen name of David N. Keightley, contributor of fiction to THE SATURDAY EVENING POST) in 1963.

The story penetrated the Iron Curtain and was discussed in the text of *The Heart of the Serpent,* a novelette by Ivan Yefremov, published in Russia in 1959. Yefremov, a Russian fossil hunter, as well as the author of several science-fiction novels, contended that Leinster's thinking was that of a decadent capitalist and that races advanced enough to have spaceships would be beyond primitive fears of war and violence. From Leinster's attitude he derived his title "Heart of the Serpent," contending through the mouth of one of his characters that ". . . in the writings of those who sought to defend the old society, proclaiming the inevitability of war and the eternal existence of capitalism, I also see the heart of a poisonous snake."

But, to display how truly harmonious, filled with sweetness and light, a first space meeting between two different intelligent races would actually be, Yefremov postulates a fluorine-breathing species on a fluorine-atmosphere planet; such a race could not conceivably covet anything possessed by earthmen.

The year *First Contact* was published, ARGOSY, now a slicked-up men's magazine, ran a Murray Leinster two-part short novel. *The Murder of the U.S.A.* This story, which followed the dropping of the atomic bomb on Hiroshima, was one of the most remarkably accurate short-range expositions ever to appear in science fiction. The United States of the near future is armed with batteries of intercontinental ballistic missiles, propelled by rockets and possessing nuclear warheads. These are situated in bombproof underground bunkers, held in reserve as a war deterrent. Then, one third of the population of the U.S.A. is destroyed by a sneak attack. Since many countries have the capacity to deliver such a blow and the rockets came over the poles, not implicating any one nation, the United States works to find out who is the international "murderer" while the whole world sweats. If the country that sent the bombs tries to follow up its advantage with an invasion, it will immediately expose itself to the retailiatory effect of the hundreds of American nuclear warheads.

The plot had initially been approved by LOOK and a tentative agreement to pay $4,000 for the completed story had been made, but when LOOK saw the final manuscript they refused it. After its appearance in ARGOSY, John W. Campbell convinced Crown Publishers to publish the short novel as a book, but they avoided calling it science fiction and instead issued it in 1946 as a murder mystery!

Leinster's thinking on modern lines proved seminal. With the age of the computer fast moving in, he wrote and had published in the March, 1946, ASTOUNDING SCIENCE-FIC-TION (under the Will F. Jenkins byline) a story titled *A Logic Named Joe,* dealing with the time when a device would be present in every home, linked in with a central univac-type "tank," which would contain all man's knowledge and would dispense information to subscribers. Naturally, there would be automatic censors. What happens when a faulty machine gets around the normal blocks, and dispenses information ranging from how to murder your wife and not be detected to the easiest way for a bank president to embezzle, makes for a brilliant and probably prophetic story.

When considering the potentialities of computers in its educational film "The Living Machine," released in 1962, The National Film Board of Canada incorporated certain observations from *A Logic Named Joe,* mentioning it by name.

Symbiosis, a Jenkins story, with the unique concept of an entire nation being infected with a disease to which they had been immunized, but which would kill other human beings with whom they came in contact, was published in COLLIER'S for January 14, 1947.

The Strange Case of John Kingman, ASTOUNDING SCIENCE FICTION, (May, 1948), dealing with the discovery of a man who has been locked up in an insane asylum for 162 years —a paranoid alien from another planet—and the attempts to cure him, is a masterpiece of the short story form and has been since widely imitated.

A complete change of pace was *The Lonely Planet* (THRILLING WONDER STORIES, December, 1949). An entire planet is covered by a single organism, called Alyx, which gradually gains consciousness from its association with men, whose most complex orders it follows blindly. Though it eventually becomes more intelligent than humanity, its motivating drive is companionship. Fearing its powers, mankind futilely attempts to destroy the creature. Its eventually successful efforts to arrive at an accommodation with the human race are touchingly and ingeniously related by Leinster.

Like the alien in *The Strange Case of John Kingman,* the science-fiction fraternity awoke one day in 1962 to the realization that Will F. Jenkins alias Murray Leinster was an unusual phenomenon. Here was a man who had again and again proved that he was leader, if not master, of the field in all its transformations and nuances. On September 1, 1963, he was Guest of Honor of The 21st World Science Fiction Convention, held at The Statler-Hilton, Washington, D.C. For more than a decade they had called him "the dean of science fiction;" now they had decided to make it official.

4

EDMOND HAMILTON

The Dean of Science Fiction Writers" is undeniably Murray Leinster, but who is heir apparent? Most certainly it must be Edmond Hamilton, one of the most underestimated (though not unappreciated) writers of science fiction.

Since 1926, not a year has passed that has not seen as many as a score of Hamilton stories appear in the science-fiction and fantasy magazines. Nor is his a fading talent which should be recognized "for *auld lang syne."* Three recent years running, science-fiction novels of his were Doubleday Science Fiction Book Club selections: *The Star of Life* (1959), *The Haunted Stars* (1960), and *Battle for the Stars* (1961). His short story *Requiem* (AMAZING STORIES, April, 1962) was, by far, the most acclaimed story of the year in that magazine. Its hymnlike mood is expressed by the spaceship commander, the last man to tread the surface of the earth before it spirals from its orbit into the sun, and culminating in his sense of outrage at the commercial professionalism of the camera crews and commentators on hand to record the mother planet's final plunge. Only slightly less applauded were *The Stars, My Brothers* (AMAZING STORIES, May, 1962), involving a dramatic choice between sentiment and rationality by a man of the present restored to consciousness in the distant future, and *Sunfire!* (AMAZING STORIES, September, 1962), where a man's pride is humbled by contact with creatures of living flame. All three stories displayed a refinement of technical skills and a maturity of outlook that added full dimension to Hamilton's long-acknowledged mastery of action and adventure.

Edmond Hamilton made his first appearance as a writer with *The Monster-God of Mamurth* back in the August, 1926, issue of WEIRD TALES; he has remained constantly on the science-fiction scene ever since.

When Hamilton's first story appeared, science-fiction magazines were only six months old; AMAZING STORIES, April, 1926, was the first. The hotbeds in which good science fiction was nurtured were ARGOSY and WEIRD TALES (which periodicals usually ran at least one, and sometimes as many as six, science-fiction tales an issue).

One of the "greats" of ARGOSY's fantasy writers was A. Merritt, and his works became literary icons for young Hamilton's worship. Using as his inspiration, Merritt's classic *The People of the Pit* (ALL-STORY MAGAZINE, January 5, 1918), a masterpiece about a lost city in an Alaskan cave, Hamilton made his first attempt to become a professional writer with a short story, *Beyond the Unseen Wall.* WEIRD TALES' editor, Farnsworth Wright, rejected it because of an unclear ending, but almost a year later, rewritten as *The Desert God,* it was accepted by him and appeared under the title *The Monster-God of Mamurth.*

By a remarkable coincidence, WEIRD TALES ran it in the same issue with the only story Merritt had ever submitted to them, *The Woman of the Wood.* WEIRD TALES rated its stories according to reader preferences and printed a monthly report on the favorite. As a head-swelling beginner's achievement, Hamilton's story scored second only to Merritt's, beating out even H. P. Lovecraft's contribution that month. *The Monster-God of Mamurth* was above-average for its period. An explorer in the North African desert discovers a legendary city protected by walls of invisibility. The long-departed inhabitants of that city worshipped a gigantic spiderlike creature, transparent as air, which, it turns out, is still alive and roams through the city's deserted buildings. Some incidents are singularly effective: one in which the hero stands visually unsupported on a 100-foot-high temple stairway; another where he gropes his way along walls and corridors he cannot see, stalked by the monstrous "god"; and, finally, the vivid imagery of his throwing a huge but optically nonexistent building block in the direction of approaching noises to pin down the menace which gradually takes shape as it splatters itself with its own blood in its desperate thrashings to escape.

Even before *The Monster-God of Mamurth* was published, Hamilton had sold to Wright *Across Space,* a three-part novel, which began in the immediately following September, 1926, WEIRD TALES. In this novel, the Easter Island statues are found to be images of Martians, still living in a city underground, who are pulling Mars close enough to earth so that overcrowding on the Red Planet can be eased by emigration. The writing and background are absorbing, but the science (reminiscent of André Laurie's *Conquest of the Moon,* 1889, in which that satellite is magnetically drawn down to earth) is embarassingly crude.

The Metal Giants followed and was illustrated on the cover of the December, 1926, WEIRD TALES. Despite the fact that it used the old Frankenstein theme (an artificial brain turns on its creator and builds tremendous atom-powered robots which devastate cities and gas their inhabitants into extinction), it received *three* times as many reader votes as its nearest runner-up. Corny but effective, it was later mimeographed in an abbreviated version by Jerome Siegel, correspondent of Hamilton's, for the Swanson Book Co., Washburn, North Dakota, who for many years dispensed the pamphlet as a premium to buyers of Swanson's mail order science fiction.

The Atomic Conquerors (WEIRD TALES, February, 1927) again was first choice of readers; it tells of a war between creatures of the micro-universe (subatomic) and of the macro-universe (of which we are but an atom) with Earth as a battleground. In the following issue, *Evolution Island,* an imaginative *tour de force,* about a ray that speeds up evolution on an island and its bizarre effects upon all life forms, including the emergence of intelligent, mobile plants, missed first place by only a few votes. At the age of 23, Hamilton was off to an auspicious writing start.

Edmond Hamilton was born in Youngstown, Ohio, on October 21, 1904, at a time when that part of the country still possessed a New England village air. His father's side of the family was Scotch-Irish and Presbyterian, and had moved into Ohio from the Shenandoah Valley of Virginia in 1820. There was also some Welsh ancestry, and a strong American Indian strain is reflected in Edmond Hamilton's features.

His father, Scott B. Hamilton, the youngest of six sons of Homer Hamilton, who owned a small steel mill, was a newspaper cartoonist. Maude Whinery, his mother, from Quaker stock of New Castle, Pennsylvania, had been a schoolteacher prior to her marriage.

The family fell upon difficult days shortly after Edmond was born, and his father tried running a farm outside of Poland, Ohio. The boy's earliest memories were of a home with no electricity, water, or gas. Automobiles were a rarity on the dirt roads. "The cows, the chickens, the sugar camps in the snowy woods which we children hung around, gave the whole feel of an old, tranquil, unchanging rural America," Hamilton recalls.

Two older sisters, Esther and Adeline, and one younger sister, ran the odds against the one boy. He found himself unmercifully bossed around.

The mother was the strength of the family, while his father was the romantic, enlisting for the Spanish-American War almost immediately following his marriage in 1898 and being shunted to Alaska for three years to build telegraph lines during the gold rush period. His mother taught school while the "man of the house" was gone.

Farm life was left behind when the family moved to New Castle, Pennsylvania, a town of 40,000, in 1911 and his father landed a job on a local newspaper. The young Hamilton was far from a recluse, enjoying a fishing, fighting, fun-raising childhood along with his schoolmates. As a student he was exceptional, entering high school in 1914 when only 10 years old and graduating, without difficulty, at 14.

The family, convinced they had a genius on their hands, rushed him into Westminster College in the fall of 1919. The tests of the freshman class rated him tops in I.Q. and expectations were high. "I started out my sophomore year as an intellectual of 15," remembered Hamilton. "I smoked a briar pipe and read Shaw, O'Neill, and Ibsen. I majored in physics. But after my first year I got bored with classes."

The difference in age between him and other students soon told. He became increasingly introverted and began collecting old books, the beginning of a lifelong passion. He had had only a minor interest in fantasy heretofore, but now ALL-STORY MAGAZINE and ARGOSY began to take on a new sheen. The marvelous fancies of A. Merritt, Edgar Rice Burroughs, Homer Eon Flint, Austin Hall, George Allan England, and Victor Rousseau quickly supplanted the more earthbound O'Neill and Ibsen. In his newfound interest was a magazine world of escape from the drag and routine of academic life. When he consistently began cutting chapel, Westminster, a Presbyterian school, expelled him during his third year.

Though bitterly disappointed, the family stood by him as

he abandoned all hope of ever contributing to the advancement of physics by accepting a job on the Pennsylvania Railroad as yard clerk. He had worked part time in similar posts during summer vacations and was enthralled by railroads. When the position was eliminated in late 1924, he sat down to write his first story, never to work for a salary again.

The fecundity of Hamilton's ideas and their high degree of originality won favor with WEIRD TALES' readers. Farnsworth Wright was delighted. Hamilton was clearly an asset in holding the science-fiction members of his audience now that AMAZING STORIES was on the scene. He might even attract new ones looking for more science fiction. In the 27 years of life that remained to it, WEIRD TALES, after that first pause in accepting *The Desert God,* never rejected an Edmond Hamilton story for any reason.

Particularly influential was Hamilton's story *The Moon Menace* (WEIRD TALES, September, 1927). It was here that Murray Leinster obtained the idea of using impenetrable darkness as a weapon (in *The Darkness on Fifth Avenue*) which caused something of a sensation when run in ARGOSY (November 30, 1929). *The Moon Menace* also made early use of matter transmitters as a method of interplanetary transport. (*Radio Mates* by Benjamin Witwer, AMAZING STORIES, July, 1927, had used it for getting about on earth.) This story won a well-deserved first place as the best in the issue.

Equally remarkable was *The Time Raider,* a four-part novel beginning in the October, 1927, WEIRD TALES. The intriguing notion of bringing together in one age a number of warriors from different eras in history had been used previously for ghastly visitants by John Kendrick Bangs in *A Houseboat on the Styx* (1895) and more scientifically by J. L. Anton in his short story *Creatures of the Ray* (ARGOSY, October 10, 1925) but it had never been explored in a full-length novel. A man from the future utilizes a time machine to go back into the past recruiting or kidnaping the army he needs for his purposes. It would remain the most notable story of its type until A. E. van Vogt's *Recruiting Station* (ASTOUNDING SCIENCE-FICTION, March, 1942). A few years later, John W. Campbell would pick up the problem of fighting an invisible airship (*Solarite*, AMAZING STORIES, November, 1930) which Hamilton had used so dramatically in *The Time Raider* and solve it in his own manner. Despite the passage of the years, *The Time Raider* still remains a superior thriller.

The entire lead editorial in the June, 1928, WEIRD TALES was devoted to Edmond Hamilton, and in the October number the editor further said: "Two examples of *genius* discovered and made public, Edmond Hamilton, supreme master of the weird scientific story, and Robert S. Carr, the apostle of the young generation and author of the popular novel *The Rampant Age,* at 19 a best seller."

This was at the time when Hamilton had launched into the superscience phase of his writing, a period when he began tossing worlds and suns around like billiard balls. This flair derived from old-timer Homer Eon Flint (*The Planeteer,* ALL-WEEKLY STORY, March 9, 1928) and Hamilton went to an extra-solar-system-scale in *Crashing Suns,* a two-part serial in WEIRD TALES (August, 1928).

Even more significant and far ahead of its time was *The Star Stealers* (WEIRD TALES, February, 1929), the first of a series which projected the reader into a far-distant time when the planets around most of the suns were inhabited and formed an interstellar council called The Council of Suns. To keep order in the galaxy and enforce its edicts, the council's tool was the Interstellar Patrol. The problem raised by the problem of diverting an invading black star is the first one solved by the patrol. *Galactic Patrol* by E. E. Smith, based on a similar concept, would not appear until the September, 1938, ASTOUNDING SCIENCE-FICTION. After that, such cosmic agencies would become science-fiction clichés.

A. Merritt was so taken with the idea of an interstellar patrol that he descended from his editorial Olympus and tried with might and main to get his own book publisher,

Boni, to issue the Interstellar Patrol Series as one volume, to no avail.

During the period 1927-1929, though the WEIRD TALES roster included such legendary notables as H. P. Lovecraft, Seabury Quinn, Robert E. Howard, Clark Ashton Smith, Henry S. Whitehead, Donald Wandrei, August W. Derleth, Frank Belknap Long, S. Fowler Wright, Gaston Leroux, Otis Adelbert Kline, E. F. Benson, Murray Leinster, Ray Cummings, Victor Rousseau, and David H. Keller, M.D., to name a few. Edmond Hamilton was *the* most popular author, as a simple adding up of first and second places in the readership polls of those years proves.

That Hamilton's stature today is not greater presents an apparent paradox—until the facts are analyzed.

There are two reasons basically. First, only a minority of the regular readers of AMAZING STORIES and, later, the other science-fiction magazines ever read WEIRD TALES at all. AMAZING STORIES claimed a readership of about 100,000. It is doubtful if WEIRD TALES had more than 50,000 readers at any time during its 30 years of publication. Of that, probably 25 percent, at a generous estimate, represented readership of both magazines. Most of the readers of AMAZING STORIES were unaware of Hamilton's fine contributions elsewhere and the truth is that the majority of ideas innovated by Hamilton were not directly copied from him at all but were *rediscovered* at a later date by other authors. Issues of the early WEIRD TALES containing his stories are so few and so rare that only a handful of people own them. As a result, even if someone deliberately adapted an old Hamilton idea, extremely few would suspect the origin.

As substantiation: when Hamilton submitted his first story to AMAZING STORIES, *The Comet Doom,* the editor bragged about discovering a great new talent, although when the story appeared in the January, 1928, issue, Hamilton stories had been appearing and had been exceptionally well received in WEIRD TALES for more than a year. A story of a race of aliens who have transferred their brains to metal bodies and do the same for an earthman, offering to take him around the universe (probably the genesis of the famed Prof. Jameson series by Neil R. Jones as well as H. P. Lovecraft's *The Whisperer in Darkness*), *The Comet Doom* was thought by the editors to be good enough for a scene from it to be used on the cover, but they did not think Hamilton's name sufficiently well known to be mentioned on that cover.

The second reason for Hamilton's comparative lack of stature lies in the repetitious plot structure of his early stories. The framework of each story was very nearly the same. A menace threatens to conquer, enslave, or wipe out the world (or the universe) and is thwarted by a single man. To this must be added a sprinkling of major scientific faults, frequently so glaring as to all but negate believability. Typical of these scientific sins of omission was the questionable premise in *Across Space* that Mars could be pulled to the very edge of the Earth's atmospheric envelope and left dangling there while Martians flew down to the surface. Even worse is the complete disregard for distances and time factors in the Interstellar Patrol series, in which ships zip past star systems thousands of light years apart in days or sometimes only hours, with no explanation from the author.

In addition, characterization was virtually nonexistent and dialogue was frequently on the Frank Merriwell level.

Despite these considerable faults, Hamilton had imaginative vitality and narrative ability of considerable power. A Stapeldonian thoroughness in delineating the history, culture, and philosophy of his aliens was not completely appreciated by the reader distracted by the vividness and swiftness of unfolding events. It was the extraordinary variety of his locales and the striking originality of his secondary themes that gave Hamilton popularity, even while some readers injected a note of criticism by bestowing on him the appellation "World Saver."

When he began writing novels for AMAZING STORIES QUARTERLY and AMAZING STORIES, he did not vary the formula that had enjoyed such success in WEIRD TALES. In

Locked Worlds (AMAZING STORIES QUARTERLY, Spring, 1929) he saves Earth from the menace of the spider men, inhabitants of a simultaneous world whose electrons move in the opposite direction from Earth's; *The Other Side of the Moon* (AMAZING STORIES QUARTERLY, Fall, 1929) finds the turtle men of the moon thwarted in their evil design to conquer the earth; in *The Universe Wreckers*, a three-part novel beginning in AMAZING STORIES for May, 1930, a marvelously enthralling and infinitely detailed account of the metal-roofed planet of Neptune cloaks the well-worn plot of the defeat of a plan to split the sun and destroy the earth.

No story of his of this genre was ever rejected by any editor, but Hamilton, almost hopelessly typed, could abide the stigma no longer. For his declaration of independence, he wrote *The Man Who Saw the Future* (AMAZING STORIES, October, 1930), a tale of a fifteenth century apothecary, transferred to the twentieth century to the accompaniment of a clap of thunder, who is sentenced to death as a sorcerer when he returns to his own time and relates the marvels he has seen. His narration of the wonders of our times, told in the figures of speech of the Middle Ages, remains memorable in its effective simplicity.

Eric Frank Russell was to popularize the bizarrely logical intimations of Charles Fort in *Sinister Barrier* (UNKNOWN, March, 1939), but it was Edmond Hamilton who had actually introduced Fortean themes to the science-fiction field ten years earlier. After reading *The Book of the Damned* (1919) and *New Lands* (1923), he had sent a batch of newspaper clippings about strange phenomena to the Bronx belittler of science, Charles Fort, and they struck up a correspondence. In one letter he asked Fort what he would do if the Fortean system were taught in the schools as right and proper. Fort wrote back, "Why, in that case I would propound the damnably heterodox theory that the world is round!"

The Space Visitors, published in the March, 1930, AIR WONDER STORIES (a short-lived experiment of Hugo Gernsback's), was taken right out of *The Book of the Damned* and tells of a gigantic scoop that periodically descends from the upper atmosphere, scraping up samples for some unimaginable group of intelligences to examine. It was a strongly Fortean symbolic effort.

More than a year later, the identical idea of *Sinister Barrier,* that "Earth is property," was used in Hamilton's *The Earth Owners* (WEIRD TALES, August, 1931) and impressed no one at all except Julius Schwartz, a specialist in science fiction, in a few years to become Hamilton's agent, who wrote a letter to the magazine.

Somewhat earlier, in AIR WONDER STORIES (November and December, 1929), Hamilton had presented another of his pioneering ideas in *Cities in the Air.* Though the concept of a floating aerial city had been used as early as Jonathan Swift's *Gulliver's Travels* (Laputa), Hamilton's spectacle of ranks of mighty cities wheeling through the air to join in stupendous conflict may well have inspired James Blish's spin-dizzy's in that author's popular series of the footloose space okies.

Hamilton did not live all of his adventures vicariously. Through correspondent Jerome Siegel he had made contact with Jack Williamson, a New Mexico writer, who had in common the fact that he was inspired to write by reading A. Merritt. The two decided to sail down the full length of the Mississippi in the manner of Huckleberry Finn, agreeing to meet in Minneapolis the first week in June, 1931, there to begin the trip.

On the way to Minneapolis, Hamilton stopped in Chicago to see the editor of WEIRD TALES, Farnsworth Wright, as well as two of that magazine's most popular authors, Otis Adelbert Kline and E. Hoffman Price. Warm personal friendships were thus formed.

In Minneapolis, Hamilton and Williamson bought a 14-foot skiff, two outboard motors, and a camping outfit. Armed with nautical ignorance, they sailed forth to conquer Old Man River. A summer of blunder, near-danger, exploration, and fun followed, until even the emergency engine sputtered its choking last cough and they completed the trip to New Orleans aboard the only remaining stern-wheel steamer still operating on the river.

The two men were a contrast in personalities: "Jack was then," Hamilton reported, "one of the most patient and restrained people alive. I was then mercurial, explosive, impatient. In spite of that we go along."

The autumn of 1933, Williamson showed up at New Castle and the two hied off to Florida, ending up as beachcombers.

There were two trips to the ranch of Jack Williamson's parents in 1935 and 1937 and the pair traveled about the Southwest and the border country regularly.

The years of good times together were also the years in which Hamilton's powers as a writer matured. Evolution had been a recurrent theme in his stories and he reached a peak in his handling of it in *The Man Who Evolved* (WONDER STORIES, April, 1931), in which the pace of natural change is artificially stepped up by a machine. A scientist experimenting on himself moves from level to level, eventually being transformed into a tremendous brain feeding itself on pure energy and capable of moving interdimensionally. Still, prodded by curiousity, the brain commands that the experiment progress. The result: protoplasm. Evolution proves to be circular. The fascination and power of the idea compensates for occasional weakness in writing.

Hamilton has written so much that it is possible to record only the most memorable of his stories. High on the list of selections is *A Conquest of Two Worlds* (WONDER STORIES, April, 1932), a strong protest against colonial psychology in dealing with the less technologically advanced creatures of other worlds that is prophetic in its weaponry.

The theme of A. Conan Doyle's Professor Challenger novelette *When the World Screamed* (in *The Maracot Deep*, 1929), that this planet is a living entity, capable of physical feeling, is made vivid in Hamilton's handling of *The Earth*

Brain (WEIRD TALES, April, 1932). In this story, a man who has tracked the intelligence center of the globe to the North Pole defies it, and is forced to flee perpetually for his life as tremors and quakes seek him out in each new hiding place and threaten destruction of the entire community unless he leaves.

The favorable reaction of readers to Laurence Manning's three-part novel *Wreck of the Asteroid,* which began in WONDER STORIES for December, 1932, a story stressing realism rather than romanticism in projecting what the world of Mars might be like, prompted Hamilton to try the same tack. While wintering in Key West with Jack Williamson in 1933, he pounded out *What's It Like Out There?* which stressed man's weaknesses, the heartbreak, the pettiness, and the political expediency, which might be part of the first expedition to Mars. Editors drew back from Hamilton's approach and the story remained buried in his trunk for nearly twenty years.

Then, at the urging of his wife, he dusted it off, did some revision and sent it to THRILLING WONDER STORIES. Editor Samuel Mines waxed poetic about "the new Edmond Hamilton" who rose, "phoenix-like, from the ashes of Captain Future." The story was acclaimed a modern masterpiece and it was said: "Now science fiction has grown up. And so has Edmond Hamilton."

"Give a dog a bad name . . ." Hamilton was no longer the "World Saver," and in the early thirties was not only writing stories of outstanding merit, but stories far in advance of the time. *The Island of Unreason* (WONDER STORIES, May, 1933) deservedly won the Jules Verne Prize Award for the best story of the calendar year 1933; *A Conquest of Two Worlds* took a similar award as the best science-fiction novelette of 1932. In the future, as Hamilton saw it in *The Island of Unreason,* American society has an island to which are sentenced all antisocial men and women who must live there for varying periods, unguarded, with their fellow malcontents, so they can experience the problems of life and survival where no law and order exist. The sociological and psychological implications of the story make it an early milestone in the maturation of magazine science fiction.

Nor were Hamilton's talents applied only to science fiction. *The Man Who Returned* (WEIRD TALES, February, 1934) has forced his way out of his tomb where he has been prematurely laid to rest and seeks to return to his family, friends, and business associates; this is at once a tale of horror and of philosophical insight. Hamilton used his real name for this one, but when the spirit moved him he was prone to spin terror yarns for WEIRD TALES under the nom de plume of Hugh Davidson.

To supplement his science-fiction writing income, Hamilton tried his hand at detective stories, selling his first to Street & Smith's DETECTIVE STORY MAGAZINE in 1932, then the leader in the field. The same year he introduced the mystery element into *The Space-Rocket Murders* (AMAZING STORIES, October, 1932), prophetically using Braun as the name of the leading German rocket scientist, who was appropriately conducting liquid hydrogen fuel experiments in Berlin. Braun is merely one of eleven savants involved in rocket research who is mysteriously murdered. The culprits prove to be Venusians disguised as earthmen; they have achieved controlled atomic power, enabling them to project their rockets across space.

No Hamilton story before 1933 had any love interest whatsoever. Very few even mention women. Hamilton was frequently quoted as being cynically against marriage. Perhaps the preponderance of sisters who outvoted him in his youth had jaundiced him; perhaps it was his mother's favorite quip whenever a man of the town got married: "Ah, he'll get his wings clipped now."

His mother's remark, however, gave him the idea for *He That Hath Wings* (WEIRD TALES, July, 1938). A child born of parents seriously affected by radiation develops wings. When he grows to maturity, the only terms under which the girl he loves will agree to marry him is if he has his appendages surgically removed. He does so and their marriage appears to be happy. Soon a child is on the way, but he notes that his wings have begun to grow back. Shortly after the birth of the child he is determined to have his new wings removed but succumbs to the desire of feeling the exhilaration of flying one last time. Airborne, he compulsively starts south, even though the long-unused pinions are rapidly tiring. Over the water his strength gives out and he finds himself "glad to be falling as all they with wings must finally fall, after a brief lifetime of wild, sweet flight, dropping contentedly to rest."

In 1940, by prearrangement, Hamilton met Jack Williamson in Los Angeles. Julius Schwartz, Hamilton's agent since 1934, was also in town with Mort Weisinger, then editing THRILLING WONDER STORIES, STARTLING STORIES, and CAPTAIN FUTURE, to all of which Hamilton was a regular contributor. They introduced him to Leigh Brackett, a young lady who had joined the fraternity of science-fiction authors only that year with *Martian Quest* (ASTOUNDING SCIENCE-FICTION, February, 1940). Hamilton and she found that they had a number of things in common: there were strains of Mohawk and Sioux in the Brackett family line; she, too, had read Edgar Rice Burroughs avidly, as early as the age of seven. Edmond returned to Los Angeles the next summer and met Leigh almost weekly at a salon presided over by Robert A. Heinlein and attended by Ray Bradbury who would eventually collaborate with Brackett in *The Lorelei of the Red Mist* (PLANET STORIES, Summer, 1946). She would write the first 9,000 words and Bradbury the remainder of a long novelette of a man who dies to find himself on Venus in the superb body of a character named Conan.

But despite mutual attraction, nothing happened between Hamilton and Brackett because he was expecting momenarily to be inducted into the armed services. Two days before his induction was scheduled to occur, a ruling was passed exempting men 38 years or older. Then both his mother and father became ill, to remain practically invalids until 1945.

When Hamilton arrived in Los Angeles in 1946 he was greeted warmly by Leigh Brackett and Ray Bradbury, and, on December 31, 1946, Hamilton and Brackett were married in San Gabriel, California. Among their close friends were C. L. Moore and Henry Kuttner, another notable marriage of science-fiction personalities with whom they motored back east in 1949, "debarking" at Kinsman, Ohio, where Hamilton had some relatives. There they became enchanted with a 120-year-old farmhouse set on 35 acres, and made it their permanent home.

Had Leigh Brackett continued writing science fiction, her achievement would have been great because she possesses unusual ability. Her forte was swashbuckling, romantic adventure set on another world, a kind of story much appreciated by readers. Parenthetically, the writer who at present is most popular for the same type of story is also a woman, Andre Norton, probably the outstanding science-fiction writer currently writing in the romantic tradition. One of the last important things that Brackett did in science fiction, before Hollywood claimed her, was a novel for Doubleday titled *The Long Tomorrow.* (1955). This was a serious work on the struggle against reaction in the post-atomic world which J. Francis McComas, reviewing it in THE NEW YORK TIMES of October 23, 1955, characterized as coming "awfully close to being a great work of science fiction."

Her screen work made her and Hamilton virtual commuters between Kinsman, Ohio, and Hollywood, where her credits include collaborating with William Faulkner on the screen adaptation of *The Big Sleep,* as well as *Rio Bravo* and *Hatari!*

While Hamilton's personal life had eventually arrived at a happy beginning, he had permitted his writing career to take a direction which was destined to put off almost indefinitely the creation of a new image for him as a quality writer of science fiction.

It came about this way. While attending The First World Science Fiction Convention in New York City, July 2, 1939, Leo Margulies, editorial director of Standard Magazines, after listening to the proceedings for a few hours, emitted his now famous line: "I didn't think you fans could be so damn sincere." He followed it with action, plotting on the spot a new science-fiction magazine. It was to be called CAPTAIN FUTURE, a pulp aimed at the younger teen-agers, each issue to feature a novel about the same character. There must be a superscientist hero. There must also be aides: a robot and an android and, of course, a beautiful female assistant. Each story must be a crusade to bring to justice an arch villain; and, in each novel, the hero must be captured and escape three times. CAPTAIN FUTURE was the pure distillation of stereotyped science-fiction gimmicks brought to bear on a single-character magazine.

Hamilton, asked to do the stories, wrote all but three of the 21 novels and novelettes in the series to a hard-and-fast formula. Thus, during a period when a new type of science fiction was coming into vogue and creating reputations for Heinlein, van Vogt, Sturgeon, and Asimov, Hamilton found himself labeled a specialist in blood-and-thunder juveniles.

Even when two Hamilton pulp novels (*The Star Kings,* 1949, and *City at the World's End,* 1951), were published in hard covers by Frederick Fell and got surprisingly favorable reviews, including THE NEW YORK TIMES, it was all dismissed as an inexplicable occurrence by hard-core scientifictionists who could not keep from thinking of Captain Future when they read the name Edmond Hamilton. Most of them were not aware that a collection of Hamilton's short stories from WEIRD TALES and the science-fiction magazines had gone into book form as *The Horror on the Asteroid and Other Tales of Planetary Horror* as far back as 1936, a period when such distinction was rare.

Throughout the fifties, Hamilton continued to turn out

a variety of science fiction for THRILLING WONDER STORIES, STARTLING STORIES, IMAGINATION, UNIVERSE SCIENCE FICTION and other titles, primarily action stories written with an originality and care atypical of the type. Since the action story in science fiction was going out of vogue, there was little comment re Hamilton until the Doubleday Science Fiction Book Club began to make his inclusion a habit, his full-length titles began to appear in paperback, and his new work for AMAZING STORIES received top reader endorsement.

The invitations to Hamilton and Brackett to appear as guests of honor at the regional Metropolitan Science Fiction Conference in New York in 1954 were extended more out of affection than as tokens of literary achievement. The reverse was true when the two were offered and accepted the same role at the 1964 World Science Fiction convention held in Oakland, California.

In these modern times, men in the arts and the industries are honored for many unusual achievements. Few can claim to have been eulogized, as Edmond Hamilton was at the 1964 World Convention, for precedents as striking as "pioneering the concept of interstellar adventure, the notion of a galactic empire and galactic police force, the use of complete darkness as a weapon, employing a time machine to recruit an army from the past, and introducing Fortean themes."

5

JACK WILLIAMSON

It is a pity that the quality of Stewart's writing is such that this "space opera" ranks only slightly above that of a comic strip adventure.

That section of a review of *Seetee Ship* by Will Stewart was brought to the attention of the editors of THE NEW YORK SUNDAY NEWS. The review, by Villiers Gerson, appeared in the Sunday book-review supplement of THE NEW YORK TIMES in September, 1951. The management of THE NEWS had been seriously worried about the effect of television on circulation and advertising revenue and were exploring various means to offset this probability. One possible solution was to feature an exclusive, nonsyndicated comic strip, but they wanted a writer a cut above average to handle the continuity.

In Portales, New Mexico, Jack Williamson's telephone rang. It was Ama Barker of THE NEWS. The editors had decided, on the basis of the review, that he was just the man to write their new comic strip. They had discovered that

Will Stewart was his pen name and called long distance to see if he would work for them.

Williamson gasped, but at last, in a leisurely Southwestern drawl, he managed to choke out his agreement.

He flew to New York where it was decided that a Sunday page to be called *Beyond Mars* would be constructed from the background of his books *Seetee Ship* and *Seetee Shock,* adventures in the mining and utilization of contraterrene matter (substances repelled by ordinary matter) in the asteroid belt. The cartoonist, Lee Elias, had previously worked with Milt Caniff on *Terry and the Pirates,* and he now employed the same style for *Beyond Mars.* Three times annually Jack Williamson would arrive in New York and work out the story line with the editors and the artist. Each week he would receive a handsome check.

The editors of THE NEWS must have checked and been aware that they were employing the services of one of the most distinguished names in science fiction. In Williamson they were getting an author who had earned a half-dozen reputations for outstanding performance in various aspects of science fiction and who had powerfully influenced several major trends. And this, the most lucrative assignment of his life, had come not on the basis of accomplishment, but as the result of hostile criticism.

John Stewart Williamson (the origin of the pen name Will Stewart is obvious) was born in Bisbee, Arizona Territory, April 29, 1908. His mother, Lucy Betty Hunt, was the daughter of a slaveholding aristocrat ruined by the Civil War. She was teaching school when she married Asa Lee Williamson, a graduate of the University of Texas, a descendent of Revolutionary War stock, who was then also teaching.

The land lured Asa Williamson and he quit teaching shortly after his marriage to take up ranching with two of his wife's brothers in Mexico. The ranch was located in such forbidding terrain on the headwaters of the Rio Yaqui in Sonora that the closest wagons could come was a day's travel away.

Though Apaches raided the ranch, mountain lions preyed on the pigs, and scorpions made foot travel uneasy, it took the uncertainties of the Mexican Revolution in 1910 to send the Williamsons scurrying back across the border.

Failing to make an irrigated farm in Pecos pay, Asa Williamson packed the family belongings into a covered wagon in 1915 and, with the livestock straggling along behind, headed for the Llano Estacado, in eastern New Mexico. They were latecomers, the best land had already been taken, and life for the family became an endless bout with poverty. The crops, if not destroyed by drought, were subject to choking sand and hail. Animals died from eating poisonous vegetation. During desperate periods Asa Williamson would take up teaching for a time or even turn to mining to see him through.

In due course, Jack had the company of a brother and two younger sisters. They milked cows, cared for chickens and turkeys, drew water, and worked in the fields. The grim contest with nature pulled the family into a tightly knit unit. Most of the children's early learning was given them by the parents at home. Daydreaming became Jack's only escape from unromantic Southwestern reality. As he became older, he verbally imparted his daydreams in a nonstop and endless radio soap opera routine to his brothers and sisters.

Regular schooling for Jack began in 1920 in the seventh grade. So long removed from contact with others than his own family, he was extraordinarily shy and introverted through high school. Though smitten with the charm of an athletic blonde, Blanche Slaten, he never gained the courage to talk to her and sadly watched her marry another boy the Christmas before his graduation in 1925. Tall and gangling, he was as ineffective at athletics as at romance and so retreated to books.

The twenties might have been roaring for others, but when Jack left school, helping out on the farm seemed his only future. One of his friends was Edlie Walker, who had become a lawyer though confined to a wheel chair. Walker, a radio ham subscribed to Hugo Gernsback's RADIO NEWS. Soon after AMAZING STORIES was started, he received the March, 1927, issue as a sample and turned it over to Jack. That issue featured *The Green Splotches,* a tale of an atomic-powered space rocket by T. S. Stribling, but what really hypnotized young Jack Williamson was the poetic and Poesque description of a civilization of nonhuman intelligences discovered in the bottom of an extinct Alaskan volcano, in A. Merritt's story *The People of the Pit.*

Appealing to his sister for aid, he scraped together enough funds to secure AMAZING STORIES regularly. His subscription started with the June, 1927, issue which contained the second installment of Merritt's *The Moon Pool.* The images that poured from *The Moon Pool*—The Shining One; Lakla, the handmaiden; The Silent Ones; Yolara, priestess of the Dweller; Olaf, the Norseman; The AKKA, batrachian-like race; the Green Dwarf; and the Ancient Ones—induced euphoria in most, but Jack Williamson they fired with a crusading fervor. There was now but one god, A. Merritt, and his prophet was Jack Williamson.

Stories began to pour out of a typewriter with a chronically pale, purple ribbon: *The Flying Flowers, The Abyss of the Scarlet Spheres, The Alien Plane, Under the Cavern's Roof, The Castle of the Seven Gates, A Prince of Atlantis* and *Via the Vacuum Tube.* Most were never finished, others were sent to AMAZING STORIES and returned. Of that early output, only an unconvincing attempt to handle a theme of physical transmutation and horror in the setting of a lost jungle city, *Crystal of Death,* has seen publication, and that in the August, 1940, issue of William L. Hamling's semiprofessional magazine, STARDUST.

Some encouragement came from winning an honorary mention for an ending submitted to an unfinished story in AMERICAN BOY. This, the idea of an undersea world, Williamson would soon use in a short novel, *The Green Girl.*

The first intimation that he had finally made the grade as a professional writer came without notice shortly after he enrolled at West Texas State Teachers College the fall of 1928 when he received the December, 1928, AMAZING STORIES. The cover, by Frank R. Paul, depicted a scene from Williamson's story *The Metal Man.* The editor clearly recognized Williamson's literary deity in his blurb: "Not since we published 'The Moon Pool' has such a story as this been published by us."

The Metal Man concerned radioactive emanations from a form of intelligent crystalline life which turn all objects into metal. While the story was a good first effort, the enthusiasm with which it was received ran far beyond its conceptual or literary qualities. However, in trying to capture something of Merritt in his writing, Jack Williamson had undoubtedly struck the right chord.

Despite the fact that he was offered a scholarship in chemistry at the end of his second year and consistently scored "A's" in his other subjects, the sale of *The Metal Man* caused Williamson to lose interest in academic pursuits. The entire Christmas vacation of 1928 was spent writing a short novel, *The Alien Intelligence,* which he sold to Hugo Gernsback's newly formed SCIENCE WONDER STORIES (July and August, 1929). It was a very competent writing job, dealing with a bizarre hidden valley in Australia. The editors appeared most impressed with Williamson's concept of a mysterious insect race whose brains had grown so large that they were sustained and transported in metal bodies. The belief that intelligence could evolve in the most alien forms was to become a trademark of Williamson's stories.

Williamson decided that education was an impediment to his drive to become a writer, particularly since he was devoting as much time to reading H. G. Wells as to his studies. He left school at the end of his second year and plunged whole-heartedly into fiction. *The Green Girl,* published as a two-part novel in the March and April, 1930, issues of AMAZING STORIES, was a success. His opening sentence—"At high noon on May 4, 1999 the sun went out!"—is frequently quoted by the school of writing that believes you should get right into your story. The story takes place in a strange world under the sea, where the roof of water is suspended in delicate balance by a gas made up of *antimatter*. "You know that science has held for a long time that there is no reason, per se, to doubt the existence of substances that would repel instead of attracting one another," one of Williamson's characters explains, and there, early in Williamson's writing career, is the seed of the contraterrence matter stories written under the Will Stewart name.

The Green Girl has atomic energy weapons, intelligent flying plants that can be trained to fight or wash dishes, with the action and colorful backdrop of the old scientific romances. Actually, Jack Williamson was to become the author bridging the gulf between the school exemplifying pure escape in the tradition of A. Merritt, Edgar Rice Burroughs, Otis Adelbert Kline, and Ralph Milne Farley, and the group then currently focusing on ideas which Hugo Gernsback strove to include in his magazine.

The influence of Merritt and, to a lesser degree, the S. Fowler Wright of *The World Below,* was to pervade most of Williamson's writing for the next three years. Yet his ability to come up with a spectacular story device, if not a new idea, gained for him the title of "The Cover Copper" in the early science-fiction fan magazines, since the subject matter of his stories provided a constant source of provocative illustrative material. Of his first 21 stories, published between 1928 and 1932, 13 gained a cover.

Typical of Williamson's ideas are the following: the notion of the Heaviside layer supporting forms of life (*The Second Shell,* AIR WONDER STORIES, November, 1929); a girl who is permitted to remain alive by a civilized race of Antarctic crustaceans because they like her singing (*The Lake of Light,* ASTOUNDING STORIES, April, 1931); a tiny artificial planet kept suspended in a laboratory (*The Pygmy Planet,* ASTOUNDING STORIES, February, 1932), a beautiful lady flying around in space asking entry into a spaceship (*The

Lady of Light, AMAZING STORIES, September, 1932).
Williamson was never without some new idea or novel
situation.

Stock devices, too, were repeated in Williamson stories.
The airplane was his favorite means of carrying his characters into action, beginning with his first story, *The Metal
Man,* then later on the cover of WONDER STORIES, May,
1931, in *Through the Purple Cloud,* and on to the ultimate
extreme in *Non-Stop to Mars* (ARGOSY, February 25, 1939),
in which he contrives a semilogical means of flying an airplane to the Red Planet.

Jack Williamson loved jewels and they are the catalyst to
the fourth dimension in *Through the Purple Cloud;* the key
to eternal life in *The Stone from the Green Star* (AMAZING
STORIES, October and November, 1931), a superscience
epic of the far galaxies related in symbols of *The Moon Pool;*
a pathway to a primeval planet in the lusty adventure *In
the Scarlet Star* (AMAZING STORIES, March, 1933). The
jewels, like the vortices of light, the outré cities inside
volcanoes, hidden valleys, other dimensions, the monsterlike
aliens with an aspect of benevolence, are all of obvious
derivation.

Perhaps Williamson's devotion to Merritt might not
have lasted so long if he had not received encouragement
from that author in the form of a letter praising *The Alien
Intelligence.* On a tour east with his correspondent and friend
Edmond Hamilton, Jack Williamson was cordially received
by Merritt at THE AMERICAN WEEKLY, where he was
Morrill Goddard's right-hand man, and they discussed
science fiction. Williamson enthusiastically suggested collaborating on a sequel to *The Face in the Abyss,* but Merritt
had already completed one (*The Snake Mother*) and turned
it over to ARGOSY. Merritt finally did agree to work with
Williamson on a novel to be called *The Purple Mountain.*
Some 20,000 words were actually written by Williamson
and mailed to Merritt in 1930. The manuscript was acknowledged but never returned.

The crown jewel of this phase of Williamson's writing was undoubtedly *The Moon Era* (WONDER STORIES, February, 1932). The protagonist, falling away from the earth in a spaceship, finds himself moving back in time and lands on the moon when that satellite is still a young world possessing water, air, and life. There he allies himself with The Mother, the last of a race of Lunarians trying to escape to the sea, with the seeds of her young in her. She is pursued by The Eternal Ones, a civilization of brains in gigantic robot bodies, who originally were an offshoot of her race. The physical and mental qualities of The Mother are sketched with such delicacy, the symbols employed to convey the desired mood so unerring, that the unfolding of the story achieves a complete suspension of disbelief in the reader, and it builds to a climax of such stirring poignancy that the reading becomes a memorable experience.

The man who would play the biggest initial role in directing Williamson away from Merritt would be Miles J. Breuer, M.D. Breuer was a successful practicing physician in Lincoln, Nebraska, who wrote science fiction for the love of it. He was no stylist, but for off-beat ideas handled with a degree of depth and maturity he ranked high. His remarkable novel *Paradise and Iron* (AMAZING STORIES QUARTERLY, Summer, 1930), portraying the ultimate in automation dominated by thinking machines, belongs with the very best stories on the subject.

Williamson greatly admired Breuer's originality and wrote him when he saw his name listed as a member of The Science Correspondence Club, of which he too was a member. Williamson was eager to learn more about the writing craft and Breuer was willing to help. Breuer suggested a novel paralleling the American Revolution but with the locale in the future and on the moon. The result was *The Birth of a New Republic* which appeared complete in the Winter, 1931, AMAZING STORIES QUARTERLY. Williamson did virtually all of the writing, but under the strictest discipline, submitting the outline of every chapter for approval to Breuer.

The result was a highly ingenious detailing of a future civilization but not a novel in any true sense, since the entire story was a blow-by-blow description of a future revolution with virtually no other story line at all.

The Cosmic Express (AMAZING STORIES, November, 1930), a spoof on interplanetary stories, was heavily influenced by Breuer and is notable for its use of matter transmitters for space travel and the brilliant prediction that westerns would dominate television.

"Breuer was an antidote to my own tendency toward unrestrained fantasy," Williamson acknowledges. "He insisted upon solid plot construction, upon the importance of real human values in character, and upon the element of theme."

Despite his reader acclaim and steady sales record, Williamson found that a writing career had failed to bring him complete satisfaction. He felt the trouble rested in his own personality. Shy, sensitive, and withdrawn, he made few friends and had neither the courage nor flourish to approach a member of the opposite sex.

He seriously considered taking up psychiatry as a profession, but was discouraged when David H. Keller, M.D., practicing in that field, and his friend Miles J. Breuer, M.D., both told him of the time and money required. He briefly flirted with the idea of becoming an astronomer, then settled for a philosophy major at the University of New Mexico, rolling into Albuquerque in the fall of 1932 on a freight car, as the finale to a summer of riding the rods.

Returning from Albuquerque in 1933, Williamson bought some paper and typewriter ribbons, secreted himself in his shack on the family ranch, and started a novel. During his entire writing career from 1928 through the end of World War II, he never found it necessary to hold a steady job. At the ranch his personal expenses would drop to virtually nothing and his writing income sustained him. His biggest coup of 1933 had been the publication of *Golden Blood,* a colorful lusty action novel in WEIRD TALES, but it brought him more prestige than sustenance, since a bank closing held up payment.

It was essential that his new novel *The Legion of Space* score effectively and quickly if life was to be conducted at some level above subsistence. Between the time the novel was started and completed, the entire complexion of the science-fiction market changed. Previously, Williamson had unerringly hit in every market he had tried, running the gamut. The best-paying market had been ASTOUNDING STORIES, which under the editorship of Harry Bates paid 2 cents a word on acceptance. In the midst of the Depression this was a princely rate, especially when it is compared with ½ cent on publication or after offered by AMAZING STORIES and WONDER STORIES, and the top of 1 cent a word on publication by WEIRD TALES. However, ASTOUNDING STORIES had ceased publication with its March, 1933, issue, which carried Williamson's *Salvage in Space,* a skillful and highly original story of men on a spaceship stalked by an invisible monster. While there was little question that other science-fiction magazines would accept *The Legion of Space,* payment might conceivably be one or more years off.

ARGOSY had for decades been buying science fiction from such well-known writers as A. Merritt, Edgar Rice Burroughs, Otis Adelbert Kline, Ralph Milne Farley, and Ray Cummings. It was a prestige market and paid good rates on acceptance, so Williamson tried them. *The Legion of Space* was returned with a note stating only that it had been seriously considered. Frustrated, Williamson providentially received a letter from Desmond Hall, who had worked for the Clayton magazine chain, announcing that he was now assistant to F. Orlin Tremaine at Street & Smith, who were about to revive ASTOUNDING STORIES. Payment would be 1 cent a word on acceptance and they desperately needed short stories. Williamson dashed out three shorts and a novelette, all of which they bought, then learned the magazine was altering its policy to run long novels. So he shipped out *The Legion of Space,* too.

The best of the short stories he sold ASTOUNDING was *Dead Star Station* (November, 1933), a touching character study of a man who spends fifty years to perfect an antigravity screen and the heroic manner in which he justifies his effort. To accentuate character, Williamson had given his aged hero a lisp. Once before, in *The Second Shell,* he had attempted to individualize a character by presenting a scientist with a stutter. It was a very small thing, but in a field of writing in which some natural phenomenon was often the lead character, and all human beings were stereotypes, this was a tremendous, perhaps daring, advance in craftsmanship.

The Legion of Space had many of the epic qualities that had made the space operas of Edward E. Smith or John W. Campbell so popular. Yet the impact it made as it rocketed along for six installments, commencing in ÁSTOUNDING STORIES for April, 1934, was predominantly due to a single character, Giles Habibula. An obese, lame, heavy-drinking, complaining old man with a sublime genius for opening locks, Habibula was characterized by a manner of speech distinctively his own:

> "Bless my bones! We can't go there! 'Tis beyond the system—six light years and more! A mortal distance, when it takes a precious ray of light six blessed years to cross it! Ah, there're ten thousand mortal dangers, life knows! I'm a brave man —you all know old Giles is brave. But we can't do that. Of all the expeditions that ever went beyond the system, only one ever came back."

The idea for *The Legion of Space* had come to Jack Williamson from a lecture by Dr. George St. Claire in a course in Great Books at the university at Albuquerque, where he learned the Polish novelist Henry Sienkiewicz had borrowed characters from Dumas' *Three Musketeers* and Shakespeare's bawdy old Sir John Falstaff for a great historical trilogy. If it worked for Sienkiewicz, Williamson thought, it might work for him. So, quite literally, in *The Legion of Space,* the Three Musketeers of Space, John Star, Jay Kalaam and Hal Samdu, accompanied by a rocket-age, lock-picking Falstaffian replica, set out to a rousing series of adventures to discover the secret of AKKA, the ultimate weapon. AKKA turns out to be little more than a ten-penny nail, but the fate of mankind depends upon it.

Like Sienkiewicz, Williamson developed a trilogy of novels, following *The Legion of Space* with *The Cometeers* (ASTOUNDING STORIES, May to August, 1936) and *One Against the Legion* (ASTOUNDING SCIENCE-FICTION, April to June, 1939). The Cometeers are a seemingly immortal race of energy creatures who control a cosmic collection of sundry worlds collected in a green comet tail twelve million miles long. They propel this interstellar conglomeration through the galaxy, feeding on the life forces of creatures of the worlds they capture. (The term "Cometeers" was eventually to be adopted by science-fiction fans for special social and business groups.)

One Against the Legion, the last of the trilogy, tells of the battle of the legionnaires to bring to terms one supercriminal and in the process ties up some loose ends of the series. All three novels were eventually put into hard covers by Fantasy Press and have become a permanent part of the nostalgia of the science-fiction world.

Through all this, Jack Williamson remained a lonely man, plagued by a variety of health problems, some of which he strongly suspected were psychosomatic. In hope of obtaining some answers he submitted himself to analysis at the Menninger Clinic, Topeka, Kansas, the spring of 1936. He continued treatment sporadically at Topeka and at Los Angeles when he could afford it, until early 1941. "Although the results of this analysis were not dramatic or spectacular," Williamson noted, "I feel that it was one of the great turning points of my life. . . . It was not so much a matter of making a change in me, as in learning to accept myself more or less as I was. . . . I had seen life as a conflict between emotion and reason . . . and I found a kind of compromise or reconciliation that ended much of the conflict."

It is quite possible that Williamson's abrupt switch to

realism in *Crucible of Power* (ASTOUNDING SCIENCE-FICTION, February, 1939) and in portions of *Non-Stop to Mars* (ARGOSY, February 25, 1939) was part of his coming to terms with himself. Realism was present in the characterization as well as in the plotting of these stories. Giles Habibula had been a milestone, but Garth Hammond, aptly labeled "a hero whose heart is purest brass," in *Crucible of Power*, was a giant step towards believability in science fiction. Hammond was the man who made the first trip to Mars and built a power station near the sun for sheer selfish, self-seeking gain. The end justified the means, and he was just as callous in romance as in business. There had never been anything as blunt as this in science fiction before.

Science fiction has never achieved much in human characterization, but what little progress it has made is as much due to Jack Williamson as any other author. After he showed the way, not-completely-sympathetic and more three-dimensional people began to appear: Granny in *Slan* by A. E. van Vogt, (1940) the uncouth title character of *Old Man Mulligan* (1940) by P. Schuyler Miller, the irascible tycoon in *Old Fireball* (1941) by Nat Schachner, and the "witch," Mother Jujy, in *Gather, Darkness* (1943) by Fritz Leiber.

Selling to ARGOSY was one of the great moments in Williamson's life, since so many of the old science-fiction "masters" had been identified with that magazine. Following *Non-Stop to Mars,* he sold them *Star Bright* (November 25, 1939), in which a harassed little bookkeeper, hit by a meteor particle, becomes capable of performing miracles in certain circumstances, and *Racketeers in the Sky* (October 12, 1940), in which a dishonest quack foils a conquest of the earth, but with no redemption in character. Williamson's practiced ability to portray something other than a cardboard hero had finally cracked ARGOSY for him.

An early tendency in Williamson's work had been a drift toward fantasy and away from scientific logic as the plot unwound. Paradoxically, he began to move in the other direction as he matured and was one of the pioneers in fictional explanation of the supernatural and witchcraft in scientific terms. His most widely acclaimed work in this area was *Darker Than You Think* (UNKNOWN, December, 1940), which suggests that human beings have the blood strain of Homo lycanthropus and that occasionally there is a throwback.

Williamson had employed the idea once before in *Wolves of Darkness* (STRANGE TALES, January, 1932), wherein his werewolves are entities from another dimension who employ a human being as a host and are able to change into wolves at will. The limited circulation of STRANGE TALES, and the fact that it was read predominantly by lovers of the supernatural, prevented the story from having any great effect, but *Darker Than You Think* exerted strong influence on Fritz Leiber, who established a reputation for translating the supernatural into logical terms, and in one specific story on James Blish in *There Shall Be No Darkness* (THRILLING WONDER STORIES, April, 1950), which meticulously explains even the conversion of fur into evening clothes and the reverse.

Early in 1942, Williamson suggested to John W. Campbell a series of stories on the engineering problems of making asteroids habitable. Campbell, who had been searching for "new" authors to replace the writers who were leaving ASTOUNDING SCIENCE-FICTION for the armed services, countered with the suggestion that Williamson combine his notion with contraterrene matter and use a pen name. The name was Will Stewart, and the results were two novelettes, *Collision Orbit* (July, 1942) and *Minus Sign* (November, 1942), and one short novel, *Opposites—React* (January and February, 1943). No one guessed the identity of the "new" author, the stories ranked high and have come to be considered the most outstanding expositions on the antimatter theme ever written.

Campbell clapped his hands in glee. Adding Will Stewart to Lawrence O'Donnell (C. L Moore) and Lewis Padgett

(Henry Kuttner), he was assembling an imposing list of "new" discoveries. Then, the unexpected. Jack Williamson, who had spent the past year in Los Angeles where he had participated in the informal Mañana Literary Society which included Robert Heinlein, Cleve Cartmill, and Anthony Boucher, selected bullets over bull sessions and enlisted in the armed forces. He served three years as a weather forecaster in New Mexico, then in 1945 was shipped out to the Solomons. He flew through a number of Marine air missions unscathed, but a routine hernia repair after his release in 1946 resulted in an intestinal obstruction which came within hours of finishing him. It took a series of operations to straighten him out.

Back to the task of making a living, Jack Williamson read the current output of science fiction, decided he was equal to it, and turned out *The Equalizer* (ASTOUNDING SCIENCE FICTION, March 1947), about an advance in technology that brings to an end the age of specialization. It was a strikingly modern and effective presentation of the technical factors that might eliminate cities, other than their destruction by atomic bombs.

If any further proof were required that Williamson was one of the most adaptable science-fiction writers alive, *"With Folded Hands . . ."* in ASTOUNDING SCIENCE FICTION for July, 1947, eliminated that need. In that story, robots are given the duty of seeing that human beings do not hurt themselves or each other. They are also dedicated to seeing that men are happy. How they go about it makes for one of the grimmest horror stories as well as one of the landmarks in modern science fiction.

The sequel was almost a command performance, and Williamson labored on a novel, *". . . And Searching Mind,"* in the isolation of the little shack he had built on his ranch. *"With Folded Hands . . ."* was almost entirely Williamson's own creation, but the new story incorporated elements of psi phenomena which Campbell had suggested as a means of defeating the robot guardians. The logical ending of benevolent enslavement had already been used on the first story, so Williamson had no alternative but to switch to a less convincing human victory in the second. There were also crudities in the dialogue which made the writing uneven, but it won first place in readers' acclaim for each of three installments in the March, April, and May, 1948, issues of ASTOUNDING SCIENCE FICTION and was published in hard covers in 1949 by Simon & Schuster as *The Humanoids.*

The forced close contact with other people in the army made a hermitlike existence more difficult for Williamson to sustain. Gordon K. Greaves, who had been a fellow student at Albuquerque, was editor of the PORTALES (New Mexico) DAILY NEWS and he offered Williamson a job as wire editor. This was to be Williamson's first regular job, and he had a special motive for accepting. While on leave from the army he had visited Portales and found, running a children's clothing store, Blanche Slaten, the girl who had broken his teen-age heart by marrying another boy before she had finished high school. She was divorced now, and bringing up two children. Approaching 40, Jack Williamson finally conquered the timidity which had hitherto blighted his life. A little over a month after their first date, the two were married on August 15, 1947.

The newspaper job lasted only six months, Williamson returning to free-lance writing out of sheer boredom. His writing was beginning to receive recognition. Fantasy Press, Reading, Pennsylvania, turned out *The Legion of Space* in hard covers in 1948. They followed it with *The Cometeers* (incorporating *One Against the Legion*) in 1949. The reissuing of *The Humanoids* as a $1 hard-cover reprint by Grosset & Dunlap in 1950 caused Simon & Schuster to snap up *Seetee Shock,* a novel in the contraterrence matter series which had been serialized in ASTOUNDING SCIENCE FICTION during 1949. It was the appearance of that book in 1950 that touched off the chain reaction that secured the *Beyond Mars* comic strip continuity with the NEW YORK SUNDAY NEWS.

While the strip was still running in 1953, Williamson had entered Eastern New Mexico University at Portales to get a better grounding in the sciences. The idea of academic life so appealed to him that when the strip failed he pushed on toward the goal of getting a degree. He received his first teaching position in English and the short story in 1956 and gradually worked his way up to an associate professorship at Eastern New Mexico University.

Summers he spent working toward completing the requirements for a Ph.D. in English Literature. With great appropriateness, his dissertation was called *H. G. Wells, Critic of Progress: A Study of the Early Fiction* (and the early fiction is mostly science fiction). Williamson sets out to disprove the prevalent belief that Wells was "a nearsighted optimist," and underscores the fact that Wells knew that progress would be "difficult and uncertain."

Teaching now became Jack Williamson's permanent career. He had not given up science fiction, and stories continued to trickle out. One reason he did not quit science-fiction writing was that he had convinced the university to permit him to teach a course in the subject and continued sales were his best credentials.

If science-fiction writing is an art that can be taught, there is probably no one in the world better qualified to teach it than Jack Williamson. His complete understanding of not only the writing techniques, but the changing approach to telling a story, has been demonstrated repeatedly by his adaptability to every shift in direction science fiction takes. Yet the record shows more than adroit adjustability and storytelling competence. It reveals an author who pioneered superior characterization in a field almost barren of it, realism in the presentation of human motivation previously unknown, scientific rationalization of supernatural concepts for story purposes, and exploitation of the untapped story potentials of antimatter.

Most certainly, students of the subject have something to learn from him.

6

SUPERMAN

Thinking sociologists find it increasingly difficult to give a well-balanced evaluation of American Culture without considering Superman. To assemble a reasonably comprehensive bibliography of important references to that adventure-strip hero has probably long since passed the point of practicability. Yet the impact of this indestructible figure, capable of flight, x-ray vision, time travel, and accelerated motion, on millions of youthful Americans each year is sustained by seven comic books, daily and Sunday newspaper strips, a daily television show, motion pictures, and an endless array of novelties, toys, games, and sundry products.

The philosophy, ethics, prejudices, preferences, and blind spots of the man who guides the story line of Superman are of importance to every parent whose child follows that character, yet as a public figure he is virtually unknown, and in the publishing world only those directly involved with producing comic magazines could identify him.

Mortimer Weisinger, mentor of the superman chronology in all of its manifestations since 1945, and for a period before World War II, does not wear a cape and did not originate the character, though he knew Jerome Siegel and Joseph Shuster, two science-fiction fans who first put the strip together in 1933, and he was aware of their five-year siege of marketing tribulations.

Mortimer Weisinger was born in Washington Heights, on New York's Manhattan Island, on April 25, 1915. While Mortimer early showed a predilection for the imaginative works of Jules Verne and Edgar Allan Poe, he balanced this tendency with a healthy interest in the Rover Boys and Motor Boy series. The fatal shift came when his parents sent him to a camp one summer and he borrowed the counselor's copy of the August, 1928, AMAZING STORIES featuring in the same issue *Armageddon 2419,* the first Buck Rogers story, by Philip Francis Nowlan, and the opening installment of *The Skylark of Space* by Edward E. Smith, Ph.D.

While in later years Weisinger's fondness for food made him the perfect person to invent a widely adopted weight-losing diet, this tendency was curbed as a teen-ager by his skipping lunch to accumulate funds to secure overpriced back issues of AMAZING STORIES, SCIENCE AND INVENTION and ELECTRICAL EXPERIMENTER from New York bookshops. The great thrill of his young life was a personal visit to Hugo Gernsback while that man was still publishing AMAZING STORIES.

His father, Hyman Weisinger, manufactured slippers in Passaic, New Jersey, and the flaming passion of his life was to see his son become a doctor. Mort was enrolled at New York University, but neglected to mention to his father that he was majoring in journalism. He showed his experimental attempts at fiction, written in longhand, to a slightly older scientifictioneer, Allen Glasser, who had sold a few minor efforts and was especially astute at winning prize contests. A single bit of advice from Glasser stayed with him: "The most important thing in writing a story or winning a contest is the *angle*; you must have an angle that no one else has thought of." The unusual story twist, the novel approach in an article, and off-beat plotting in comic strip continuities were to become Mort Weisinger's trademarks and the foundation of his later success.

While the science-fiction magazines fascinated him, he felt that an *esprit de corps* was lacking. This same feeling was held by others. A Chicago science-fiction fan, Walter Dennis, together with Raymond A. Palmer of Milwaukee (who had not yet cracked the professional science-fiction market), helped to organize the Science Correspondence Club in 1929. This was intended to further the discussion of science through correspondence among interested science-fiction readers, particularly authors. The first issue of a mimeographed bulletin called THE COMET (later COSMOLOGY) from this club was dated May, 1930.

Allen Glasser corresponded with Walter Dennis about the Science Correspondence Club and decided to form a similar organization, which he called The Scienceers. The charter meeting, attended by four, was held in the Bronx on December 11, 1929. The first elected president of The Scienceers was Warren Fitzgerald, a Negro professional, about thirty years of age, at whose home in Harlem meetings were held. Weisinger joined immediately upon hearing of the group and became one of the most active members, serving as treasurer and pressing for the publication of a club bulletin.

This materialized as THE PLANET (first issue dated July, 1930), with Glasser as editor and Weisinger as associate editor. While the Science Correspondence Club's COMET was mainly a sophomoric rehash of fundamental science, The Scienceers' PLANET in a sprightly fashion, placed more emphasis on *science fiction*. THE PLANET (which lasted six issues) was actually the first of the science-fiction fan magazines, which today number perhaps 300.

The club received a publicity break when Allen Glasser won a $20 third prize in SCIENCE WONDER QUARTERLY's competition, "What I Have Done To Spread Science Fiction." His prize-winning entry, which appeared in the Spring, 1930, issue described the club and attracted inquiries from many parts of the country (the founding of two other chapters was attempted), and was responsible for the valuable addition to the club roster of Julius Schwartz, a noted collector of science fiction. Schwartz formed a friendship with Mort Weisinger which was to become lifelong.

Hugo Gernsback, publisher of WONDER STORIES and SCIENCE WONDER QUARTERLY, became interested in the group and made arrangements for a meeting to be held at New York's American Museum of Natural History. He sent to that meeting his editor, David Lasser, who had just formed The American Interplanetary Society, which then seemed even more crackpot and far out than a literary discussion group on science fiction. For that matter, the first issue of THE BULLETIN OF THE AMERICAN INTERPLANETARY SOCIETY (June, 1930) was a four-page mimeographed affair, even less pretentious than The Scienceers' PLANET.

Lasser exerted considerable pressure on The Scienceers to merge with The American Interplanetary Society. Only the older Warren Fitzgerald joined. When the other Scienceers members appeared reluctant, payment for rental of the hall failed to materialize from WONDER STORIES. The club broke apart in violent disagreement as to whether they should foot the obligation. In retrospect, of course, a merger with The American Interplanetary Society, which has since become The American Rocket Society, the world's most respected civilian rocket group and publisher of ASTRONAUTICS, a magazine almost as impressive in size as GOOD HOUSEKEEPING, would scarcely have been called a sad fate.

While notices of The Scienceers had appeared every Friday in the now defunct NEW YORK WORLD, Glasser and Weisinger yearned for greater recognition. One day they called up THE BRONX HOME NEWS (now combined with THE NEW YORK POST) and informed the editor that the great British savant, Sir Edgar Ray Merrit, was to speak before the next meeting of The Scienceers, the only American speaking engagement he had agreed to. The name had been cobbled together from Edgar Rice Burroughs, Ray Cummings, and A. Merritt, but the BRONX HOME NEWS didn't know that, and the paper ran fourteen column-inches about the glories of The Scienceers and their distinguished guest speaker.

This tomfoolery was a prelude to more constructive things. Prominent readers, writers, and collectors of science fiction received a circular announcing the monthly publication of THE TIME TRAVELER, the first fan magazine devoted *entirely* to science fiction and intended to fill the void left by the PLANET's demise. Allen Glasser and Julius Schwartz held top editorial posts, but Mort Weisinger, as associate editor, was one of the publication's mainstays. He attempted the first history of science fiction on record, *beginning* in the February, 1932, issue of THE TIME TRAVELER with Part II (the mystery of what happened to Part I has never been explained), and creditably carried through as far as Jules Verne, where he terminated it after eight published installments. Winchell-type reporting was introduced to science fiction by Weisinger with his lively news column "Out of the Ether," which reflected a wide correspondence with popular contemporary science-fiction writers.

The arrival in New York of Conrad H. Ruppert, a young printer from Angola, Indiana, who enjoyed the enviable distinction of having won a $50 second prize in the "What I Have Done to Spread Science Fiction" contest with his suggestion of "Science Fiction Week," offered an opportunity to broaden THE TIME TRAVELER's horizons. He agreed to set up in type and print the periodical for nothing more than the cost of paper. This offer he implemented with action, and the March, 1932, issue was turned out on a printing press.

Weisinger saw other potentialities in the printing press. Taking the best of his handwritten manuscripts, *The Price of Peace,* he sneaked into his father's factory after hours and used an office typewriter to put it into proper form for submission. He gained moral support from Dr. Robert B. Dow, a professor of English at New York University, who made some minor corrections and suggested that the story might be salable.

He had been anticipated. When Ruppert, as Solar Publications, turned the first of a series of pamphlets off the press, the title read *The Cavemen of Venus* by Allen Glasser. Weisinger's *The Price of Peace* followed it a few months later. In this tale, an American scientist announces he has discovered a green ray which will cause an atomic explosion. A number of U.S. naval vessels disintegrate in a great billow of smoke as the world watches. Major wars end out of fear of the "ultimate" weapon. But the entire test had been a hoax, believed only because of the scientist's reputation.

Encouraged by the friendly comments of those who paid the full retail price of six cents in stamps for the pamphlet, Weisinger took the story over to AMAZING STORIES' editor, T. O'Conor Sloane, who accepted it and published it in the November, 1933, issue. The $25 Weisinger got for the story was invested in a second-hand typewriter and thus began a career.

But Allen Glasser again had beaten Weisinger to the punch in this official contest between them by placing a short story, *Across the Ages,* in which a man imagines himself back in Rome during a New York heat wave, in the August-September, 1933, AMAZING STORIES. When the story appeared, readers protested to Editor Sloane about the very close similarity between Glasser's story and *The Heat Wave* by Marion Ryan and Robert Ord, which had appeared in the April, 1929, issue of MUNSEY'S MAGAZINE. A careful check of the two stories indicates that very few changes were made in Glasser's story.

Sloane was fit to be tied. He had just been through apologizing in print to A. Merritt (AMAZING STORIES, June, 1933) for "many similarities in descriptions, characterization and situations" in the story *Beyond the Veil of Time* by B. H. Barney, published in the Fall-Winter, 1932, issue of AMAZING STORIES QUARTERLY, to those in two of Merritt's books, *The Moon Pool* and *The Face in the Abyss.*

Sloane was at the moment involved in the very embarrassing situation of having published in his February, 1933, issue a story called *The Ho-Ming Gland* by Malcolm R. Afford, which was identical with *The Gland Men of the Island* by the same author published by WONDER STORIES two years earlier in its January, 1931, number. It developed that Afford had *first* sent the story to Sloane more than four years before. When after a year it did not appear, he mailed a copy to WONDER STORIES, who accepted and published it. Characteristically, Sloane had just gotten around to pulling it out of inventory. This latest situation with Glasser, following on the heels of the others, was just too much. Any of Glasser's friends with professional aspirations were not welcome.

This made final a split that had begun earlier when Weisinger, Schwartz, Ruppert, Maurice Ingher, and Forrest J. Ackerman had formed a corporation for the publication of SCIENCE FICTION DIGEST, a semiprofessional magazine along the lines of THE TIME TRAVELER. Publication of the new magazine began with its September, 1932, issue. The October, 1932, issue incorporated THE TIME TRAVELER but without Glasser.

THE SCIENCE FICTION DIGEST (later called FANTASY MAGAZINE) was a remarkable publication. Until its demise with the January, 1937, number, its pages comprised a virtual encyclopedia of information concerning the science-fiction world: news, biography, bibliography, criticism, exposes, as well as pastiches, poetry, and fiction. Professionals contributed fiction gratis, much of which later found its way into the newsstand magazines. Its most impressive achievement was assembling a round-robin story titled *Cosmos,* each part complete in itself, written by eighteen authors and running 5,000 to 10,000 words an installment. The contributors read like a "Who's Who" of the period, including A. Merritt, E. E. Smith, John W. Campbell, Ralph Milne Farley, Otis Adelbert Kline, David H. Keller, Edmond Hamilton, Raymond A. Palmer, Arthur J. Burks, Eando Binder, P. Schuyler Miller, Francis Flagg, Bob Olsen, L. A. Eshbach, Abner

J. Gelula, J. Harvey Haggard, E. Hoffman Price and Rae Winters (a pen name of Palmer's).

The key idea man of the publication was Weisinger. He gathered much of the hot news and showed considerable skill at interviews of well-known authors, editors, and artists. As a by-product of this labor of love, he uncovered numerous pen names of well-known authors and used this material as the basis of the article "Why They Use Pen Names," published in the November, 1934, AUTHOR & JOURNALIST. Willard E. Hawkins, the publisher, while sympathetic to science fiction, as an occasional writer himself, was unable to pay Weisinger for the article, but offered free advertising space in exchange. Weisinger suggested to Julius Schwartz that they seize the offer to create and promote The Solar Sales Service, a literary agency specializing in the placement of fantasy. Their "stable" of authors grew as that advertisement got results, including Earl and Otto Binder, the two brothers who then cooperatively wrote under the name of Eando Binder, J. Harvey Haggard, H. P. Lovecraft, Ralph Milne Farley, David H. Keller, Henry Hasse, Henry Kuttner, Robert Bloch, and Edmond Hamilton. Several of the stories they received were rejects which the authors had been unable to sell. For these, the ingenious agents resorted to the technique of changing the titles and retyping the first few pages, then resubmitting them. The results were creditable.

Their most outstanding achievement was handling the output of the brilliant young science-fiction star, Stanley G. Weinbaum. They sold Weinbaum consistently to the leading market of the day, ASTOUNDING STORIES. Their adroitness with that talented author, who was to leave his mark on an entire generation of writers, attracted other high caliber clients, including John Taine (the science-fiction pen name of Eric Temple Bell, well known as a mathematician and historian of mathematics) whose *Twelve Eighty Seven* they placed in ASTOUNDING STORIES.

Added to his editorial experience of working on THE PLANET, THE TIME TRAVELER, and SCIENCE FICTION DIGEST,

Weisinger also had background as editor of New York University's daily newspaper and the NYU MEDLEY, the institution's magazine. Editing as a career now interested him. He was also steadily making sales to professional magazines including *The Prenatal Plagiarism* (WONDER STORIES, January, 1935), about a present-day author ruined by pre-publication of his novel before his birth; and *Pigments Is Pigments* (WONDER STORIES, March, 1935), built around the use of a drug that can turn a white man's skin black over night.

But Weisinger was not primarily interested in becoming a fiction writer, though he qualified for the American Fiction Guild, where eligibility required the sale of 100,000 words of fiction, and became its secretary. One evening, at a meeting, he heard that one of the editors of Standard Magazines had quit. Editorial director at Standard was a former literary agent named Leo Margulies, who guided the destiny of between forty and fifty pulp magazines. Weisinger had previously entered a contest sponsored by POPULAR DETECTIVE, one of Margulies' brood, which paid five cents a word for each word *short of* 1,000 in which a good whodunit could be written. He made a favorable impression on Margulies by compressing a salesworthy plot into 500 words for a story called *Rope Enough*. When he approached Margulies at a meeting and asked for the job, he got it, at $15 a week. At the age of twenty, Mort Weisinger was on his way.

Now fate played a hand. Hugo Gernsback's WONDER STORIES, which had survived six years of the worst depression in the nation's history, could no longer pay its way. Standard Magazines purchased it early in 1936.

Weisinger was the logical man to edit the publication, except that Standard Magazines had a policy that every story had to be approved by *three* editors. A limited pool of harried and overworked men were cumulatively editing over forty magazines and none of them knew anything of science fiction except Weisinger. They tended to OK anything he wanted without even giving it a reading. Thus Weisinger "beat the system" and became editor of the magazine in fact as well as theory. Because of tough competition in adult science fiction from ASTOUNDING STORIES, Margulies and publisher Ned Pines decided to aim for the teenage market. They changed the title to THRILLING WONDER STORIES (Standard Magazines were trademarked as the "Thrilling" group), and established a policy of action covers, preferably with a monster involved. So frequent and varied were the monsters on THRILLING WONDER STORIES' covers, and so bulging their eyes, that the term Bug Eyed Monster (BEM)· originated and was fostered in that publication.

Despite the raucousness of the covers and the juvenile slant, Weisinger, through his knowledge of the field, managed to retain the magazine's readers by securing authors of considerable appeal. From the pages of SCIENCE FICTION DIGEST he reprinted two A. Merritt stories that had never previously appeared in a professional magazine. He secured original stories from Otis Adelbert Kline, who had achieved a substantial following for his imitations of Edgar Rice Burroughs. Posthumously, works of Stanley G. Weinbaum were run, and John W. Campbell became a regular contributor.

Until then, editing a science-fiction magazine had consisted of reading the manuscripts that were submitted and picking the best. Weisinger switched to feeding authors ideas and ordering a story of predetermined length built around an agreed-upon theme. Serials were out of the question for the bi-monthly THRILLING WONDER STORIES, so authors were encouraged to write series using proven popular characters. Henry Kuttner, who had hitherto written only weird stories, was induced to try science fiction and was given the idea for a group of stories on the theme of a Hollywood on the Moon; Eando Binder enthralled readers with the adventures of Anton York, an immortal man, at the same time that he was building a reputation for the nom de plume of Gordon A. Giles for a sequence of interplanetary adventures, the "via" stories; John W. Campbell used a light touch in popularizing Penton and Blake, who cavorted around the solar system because they were wanted by the authorities on Earth; a wild animal hunter for earth zoos, Gerry Carlyle, provided an excellent base for an interplanetary series by Arthur K. Barnes; and Ray Cummings revived "Tubby," a paunchy character he had popularized fifteen years earlier, who dreams wild scientific adventures.

Weisinger found that discovering a good cover situation in a story was not always possible; so his policy was to give a provocative idea to an artist and then have the author write a story around the artwork. This was to become a common practice.

Anticipating teachers' reservations about their students reading anything as garish as THRILLING WONDER STORIES, Mort Weisinger bluffed the educators into a state of open-mouthed bafflement by featuring, on the same cover as *Dream Dust of Mars* by Manly Wade Wellman, an article by Sir James Jeans on *Giant and Dwarf Stars* (February, 1938). Along with *Hollywood on the Moon* by Henry Kuttner, young readers were initiated into the mysteries of *Eclipses of the Sun* by no less an authority than Sir Arthur Eddington (April, 1938).

By mid-1938 THRILLING WONDER STORIES' sales were encouraging enough to warrant either more frequent (monthly) publication or a companion magazine. The publishers decided on a companion to be titled STARTLING STORIES, a title Weisinger had created in his short story *Thompson's Time Traveling Theory* (FANTASY MAGAZINE, January, 1937).

Remembering the popularity of the complete novels in the old AMAZING STORIES QUARTERLY, Weisinger instituted the same policy for the new magazine, leading off its first, January, 1939, issue with *The Black Flame,* a previously unpublished work by Stanley G. Weinbaum. The new magazine was an instant success, frequently outselling THRILLING WONDER STORIES.

When Weisinger took his editorial post with Standard, he sold his interest in the Solar Sales Service to Julius Schwartz, who was still editing FANTASY MAGAZINE. Business forced Conrad H. Ruppert to cease gratuitous printing of the publication, and after a switch to another printer for a few issues, the magazine quit publication with the January, 1937, number. The science-fiction fan world collapsed into dwindling juvenile pockets of interest with the removal of this central focus.

But Weisinger played a major role in reviving science-fiction fandom in late 1938 when he made appearances at local and regional meetings, and most particularly when he decided to review science-fiction fan magazines, giving prices and addresses, as a regular column in STARTLING STORIES.

He also gave major support to The First World Science Fiction Convention, held in New York in 1939, by contributing publicity, money, auction material, and program talent, and by bringing Leo Margulies and a dozen big-name authors to the affair with him. It paid off when TIME and the NEW YORKER gave major write-ups to the event. It was at this convention that Margulies went into a huddle with Weisinger in back of the hall and conceived CAPTAIN FUTURE, a quarterly based on the adventures of that heroic character.

Weisinger also developed new writers by conducting an Amateur Story Contest. His most notable find was Alfred Bester, who was to become internationally known for his *The Demolished Man.* Bester's first story, *The Broken Axiom,* a tale of the possibility of two objects simultaneously occupying the same space, appeared in the April, 1939, THRILLING WONDER STORIES. Another accomplishment was convincing the sons of Edgar Rice Burroughs, John and Hulbert, to write *The Man Without a World* (June, 1939) one of the earlier tales of the thousand-year spaceship and the first of a number of stories they did for him. He was also responsible for introducing Alex Schomburg, master of the air brush, to science-fiction illustrating.

From 1939 to 1941, while Weisinger was performing a yeoman editorial job for Standard, comic books had mushroomed into a publishing phenomenon. From the first of the "modern" comic books, FUNNIES ON PARADE, published in 1933 by M. C. Gaines of Dell, until 1939, growth in this field had been of only modest proportions. Most comic magazines were reprints of nationally syndicated strips until the appearance of DETECTIVE COMICS, dated January, 1937, by the National Company, which had entered the comic magazine business in 1934. Historians tend to lose perspective of *why* original comic features came into existence in the comic magazines. It was not out of any desire to be creative but because most of the obtainable worthwhile syndicated daily and Sunday strips were contracted for. As the field broadened, it became increasingly difficult to obtain suitable reprints.

But the comic field found a life-giving new formula with the introduction of the character of Superman in ACTION COMICS, June, 1938, resulting in a sellout of that magazine, and in the appearance of SUPERMAN QUARTERLY MAGAZINE in May, 1939. Original scripts based on heroic figures, preferably with a dash of superscience and fantasy, became the rage, and nothing could hold the lid on.

The two men responsible for the creation of the Superman strip, Jerome Siegel, the writer, and Joseph Shuster, the artist, were old science-fiction fans and long-time friends of Mort Weisinger. Jerome Siegel produced in October, 1932, a crudely mimeographed magazine called simply SCIENCE FICTION. To obtain readers he exchanged advertisements with THE TIME TRAVELER. This magazine contained stories under various pen names by the editor, plus some cast-offs contributed by kindly authors. From its second issue on, it featured some professional quality cartooned illustrations by Joseph Shuster. Siegel, writing under the name of Bernard J. Kenton, had placed a story with AMAZING STORIES, *Miracles on Antares*. It was held for five years and then returned as no longer suitable. In informing his readers of this fact, Siegel wrote that Kenton "was at present working upon a scientific fiction cartoon strip with an artist of great renown." The artist was Joseph Shuster, the year was 1933, and the strip was Superman. In the same undated fifth and last issue of SCIENCE FICTION, Mort Weisinger had a Winchellian news column under the pen name of Ian Rectez, which was a partial anagram of his name.

For five years Siegel and Shuster tried to peddle the Superman strip, meeting rejections at every turn. Among the editors who turned it back was M. C. Gaines. He left Dell to work for National in 1938, and when ACTION COMICS was projected thought it might prove suitable. Siegel and Shuster had been doing a variety of well-received originals for DETECTIVE COMICS and ADVENTURE COMICS, and they were available and cooperative. Superman was given a chance and literally created the comic book industry as an important publishing business.

By 1941 the various Superman comic books were selling so well that the editorial director of National Comics, Whitney Ellsworth, decided they could use another editor. Since the entire success of Superman was based on a background of science fiction, Ellsworth felt Weisinger was ideally qualified. Negotiations were conducted through Leo Margulies, who wisely counseled Weisinger that comic magazines had a greater future than pulps. But almost simultaneously, Mort Weisinger received a letter from Ziff-Davis offering him the editorship of a new slick paper magazine they were planning to issue, POPULAR PHOTOGRAPHY. Weisinger was on the horns of a dilemma. The Ziff-Davis offer carried with it full editorship, a challenge, and prestige, but the field was unknown to him. Superman, which required a strong facility at plotting and a comprehensive background in science fiction, was right down his alley. In March, 1941, he decided to stay with Superman.

Then World War II abruptly terminated his stint at National Comics. Happily, his old friend Julius Schwartz, turned down by the army because of poor vision, was taken on as interim editor. In the armed forces, it was *Sergeant* Mort Weisinger who was assigned to Special Services, working at New Haven as associate editor of Yale's lively paper called THE BEAVER. It was on the train to New York, where he wrote the script for an Army radio show, that he met a tall, attractive registered nurse, Thelma Rudnick. He proposed on the train, and they were married on September 27, 1943. They have two children, a boy and a girl.

Following his discharge shortly before the end of the war Weisinger took a whirl at nonfiction. His talent for the offbeat and his skill at finding the unusual angle made him a winner from the start. He sold four major articles in one week, including one to CORONET, a prestige market. All the research experience, and familiarity with interviewing techniques gained on THE TIME TRAVELER and THE SCIENCE FICTION DIGEST paid off as Weisinger grew to become one of the nation's leading article writers, appearing in READER'S DIGEST, COLLIER'S, SATURDAY EVENING POST, LADIES HOME JOURNAL, ESQUIRE, COSMOPOLITAN, THIS WEEK, HOLIDAY, REDBOOK, and most of the rest of the galaxy of great American magazines. Eventually a paperback he wrote, *1001 Valuable Things You Can Get Free,* would go into endless editions and be used as the basis of a weekly feature in THIS WEEK. Weisinger had settled down to a career of free-lancing when SUPERMAN COMICS called up and asked when he was coming back to work. Reluctant to part with his newfound prosperity, he finally succumbed to the lure of an all-expense sojourn for himself and family to work on the plotting of a Superman movie in Hollywood as a prelude to his resuming editorial work.

The story has often been told of the FBI's unsuccessful attempt to stop John W. Campbell from printing atomic energy stories in ASTOUNDING SCIENCE-FICTION. The story has also been told of the successful mothballing of a Philip Wylie atomic energy story, *Paradise Crater,* sent to BLUE BOOK during the war. To those stores may be added two about Superman strips with atomic energy plots which the government stopped Mort Weisinger from printing in 1945. So he was off to a lively start.

The prosperity of Superman had encouraged imitators,

the most popular of which was CAPTAIN MARVEL, published by Fawcett with continuities written by Eando Binder. National Comics, before World War II, sued Fawcett to "cease and desist" from using that type of character. (Their counsel was the distinguished attorney Louis Nizer.) For nearly a decade the case dragged through the courts. As the years rolled past, many of the Superman imitators disappeared, unable to sustain novelty and originality in their story lines. Finally Fawcett settled out of court. It was suggested that Fawcett felt the vogue had passed and there was little money to be made from CAPTAIN MARVEL and that Superman had won a pyrrhic victory.

National's answer to that was Mort Weisinger. Rallying his vast background of science-fiction plotting, he began to reshape the history of Superman to make it possible for new, more fascinating adventures to occur. There was precedent. Originally, Superman covered ground by tremendous leaps. When the first movie was made, it became obvious that this would make him appear like a kangaroo on the screen, so he was given the power of flight. A new generation of readers was indoctrinated with a background that lent itself to greater thrills.

Ancient evildoers of Krypton, men with powers approaching that of Superman, readers now learned, had been banished to "The Phantom Zone" from which they could be released as needed to add zest to the continuities. The "worlds of if" device was introduced. This featured things that Superman *might* have done and what would have happened if he followed that course.

Most sensationally popular of Weisinger's innovations in the comic was the device of time travel. This astounding new Superman talent opened another dimension of adventure, making it possible for our hero to go into the past and introduce Hercules, Samson, and Atlas into the adventures, or to reach into the future to foil a menace that would not arrive for 1,000 years.

Frequently, associational characters built a following. This resulted in a proliferation of the Superman Group. The big gun, SUPERMAN, was published eight times a year and averaged one million circulation. Added to this was ACTION COMICS, featuring Supergirl; WORLD'S FINEST COMICS, where Superman appears with Batman, another famed adventure strip hero, whose destinies are guided by Weisinger's friend, Julius Schwartz; Jimmy Olsen, teen-age pal of Superman, has his own magazine, as has Lois Lane, Superman's girl; SUPERBOY features the adventure of Superman as a boy; ADVENTURE COMICS has Superboy and the Legion of Super Heroes. Special adventures have featured Krypto, the Super Dog. This variation on a theme has prevented youngsters from becoming jaded with a single character.

Presiding over the entire retinue is Mort Weisinger, who directs the continuity writers (including such science-fiction veterans as Edmond Hamilton, Eando Binder, and the originator, Jerry Siegel, who is still active) into the channels he considers most appealing to his audience. Thus, in the most direct way, from origin to present-day, the Superman strips and books are the spawn of the science-fiction magazines; created by a science-fiction fan, from ideas obtained from science-fiction stories, run by a former science-fiction editor and to a great degree written by science-fiction authors.

Theoretically, popular SUPERMAN should repay its debt to science fiction by a feedback system as its readers outgrow the comics. The reason this has not happened to any great degree since 1952, when science-fiction went sophisticated, is because no "bridge" magazines exist to wean the jaded away from the comics and into slick science fiction. Weisinger's THRILLING WONDER STORIES, STARTLING STORIES, and CAPTAIN FUTURE performed that role earlier buttressed by AMAZING, FANTASTIC ADVENTURES, and PLANET STORIES. Should such magazines come back on the scene, they will find Mort Weisinger with his Superman Group conscientiously continuing to do the spadework for them.

7

JOHN WYNDHAM

The entire world, except for a few fortunates, is blinded by a pyrotechnic display of green light in the sky—origin unknown. Millions of giant, walking plants—offshoot of some misguided experiment—move into cities to kill and eat the helpless masses. On the face of it, something ground out by some early science-fiction pulpster, *The Revolt of the Triffids* by John Wyndham was scarcely the stuff the mass readership of the January 6, 1951, issue of COLLIER'S might be expected to find as a five-part novel, illustrated in full color.

Who was John Wyndham?

A quick check revealed that John Wyndham had appeared for the first time in the September, 1950, AMAZING STORIES, as author of *The Eternal Eve,* a story of a Venusian maid so revolted by the notion of female dependence upon the male that she shot all of the opposite sex who came within rifle range of her cave hideout until the "right" one happened along. The rest of the case was quickly cracked. Howard Browne, AMAZING STORIES' editor, admitted Fred Pohl was the agent. Pohl, in turn, felt it was no secret that the man behind the nom de plume John Wyndham was none other than John Beynon Harris. To most new readers who followed the story's history, as with a title change (to *The Day of the Triffids*) it was published in hard covers by Doubleday in 1954, appeared in paperback from Popular Library in 1952, and was evaluated for moving picture production, this merely deepened the mystery.

Who was John Beynon Harris?

The baptismal name was John Wyndham Parkes Lucas Beynon Harris, improvised politically to keep all branches of the family happy after the birth of its recipient July 10, 1903, in the village of Knowle, Warwickshire, England. The father George Beynon Harris, was a barrister at law of Welsh descent and the mother, Gertrude Parkes, was the daughter of a Birmingham ironmaster, one of the last of a then vanishing breed.

There was one other child in the family, a brother, Vivian, who arrived two and one-half years later, so there was companionship and real friendship. Eventually, Vivian would attend The Royal Academy of Dramatic Art and tread the boards for a period. While he was not lonely, in other respects John's early life was chronically unsettled.

His parents separated when he was eight. He saw his mother primarily during school holidays and attended seven schools in all as she impulsively changed her places of residence. By the time he was 11, John learned that the easiest way to get along with other children, or other adults for that matter, was to pretend enthusiasm for majority interests.

Out of school at 18, he was a farm pupil for a while, then thought he might follow his father's footsteps into law. An Oxford tutor was obtained to help him prime for entrance exams. These he failed because he spent too much time in the Science Museum at Oxford.

A small allowance from his parents minimized the urgency

of earning a livelihood, but he nevertheless attempted to make a go in advertising. This helped develop some of his writing skills, which he utilized to phrase occasional bits of fiction. Most were rejected, but a few minor pieces were published in London newspapers.

The writing of weird fiction fascinated him and he tried a good many stories with singular lack of success. The turning point in his writing career came in 1929, when he happened to pick up a copy of the American magazine, AMAZING STORIES, which had been left in a London hotel lounge. He was fascinated by the believability of the stories and searched out others in Woolworth's for 3d each (about 7 cents), less than British juvenile paperbacks cost. The reason for the low price was that out-of-date American magazines returned to the publishers were used as ballast on ships going to England, Australia, and South Africa, which incidentally created a science-fiction audience in all of those nations.

As a youngster Harris had read H. G. Wells "with devotion." At 13 he had written a superscience masterpiece involving flying armored cars which brought down Zeppelins bombing London by firing enormous fishhooks at them.

His first sale to a science-fiction magazine was a "slogan." The February, 1930, AIR WONDER STORIES offered "One Hundred Dollars in Gold" to the reader who could come up with a catchy phrase that best typified its contents. The announcement that John Beynon Harris had won first prize with "Future Flying Fiction," as well as his letter explaining why he had selected the alliterative phrase, was published in the September, 1930, WONDER STORIES, but it was a somewhat hollow victory since AIR WONDER STORIES combined with WONDER STORIES after its May, 1930, issue, and the slogan was never used.

Greatly encouraged, nevertheless, Harris sat down to write for the science-fiction magazines in earnest. The paradoxes evidenced by Wells' *The Time Machine* had always fascinated him, so he wrote a story in which men of the distant future forcibly evacuated their ancestors from an earlier time period to secure a lusher planet for themselves. The working title of the story was *The Refugee*. It was announced as *Two Worlds to Barter* and published as *Worlds to Barter* in the May, 1931, WONDER STORIES. Considerable controversy arose as to its plausibility, spearheaded by the teen-age Henry Kuttner, who would eventually be guilty of many blatant, perforce ingenious time travel paradoxes himself.

A series of remarkable stories from Harris followed in quick succession. The first was *The Lost Machine* (AMAZING STORIES, April, 1932), concerning a Martian robot stranded on earth, who is so appalled by the hopelessly backward state of civilization that he commits suicide. This story was one of the earliest attempts at treating the robot sympathetically, and, in the process, offering social criticism. Eventually his approach would all but replace the notion of the robot as a Frankenstein monster, as the concept was developed by John W. Campbell, Jr., Eando Binder, Lester del Roy, and Isaac Asimov.

The Venus Adventure (WONDER STORIES, May, 1932), was an interplanetary adventure that placed the stress on the sociological results of the impact of an alien environment on diverse philosophical outlooks. *The Venus Adventure* was remarkable even by today's standards for both content and story.

Superlatives were definitely in order for *Exiles on Asperus,* Harris' next story, a novelette in WONDER STORIES QUARTERLY, Winter, 1933. For that year, the story can honestly be termed *avant garde*. Earthmen discover members of their race who have been enslaved for several generations by aliens on whose world they have crash landed. They defeat the batlike otherworlders, but find that those born in bondage are so conditioned to their masters by religious doctrine that they will fight to the death rather than be freed. The "liberators" from earth have no alternative but to leave them in slavery.

Openly in *Exiles on Asperus,* more subtly in certain other of his stories, Harris flays hypocrisy in religious teaching. Though his early work possesses the strong element of action then preferred by the science-fiction magazines, they are, nevertheless, grimly serious social and religious satires and turn on philosophic and psychological pivots. Harris started at a level which most of his contemporaries would never attain, either in content or style.

Not all of Harris' stories of the 1933 and 1934 period were winners. Many had been written as early as 1931, rejected, and then accepted upon resubmission. One such story, *The Moon Devils* (WONDER STORIES, April, 1934), was originally prepared as a straight weird-horror story, rejected by WEIRD TALES, and then redone as an interplanetary with a lunar locale. Somehow Harris never seemed to be able to make it as a weird story writer, one of his few stories of that type to be published. The Cathedral Crypt (MARVEL TALES, April, 1935), involving the sealing alive in mortar by six monks of the two witnesses to their similar entombment of a nun, appeared only because it was *donated* to the publication.

The best of his early time travel stories was *Wanderers of Time,* wherein four different groups of humans from progressively distant eras of our future assemble in a period when the ants are the supreme rulers of the earth's surface, commanding elaborate robots to enforce their domination. The concept that man would not continue to evolve and prevail was a shocker in its day.

The first phase of Harris' American writing career ended on a high note with *The Man From Beyond,* the cover story of the September, 1934, WONDER STORIES. In this story, centaurlike Venusians discover that a specimen they have found in a lost valley, and subsequently caged in a zoo, is actually an intelligent mammal from Earth. The transition of this man's bitterness at the mercenary kinsmen who deliberately abandoned him on an unexplored world, to grief when he learns that he has been in suspended animation for millions of years and that Earth is no more, is played out with skill and poignant delicacy.

The departure from the American scene was brought about by Harris' decision to test his ability in the novel. Upon finishing a long effort under the working title of *Sub-Sahara,* he felt the theme was too elementary for the American market. It dealt with a future where the Sahara is being flooded by water pumped from the Mediterranean. A rocket plane with a man and a women aboard suffers a power failure over the new project and is sucked into gigantic underground caverns by a whirlpool. There, a semicivilized pygmy race fights to seal off the waters that threaten them with extinction, while at the same time they hold in bondage nearly 1500 men who have blundered through the years into their realm from the surface. In addition to high literary technical skills, a remarkable sense of pace and a storyteller's instinct were evident in Harris' narrative flow.

The novel was submitted to THE PASSING SHOW, a magazine which hoped to become the British equivalent of THE SATURDAY EVENING POST. It had already published *When Worlds Collide* by Edwin Balmer and Philip Wylie, as well as *The Pirates of Venus* and *Lost on Venus* by Edgar Rice Burroughs. Harris' novel was just their cup of tea and they accepted it, changed the title to *The Secret People,* and ran it as a nine-part serial beginning in July, 1935, illustrated by an extraordinarily talented artist named Fortunino Matania.

That was credentials enough for the book publisher Newnes of London, who put the novel into hard covers the same year. The story was then serialized by THE TORONTO STAR WEEKLY.

British readers who had followed John Beynon Harris in the American magazines were puzzled by the byline, which read merely "John Beynon." When Harris had originally submitted stories to American magazines, he intended to use the name John Beynon, but the editors had run his last name. He had always felt that Harris was too common a name in Britain and that John Beynon would have a more literary ring.

Emboldened by his literary achievement, Harris broadened his endeavors and got Newnes to publish *Foul Play Suspected,* a detective novel, in 1935.

Then he set to work on an interplanetary epic, *Stowaway to Mars,* a penetrating philosophical documentary of a space race to Mars, and probably the first important science-fiction work to see the Russians as major contestants, Martian robots similar to the one in *The Lost Machine* are encountered by the earthmen; they turn the earthships back because of the danger of mutual bacterial contamination.

Stowaway to Mars was also serialized in PASSING SHOW, beginning in May, 1936. It was even more popular than *The Secret People* and it was immediately rushed into hard covers as *The Planet Plane* by Newnes, and a year later reprinted in a popular science weekly, MODERN WONDER, beginning in the issue of May 19, 1937, under the title of *The Space Machine.* For no apparent reason, the editors of MODERN WONDER changed one of the men in the story to a woman, only to encounter an irresolvable dilemma as they moved into the final installment, which forced them to call upon the author to write a new ending to take care of the situation.

These achievements made Harris the toast of London's science-fiction circles. In an interview in the January, 1937, issue of SCIENTIFICTION, "The British Fantasy Review," Walter H. Gillings hailed "John Beynon (Harris) on his British triumph" and made the assessment that "judged from the standpoint of literary ability, Harris is probably the best of our modern science-fiction authors."

At the time this seemed a daring assumption, for another British author, W. J. Passingham, had appeared in PASSING SHOW with a science-fiction novel, *When London Fell,* and contemporaries Benson Herbert, Festus Pragnell, and J. M. Walsh were achieving the eminence of hard covers in Great Britain for novels that had run in American science-fiction magazines. None of these others was destined to sustain his writing efforts, however, so Gillings' appraisal, in hindsight, was essentially justified.

When Gillings succeeded in convincing World's Work to issue a test science-fiction magazine, TALES OF WONDER, in 1937, Harris contributed a humorous farce, *The Perfect Creature,* to the first issue. Far more substantial, however, was his writing to order a sequel to *Stowaway to Mars,* titled *Sleepers of Mars,* in 1938, for the second issue of TALES OF WONDER. This sequel told the details of the fate of the Russian expedition to Mars and may well have contributed substantially towards the establishment of TALE OF WONDER, for a regular quarterly schedule was thereafter announced. This coup was destined to prove nonexclusive, for George Newnes Ltd., possibly encouraged by TALES OF WONDER's acceptance, decided to experiment with a British science-fiction magazine of their own, FANTASY, edited by T. Stanhope Sprigg, the first issue of which reached the newsstands on July 29, 1938. Newnes was thoroughly experienced in periodical sales as owner of the renowned magazine WIDE WORLD, as well as a number of other adventure magazines. When Harris was asked to contribute, he could scarcely refuse his book publishers.

The first issue of FANTASY contained his *Beyond the Screen,* concerning the invention of an electronic screen that projects an attacking armada of 1200 Nazi and Fascist planes into the far future. Under the title of *Judson's Annihilator,* this story was reprinted in the October, 1939, AMAZING STORIES, and was the first appearance of the John Beynon pen name in the United States.

Hitler's attack on Poland and the entry of England and France into the war put an end to the new magazine, FANTASY, after only three issues. Harris had a story under the Beynon name in each of them, and a fourth, *Child of Power,* under the nom de plume of Wyndhame Parkes in the third issue. That story, a smoothly written tale of a child born with the ability to hear radio waves, even those from outer space, ended with a flash of lightning and a clap of thunder "blinding" the extra sense. "That's all," the youth had said, "that was the end of it."

So it was for Britain's bid to develop a science-fiction market of its own. For all practical purposes it was also to prove the end of the John Beynon pen name.

The excitement, the pressures, the uncertainties of war made writing difficult. Civil liberties taken for granted during peace time were restricted, and Harris, working in civil service in Censorship from August, 1940, to November, 1943, participated in their curtailment. Then, at the age of forty, he found himself a Corporal with the Royal Signal Corps, working as a cipher operator. He next was deposited on the beaches of Normandy. Many of his past science-fiction stories had dealt with war: *The Third Vibrator, The Spheres of Hell, Beyond the Screen* and *Trojan Beam,* but all of them had been composed within the subjective atmosphere of his study. This was the real thing.

"I had a constant feeling I was there by mistake," he recalls. "Possibly that was because I had spent much of my schooldays expecting in due course to be in the Kaiser's war, though it ended when I was still too young. Nevertheless, I could not get rid of the feeling that *that* had been my war, and now I had somehow got into the wrong one. It produced odd moods of detached spectatorship, shot with flashes of *déja-vu.* I took to writing sonnets because you can't carry a lot of paper on a campaign, and they are more interesting than crosswords. When things grew more static, I tried my hand at translating a French play or two, but lost the translations somewhere in Germany."

Through the entire war period only one story appeared, *Phony Meteor,* in AMAZING STORIES for March, 1941, telling of a tiny spaceship mistaken first for a Nazi secret weapon and then for a meteor. All its passengers, minute buglike creatures sent to establish a colony on earth, are destroyed by insect spray without there ever being the slightest realization of their intelligence.

During his army sojourn, Harris came to the decision that he would work in fantasy, not science fiction, when he resumed writing, because of the wider latitude it permitted. Upon his release in 1946, he gave himself two years to make good, but as the allotted time passed and the rejections mounted uninterruptedly, he faced an agonizing reappraisal. His accumulated savings were virtually exhausted and he either must write something that people would buy or try to get a post in the civil service again.

Science fiction had changed greatly since John Beynon Harris, reborn John Beynon, was first choice for England's leading science-fiction writer. A more sophisticated brand of fiction, much more comfortable in the depths of the galaxy than in the solar system or on the planet Earth, prevailed. In this new fiction, action was often only implied and the plot could turn on a psychological quirk, a Freudian slip, or a philosophical misinterpretation. The circumstances leading up to the story were frequently taken for granted, resulting in stylized backgrounds. Explanations, logical or otherwise, of the wonders that abounded, were often simply omitted.

In a good many respects it was superior to the type of science fiction most popular before World War II, though in the process of refinement some of the substance had been lost. Harris wasn't sure he could write it, and wasn't sure he wanted to write it, but it began to look as if he would have to try. The last science-fiction story he had seen published was a novelette, *The Living Lies,* a rather obvious allegory of color and racism on the planet Venus, in the second issue of NEW WORLDS in 1946. To write himself back into shape would take time and money.

Then, one of his near-to-life fantasies, *Jizzle,* a short story of an artistically vindictive female monkey (a variation of the female pig in John Collier's *Mary*), was sold to COLLIER'S in the United States and was published in the January 8, 1949, issue under the John Beynon byline. The parallel in Harris' situation was remarkably close to that of the dying man in *Technical Slip* (ARKHAM SAMPLER, Spring, 1949), (one of Harris' few postwar fantasies to see print), who had

a special arrangement whereby for 75 per cent of his accumulated wealth he would be permitted to replay his life from
boyhood.

This was a second chance to make it. First he was to try
his neglected skills as a science-fiction writer on a short-
length story. The result was *Adaptation* (ASTOUNDING SCI-
ENCE FICTION, July, 1949), a delicately wrought, superbly
handled, heartstring-tugger about a baby girl who is scientifically adapted to live on another world. No question now existed of Harris' ability to compete with the best writers of
modern science fiction.

It was in the novel that Harris had made his greatest success prior to World War II, so now he proposed to try a new
one. He joined two ideas in his files, one on the theme of
universal blindness and the other on a plant menace. The
latter was illuminated in his mind when he was startled one
night by the manner in which the wind made a sapling in a
hedge appear to be making jabs at him. Other stories that
may well have influenced his handling of the two major plot
situations in *The Day of the Triffids* were *Seeds from Space*
by Laurence Manning (WONDER STORIES, June, 1930), with
its intelligent plants grown from unknown spores, and Edgar
Wallace's short tale, *The Black Grippe,* from the March,
1920, Newnes' STRAND MAGAZINE, in which the entire world
is stricken blind for six days.

On the surface, the ideas were old ones and the approach
"pulpish." In execution, the novel exhibited stylistic strengths
which were instantly recognized by the reviewers and a
Gibraltar-like foundation of scientific logic that was not. This
last, to a degree, was developed by reverting to Hugo Gernsback's insistence on detailed explanation and background in
WONDER STORIES.

Harris' ideas for *The Day of the Triffids* and the many
works that followed were adapted from many sources, since
he was a regular reader of science fiction and thoroughly
familiar with its various gambits. His rhetoric, on the other
hand, appears to have been persuasively influenced by only

one major writer, H. G. Wells. Great ingenuity at approaching an old idea from a fresh slant was characteristically his own contribution.

Almost instantly following the appearance of *The Revolt of the Triffids* in COLLIER'S, a spate of short stories by John Wyndham began to appear in U. S. science-fiction magazines. There was little question that Harris could now sell anything he wrote. However, he calculatedly decided to stick with the novel and the world menace theme. *The Kraken Wakes* appeared in boards in England with the Michael Joseph imprint, and in the United States in paperback as *Out of the Deeps*. With echoes of Karel Capek's *War with the Newts,* it chronicles in fascinating detail the attempts of an alien race, who have settled in our ocean depths, to destroy humanity. As in *Revolt of the Triffids,* Harris has no final answers, but merely· acts as an overly literary reporter. His penchant for walking away from a resolution of the problems he proposes has been criticized, but his stories succeed in spite of this tendency.

The Kraken Wakes quickly multiplied editions in England, and was followed by *The Chrysalids* from the same publisher (issued in the United States by Ballantine Books as *Re-Birth*). Here, a postwar remnant of civilization ostracizes and attempts to destroy any creature, plant or human, showing variance from the norm. A six-toed girl thus finds herself in deadly peril until she finds she is one of a new telepathic race which is slowly evolving.

Those years that Harris did not have a new novel for the book publishers they put together collections of his shorts (*Jizzle,* 1954; *The Seeds of Time,* 1956) which, astonishingly, seemed to sell nearly as well as his novels.

Harris had written a dozen or more stories with a time travel theme. It seemed to be his private form of fun and relaxation, and the best of these stories, such as *Pawley's Peepholes* (SCIENCE-FANTASY, Winter, 1951), where prying intangible tourist buses from the future are sent scuttling back where they belong by the use of vulgarity, appeared to have nothing else in mind but light entertainment. ·

Not so with the time travel story, *Consider Her Ways,* a new novelette, specially written for a Ballantine collection, *Sometime, Never,* in 1956. Through the use of drugs, a woman doctor of our time turns up in the future as an obese "mother" in a world without men, where selected females produce children like the queen bees. The high point of the story is the dialogue on whether the world is better off with or without men, which introduces a highly original and disturbing point of view (at least, to a man) on the subject.

Because of the international success of *Day of the Triffids,* the feeling was prevalent that Harris had made his mark with that novel and everything that followed was to be anticlimactic. In fact, it was felt that whatever opening of doors there was to be in the future could only be done by using the phrase, "by the author of . . . ."

That was when Harris set off another time-bomb. A new novel of his, *The Midwich Cuckoos,* had been shown in manuscript to Metro-Goldwyn-Mayer and purchased for what would eventually appear as the motion picture *Village of the Damned* (1960).

A flying saucer lands on the green of the British town of Midwich and twenty-four hours are blotted from the memories of everyone in the community. As of the following day, every woman in the town turns out to be pregnant. When the children are born they are distinguished by great golden eyes. By the time they are nine they have developed a community mind and a community will, special powers which they admit will ultimately doom mankind. Disposing of them poses a seemingly insoluble technical as well as moral problem until they are destroyed through their trust in the man who has educated them.

Wyndham, for this story, reworked the plot of *The Chrysalids,* directing the sympathy of the reader away from the children and toward humanity. He accomplished this by making the method of their conception illegitimate and nonhuman, and their actions so cold-bloodedly extreme as to divorce them from reader sympathy. The devices of the amoral superior child and the desirability of the community mind both seem to have been adapted from Olaf Stapledon.

The motion picture proved to be extraordinarily effective and was followed by a much inferior sequel, *Children of the Damned*. It may well be that in these sinister children a new menace has been created which will evolve into a nonstop series similar to those following the appearance of *Frankenstein* and *Dracula* on the screen.

As successful as *Village of the Damned* as a film is *Day of the Triffids,* released by Allied Artists in 1963. A reasonably faithful approximation of the novel, it is fulfilling its destiny by frightening audiences around the world.

The realization that he was becoming typed as a horror writer may well have caused Harris to write four connected interplanetary novelettes, all appearing in NEW WORLDS during 1958. The novelettes deal with the contributions of four generations of the Troon family in the building of a space station and in the first explorations of the Moon, Mars, and Venus. Atomic war comes, new powers emerge, but progress continues. Published as *The Outward Urge* by Michael Joseph in 1959, the book was represented as a collaboration of John Wyndham and Lucas Parkes. The reason for the collaboration was to head off John Wyndham's propensity for producing such phenomena as Triffids, Krakens, or golden-eyed children, "and keeping him to the more practical problems of tomorrow." Since "Lucas Parkes" uses but two of Harris' generous supply of middle names, this may well be one of the few official collaborations of an author with himself.

The next fictional problem Harris occupied himself with was that of how to go about informing the public of a means of doubling or even tripling the life span, without creating a world catastrophe. The book was published by Michael Joseph as *Trouble With Lichen* in 1960. In the novel, the public would be offered a second full start. Harris found he had to cope with the problem himself. At the age of 60, he helped Grace Isabel Wilson "celebrate her retirement from teaching English to the young," by marrying for the first time, in July, 1963.

The Wyndham method was not lost on the new generation. The brightest pupil of a number was John Christopher (pen name of Christopher Samuel Yond), possibly urged along by Michael Joseph, publisher of the Wyndham books. The most successful Christopher stories in the Wyndham vein were *No Blade of Grass* (serialized in THE SATURDAY EVENING POST and sold to the films) and *The Long Winter*.

Perhaps the most unexpected turn of John Wyndham's success, was that the moving picture approach to his novels, coupled with the reportorial believability of his writing approach, created a special type of terror—one based solely on a scientific buildup—that proved far more effective and memorable than any previous horror stories he had attempted utilizing stock fright devices.

8

ERIC FRANK RUSSELL

There are some tales so good that one hates to see them die. Among them is the fiction that Eric Frank Russell's submission of the novel *Sinister Barrier* to John W. Campbell inspired the publication of a new magazine, UN-KNOWN. It is easy to find circumstantial evidence to "support" the story. Immediately prior to the appearance of the first issue on February 10, 1939 (dated March), featuring *Sinister Barrier*, giant posters reproducing its covers were carried on the sides of the delivery trucks of the American News Company, a promotion if not unprecedented for a new pulp magazine at least distinctly uncommon. *Sinister Barrier* was billed in advance by its publishers as "The greatest imaginative novel in two decades!"

"Swift death awaits the first cow that leads a revolt against milking," were the opening lines of *Sinister Barrier*. Quoting Charles Fort, "I think we are property," Russell built his story on the realization by humans that the planet Earth is "owned" by alien globes of light called Vitons, who "breed" us like cattle and influence our history for their own purposes.

The origin of the magazine and the publication of the novel seemed too happy a wedding to be fortuitous. Nevertheless, it was.

The novel had been submitted to Campbell in 1938 as *Forbidden Acres*. He was enthralled by the first half but felt that the narrative lost all momentum as it moved to a close. He returned it to Russell for rewriting.

Russell, who had been selling science fiction intermittently for only a little over a year, accepted the challenge. He decided to rewrite the novel from end to end, utilizing as his technical model the Dan Fowler stories which ran in G-MEN, a popular pulp magazine of the period. Campbell, on accepting the revision, openly admitted that he was astonished that Russell, with his limited writing experience, had been able to do the difficult theme justice.

The novel was first scheduled for ASTOUNDING SCIENCE-FICTION, then shifted to UNKNOWN when the plans for that magazine had completely jelled.

In retrospect, the major impact of the novel depended almost entirely on its daring concept. Unnecessary action extends the length of the story. The reader frequently finds himself losing track of the identity of the characters, so inadequately are they sketched. The logic becomes gossamer-thin at points.

What was seemingly its great strength, its apparent originality of theme, was exposed when Thomas S. Gardner, Ph.D., writing in the March 5, 1939, issue of FANTASY NEWS, pointed out: "The same plot was developed with an unusual twist that Russell's *Sinister Barrier* does not contain in a short story by Edmond Hamilton in WEIRD TALES. The story was *The Earth Owners* and was published in the August issue in 1931. Even the same quotation from one of Fort's books is used in both stories. In order to appreciate

Sinister Barrier one should also read Hamilton's story and notice the difference in the endings."

Hamilton's plot has one group of radiant globes (similar to the Vitons) as protectors of the earth against raiding black clouds who feed on humans. The implication is that Earth is being shielded from harm until man achieves a state of development in which he can fend for himself. Hamilton's short story, extraordinarily off-beat for the period, made no reader impression, having had the misfortune to appear in the same issue with *The Whisperer in Darkness,* the wildly acclaimed H. P. Lovecraft science-fiction novelette.

Russell disclaimed any prior reading or knowledge of Hamilton's effort, attributing the plot similarity to both authors having read Charles Fort independently; both were members of the Fortean Society. It is the oft-repeated case of the first man to use the idea not always being the one to popularize it. As far as the science-fiction world is concerned, Russell and the "I think we are property" theme are synonymous. There is no question that the widespread use of Fortean material in science fiction begins with the publication of *Sinister Barrier.*

Eric Frank Russell, descended from Irish stock, was born January 6, 1905, in Sandhurst, Surrey, England, where his father was an instructor at the Military College. The family moved frequently, residing at various times in Chatham, Croydon, Bradford, Aldershot, Longmoor, Portsmouth, Weymouth, Pembroke Dock, Brighton, and Southport, and part of Russell's childhood was spent in Egypt, where he was close enough to the natives to learn Arabic (which he gradually forgot). In Egypt and the Sudan he lived in Alexandria, Cairo, Khartoum, and Port Tewfik. His education was apparently a good one, predominantly obtained at schools for sons of British officers. The list of courses is impressive, including chemistry, physics, building and steel construction, quantity surveying, mechanical draughtsmanship, metallurgy, and crystallography.

So reticent is Russell about his parents that one is tempted to speculate, perhaps unfairly, on a personal application of the passage in his short story *I Am Nothing* (ASTOUNDING SCIENCE FICTION, July, 1952) where he offers an almost extraneous background illumination of dictator David Korman's filial relationship: "When a child he had feared his father long and ardently; also his mother."

Moves from place to place and intensive study did not stunt his growth. He grew to be six foot two, 180 pounds, with great hands and a cocksure smile. While in the process of finding himself he worked as a soldier, telephone operator, quantity surveyor, and government draughtsman. He met and married a nurse who bore him a baby girl which they named Erica, because she was born on his (Eric's) birthday, January 6, 1934.

Interest in science fiction was a lifelong process for Russell, beginning with fairy tales, mythology, and English legends and continuing to the discovery of the science-fiction magazines. The earliest science-fiction stories that appear to have made an impression upon him are *The Gostak and the Doshes* by Miles J. Breuer, M.D. (AMAZING STORIES, March, 1930), a truly remarkable precursor of Alfred Korzybski's *General Semantics,* and Paul Ernst's *The Incredible Formula* (AMAZING STORIES, June, 1931), a tale of the social implications of the living dead. Later the brief but influential talent of Stanley G. Weinbaum, the even briefer spark of youthful suicide David R. Daniels, as well as individual stories of Alexander M. Phillips and Norman L. Knight, left their mark on his mind. His preferences appear to run to specific stories rather than favorite authors.

When he took up a post as technical representative and trouble shooter for a steel and engineering firm in Liverpool, Russell set into motion the series of circumstances that would bring him into contact with the inner-circle group of the science-fiction movement and, through his association with them, make his bid as a professional writer.

Two men had been primarily responsible for the formation

of the British Interplanetary Society in October, 1933. The
first of these was P. E. Cleator, the multidegreed acting
president, whose writing ability would prove a major factor
in recruiting members to the society. The other was Leslie
J. Johnson, a youthful Liverpool scientifictionist. A press
story planted by Cleator attracted the attention of Russell.
The May, 1935, issue of THE JOURNAL OF THE BRITISH
INTERPLANETARY SOCIETY not only lists Russell as a new
member, but it acknowledges that the cover photo, an astronomical shot of the planet Jupiter, was used by his courtesy.

Johnson, upon meeting Russell, was fascinated by the self-
assured demeanor, the direct and earthy personality of the
older man. Russell was already contributing articles to trade
magazines and house organs. In addition, he was placing
poetry in the local newspapers, mostly anonymous shafts
directed at topical subjects and politicians, and he had done
a series of articles on "Interplanetary Communications"
(based on the writings of the Russian Konstantin Tsiolkovsky) for a private periodical of limited circulation.

Impressed by Russell's writing skill, Johnson urged him
to try science fiction, suggesting a plot for a story to be called
Eternal Re-diffusion. Russell completed it and sent it to F.
Orlin Tremaine, editor of ASTOUNDING STORIES. When it was
rejected as being too difficult for the reader to grasp, Russell
started to tear it up, but Johnson, horrified, claimed the story
and retained it as a souvenir. It has never been published.

A second attempt, *The Saga of Pelican West,* a novelette
done by Russell on his own, appeared in the February, 1937,
issue of ASTOUNDING STORIES. The influence of Stanley G.
Weinbaum permeates the story, most obviously in the person
of Alfred, a talking "Callistrian domestic *ulahuala,* or re-
ticulated python," but also in the light air of humor and the
boy-meets-girl banter which pervades the superficial plot.

During a period when science fiction could best be described as "dull," *The Saga of Pelican West* was refreshingly
sharp. Though the literary influence was obvious and the plot
insubstantial, readers on both sides of the Atlantic instantly

recognized the flicker of an unusual talent. The only adverse comments from readers referred to the weakness of some of the science. To these Russell replied, in the June, 1937, SCIENTIFICTION, the British Fantasy Review, that plausibility rated higher than pure scientific accuracy in writing science fiction.

Russell immediately followed with *The Great Radio Peril,* a short story published in the April, 1937, ASTOUNDING STORIES, actually a social satire aimed at the mushrooming radio networks. The quantity and strength of radio waves stunt crops, threatening the world with starvation. An international code limiting the number of stations and the power of transmitters is forced upon the world. These restrictions are effected almost like a disarmament arrangement. However, television has since hopelessly outdated any physical or social "danger" from radio.

The only British science-fiction magazine published up to that time had been SCOOPS, a juvenile weekly that ran for twenty issues from February 10th to June 23rd, 1934. When Walter H. Gillings announced early in 1937 that he would edit a quarterly periodical, printed on book paper, to be entitled TALES OF WONDER, it was treated as a literary event and he was flooded with manuscripts from British authors. The appearance of the first issue on British newsstalls, June 29, 1937, found a Russell story, *The Prr-r-eet,* in the contents. Reader reaction made it the most popular story in the issue. Again, Russell had borrowed from Weinbaum, of whose famed Martian ostrich Tweel, so named because of the sound he uttered, "Trrweerrill," he created another acoustically named alien being, "Prr-r-eet." The story evoked a feeling of empathy for the "humanity" of the creature, despite its bizarre form. Before it leaves Earth, it gives its Homo sapiens contacts a device for simultaneously blending color and sound into a new type of music. This idea was supplied by Arthur C. Clarke, who had met Russell at a London meeting of the Science Fiction Association, and he received 10 percent of the proceeds for his contribution, something under three dollars, but was the first money Clarke ever earned from science fiction.

Russell's greatest success of 1937 was a 17,000-worder written around an idea supplied by Johnson and titled *Seeker of Tomorrow*. As Johnson originally wrote it, it was called *Amen*. Later he succeeded in getting a professional writer of his acquaintance to revamp it as *Through Time's Infinity*. It still didn't go, so he showed it to Russell, who, impressed, rewrote it and sent it to Newnes, then contemplating a British science-fiction magazine. The idea of the magazine fell through, so Julius Schwartz, Russell's agent in the United States, took it to F. Orlin Tremaine, who bought it. The title appeared on the cover of the July, 1937, ASTOUNDING STORIES with the names of both authors beneath it. Somehow the magazine carried Johnson's middle initial as "T" instead of "J," which later brought up the question of whether there were two Johnsons. The story was a simple but absorbing retelling of H. G. Wells' *The Time Machine,* with two temporal technicians exploring the future in a series of fascinating hops.

Russell made a working agreement with a Spanish author friend, Antonio Moncho y Gilabert, of Valencia, who wrote under the pen name of Miguel Gautisolo, to rewrite each other's stories in their respective languages and attempt to sell them. However, Gilabert disappeared forever in the maelstrom of the Spanish Civil War.

A sequel to *The Saga of Pelican West* was undertaken and submitted under the title of *They Who Sweep*. The story dealt with the adventures of Pelican, the lead character of *Saga,* on Pallas "where the air is so high explorers must wear nose plugs." The title was taken from a Russell poem of space travel. Rewritten three times, the story finally was literally consigned to the flames, and an incredulous Johnson castigated Russell as a "madman" when he found out.

A 20,000-word effort, *Trumpeter, Sound the Recall!* "a

story of future warfare in which 100 million men get killed because one man throws away a banana skin," suffered a like fate.

Submicrowave Hypnosis, "showing how thought control is put on a business basis," was discarded two thirds of the way through when someone beat Russell into print with the plot.

The Atompacker, a tale in which the "menace from outer space" theme is treated lightly, couldn't seem to find a home in any of the magazines.

All these represented a substantial amount of time and effort that could have been spent by Russell with his family or in just plain pleasurable reading. Writing began to look much less attractive to him. Nevertheless, he persisted and a very brief and poetic story titled *Mana* in the December, 1937, ASTOUNDING STORIES proved to have influence beyond its immediate popularity, which was negligible. It told of the last man on Earth, who steps up intelligence in ants to the point where they are on the road to civilization with little wheelbarrows, bows and arrows, and fire. The similarity to Clifford D. Simak's cart-pulling and ore-smelting ants in *Census* (ASTOUNDING SCIENCE-FICTION, September, 1944), second in the famed "Cities" series, is obvious.

George Newnes Ltd., the periodical publisher who had been postponing plans for years, finally placed FANTASY on sale July 29, in competition to TALES OF WONDER. Again Russell had the distinction of appearing in the first issue of a new British science-fiction magazine, this time with *Shadow-Man,* a brief short of a criminal who is caught despite his power of invisibility because his shadow betrays his presence. This was the first Russell story utilizing the surprise or "O. Henry" ending and it was to become a standard trick in his repertoire.

At almost the same time, his short story, *The World's Eighth Wonder,* appeared in the Summer, 1938, TALES OF WONDER. Russell sardonically speculates that if the Martians were ever to land on Earth and were to look anything like humans, no one would believe them and they would be placed in a circus as side-show freaks. The idea was not original with him, having been reworked from *The Martian* by Allen Glasser and A. Rowley Hilliard (WONDER STORIES QUARTERLY, Winter, 1932), and the "Americanese" of Russell's dialogue looked strange in the British publication in which it appeared. Where Russell had picked up his American idiom (possibly from U.S. pulps) is not quite certain, but his style was definitely American, as were most frequently his locales and heroes, and this was to remain constant.

Substantiation of his very friendly feeling toward England's former colony was to be found in his later philosophical sketch in TALES OF WONDER for Autumn, 1940, where he eulogized: "A temporarily suppressed gland America commenced to function coincident with mass humanity's need. Twin rails crawled across virgin desert like nerves creeping through the new flesh of a growing thing."

However, his only appearance in the United States in 1939 was with *Impulse* in the September issue of ASTOUNDING SCIENCE-FICTION. It was a very weak effort concerning "possession" of a cadaver by an intelligence from outer space and reflected some of the elements of the living dead in Paul Ernst's *The Incredible Formula*.

The evidence up to this point was overwhelming that Russell showed much greater promise stylistically than creatively. Most of the stories he had sold were derivative in plot or method from other authors or were collaborations where the idea was supplied to him and he "put the flesh on the skeleton."

Russell's obvious weakness may have come from his philosophical outlook. Dissenting to a reviewer's opinion of a book he characterized himself in a letter dated June 24, 1937, and published in the July, 1937, issue of NOVAE TERRAE, a British science-fiction fan magazine, as "another young rationalist of 32 years of age." "Rationalism" is an outlook that recognizes only what is demonstrable to the human intellect. Its adherents believe reason is the best means of attaining ultimate knowledge. It accepts nothing on faith and rejects the emotions and imagination as means of intellectual advancement. It does not, automatically, deny the existence of God or the immortality of the soul, since St. Thomas Aquinas is considered one of the great rationalists. It is a philosophy of skepticism, which urges its adherents to doubt everything.

The weakness of the rationalist viewpoint is that it promulgates no ideas of its own; it waits to be shown. Stubbornly waiting to be shown, Russell was retarded in conceiving plot deviations and depended for intellectual nutrient completely on others.

Paradoxically, the two greatest influences on his thinking were men noted for their attempts to shatter complacency and broaden the scope of men's thinking. The first of these was Olaf Stapledon, a respected philosopher of this century, who, in his book *Last and First Men* (1930), supplied many of the basic concepts on which the latter-day school of science fiction is founded. Stapledon had sent a letter of inquiry to the British Interplanetary Society the summer of 1936 (he eventually joined). Russell saw the letter and the proximity of Stapledon, who was then Professor of Philosophy at Liverpool University, prompted him to visit the man. He introduced Stapledon to the science-fiction magazines, bringing over a stack to read. Stapledon had not intended to write science fiction but merely to find the proper vehicle to convey his philosophical ideas. The two men saw one another at long intervals some six more times before Stapledon's death.

The second and more obvious influence was a strange little Bronx, New York, man named Charles Hoy Fort, who spent a lifetime assembling 40,000 clippings on seemingly inexplicable events; poltergeists; red rain; rains of frogs, fish, stones; strange lights in the sky; disappearances; levitation; and related bizarre and unusual phenomenon. He was not satisfied with documenting such notices, but offered his own interpretation, displaying so vast an imaginative resource as to become a seemingly bottomless reservoir of science-fiction plots. Many of his clippings and observations were presented in four books, the first of which, *The Book of the Damned,* was published in 1919 by Boni & Liveright. The most famous of the four was *Lo!* issued in 1931 by C. Kendall and reprinted in full in ASTOUNDING STORIES, April to November, 1934, inclusive. Together with his other two volumes, *New Lands* (1923) and *Wild Talents* (1932), these were collected by Henry Holt and issued in 1941 as *The Books of Charles Fort.* This volume became the bible of The Fortean Society, a group of acolytes organized by novelist Tiffany Thayer who edited a periodical titled DOUBT, dedicated to continued presentation of Fortean-type material.

Russell had read *Lo!* in ASTOUNDING STORIES, but it had made no impression at the time. However, when he stumbled across a British edition of *Lo!* in a secondhand book shop he went quietly mad. His lifelong ambition became the resolve to obtain the three other books. He wrote to American antiquarian dealers and secured all but *New Lands.* For *Wild Talents* he paid $27, an amount which represented two weeks' pay for the average Britisher in the 1930's; in terms of today's purchasing power this amounted to paying $270 for a book published in the not-too-distant past.

From *Lo!* he took the plot nucleus for *Sinister Barrier,* and from Olaf Stapledon's *Last and First Men* he acknowledged taking the theme of symbiotic relationship—two intelligent life forms interdependent as the humans and Vitons were on earth.

The $600 he received for *Sinister Barrier* added to $100 of his own enabled him to visit America with his wife in May, 1939. He mortgaged his vacations for the next two years with his employers so that he could make an extended stay of six weeks. He urgently wanted to come because he was convinced that war was imminent and that this might be his last opportunity for some time. In the United States, he spent most of his visit in and around the Greater New York area. He spoke at the May 7, 1939, meeting of the Queens Science Fiction League, where he expressed his disappointment at the lack of support given science-fiction projects both amateur and professional in England. His talk left no question that he was a "fan" of science fiction as well as a professional author.

Talkative and likeable, he would thread his conversation with four-letter words, the shock value of which appeared to amuse him. If permitted to introduce himself he could prove direct to the point of rudeness! For example:

"You're a Jew, aren't you?"

"Quite evidently you're on the dole."

In America he met Edmond Hamilton. The two had in common, in addition to an interest in science-fiction writing, membership in The Fortean Society. Hamilton gave him his own copy of *New Lands,* completing Russell's Fort collection, as well as a letter from and a photo of Charles Fort. This remained the high spot of the American visit in Russell's memory.

The Atompacker was sold to and appeared in the undated (1939) second issue of FANTASY as *Vampire from the Void.* The final and third issue of that magazine, before the wartime paper shortage caused it to fold, carried Russell's tale *Mightier Yet,* apparently influenced by war psychology in its theme of the Nazis using a machine capable of hypnotizing soldiers over a distance of a number of miles. The only other published Russell item during 1939 was an article describing newly reported Fortean phenomena which appeared in the September, 1939, UNKNOWN as *Over the Border.*

Whether wartime responsibilities now limited his time (he took radio courses at Northern Polytechnic, London, and the Marconi College, Chelmsford) is not known, but 1940 saw the appearance of only two items, *Spontaneous Frognation* (UNKNOWN, July, 1940) (non-fiction) and *I, Spy* in the Autumn, 1940, TALES OF WONDER, a superbly handled novelette of a Martian capable of simulating any living form —plant, animal, or human being—who is loose on Earth. The tale evolves into an adroit detective story, reminiscent of Campbell's *Who Goes There?* but distinctive enough not to be considered an imitation. The story ends in an ingenious burst of inspired writing.

One of Russell's author friends in England was Maurice G. Hugi, a writer of modest ability who had sold a few stories to TALES OF WONDER. One of his stories just couldn't make the grade. He showed it to Russell, who liked the plot and offered to rework it. The actual writing is said to have occurred in the fall of 1940 during a bombing raid on Liverpool, with Russell on the floor beneath the bed or the table (versions differ) pounding away on a typewriter.

What emerged was *The Mechanical Mice,* published under Maurice G. Hugi's name in the January, 1949, ASTOUNDING SCIENCE FICTION. The story involves a man who extracts from the future the idea of a machine, which when built, mothers tiny mechanical mice which steal materials necessary for it to reproduce itself. The story is brilliantly told and is considered one of the small masterpieces of science fiction, quite probably the inspiration of Lewis Padgett's *Twonkey.*

The birth of the most famous character created by Russell came about, he recalls, "when I was seeking a plot and realized I had never attempted a robot yarn." The result was Jay Score, outwardly having the appearance of a giant human, who first appeared in a story appropriately titled *Jay Score* (ASTOUNDING SCIENCE-FICTION, May, 1941). The spaceship crew in the story, including a group of many-tentacled Martian chess masters, provided a cast of characters as engaging as any seen since the entourage of the Doc Savage stories. The heroic efforts of Jay Score, together with the special talents of the Martians, save the spaceship from a fiery death in the bosom of the sun in a rather routine adventure.

Seat of Oblivion (ASTOUNDING SCIENCE-FICTION, November, 1941) was a third attempt at the plot of *Impulse* and *I, Spy.* A device is used by a criminal to take possession of successive individuals for ulterior motives. He finally is tricked into entering the body of a notorious killer minutes before the killer is apprehended by the police.

An attempt at fantasy, *With a Blunt Instrument* (UN-KNOWN, December, 1941), involving the use of Australian native magic to kill men for insurance purposes, proved a dud. The same month, the pen name of Webster Craig was used for *Homo Saps* in ASTOUNDING SCIENCE-FICTION (December, 1941), in which Martians tip the protagonists to the fact that camels are telepathic and smarter than people.

The cast of *Jay Score* returned in a sequel, *Mechanistria* (ASTOUNDING SCIENCE-FICTION, January, 1942), to engage in an exciting adventure on a planet dominated by a civilization of diverse machinery, ruled by a computing machine. The plot was reminiscent of *Paradise and Iron* by Miles J. Breuer, M.D. (AMAZING STORIES QUARTERLY, Summer, 1930), but with an element of humor.

The most influential of the Jay Score stories was *Symbiotica* (ASTOUNDING SCIENCE-FICTION, October, 1943). Stapledon's concept of interdependent life forms was utilized to show a world where humanoids lived in symbiosis with trees and indirectly with other life forms on their planet. Great imagination was displayed and the vividness of the narration would seem to have been the inspiration of Harry Harrison's novel *Death World*. Beyond that, the story appears to have been the springboard from which the writers of most of the important science-fiction stories involving symbiosis as the basis of their plots have taken off.

Only a single Russell story appeared in each of the next three years. *Controller* (March, 1944, ASTOUNDING SCIENCE-FICTION) and *Resonance* (July, 1945, ASTOUNDING SCIENCE-FICTION), both inconsequential war stories aimed contemptuously at the Japanese. The war in Europe finally ended with Russell dogging General Patton's army in command of a Royal Air Force mobile radio unit.

Until now, almost all of Russell's plots had been carried along on a stream of physical action. In the short novel *Metamorphosite,* his sole contribution for 1946, which appeared in the December, 1946, ASTOUNDING SCIENCE FICTION, he constructed an absorbing plot in which a Galactic empire seeks to annex a world of apparent humanoids, only to learn, in a revelation ingeniously impacted by indirection, that evolution has made this impossible. As a result of this story, Russell's stock rose in the literary marketplace.

Twist endings were a Russell specialty. He showed it again when Walter Gillings coaxed the Temple Bar Publishing Co. of London into getting out the first postwar British science-fiction magazine, with Russell's contribution, *Relic,* in the second (April, 1947) number. The mystery of a meteor-scarred spaceship which lands in England is solved when it released a robot, which after taking its bearing plunges into the ocean "returning to the Lemurians' Fathers' fathers."

Hobbyist (ASTOUNDING SCIENCE FICTION, September, 1947) ended on an even more ironic note when a terrestrial and his pet macaw make a naturalist's study of a strange planet, departing unaware that a superior intelligence has duly recorded both of them during a routine card-indexing of life on that world.

Russell's most spectacular success in the forties proved to be the novel *Dreadful Sanctuary* (ASTOUNDING SCIENCE FICTION, June-August, 1948), built around the activities of The Normans, a secret society representing themselves as the only completely sane inhabitants of earth (all other races are the lunatics dumped here by other worlds). They are dedicated to sabotaging progress, fomenting wars, and generally creating hob, until such a time as natural evolution improves the breed. They turn out to be the true madmen, as might be surmised, and when they are deposed the way for the first landing on the moon is open. Well written and fast paced, *Dreadful Sanctuary* betokened the fact that Russell had written himself back into the front rank of science-fiction writers.

Stories from his typewriter now began to increase in frequency, with emphasis on clever endings. A typical example was *U Turn,* published under the pen name of Duncan H. Munro in the April, 1950, ASTOUNDING SCIENCE FICTION, in which those who apply for euthanasia on a "perfect" but dull earth wind up as guinea pigs for matter transmitters, with survivors deposited as pioneers on Callisto.

In these stories, Eric Frank Russell was, to some degree, writing for the market. This was not the case with *Dear Devil,* submitted to John W. Campbell for ASTOUNDING early in 1950. Campbell returned it, suggesting some changes to strengthen the ending. Instead of obliging, Russell sent the story to Raymond A. Palmer, who had recently started a new science-fiction magazine in Chicago, OTHER WORLDS SCIENCE STORIES. As the cover story for the May, 1950, issue of that magazine, *Dear Devil* was most enthusiastically received and was nominated for the unofficial distinction of best novelette of the year.

"Dear Devil" is a Martian poet and artist who elects to stay behind when an exploring party finds Earth a war-blasted, nearly lifeless world. Hideously blue in color, with gigantic tentacles instead of hands, he overcomes the repugnance of a group of deserted earth children in an exercise of kindness, and guides them as they grow up to build a new civilization. Related tenderly and compassionately, the story is one of the most effective calls for racial tolerance ever to appear, in or out of science fiction.

Even more moving was *The Witness* in the September, 1951, OTHER WORLDS SCIENCE STORIES. An intelligent reptilian creature, which has landed from outer space on a farm, is put on trial as a menace to the human race. The legal twists through which prosecution makes innocent acts appear ominous are cleverly presented, as are the methods of the defense attorney, who shows the alien to a telepathically endowed immature female of her species, fleeing from injustice and seeking asylum. The final passages contain great beauty of thought superbly handled.

The same theme of tolerance pervades *Fast Falls the Eventide* (ASTOUNDING SCIENCE FICTION, May 1952). In the distant future Earth has become a training school from which humans are sent by quota to live among diverse races of

the galaxy, teaching by their very presence universal brotherhood, regardless of form. It has been suggested that this
story, like *Dear Devil* and *The Witness,* is not actually a
parable of racial tolerance at all, but merely an expression
of Russell's encompassing love of most birds, animals, and
even insects. Russell has admitted to having "friends" in
his garden and to prolonged "discussions" with them. He has
also let slip that he is frequently an object of suspicion
at zoos. In the future of *Fast Falls the Eventide,* even
the insects have advanced in intelligence and listen intently
if not comprehendingly to human talk directed at them.
We read:

> The children of this world were bugs.
> And birds
> And bipeds
> Moth, magpies and man, all were related.

When Russell writes, "Thus it was in no way odd that
Melisande should talk to a small beetle," he is writing of
himself.

The concept that other forms of life are not inferior merely
because they are different remains constant throughout Russell's writing. It is the central theme of the early story *The
Prr-r-eet,* it appears in *Mana* and again in *The Eighth
Wonder.* It even extends to a robot, such as Jay Score, and
most certainly to his unusual Martian shipmates. It is the
none-too-subtle message conveyed by the discovery of the
telepathic power of camels in *Homo Saps* and is distinctly
present in *The Hobbyist.* It is certainly Russell's point in the
poignant *Postscript* (SCIENCE-FICTION PLUS, October, 1953),
in which an old man finds he must adjust to the realization
that a creature from a distant star system, with whom he has
corresponded all his life and whose letters display an outlook
of femininity, is actually a fungoid growth.

Russell's total output across the years has not been great,
though his most cherished ambition is to become a professional writer. Yet he won a Hugo for the best short science-

fiction story of 1955, presented at the 13th World Science
Fiction Convention, September 3, 1955, for *Allamagoosa*
(ASTOUNDING SCIENCE FICTION, May, 1955). And despite
the limitations and diffuse spread of his output, Russell's
influence has been substantial. For good or bad, the astonishing bulk of science fiction plastered around Fortean phenomena, and verging logically off into strange talents, stems
from him. In fact, Russell virtually parodies the genre in
his novel *The Star Watchers* (STARTLING STORIES, November,
1951), which includes twelve major mutations each enjoying
a variation in special powers. In addition, he has acted as a
bridge to carry many of the ideas of Olaf Stapledon into
the science-fiction magazines.

Most significant of all is the final impression the works
give of the man. The display of outward toughness of manner,
speech, and philosophy is a façade. A man who feels not only
a reverence for but a communion with life, who transmits
those feelings and with them his protests against prejudice
in terms of poetry and parable—such a man is not a rationalist.

The point is underscored in *I Am Nothing,* where the dictator who has started a war for conquest and power reads
the childish scrawl of an orphaned "enemy" girl: "I am
nothing and nobody. My house went bang. My cat was
stuck to a wall. I wanted to pull it off. They wouldn't let
me. They threw it away." The dictator loses his appetite
for the war and negotiates a peace. This is not an appeal from
intellect to intellect. This is an appeal from emotion to
emotion.

9

L. SPRAGUE de CAMP

There have only been two humorists capable of effectively using satire who achieved their development in the science-fiction magazines. The first was Stanton A. Coblentz, introduced by AMAZING STORIES QUARTERLY with his novel of Atlantis, *The Sunken World* (Summer, 1928), and the other was L. Sprague de Camp, who made his bow with *The Isolinguals* in ASTOUNDING STORIES for September, 1937.

Coblentz, a poet and literary critic, did his best work from 1928 through 1935, particularly in the novel. Though at times he was crude and obvious, *After 12,000 Years, The Blue Barbarians, The Man from Tomorrow,* and *In Caverns Below* have moments not only of hilarious satire but of real prophecy.

De Camp's blend of humor and criticism was akin to Mark Twain's. *A Connecticut Yankee in King Arthur's*

Court served as the model for de Camp's most successful novel, *Lest Darkness Fall* (UNKNOWN, December, 1939). While de Camp acknowledged the shortcomings of our present civilization, he used satire to show that it was still better than any previous and possibly even better than most to come, and buttressed his opinion with impressive scholarship.

In *Lest Darkness Fall,* a lightning bolt sends archaeologist Martin Padway back to decadent Rome in the sixth century A.D. His attempts first to survive and then to use his scientific knowledge to halt the decline of Rome parallel the adventures of Twain's Yankee. De Camp's novel proved the most lighthearted exercise in the manner of Mark Twain since ARGOSY began serialization of William Wallace Cook's *Marooned in 1492* in its December, 1904, issue. Others who wrote on this theme, such as Robert W. Chambers in *The Demoiselle d'Ys* (1895), A. Merritt in *Three Lines of Old French* (ALL STORY, August 9, 1919), and John L. Balderson and J. C. Squire in *Berkeley Square* (1928), dealt principally with romantic tragedy. Reference to the similarity of *Lest Darkness Fall* to *A Connecticut Yankee in King Arthur's Court* did not bother de Camp (or hurt his popularity), but being labeled a satirist for this and other works elicited an incisive response.

"People sometimes accuse me of writing satire," he began in the introduction to his first short story collection, *"The Wheels of If,* published by Shasta in 1948. "This, if not exactly a vile canard, is at least an inaccurate statement, because in the strict sense satire is ridiculing established conditions, conventions, or institutions by exaggeration or burlesque in the hope of changing them. In other words, it has social significance, which is just the thing I studiously avoid in my stories. These yarns are meant purely to amuse and entertain, and neither to instruct, nor to incite or improve."

Despite the fact that the family owned 20,000 acres in the Adirondacks (Herkimer County) which his father, Lyon de Camp, had inherited, Lyon Sprague de Camp was born in an apartment on 93rd Street, in congested New York City, November 27, 1907. The de Camps were not affluent, and the sale of parcels of land for the construction of summer camps as well as the ownership and operation of a sawmill were important sources of income. He was the first of three boys borne by his mother, Beatrice Sprague, daughter of the distinguished Civil War hero, educator, inventor, banker, economist, and linguist, Charles Ezra Sprague, founder of The School of Commerce at New York University, where a plaque has been erected in his memory.

The boy enjoyed his summers in the Adirondacks, canoeing, around the swamps, digging up specimens and examining them under the microscope. His parents were practicing Episcopalians, which led to his being sent to Trinity School in New York because of its connection with that church.

He was a difficult child, stubborn and insisting on his own way in everything. Figuring to take some of the contrariness out of him, the family decided to send him to an institution with military discipline, Snyder School in North Carolina. There young Sprague really ran into trouble. He was precociously intellectual, already a master of the snide remark, and his tongue helped get him clobbered every day for ten years. Awkward and thin, he was an ineffective fighter and become a safe target for every bully on the campus. This perpetually humiliating personal agony described in *Judgment Day* (ASTOUNDING SCIENCE FICTION, August 1955), resulted in a protective veneer of unemotional impersonality which he found difficult to discard as he matured. He cultivated a smiling, agreeable manner but kept his feelings so well covered that all but his close friends regarded him as cold.

He was a good student, but not an exceptional one. His earliest passion was the study of bugs. Later, he hoped to become a paleontologist. These were put aside to make way for the more practical prospects of aeronautical engineering, for which purpose he enrolled in the California Institute of Technology. He was delighted to find none of the persecutions of grade and high school in the intellectual atmosphere of the university and quickly achieved editorship of the college paper and even a small athletic distinction as a member of the fencing team.

When he graduated in 1930, he went to work with his father in the Adirondacks. The strenuous activity, including surveying, strengthened him physically. He decided to go for his Master's degree at Stevens Institute, Hoboken, New Jersey, and secured it in June, 1933, majoring in engineering and economics.

His first job was with the Inventors Foundation Inc., Hoboken, where he gave a course in patents for inventors. The school was taken over by the International Correspondence Schools, and he went to work for them in Scranton, Pennsylvania. When he resigned in 1937 he held the title of Principal of the School of Inventing and Patenting. Several years earlier he had collaborated with Alf K. Berle on a book which appeared as *Inventions and Their Management,* published by the International Textbook Co., Scranton, in 1937. This was his first professional work; a standard reference on the subject, it has gone through a number of revisions and editions since then, and has been cited in at least one Supreme Court action.

As early as 1936 he had attempted writing fiction. His first was *The Hairless Ones Come,* a prehistory tale eventually published in the January, 1939, issue of the short-lived GOLDEN FLEECE, though it had been rejected by several periodicals previous to that.

While in college he had roomed with John D. Clark, an avid science-fiction reader who knew many of the authors and editors. Clark introduced him to P. Schuyler Miller, a popular writer in the field, who had entered science fiction in the early thirties. De Camp collaborated with Miller on *Genus Homo,* a story of a busload of men and women who are buried in a tunnel cave-in and awake in the far future when no human remains and intelligent apes are the dominant species. The early part of the novel is a straight action adventure reminiscent of Murray Leinster's *Red Dust*. The latter part, describing the culture of the apes, contains all those elements of satire, humor, and dialogue that have become de Camp's trademark. It is difficult to understand why the story did not sell at the time, but publication eluded it until March, 1941, when it appeared in SUPER SCIENCE STORIES, paid for at the rate of a half cent a word.

Clark's success in selling several things to ASTOUNDING STORIES stimulated de Camp's efforts to break into professional science-fiction ranks. A first sale came sooner than he really expected. *The Isolinguals,* a story of a machine which caused ancestral memories to prevail over current ones, was picked up by F. Orlin Tremaine and published in the September, 1937, issue of ASTOUNDING STORIES. Ironically, Stanton A. Coblentz, the earlier king of science-fiction satire, made his last appearance in ASTOUNDING STORIES in that same issue with a serious story, *Gravity Unaffected.*

Now a member of the "establishment," de Camp attended a meeting at the apartment of John D. Clark in New York, where he was introduced to such notables as Julius Schwartz, literary agent; Mort Weisinger, editor of THRILLING WONDER STORIES; Henry Kuttner, another aspiring author; and John W. Campbell, Jr., soon to become editor of ASTOUNDING STORIES. This was all very exciting, but a single sale wasn't enough to retire on, so in December, 1937, de Camp took a job as assistant editor on a trade magazine, FUEL OIL JOURNAL. A wave of economy beached him after only three months and he found himself unemployed. There was little to do but take another crack at science fiction.

Tremaine was still with Street & Smith, but Campbell was running ASTOUNDING STORIES as he liked and bought *Hyperpilosity,* an entertaining episode on the sociological impact of the spontaneous growth of a furlike coating of hair on all men and women (ASTOUNDING SCIENCE-FICTION, April, 1938). Reader reception was only mild.

De Camp scored his first literary hit with an article, *Language for Time Travelers,* which appeared in the July, 1938, ASTOUNDING SCIENCE-FICTION. Tales of temporonautical excursions into the future had long been common, but no one had considered the problems of communication that would arise from the gradual change in pronunciation and semantics. With humor and deft style cloaking his scholarship, de Camp's *Language for Time Travelers* was the first nonfiction to be voted by the readers top monthly honors over fiction in the history of ASTOUNDING SCIENCE-FICTION.

As if he were anticipating this reaction, Campbell had interrupted the program of the First National Science Fiction Convention held in Newark, New Jersey, May 29, 1938, to put de Camp on display. From the platform de Camp pinpointed the area of the United States from which various members of the audience came by the peculiarities of their speech. The more than 100 present recalled this interlude as a revelation into the extent of research that de Camp devoted to giving his humor an authentic background.

The next time in print de Camp scored a runaway first place with his fiction *The Command* (ASTOUNDING SCIENCE-FICTION, October, 1938), which introduced Johnny Black, the bear with the souped-up brain and a compulsion to master chemistry. The title was prophetic, for by popular command de Camp was forced to turn out three sequels concerning his genius-rated bruin.

The high rating of *The Command* won him the cover of the December, 1939, ASTOUNDING SCIENCE-FICTION for *The Merman,* a deft chronicle of a man who invents a chemical that makes it possible to breathe under water. This also tied for first place, beating out competition as formidable as Lester del Rey's *Helen O'Loy.* In the brief period of but fifteen months de Camp had moved into the front rank of science-fiction writers.

The influence of Mark Twain, which was to become so obvious in *Lest Darkness Fall,* was earlier evident in *Divide and Rule,* a two-part novel which ran in UNKNOWN in April and May, 1939. A kangaroolike race of aliens conquers the earth and restores knighthood as a means of keeping mankind in subjugation. Though the writing was choppy in spots, the details of an utterly unique social set-up, complete with its own slang, was engrossingly worked out and chuckle-provoking. That de Camp was the funniest writer in science fiction was proved in a letter he wrote in the June, 1939, UNKNOWN, hilariously delineating the scientific effect of yoga exercises on the human body and using the spiritual terminology employed by its practitioners.

UNKNOWN was to become almost legendary for a new type of logical fantasy for grownups, and de Camp was to play a major role in its reputation. Immediately following *Divide and Rule,* his *The Gnarly Man* (UNKNOWN, June, 1939), telling of the discovery of a 50,000-year-old Neanderthal man who is making a living as a "wild man" in a side-show, broke ground for an entirely new approach to such material, most notably emulated by Philip José Farmer in *The Alley Man.*

Called in by Campbell as a trouble shooter to rescue a novel, *None but Lucifer,* submitted by H. L. Gold, he rewrote the story from end to end, and readers of the September, 1939, UNKNOWN were treated to the shockingly original concept of a man who so outdoes the devil that he replaces him.

During the period when he was writing his way to reader acceptance, de Camp roomed in bachelor quarters with Robert N. Lyon, a junior engineer. At a New Year's Eve party given by Lyon he was introduced to Catherine Crook, who taught at a private school for teen-agers. Isaac Asimov was later to note that she "looks like the younger daughter of a British peer. I have long considered her the most beautiful blonde in science-fiction. I can say this safely, as my own wife is a decided brunette."

On their third date de Camp proposed. The problem now was to find money for a honeymoon. De Camp vigorously launched into the final draft of *Lest Darkness Fall.* The more he wrote the longer the novel seemed to get, and it appeared that marriage and honeymoon would be indefinitely delayed. Then Catherine suggested that there was no reason why he could not finish it after their marriage. So the ceremony took place August 12, 1939, and for the next two days de Camp pounded the typewriter in the hotel room, finally bringing the manuscript over to Campbell who got him a check while he waited. Only then were the de Camps off on their honeymoon trip.

Among those impressed by de Camp's sprightly and entertaining scholarship was Fletcher Pratt, a tiny man with a pointed beard who had gained a reputation as a military expert and had published a number of much-praised volumes on American and European history. As early as 1928 he was a contributor to AMAZING STORIES and had been a dilettante author in science fiction through the years, most frequently with a collaborator. In common with de Camp, he had a great interest in languages and had translated many science-fiction stories from German and French for Hugo Gernsback's magazines.

The two were introduced by John D. Clark, and in no time at all they began plotting a fantasy for UNKNOWN based on the Norse legends. The result was the creation of Harold Shea, a bored psychologist who uses a principle suggested by one of his colleagues to whisk himself off to a time and land where the "natural" laws are magic and almost anything can happen. De Camp wrote the first draft of *The Roaring Trumpet* and Pratt polished it. The result appeared in the May, 1940, UNKNOWN, and was instantly recognized as a milestone among many milestones in the history of that honored magazine.

Shea was immediately afterward shuttled off to the land of Spenser's *Faerie Queene* in *Mathematics of Magic,* a sequel which appeared in the August, 1940, UNKNOWN. This proved less popular with the readers, possibly because Spenser's work was not as familiar as the Norse myths.

The two novels were combined into a book and published

in 1941 by Henry Holt as *The Incomplete Enchanter*. The same year Holt put *Lest Darkness Fall* into hard covers. This was an era when fantasy pulp authors still were not literarily respectable, and de Camp's feat in achieving two trade books from an important book publisher in a single year carried monumental prestige. The volumes received good reviews and the sales, though modest (probably not over 1500 apiece), were passable for that era. The result was that another collaboration with Fletcher Pratt, *Land of Unreason* (UNKNOWN WORLDS, October, 1941), went into hard covers under the Henry Holt imprint in 1942. This time, Fred Barber, a member of the U.S. diplomatic corps, resident in England, drinks milk from a bowl left outdoors for the little people and refills it with Scotch. A drunken brownie mistakes him for a changeling and carries him off to the fairyland of Shakespeare's *A Midsummer Night's Dream*. This volume was a failure in the market and was remaindered. De Camp attributed the failure to the fact that the book was in part an allegory of international politics spoofing Mussolini and it appeared just as the United States entered the war. No one thought it was very funny.

Nevertheless, of the fifteen stories de Camp had published in UNKNOWN and UNKNOWN WORLDS from April, 1939, to August, 1942, inclusive, all but one, *None but Lucifer,* would eventually appear between hard covers, a tribute to his ability at popularizing the whacky variety of fiction that appeared in that magazine.

Despite his preoccupation with fantasy, de Camp was holding his own against a formidable array of competition in science fiction that included Robert A. Heinlein, A. E. van Vogt, Theodore Sturgeon, and Isaac Asimov. *The Stolen Dormouse,* a two-part novel in the April and May, 1941, issues of ASTOUNDING SCIENCE-FICTION, in its image of American big business hardening into feudal casts, was as clever and adroit as anything his contemporaries were doing in their specialties at the time.

How well de Camp would have stood up in a continuous

literary competition with this group was never to be tested. A friend and classmate of Robert A. Heinlein's, Lt. Commander A. B. Scoles of the U.S. Navy, wanted science-fiction writers as engineers at the Naval Aircraft Factory in Philadelphia. Heinlein, de Camp, and eventually Asimov were to be employed at the Philadelphia Naval Yard as civilian engineers; but de Camp, who entered on July 15, 1942, and took the naval training courses at Dartmouth, emerged a full lieutenant in the United States Naval Reserve. He was assigned to do test and development work on parts, materials, and accessories for naval aircraft, which included cold-room and altitude-chamber work.

During the war years his writing virtually ceased, but another attribute of his nature came to the fore: a passion for research. This penchant was obvious in his fiction and even more pronounced in the rather frequent articles he had done for ASTOUNDING SCIENCE-FICTION on subjects as diverse as brown rats (*The Long-Tailed Huns,* ASTOUNDING SCIENCE-FICTION, January, 1942) and the development of the armored tank (*Come and Get Under,* ASTOUNDING SCIENCE-FICTION, December, 1942). He was one of the few science-fiction writers of the time whose nonfiction was every bit as good as his fiction.

He researched continuously for "a book on magic, witchcraft, and occultism," which was originally scheduled for publication by Henry Holt. One chapter of this book, *The Unwritten Classics,* was the feature article of the March 29, 1947, SATURDAY REVIEW OF LITERATURE. It concerned imaginary works which were almost as well known as the real classics of occult literature, but were what de Camp termed *pseudobiblia,* fake bibliographical references. Included were such titles as *The Book of Thoth, The Story of Setnau, The Book of Dzyan,* and of course *The Necronomicon.* A financial crisis at Holt aborted publication of the magic book, but de Camp has since used most of the material in articles and in other books.

Earlier an article had appeared in the May, 1947, NATURAL

HISTORY titled *Lost Continents.* This would eventually be included as part of *Lost Continents,* a book originally set in type by Prime Press (Philadelphia), but after the collapse of that company, published by Gnome Press (New York) in 1954. De Camp not only explored the legends concerning Atlantis, Mu, and other "lost continents," but did an exhaustive analysis of the literature, including fiction, concerning the topic. The result was unquestionably the finest single book produced on "The Atlantis Theme in History, Science and Literature," and has become the basic guide to serious research in that aspect of science fiction.

Lost Continents was written after de Camp left the Navy Yard in January, 1946. During this period he attempted a spoof in the P. G. Wodehouse style, which proved unsalable. These were lean times for the de Camp family, now permanently resident in the suburbs of Philadelphia. Research and literary experimentation might provide food to nourish de Camp's intellect but it put little on the table. The death of his father in 1945 gave him a small income (his mother had died in 1927 at the age of 39) which helped, but it was inadequate to carry the total financial burden.

To get back into the routine of writing fiction proved difficult. *The Ghosts of Melvin Pye,* a very weak fantasy concerning the dual ghosts of a split personality who haunt the same building, appeared in the December, 1946, THRILLING WONDER STORIES, but it was the only work of fiction by de Camp to see publication in the years from 1943 to 1948 inclusive.

In 1948, a collection of short stories, *The Wheels of If,* appeared, led off by an amusing short novel of a half-dozen alternate worlds (UNKNOWN, October, 1940). De Camp at last got the kind of press he needed. Among the short stories in the volume was *The Gnarly Man,* and de Camp made his fictional comeback with a variation on the theme. In *Throwback,* published in the March, 1949, ASTOUNDING SCIENCE FICTION, giant ape-men are bred through the kind of reverse genetics that in reality was used to bring back the European bison and the nine-foot brutes are kept on reservations. Though the style was well up to de Camp's best standards, his handling of the potential in the situation was so limited that of six stories in the magazine *Throwback* rated sixth with the readers.

A second try, *The Animal Cracker Plot* (ASTOUNDING SCIENCE FICTION, July, 1949), managed to take only third place in the ratings, but it marked the beginning of a new series known as the *Viagens Interplanetarias* (Portuguese for "interplanetary tours").

Why Portuguese?

Well, in the hypothetical future de Camp propounds, Brazil is the dominant power in the world and naturally spearheads space travel. And that country is Portuguese-speaking.

Much of the action of this series was to take place on three planets: Vishnu, Krishna, and Ganesha. The stories have frequently been called *in toto* the "Krishna" stories.

The first short novel of the group, *The Queen of Zamba* (ASTOUNDING SCIENCE-FICTION, August, 1940), is set on Krishna. No mechanical devices of any sort are permitted on this world, for the inhabitants (almost human in appearance) are intelligent enough to imitate them but not sufficiently socially advanced to use them for good. The concept offers de Camp the opportunity to engage in cloak-and-dagger action with much swordplay. The background provides an excuse for getting a standard historical adventure into a science-fiction magazine. The early stories were popular, but while de Camp was excellent at preparing the setting he lacked ingenuity in creating novel situations from his initial premises, and as a result few of the series were outstanding. One notable exception was *Rogue Queen*, a novel which saw first publication as a Doubleday book in 1951. A planet where humanoids have set up a society with a sexual arrangement not unlike that of the bees on earth is outlined with thoroughness and originality. The efforts of this society to cope with the technology and philosophy of earth men from a spaceship that has landed on their world results in its overthrow. This novel, more than any other postwar work, fulfilled the expectations that prewar readers held for de Camp. Because the entire plot was integrally involved with the sexual basis of the alien community, de Camp was highly praised for his skilled handling of this subject matter. Actually, sex formed a part of and was handled with great competence in many prewar de Camp stories. *Rogue Queen* is one of the few science-fiction stories that might conceivably have made some impression on Philip José Farmer in preparing *The Lovers,* which was to break through the sex taboo in the science-fiction magazines the following year.

The advent of THE MAGAZINE OF FANTASY AND SCIENCE FICTION in 1949, which paid two cents a word, double that of any previous magazine stressing fantasy, reopened the market for nonscientific extravaganzas. To breach this market, de Camp again teamed up with his old friend Fletcher Pratt. The first story they sold to the magazine, *Gavagan's Bar,* appeared in its second (Winter-Spring, 1950) issue and sparked a series eventually to be collected as *Tales from Gavagan's Bar,* published by Twayne in 1953. The brief tales were obviously fashioned after the popular Jorkens series of Lord Dunsany, every yarn starts in a pub. The Gavagan stories were for the most part not only failures as stories, but tedious and dull.

A far more successful collaboration with Willy Ley produced *Lands Beyond,* a book published by Rinehart in 1952. Here some of the research for *Lost Continents* was used and two ranking writers of science nonfiction teamed up to apply scholarship to the stories of Atlantis, Sinbad, Prester John, the ten lost tribes of Israel, among other amazing and romantic elements of history and literature, to produce an absorbing and worthwhile book.

De Camp's literary diggings for *Lost Continents* intrigued him with science fiction as a literature. In a symposium with Robert A. Heinlein in the February, 1952, GALAXY SCIENCE

FICTION, he contributed *Where Were We?* evaluating the prophetic qualities of science-fiction works of the past and concluding they had been too conservative. The future, he held, was likely to be much more, not less, remarkable than science fiction thought it would be.

Hermitage House, a New York publishing firm which during its existence enjoyed the distinction—and profits—of publishing L. Ron Hubbard's best-selling *Dianetics,* was building a series called "The Professional Writers Library." They already had four titles in the series and decided they would like to have one on science fiction. De Camp heard about it from a friend and outlined his qualifications to Hermitage. The result, produced in 1953, was *The Science Fiction Handbook,* which proved to be much more than the customary volume of half-baked writing advice. It had chapters on the history and philosophy of the literature, biographical sketches of its leading practitioners, and bibliographies of recommended readings. It was suitable as a college text on the subject and was used in extension classes at The College of the City of New York in Creative Science Fiction Writing during 1953, 1954, and 1955.

The similarity of sequences in de Camp's *Viagen's* stories to the flash and vigor of Robert E. Howard's sword-and-sorcery epics of Conan the Cimmerian is no accident. Reading Howard was urged on de Camp by his two good friends, John D. Clark and P. Schuyler Miller (who had collaborated on *A Probable Outline of Conan's Career* in 1938). De Camp's analytical intellect told him that Howard's premises were implausible but his emotions were overpowered by the sagas so vividly visualized that they came to "furious and gorgeous life."

When he was told on November 30, 1951, in a telephone conversation with Donald A. Wollheim, that a box of Howard's unpublished manuscripts were at the home of literary agent Oscar J. Friend, De Camp virtually took possession of them. He proceeded to revise and edit Howard's unpublished work, readying it for the printed page. Three stories went into the magazine or book almost immediately: *The Frost Giant's Daughter, The God in the Bowl,* and *The Treasure of Tranicos.* Four other straight oriental adventure novelettes de Camp converted into Conan stories, adding elements of the supernatural, and they were collected as *Tales of Conan* by Robert E. Howard and L. Sprague de Camp (Gnome Press, 1955). When a Swedish author, Björn Nyberg, wrote a novel called *The Return of Conan,* de Camp put it into shape for book publication by Gnome Press in 1957. For his efforts he was elected on November 12, 1955, Royal Chronicler of the Hyborian Legion, a loose-knit association of admirers of Robert E. Howard's work. Through Conan, the bullied weakling of school days now vicariously but happily beheaded and skewered the tormenters of his youth, only lightly disguised with the armor and speech idioms of an unrecorded period in mankind's history.

But Conan apart, de Camp's ventures into fantasy fiction were growing less frequent and his plots less incisive. An outstanding exception was *A Gun for Dinosaur* (GALAXY SCIENCE FICTION, March, 1956) which, in a time travel story, discussed with an air of quiet authority the problem of what type of gun and what methodology were best suited to shooting dinosaurs.

De Camp's love of historical research and his zest for swordplay finally met in a happy marriage in *An Elephant for Aristotle,* a novel of the ingenuity and adventure involved in walking a pachyderm from its natural habitat to the city of the great Greek philosopher. Critical reviews were excellent when Doubleday issued the novel in 1958. A second book, *The Bronze God of Rhodes,* followed in 1960, and for a third, *The Dragon of the Ishtar Gato* (1961), de Camp traveled to Africa to absorb local color, his real-life adventures included being chased by an enraged hippopotamus. This tale of the search on the south side of the Mediterranean for the ingredients of the elixir of life was de Camp's favorite, but it proved to be the poorest seller and endangered the continuation of the series. De Camp, however, has a contract for another historical swashbuckler and means to have at least one more try at the genre. All three novels harmoniously combine the scholarship, humor, and action which are de Camp's forte.

At the same time, de Camp wrote a number of illustrated juvenile books on power machinery, biology, and other scientific and historical subjects. He also did a book on *The Heroic Age of American Invention* for Doubleday in 1961. This sold well enough to warrant a follow-up nonfiction title, *The Ancient Engineers* (1963), deservedly praised as a sprightly rendition of the building feats of the ancient Romans, Greeks, and Egyptians, as well as other early civilizations. It has outsold all thirty-seven of de Camp's previous books —with over 12,000 copies in print at last count—and seems to epitomize a new, more dignified phase in his writing career. Appropriately the book was dedicated to his wife, Catherine Crook de Camp, for whose sake and that of their two sons he had persisted so dedicatedly at the writing game, and who had been doing more and more editorial work on his copy.

Given his choice of what he preferred to write, he would dearly love to have another crack at the Conan-type story.

Given his choice of professions, more than anything else de Camp would have preferred a professorship at some college or university, where he could delve endlessly into the library, to emerge with nuggets of fascinating lore which he would impart with wry humor to an endless succession of classes. If on occasion an ancient incantation, from a dusty old tome, actually delivered as promised, all to the good; if not, the magic of his typewriter would serve equally well.

10

LESTER del REY

An accident in an atomic energy plant. The chance formation of an isotope which upon reaching critical mass could
blow half the United States off the map. The only man who
might save the situation buried in the radioactive debris.
Government inspectors on the premises engaged in an investigation to decide whether the plant should be relocated
from the urban area which had grown up around it. There
you have the taut situation in Lester del Rey's *Nerves* in the
September, 1942, ASTOUNDING SCIENCE-FICTION.

The story's value as prophecy is self-evident. It was an
attempt to write a "realistic" drama in the setting of a hypothetical atomic energy plant at a time when the Manhattan
Project had barely gotten underway. There had been other
stories on the same theme, notably *Blowups Happen* by
Robert A. Heinlein (ASTOUNDING SCIENCE-FICTION, Septem-

ber, 1940), but none of them possessed the crisp immediacy of this tale which built in suspense page by page.

What amazed readers most was that the story was the work of an author whose reputation had been built on tearjerkers threaded with passages of somewhat purplish prose that verged on poetry. So chilling a blast of "realism" from his typewriter called for a reevaluation of Lester del Rey.

Ramon Felipe San Juan Mario Silvio Enrico Smith Heathcourt-Brace Sierra y Alvarez del Rey y de los Uerdes' mother died a few days after his birth, June 2, 1915, and he never forgave her. Twenty-nine years later, writing as Lester del Rey, *Kindness,* his short story in the April, 1944, ASTOUNDING SCIENCE-FICTION, echoed his feelings: "Danny was only a leftover, the last normal man in the world of supermen, hating the fact that he had been born and that his mother had died at his birth to leave him only loneliness as his heritage."

This had been the third marriage for his father, Francisco Sierra y Alvarez del Rey, a 55-year-old carpenter, tenant farmer, and Northern sharecropper, who had lost an arm in the Spanish-American war. Despite the name, the father's background was only partially Spanish. He came from a line of militant athiests in Spain, his great-grandfather having left that country for France after hanging three priests who came out to question him during the time of the Inquisition. The family came to America before 1750 and through the generations acquired a sprinkling of English, Scotch, German, and Indian blood. Lester's mother, Jane Knapp, was English and New England Methodist Yankee.

There were no children from his father's first marriages and since a girl born a few years earlier was barely toddling about, the problem of taking care of a motherless baby boy became a desperate one. The woman who acted as nurse at the time of the mother's death stayed on for a time and Francisco Sierra y Alvarez del Rey convinced her it might be a good idea if they married. This seemed to take care of the immediate needs of raising an infant and a little girl but it actually was the start of the family's problems.

The sod-floor shack they lived in was so vermin-ridden that the boy and his father frequently slept outside in a tent during the summer. As a child of a dirt farmer, Lester del Rey literally did not have enough to eat, let alone a balanced diet. The days were never-ending bouts with malnutrition that left him a delicate wisp of a child in contrast to his father, who despite a missing arm, was physically a powerful man.

Because of his slightness, fear of physical violence balanced between desperation and cowardice in the boy. One day, when he was only four, his stepmother threatened physical discipline. Almost frantic, tiny Ramon grabbed a kitchen knife and held her at bay until his father got home. The stepmother washed her hands of him after that and an uneasy state of coexistence was established with the boy as a completely independent spirit, answerable only to his father. As he grew older he frequently prepared his own meals.

Despite the birth of a half-brother and a half-sister, the stress of economics and incompatibility made the marriage relationship between his father and stepmother an increasingly strained and unhappy one.

Within the family, his full sister was completely obedient to his stepmother and had little to do with him, while his half-brother was subject to outbursts of temper, on several occasions striking Ramon with metal implements that left life-long scars. The half-sister maintained an air of neutrality. Except when his father was home, he was an outsider living in the home on sufferance.

While his father was poorly educated, he did respect learning and was surprisingly well read. He introduced the boy to the theories of Charles Darwin and taught him algebra. An atheist, he nevertheless felt that his son should have religious training and arranged to have him attend Catholic Sunday School.

Lester entered grade school at Utica, Minnesota, when he was seven, and was fortunate in going to the two-room school house of an old schoolmarm of outstanding ability who understood him and saw him through the fourth grade.

In relation to other children he was somewhat of a loner, introspective and tending to read a great deal, rather than to engage in games. Being small and thin he was fortunate, inasmuch as the bigger boys did not seem to regard him as worth bullying.

His school attendance was irregular, for he worked with his father in carpentry and was paid in ratio to what his father received. From this money he bought his own clothes. Though there was mutual respect between them, the father was always more of a co-worker than a pal.

Somehow he managed to finish grade school by twelve, frequently completing two terms concurrently. His father let him go off with a circus that came to St. Charles, Minnesota, to work all that summer of 1927 replacing milk bottles knocked down by ball-throwing customers. For the first time in his life he got three regular meals a day.

He returned to Fremont, Minnesota, for one year of high school, and when the school term ended, now thirteen, he hitchhiked to Yakima, Washington, where he picked fruit, carried water to the men harvesting grain, and later served as water boy to lumberjacks in Idaho, finally returning to his father's home in St. Charles.

This became the pattern of his life. After attempting to catch up on his schooling he was off again, this time to Chicago, where he survived by accepting any odd job offered him, including bootblack and newsstand attendant.

His next trip was to California, where his questionable ability to cook his own meals secured him employment as a short-order cook. Then he was off to Mexico for three weeks with a friend, returning to read a romantic tale of Alaska by William MacLeod Raine which prompted him to get a job as a steward on an Alaskan steamer. A single day in

Alaska convinced him that most of its glamor reposed in Raine's fancy and he turned around and came back.

An omnivorous reader of fiction as an escape from his far-from-ideal existence, del Rey had read Jules Verne and H. G. Wells and, beginning with *Tarzan and the Jewels of Opar,* periodically ordered Burroughs' Tarzan novels at 49 cents each from a Sears, Roebuck catalogue.

He really went overboard on science fiction when a friend in St. Charles loaned him a copy of the Fall, 1929, SCIENCE WONDER QUARTERLY which featured Otto Willi Gail's *The Shot into Infinity,* a remarkable novel translated from the German, accurately based on the rocket theories of Herman Oberth. His mail-order book buying now expanded to include Burrough's Martian novels.

Working with bootleggers in a New Mexico town in 1930, he met a girl and proposed to her the same day. He was only fifteen but he managed to convince officials that he was older; the girl was legal age. The marriage ended in tragedy three months after it began, when his wife was thrown from a horse and died of injuries.

Once more he returned to Minnesota, where, in the summer of 1931, with the aid of friends he managed to get a certificate of completion of high school, though he never formally graduated or received a diploma. The librarian at St. Charles encouraged him to go to college. Carlton College in Minnesota had been given money by del Rey's grandfather and it was thought that they might be willing to offer him a scholarship to return. Del Rey's father also wrote to his half-brother, George L. Knapp, in Washington, D.C., to see what he might do. Both approaches paid off. Carlton College offered a scholarship and Knapp volunteered to put up the tuition for the teen-ager at George Washington University and house him in his own home.

The latter offer was accepted and del Rey found that Knapp, who had a daughter with a Ph.D. in chemistry but no son, treated him with fatherly kindness. There was something else they would eventually have in common. Knapp was the editor of a railroad brotherhood weekly newspaper called LABOR. He had been a writer and among his published works was a science-fiction novel, *The Face of Air,* published by J. Lane, New York, in 1912, as well as a quartet of shorter science-fantasies published in BLUE BOOK in 1926 and 1927: *The Black Star, McKeever's Dinosaur, Father of the Buffaloes,* and *The Juice of Power.* (*McKeever's Dinosaur* was reprinted in the August, 1943, BLUE BOOK.)

At George Washington University, technically majoring in journalism, del Rey actually followed a general course in the sciences. He attempted to earn his keep by doing typing for his uncle and he made side money by writing themes for other students, but he did not have the slightest conception of what he wanted to be. He lost confidence in the value of school when he tried to apply the geometry and trigonometry he had been taught and found he really had no knowledge of the subject. As a result, after two years, 1931-32 and 1932-33, he dropped out.

He decided to take a one-year course in the secretarial skills, shorthand and typing, as a means of gaining entry to firms where he might find the type of work he liked. The best it did for him, during the Depression years, was to help him get a job in 1934 as an office boy and comptometer operator at the Crane Plumbing Co. in Washington, D.C., a job he would hold until 1937.

Then occurred one of those freak bits of luck. He went out to a Maryland gambling house one day in 1934 with $100 and began to play roulette. He wound up with $6,000 and bought a little restaurant, employing others to run it. In a declaration of independence, he left his uncle's home for his own lodging.

His luck didn't last long. Letters from home told of personal problems that urgently required substantial sums of money. On top of that, his poor eating habits and the acquisition of a taste for drink were playing hob with his none-too-hardy constitution. To raise the money for his family's problems and finance his own, he was forced to sell the restaurant in 1935. Then the news came that his father and his entire family except his full sister had died in an auto accident. Eventually, he became so ill that only a major operation involving new techniques saved his life, and then he found himself without the physical energy to do an effective day's work at his job with the Crane Plumbing Co. He was let go and, what with the expense of burying his family and his prolonged illness, he was penniless.

To survive, he sold magazines door to door, worked in restaurants, and did research for a man working on a WPA bibliography of music in the United States. All told, del Rey averaged five to six dollars a week and somehow managed to subsist, though the future appeared anything but bright.

During this period del Rey was not without his literary interests and literary aspirations. He had a deep love of poetry, his favorite being Algernon Charles Swinburne, whom he enjoyed for "making the right sounds in the right order." Others he read carefully were Robert Browning, Robert Burns, John Milton, and Rudyard Kipling. Among American poets, Stephen Vincent Benèt was his favorite. Although he decried Henry Wadsworth Longfellow, a number of the titles of his stories are quotations from that poet, for example, *The Day Is Done* and *The Wings of Night*.

During 1933, he began writing verse and says he sold twenty poems under pen names to magazines as prominent as LADIES' HOME JOURNAL and GOOD HOUSEKEEPING. Then he abruptly decided he wasn't a poet and quit writing poetry for good in 1936.

When he picked up the August, 1932, AMAZING STORIES, which included W. Campbell's *The Last Evolution,* he resumed buying science fiction regularly. His interest in fantasy was wide enough to include WEIRD TALES. But, by all odds, the science-fiction magazine that was his favorite was ASTOUNDING STORIES, which included Campbell's mood stories under the name of Don A. Stuart, Raymond Z. Gallun's superbly sentimental offerings (*Old Faithful,* December, 1934, *Davy Jones Ambassador,* December, 1935), Jack Williamson's suspenseful space operas, and Stanley G. Weinbaum's delightfully refreshing alien tales (*Parasite Planet,* February, 1935; *The Lotus Eaters,* April, 1935). The influence of all these writers is clearly revealed in his early fiction, but in the efforts of his relatively more mature years no influence is as evident as that of Clifford D. Simak, who made an enduring impression on del Rey with *The Creator,* a novelette published by the semiprofessional magazine MARVEL TALES (March-April, 1935), in which the universe is said to be the experiment of a creator of macrocosmic size rather than the handiwork of God.

During this period in the development of science fiction, science-fiction fan magazines were few and its followers gained renown by the frequency of their letters in the reader's columns of the magazines. Del Rey was among the most prolific of the letter writers. The readers' correspondence section of ASTOUNDING STORIES was called "Brass Tacks" and, beginning in the March, 1935, issue, letters signed Ramon F. Alvarez del Rey became a regular feature of the section, winning him a place in the "inner circle" and leading to his discovery of the science-fiction fan magazines.

While del Rey enjoyed seeing his letters in print he had felt no compulsion to become a writer. The transition occurred as a result of an argument with a girl friend. In the course of a discussion he had strongly criticized Manly Wade Wellman's handling of the story of a near-human ape in *Outlaws of Callisto* (ASTOUNDING STORIES, April, 1936).

"If you think you are so much better, let's see you write one that ASTOUNDING will take," she taunted.

"Will you settle for a reply from the editor saying he liked the story?" del Rey asked.

The girl agreed.

Del Rey figured that on the strength of his letter-writing reputation he might be able to swing that much. He sat down and wrote *The Faithful,* a tale of intelligent dogs made nearly human by the experiments of the last human survivor of a plague. The dogs remain instinctively loyal to him, for after 200,000 years of domestication the dogs need some-one they can serve. Before the man dies, he brings them together with semicivilized apes who will serve as their "hands." Del Rey had kept to the task of rewriting Well-man's story in his own manner.

Originally 8,000 words in length, *The Faithful* was slashed to 4,000 before it was submitted. Instead of a letter, a check for $40 arrived in January, 1938, which del Rey triumphantly showed his girl.

Understandably enthusiastic about writing, he plunged into another story which grew into a 12,000 word novelette about mining ice on Mars. Campbell rejected it, and the story has since been lost.

Feeling that possibly the novelette was not his forte, del Rey returned to the short story with a second-person yarn in future tense on the circle-in-time theme. Campbell didn't like that one either and rejected it. Years later it was re-written from memory for GALAXY SCIENCE FICTION (February, 1951) as *It Comes Out Here.*

Now discouraged, del Rey gave up on fiction and turned to other pursuits, but when *The Faithful* appeared in the April, 1938, ASTOUNDING SCIENCE-FICTION, reader reaction placed it second only to *Three Thousand Years,* a new novel by Thomas Calvert McClary, author of the all-time science-fiction classic, *Rebirth* (in 1934). As a result, del Rey received a letter from Campbell urging him to do more. Once again encouraged and determined to please, del Rey consulted WRITER'S YEARBOOK for Campbell's requirements. Among them he found: "Even if the story is about a robot, there should be a human reaction."

Translating the suggestion into fiction, del Rey displayed a technical craftsmanship which at the age of twenty-three made him the equal of any contemporary writer in his field. *Helen O'Loy* was the story of an atom-powered thinking machine, made of metal with spun plastic exterior fashioned minutely to resemble a woman. Feminine impulses were electronically built into the device. Upon being motivated, the mechanism falls in love with the man who owns her and through a tender series of circumstances succeeds in getting him to accept her as his wife.

Such a plot obviously provided quicksands of bathos that were not avoided but bathed in by the author, whose facility at handling sentiment with empathic realism proved virtually unsurpassed in the history of science fiction. The idea was not new; a robot vamp plays an important part in Thea von Harbou's novel *Metropolis,* from which the famed German motion picture was made by UFA in 1926. Del Rey's contribution in *Helen O'Loy* was artistic and stylistic.

While the immediate reaction to the appearance of that story in December, 1938, ASTOUNDING SCIENCE-FICTION was very good, particularly among the authors of science fiction it rated in reader's approbation below two other stories in the issue: *A Matter of Form* by H. L. Gold and *The Merman* by L. Sprague de Camp. Its standing in science fiction as one of the masterpieces on the robot theme results from second looks by the readers. Actually it was the tale's second appearance in Lester del Rey's first hard cover collection, "*. . . And Some Were Human,*" published by Prime Press, Philadelphia, in 1948, that won it critical acclaim.

In retrospect, *The Faithful* was far more influential than *Helen O'Loy*. It is almost a certainty that Clifford D. Simak's poignant development of the dogs in *City* took its cue from *The Faithful*. While the notion that a canine civilization can be developed to replace that of humanity played a role in the space epic *Invaders of the Infinite* by John W. Campbell (AMAZING STORIES QUARTERLY, Spring-Summer, 1932), it was del Rey's treatment that popularized this concept. Quite probably, also, L. Sprague de Camp's popular series about Johnny Black, the intelligent book-loving bear, may have received some of its ideas from *The Faithful*. Similarly, the civilized monocled apes of L. Sprague de Camp and P. Schuyler Miller's novel *Genus Homo* (SUPER SCIENCE STORIES, March 1941), conceivably may have obtained some substance from those described in *The Faithful.*

When del Rey decided to test how well he could do as a full-time writer, Campbell suggested that he take the theme of de Camp's *The Gnarly Man* concerning the problems of a Neanderthal man in adjusting to modern civilization and see if he could find a different approach. The result was *The Day Is Done* (ASTOUNDING SCIENCE-FICTION, May, 1939), in which the last Neanderthal man, living off the charity of the early tribes of "modern man," dies of a broken heart, a minor masterpiece.

ASTOUNDING SCIENCE-FICTION's companion magazine was UNKNOWN, whose stock in trade was "fairy tales for grown ups." Del Rey tried to make its pages with *A Very Simple Man,* a story about a man who fishes up a Nereid (a lake spirit) and is granted three wishes. He eventually decides to return the wishes and paddles off in his boat. The story was rejected and del Rey has since lost it.

His next attempt, *Forsaking All Others,* a tender poetic tale of a little dryad who falls in love with a man and sacrifices her immortality and the life of her tree to consummate their union, did get into the May, 1939, issue of UNKNOWN.

Del Rey's opportunity to sell a longer story came with *The Luck of Ignatz* (ASTOUNDING SCIENCE-FICTION, *August,* 1939), a novelette in which an intelligent Venusian reptilian pet brings ill luck to a space pilot and anyone close to him. Originally it had been a dog instead of a Venusian, but the more Weinbaum-like creature was substituted during revision. The story line was hackneyed, but a lengthy sequence where the space engineer redeems himself by running the ship manually for sixty hours, after the automatic controls are knocked out, possessed elements of the tense drama that would later make *Nerves* a hit.

The humanistic qualities of del Rey at their finest came

through in *The Coppersmith* (UNKNOWN, September, 1939), as the adventures of a proud and industrious elf to find a place for himself in a world where his solder and tools are no longer effective on the modern metals used in pots are sympathetically presented. A sequel, *Doubled in Brass,* appeared in UNKNOWN, for January, 1940.

Growing in confidence, del Rey began to experiment with themes and techniques. In *Habit,* (ASTOUNDING SCIENCE-FICTION, November, 1939), he wrote a straight sports story of the future about racing rockets; *The Smallest God* (ASTOUNDING SCIENCE-FICTION, January, 1940) was an entertaining tale of a rubber doll that turns into an animated creature when stuffed with a by-product of atomic fission, and how this new intelligence yearns for and finally attains a full-sized, near-human body. *Reincarnate* (ASTOUNDING SCIENCE-FICTION, April, 1940) was based on an idea suggested to Campbell by Willy Ley. Dealing with the transference into a mechanical body, of a man whose limbs are lost and whose body is charred, it may well have served C. L. Moore as the inspiration for her masterpiece, *No Woman Born. Dark Mission* (ASTOUNDING SCIENCE-FICTION, July, 1940) was concerned with a Martian who comes to earth to delay the first flight to that planet until the germs of a deadly plague have dissipated.

The most successful story of that period of del Rey's career was *The Stars Look Down* (ASTOUNDING SCIENCE-FICTION, August, 1940) in which two opponents, one with liquid rocket fuels, the other with atomic engines, race to be the first in space. Like Moses in the Bible, the "winner" finds that because he has a bad heart he can never pilot the ship into "the promised land." Even at that time it was recognized as a variant of Robert Heinlein's *Requiem,* and the passage of years has badly dated it.

In the same issue, del Rey used the pen name Philip St. John for a short story, *Done with Eagles,* in which a blind space pilot and a four-armed mutant set a spaceship safely down on Mars without any scientific guidance. Another pen name, Philip James, was employed for *Carillon of Skulls*, (UNKNOWN, February, 1941), a weird tale of incantations and spells based on an idea supplied by James H. Beard, who had previously been responsible for feeding two ideas to Theodore Sturgeon. Del Rey's special magic infused the story with a touch of pathos.

Del Rey's first anthology recognition (*The Other Worlds*, edited by Phil Stong, and published by Wilfred Funk in 1941) was for his story *The Pipes of Pan* (UNKNOWN, May, 1940), in which the last disciple of the ancient god Pan dies, forcing the deity to make a living playing his pipes for a jazz band. Of this story Stong said: "Numbers of people have written modernizations of myths, or myths translated to modernity; of these, the most sympathetic in immediate writing seems to me to be Mr. del Rey's 'Pipes of Pan.' "

The middle of 1940 marked the end. of a phase in del Rey's career. He began to lose interest in writing as he became involved in photography, spending most of his time in the darkroom. Soon he was earning his subsistence money by making enlargements of five- and ten-cent photos which he hand-colored himself. Only one story other than *Carillon of Skulls* appeared in 1941, and that was his ironic fantasy *Hereafter* (UNKNOWN, December, 1941), about a little man whose circumscribed lifelong philosophy converts his heaven into hell after death.

Campbell tried hard to get him to write more, but del Rey would only come through with a story when he needed money for a special project; otherwise he puttered happily in his darkroom. One of these infrequent stories was *The Wings of Night* (ASTOUNDING SCIENCE-FICTION, March, 1942) concerning the last living moon "man" who needs copper in order to reproduce his race. Told in del Rey's most sympathetic vein, it proved very effective and variations on the theme have shown up periodically since then.

Del Rey was particularly fond of *My Name Is Legion* (ASTOUNDING SCIENCE-FICTION, June, 1942) in which he thought up a hellish circle-in-time fate for Adolf Hitler, but his banner story for the year and one of the best he ever wrote, *Nerves,* grew from a suggestion of John Campbell's, who gave him a bonus for the story. The results of the readership poll which were published two issues later showed that it had been rated first in the issue by 100 per cent of the respondents. The story was lengthened from 34,000 to 57,000 words for the Ballantine Books paperback published in 1956, the expanded version heightened by a superb character sketch of the key scientist, Jorgenson, before he is enveloped by an atomic miscalculation. The original version, however, had been reprinted in Random House's 1946 anthology *Adventures in Time and Space,* edited by Raymond J. Healy and J. Francis McComas.

Ignoring the impact created by *Nerves,* del Rey traipsed from Washington, D.C., to St. Louis to be near a girl who had been transferred there. He completed *Lunar Landing* in St. Louis, on commission for the cover of the October, 1942, ASTOUNDING SCIENCE-FICTION, in which a rescue operation for the first earth ship on the moon finds others there ahead of them. In St. Louis, del Rey went to work at McDonald Aircraft Co. as a sheetmetal worker and handformer and stayed on the job until April, 1944.

The desire for anonymity must have burned bright in 1943 for of the three short science-fiction stories del Rey produced that year, two were published under pen names. *The Fifth Freedom* (ASTOUNDING SCIENCE-FICTION, March, 1943) by "John Alvarez" was a plea for more enlightened treatment of conscientious objectors. Much more effective was *Renegade,* published under the nom de plume "Marion Henry" (ASTOUNDING SCIENCE-FICTION, July 1943), a moving and tender story of the affection of a community of civilized apes in Africa for an ex-playboy who has tutored them. *Whom the Gods Love* (ASTOUNDING SCIENCE-FICTION, June, 1943), a mystical story of a World War II Pacific fighter pilot given a second chance to justify his dead buddies, had del Rey's name attached to it.

Almost unknown is the fact that del Rey sold a short-

short and a short love story to COLLIER's in 1943, neither one a fantasy tale.

St. Louis was the home of Robert Moore Williams, much admired by del Rey for his story *Robot's Return* (ASTOUND-ING SCIENCE-FICTION, September, 1938), in which robots return from space to a deserted earth to discover that they were originally created on that planet. Del Rey, in appreciation, wrote a prelude to it titled *Though Dreamers Die* (ASTOUNDING SCIENCE-FICTION, January 1944).

Back east in New York in 1944, del Rey took a job as a counterman selling hamburgers in a White Tower restaurant. He succeeded in selling Campbell one story, *Kindness* (ASTOUNDING SCIENCE-FICTION, October, 1944), which despite an unconvincing ending, is a superior effort, depicting the plight of the last normal boy on earth, raised in a world of kindly supermen.

Now 30 and lonely, he dated Helen Schlaz, a Lithuanian girl who worked in another White Tower. Repeating the pattern that led to his first marriage, he proposed on their first date and they set up housekeeping in 1945. He quit the White Tower chain to make another try at science fiction when *Nerves* was anthologized in *Adventures in Time and Space*. But six stories in a row were rejected by Campbell, reducing del Rey's confidence in his writing ability to its nadir.

His flagging spirits were raised when Prime Press contracted for a collection of his stories for hardcover to be titled "*. . . And Some Were Human.*" The publication of the book in 1948, containing some of his best work, bolstered a fading reputation. Though the sale was modest, the book was widely hailed in science-fiction circles.

Attending the Fifth World Science Fiction Convention in Philadelphia, August 30 – September 1, 1947, at the invitation of Prime Press, del Rey was introduced to Scott Meredith, a science-fiction fan, who had set up a literary agency in New York. Meredith took him on as a client.

Shortly afterward, while aiding in the formation of the

Hydra Club (an organization composed primarily of professional science-fiction writers, editors, and authors) with Fred Pohl and Robert W. Lowndes, he was informed by the latter that Meredith was looking for someone to work in the agency. He applied for the job and went to work for Meredith, grinding out sports stories for the pulp magazines in his spare time.

His second marriage broke up in 1949, his wife marrying another science-fiction writer, Damon Knight.

The same year, the del Rey name came back into the spotlight in another manner. A 21-year old biology major at Canisius College, Buffalo, Richard I. Hoen, had sent a letter, published in the November, 1948, issue of ASTOUNDING SCIENCE FICTION, proposing authors and as yet unwritten stories for an all-star November, 1949, issue of that magazine. Campbell surprised his readers by undertaking to make that issue a reality.

Among the stories requested was one by Lester del Rey to be titled *Over the Top*. Del Rey wrote this story to order and, though it was a rather mediocre tale of the first space explorer stranded on Mars, it proved professionally important by placing del Rey's name in the company of Robert A. Heinlein, A. E. van Vogt, Theodore Sturgeon, L. Sprague de Camp, and other prominent authors in the issue.

There was a "boom" in science fiction underway. Del Rey dug his rejects out of the trunk and begun offering them around. They sold with astonishing speed. Encouraged, he decided to leave Scott Meredith and try his luck again at free-lance writing.

Some of his old skills began to return. Among the stories he sold in 1951 was one to ARGOSY, *The Monster,* a remarkably effective statement of the mental agony endured by an intelligence that discovers it is actually a robot which is to be animated for a brief period of usefulness and then eliminated. That year he sold the first of a series of science-fiction teen-age novels to Winston, *Marooned on Mars,* which won the 1951 Boys Award for Teen-Age Fiction.

A New York publisher, John Raymond, asked del Rey to write a story for a projected new science-fiction magazine, SPACE SCIENCE FICTION. When del Rey delivered the story in person, Raymond offered him the editorship of the magazine and del Rey accepted. The first issue (May, 1952) carried del Rey's *Pursuit*, a "chase" fantasy involving wild and unbelievable psi powers. Soon three other magazines, SCIENCE FICTION ADVENTURES, ROCKET STORIES, and FANTASY MAGAZINE, were added to the Raymond group. Del Rey wrote a great deal for the magazines he edited, his most controversial story proving to be *Police Your Planet* (under the pseudonym Eric van Lihn), an attempt to capture grim realism in depicting the social and economic life of early Martian city dwellers.

He proved to be a very fine editor, but conflict with the publisher over payment policies resulted in his resignation in late 1953. He was replaced by Harry Harrison, a continuity writer for the comic magazines who would later win distinction for the novel *Death World*, serialized in ASTOUNDING SCIENCE FICTION in 1960, which received a Hugo Award nomination.

Del Rey's third marriage, on July 23, 1954, was to Evelyn Harrison, the former wife of Harry Harrison whose acquaintance he had made at meetings of The Hydra Club. She was to prove the greatest stabilizing influence of his life, standing by him through a series of financial crises and several major illnesses. A few years after their marriage they bought a small home in River Plaza, New Jersey, only blocks away from the residence of Fred Pohl, with whom del Rey had maintained an unbroken friendship since the formation of The Hydra Club.

At this time, GALAXY SCIENCE FICTION had announced a contest in conjunction with book publisher Simon & Shuster for a prize of $6,500 for the best science-fiction novel by a new author submitted to them within the next year. As the months passed, GALAXY's editor H. L. Gold became sickeningly aware that his problem was not going to be getting a good novel by an unknown. His problem was to get *any* novel at all. Even though the amount offered was the largest in the history of the science-fiction magazines, it was becoming obvious that there would be no takers.

Since Fred Pohl had scored one of the really big hits of the magazine's history with *Gravy Planet* (in collaboration with Cyril Kornbluth) in 1952, Gold commissioned him to be "discovered" again in 1955. Pohl, in turn, asked Lester del Rey to assist him with the writing. The result was *Preferred Risk,* which ran as a four-part serial beginning in the June, 1955, GALAXY SCIENCE FICTION under the name Edson McCann and was published in hard covers by Simon and Shuster the same year.

Few saw through the deception, despite the fact that the basic concept of *Preferred Risk,* insurance companies running the world endangered by bankruptcy when a cobalt bomb threatens the life of a major part of the earth's population, was very similar to the idea of *Gravy Planet,* in which advertising agencies run the world.

A major reason for the ruse's not being uncovered was that del Rey wrote the greater part of the text, the style thus being quite different from that of *Gravy Planet,* even to the point of greater dependence upon action to carry the story.

Pohl was also engaged in editing a series of science-fiction anthologies for Ballantine Books made up entirely of original stories. He commissioned del Rey to write a novelette for *Star Short Novels,* a paperback issued in 1954. Del Rey's contribution was a shocker, *For I Am a Jealous People,* in which earth is attacked by aliens, who have the might of "Our God," the God of Abraham and Moses, behind them, for He has rejected man. Though the story depends too much on action in conveying its spiritual and philosophical content, the closing lines are memorably sacrilegious: " 'God has ended the ancient covenants and declared an enemy of all mankind,' Amos said, and the chapel seemed to roll with his voice. 'I say this to you: He has found a worthy opponent.' "

This was the cynical, hard line that people now began to associate with del Rey. It had been increasingly reflected in his fiction since *Nerves.* It was even more evident in his public-speaking appearances, beginning at The Eastern Science Fiction Association (Newark, New Jersey) meeting of February, 1948, when he revealed a strong speaking voice and a rare ability to organize and expound his arguments extemporaneously. This talent eventually made him a regular guest on The Long John Nebel Show, a radio "Talk" program over WOR, New York, which ran nightly for five hours from midnight to 5:00 A. M. In over 300 appearances from the late fifties through 1965 del Rey incisively lampooned flying saucers, Shaverism, Dianetics, abominable snowmen, telepathy, and psionics, as well as the broader spectrum of the many superstitions and misconceptions to which the human race is heir.

This created the image of Lester del Rey the rebel, reformer, and iconoclast, an illusion which his actions encouraged but which the facts refused to support. Del Rey's stories rarely involved social protest and, particularly in the beginning, were repeated pleas for society to make a place for the independent spirit. They are pilgrimages of loneliness. The characters do not ask for reform and do not ask for favor. They ask only for acceptance.

Del Rey never blames society for his problems, rather he blames the limitations of his physical equipment. "The Smallest God," though superior in intelligence, chafes at his size and works toward and achieves his goal transference into the body of a six-foot artificial man; Dave Mannen, in *Over the Top,* when stranded on Mars with seemingly no hope of rescue, bitterly reflects: "With a Grade-A brain and a matinee idol's face, he'd been given a three-foot body and the brilliant future of a circus freak. It had looked like the big chance, then. Fame and statues they could keep, but the book and the endorsement rights would have put him where he could look down and laugh at the six-footers. And the guys with the electronic brains had cheated him out of it."

Yet essentially his works reflect optimism. Like those of another major science-fiction writer born and raised on a farm, Clifford D. Simak, Lester del Rey's stories hold forth hope for the individual and hope for man. His personal hardships appear to have stirred in him deep feeling for, not hatred or resentment toward, the human race. Most of his endings are "happy" ones, though they frequently are the result of extraordinary compromises on the part of the characters.

His rages are directed at patterns of thought which he feels threaten the progress of mankind, but not at individuals or institutions. Even his novel *The Eleventh Commandment* (Regency Books, 1962), which appears to be a no-quarter-given attack on the Catholic Church's birth control policy, turns out to be sleight-of-hand misdirection, since it ends with the policy proven right in the hypothetical future situation created in the book.

His work has exhibited elements that have influenced the course of science-fiction and gained him a personal following and a certain respect from his contemporaries. His greatest drawback is that he has been unable to acquire self-discipline. When confronted with a difficult problem, whether personal or occupational, he has tended to retreat to the quiet of a photographic darkroom or its equivalent.

The façade of toughness appears to have been fabricated more to maintain his own self-estimation than as a defense against the world. Nevertheless, its manifestation in his writing represents a psychological conflict that wells up in a spring of compassion that makes a certain part of his earlier work memorable.

11

ROBERT A. HEINLEIN

On October 23, 1960, an event of special significance for the literary acceptance of science fiction occurred. Marion Shelby's weekly program, "Young Book Reviewers," broadcast by radio station WMCA, New York City, carried a half-hour panel discussion on a book about interstellar warfare, Robert A. Heinlein's *Starship Troopers*. The panelists were all students of Teaneck, New Jersey, High School and the moderator was Alice Kelleher of Jersey City State College.

Considering that mankind was about to enter what is romantically called "The Space Age," it seemed entirely in order than an educational program, customarily devoted to discussions of important or timely books, should permit teenagers to enjoy an enthusiastic appraisal of the world of the future, space exploration, and exciting adventure, except those subjects weren't what they were talking about.

If a listener had tuned in in the middle of the program he

might understandably have thought that the topic was "The Philosophy of Government." The students were evaluating Heinlein's proposal that the professional soldier become the basis of government. The discussion picked up Heinlein's premise that citizens should be made to earn the right to vote by serving their country for two years in the armed services. Some way would be found for everyone who volunteered to serve, no matter how disabled. Heinlein projected the thesis that since the armed forces taught that the individual should place the group above self, the discipline-trained citizen would tend to display that same selflessness in his voting decisions, for the betterment of all.

Beyond that, Heinlein urged that we dispense with romanticism and base our morality upon the fact that we are fundamentally "wild·beasts" driven by the need for survival. The morality of the lion, by its very nature, must differ from that of sheep. It cannot be immoral for the lion to kill for food or he would starve.

Something new was happening here. For years, it was the vogue to show what those mainstream writers who had worked in science fiction had contributed to the art as it is practiced today. Now, a product of the science-fiction pulp magazines, Robert A. Heinlein, by his unique talents, was influencing the thinking of the mainstream.

True, in this instance it was on the teen-age level, but a few years earlier, through his stories of science fiction in THE SATURDAY EVENING POST and the motion picture based on one of his works, *Destination Moon,* he had demonstrated to adults that the themes of science fiction were their problems in a world only as far away as tomorrow.

Among the writers and devotees of science fiction, Heinlein frequently was envied and admired as being on the top rung in ability and influence among writers of "modern" science fiction, "modern" being used as a term to designate those writers and methods in science fiction that had reached their greatest vogue since 1940. This same inner circle now presented a paradox. In dozens of the mimeographed journals that are known as "science-fiction fan magazines," and on the platforms of regional science-fiction conventions, the controversy raged as to whether Heinlein's philosophy in *Starship Troopers* was "evil," or valid, or merely an author's device to spur reader interest. The majority seemed to regard the philosophy of *Starship Troopers* as Heinlein's personal belief and condemned it.

On the other hand, despite the furious disputes, they joined ranks on the question of Heinlein's literary artistry. In a poll of the members of the 18th World Science Fiction Convention, Pittsburgh, 1960, for the best science-fiction novel of 1959, *Starship Troopers* (Putnam) obtained a decisive plurality and its author, for the second time in his writing career, received the coveted Hugo. Four years earlier, Robert Heinlein's novel *Double Star* (Doubleday, 1955) also copped a Hugo at the 14th Annual Convention of the World Science Fiction Society, Inc., in 1956. He was to receive still another for *Stranger in a Strange Land* (Putnam, 1961) at the 20th World Science Fiction Convention in 1962.

Robert A. Heinlein is an author who for twenty-five years has held major status as a writer of science fiction. His views are frequently berated, but as a major shaper of the direction of science fiction he is also beloved. The three Hugos, in a very real sense like the coveted Nobel Prize, were given him in consideration of past as well as current performance.

Robert Anson Heinlein was born July 7, 1907, in Butler, Missouri, the son of Rex Ivar Heinlein and Bam Lyle Heinlein. As one of seven children, there were distinct checks and balances on his ego as a result of the type of discipline that children in large families impose on one another.

His elementary education was in the public schools of Kansas City, Missouri, and he graduated from Central High School there in 1924.

A major if not pivotal influence on his thinking was his naval career. He graduated from the U.S. Naval Academy at Annapolis in 1929 and served on aircraft carriers when they were still science fiction as far as proving themselves in actual combat was concerned. A crack gunnery officer, he ignored a severe illness while on active duty in 1934 and ended the season with a superb record but with his health so undermined that he was retired that year as permanently disabled.

The second most important influence on his writing was his continuous and generous reading of science fiction from his earliest days, starting with second-hand copies of FRANK READE WEEKLY, a dime-novel paper devoted to a young inventor similar to Tom Swift, as well as Tom Swift himself and everything purchasable from the stands from 1916 on. To a "classic" background in Wells, Verne, Haggard, and Burroughs he added regular purchase of ARGOSY ALL-STORY and Hugo Gernsback's ELECTRICAL EXPERIMENTER. When science-fiction magazines appeared, he bought and read them all. He was literally saturated in the popular periodical background of American science fiction. This broad knowledge of his medium was later reflected in the familiarity with which he combined and refined the diverse and intricate themes of magazine science fiction into his own work.

Heinlein did not have to surmise when he struck a new chord in science fiction; he positively knew. Echoes of dozens of popular pulp science fiction writers sounded in his work but no single note called his direction. His role was to lead, not to follow.

The only mainstream writer to whom Heinlein acknowledges a debt is Sinclair Lewis, and it is not for literary style. Lewis laid out extensive backgrounds for his work which did not directly appear in the story. That way he understood how his characters should react in a given situation, since he knew more about them than the reader did. In Heinlein, this ultimately grew beyond the bounds intended by Sinclair Lewis, whose characters performed against a setting with which the reader might be familiar. The Sinclair Lewis method couldn't work for science fiction unless an entire history of the future was projected; then individual stories and characters in that series could at least be consistent within the framework of that imaginary never-never land.

In following just this procedure, Robert A. Heinlein inadvertently struck upon the formula that had proved so successful for Edgar Rice Burroughs, L. Frank Baum, and, more recently, J. R. R. Tolkien. He created a reasonably consistent dream world and permitted the reader to enter it. Heinlein's Future History has, of course, a stronger scientific base than Burrough's Mars, Baum's Oz, or Tolkien's land of the "Rings," but it is fundamentally the same device.

A retired naval officer at 27, disabled or not, Heinlein could not simply sit and vegetate, so he enrolled at U.C.L.A. graduate school in California to study mathematics and physics. His health failed again before he could complete his studies, but the time spent there gave him an insight into the sciences which were to give his work an added note of verisimilitude.

In the next few years he tried his hand at many things: politics, real estate, architecture, and mining; regardless of his personal success at any of them, elements of each are reflected in his stories. We find Heinlein speaking with a note of authority on the nature of politics in *"If This Goes On . . ."*; the art of selling real estate and architecture both figure in *" . . . And He Built a Crooked House";* only mining, of all his background, seems conspicuously absent from his works.

John W. Campbell, Jr., editor of ASTOUNDING SCIENCE FICTION, used to say that the best way to get Heinlein writing was to interest him in something that cost money. The year that Robert Heinlein first appeared as a professional writer was a depression year, 1939. He needed money to pay the mortgage on his home. Carefully nursing his delicate health, he decided to investigate writing as a method of making money. And as an unrepentant lifelong reader of science fiction, for him to write in science fiction was a logical step.

In 1939 the genre was on the upward swing of the pendulum. The boom started in mid-1938 when Red Circle Publications experimentally issued MARVEL SCIENCE STORIES, which, powered by *Survival,* a remarkable novel by Arthur J. Burks of the remnants of a defeated America tunneling into the Rockies to escape their Asiatic conquerors, immediately made money. The revival accelerated by the purchase of RADIO NEWS by Ziff-Davis Publications from Teck Publications, who required that Ziff-Davis take the failing AMAZING STORIES as part of the deal. Under the new ownership, AMAZING STORIES climbed quickly in circulation.

Ziff-Davis soon issued a companion to AMAZING STORIES entitled FANTASTIC ADVENTURES; Standard Magazines offered a running mate to the long-established THRILLING WONDER STORIES under the title of STARTLING STORIES; Street & Smith's ASTOUNDING SCIENCE-FICTION announced a brother to be titled simply UNKNOWN; Blue Ribbon Publications decided to call the genre by its first name and began publishing a magazine identified as SCIENCE FICTION; Frank A. Munsey, publishers of ARGOSY, evaluating the situation, concluded it was time to offer classics from its files going back nearly fifty years in a reprint periodical, FAMOUS FANTASTIC MYSTERIES. And that was only the beginning!

An expanding field is good for the beginning writer and editors were anxious to encourage. ASTOUNDING SCIENCE-FICTION in its July, 1938, issue had an editorial titled simply "Contest." Briefly, this editorial told the readers how to submit stories, what the "prizes" were for the "winners," and announced a perpetual contest was in effect for talent. Heinlein decided to submit something to them.

His first story, *Life Line,* after an unsuccessful try at COLLIER'S, was offered to ASTOUNDING SCIENCE-FICTION, accepted, and published in the August, 1939, number. It would be nice to say that Heinlein "wowed them" from the first, just as Stanley G. Weinbaum had exploded like a nova five years earlier with *A Martian Odyssey,* but it didn't happen that way. *Life Line,* though well written, was on the borderline of acceptability. It concerned one Dr. Hugo Pinero, who builds a machine that can tell a man how long he will live. The machine functions on the premise that the future, present, and past exist simultaneously; that time is a dimension and therefore one's duration in that dimension may be electrically measured. The climax comes with the realization that the inventor has calculated his own time of death and philosophically accepted it. This story is science fiction only by courtesy, and in style and plotting resembles stories of the World War I period in ARGOSY and ALL-STORY WEEKLY.

There were also a few distractions that kept readers from recognizing this new major talent. The month before, July, 1939, ASTOUNDING SCIENCE-FICTION's cover had featured a writer named A. E. van Vogt with a dynamic first story, patterned on Campbell's *Who Goes There?* called *Black Destroyer.* The issue following, September, 1939, the magazine published a decidedly adroit first story, *Ether Breather,* by another capable young man named Theodore Sturgeon.

The competition wasn't asleep either. A few months earlier THRILLING WONDER STORIES had announced the first-prize winner in their amateur author contest, a promising neophyte by the name of Alfred Bester whose *Broken Axiom* appeared in the April, 1939, issue. The month before that, AMAZING STORIES, reaching into its slush pile, came up with an acceptable effort of an ebullient New York science-fiction fan named Isaac Asimov, *Marooned off Vesta.* As far as magazine editors were concerned, things were good all over.

Misfit, Heinlein's second published story, in the November, 1939, ASTOUNDING SCIENCE-FICTION, has usually been given short shrift by reviewers as a minor effort imperfectly told. True enough as far as intrinsic merit is concerned, but with the critical advantage of hindsight, it can be seen to be of great importance as a precursor of Heinlein's method. The story concerns a group of maladjusted boys who are taken to an asteroid by the government for reorientation. Among them is a youth from the Ozarks who develops into a mathematical genius, capable of matching an electronic computer without pen or paper. The boy, Andrew Jackson Libby, saves the ship when the calculator fails and he accurately functions in its stead.

Misfit is Heinlein's first juvenile. It fits the pattern of the juveniles of Heinlein's post World War II writing career: the teenage hero, the firm but fundamentally benevolent military man, an elementary skeleton of a plot (misfit boy proves himself) set against a casually detailed background developed as though it could happen today. The gifted boy later becomes an important factor in Heinlein's novel *Methuselah's Children,* helping to perfect a near-the-speed-of-light drive for a starship.

Heinlein came into his own, after a very brief apprenticeship, with the short story *Requiem* in the January, 1940, ASTOUNDING SCIENCE-FICTION. The hero of that story is an old man with a bad heart, whose drive, ingenuity, and capital made the first manned space flight to the moon possible. He should never go himself, because the acceleration and other rigors of space travel will kill him. But he convinces two hard-up space men to take him to the moon. Evading all attempts by associates and government officials to stop him, he survives the trip and lives just long enough to touch the moon's surface.

Here, the student of writing techniques becomes aware of the caliber of Heinlein's craftsmanship. The phrase "art that conceals art" applies pointedly to *Requiem,* as it does to a large number of Heinlein's stories. The reader is not aware that there is a "style." Everything is subordinated to the story, which is carried along almost invisibly by clear prose, natural sounding dialogue, and a careful integration of detail concerning the times, the society, and the past of the characters that never disturbs the flow of the narrative. This extraordinary talent is at once Heinlein's triumph and sorrow. It can achieve memorable poignancy as in the case *of Requiem,* yet no one ever refers to his prose as poetic, because the details are incorporated with such cool efficiency that few realize the author has sacrificed the aesthetics of the individual passage to achieve the unified poetry of the whole.

Requiem is unusual in still another respect. It is a sequel to a longer story that was not written until ten years later. The trials and tribulations of Harriman in financing and launching the first moon rocket, casually referred to in *Requiem,* are detailed in *The Man Who Sold the Moon,* the 30,000-word title story in the first hard-cover collection of Heinlein's Future History series, published by Shasta in 1950. Though relatively recent, this story, which never appeared in a magazine, being written especially for the book, is already hopelessly outdated from the standpoint of history.

In the issue in which *Requiem* was published, editor Campbell announced gleefully two forthcoming novels. The first, by Heinlein, was *"If This Goes On. . . ."* The second, *Final Blackout,* was by the brilliant pulp writer L. Ron Hubbard, who would disappear from the ranks of science fiction some years later to devote his time to his dual creations of Dianetics and Scientology. The latter story was distinctly the better of the two, powerfully written, prophetically warning, with the principal character magnificently drawn. Yet, Heinlein's story was destined to have by far the more permanent effect on the pattern of future science fiction.

"If This Goes On . . ." fell in with Campbell's new policy of stressing the sociological implications of the changes of the future in preference to advances in technology. It was a return to the old "Utopias" with the difference that this was a "warning" story, a "Utopia in reverse" or "Misutopia."

The pattern of thought shaping, television spying, and studied psychological and physical torture to keep the masses in line and maintain power, all precede the horrors of George Orwell's *1984,* published nine years later in 1949. Not that Heinlein originated the theory of the methods but something must be said for the writer who brings inadequately considered areas of thought under scrutiny.

Most important, *"If This Goes On . . ."* showed one possibility by which a state-imposed religion might effectively play a role in the future as a cover for tyranny. Science fiction in the magazines had stayed clear of theocracy, but that policy was now to end, opening a rich field of exploration which would help create at least two reputations: those of Fritz Leiber, Jr., upon the appearance of *Gather, Darkness!* (1943), and Walter M. Miller, Jr., in *A Canticle for Leibowitz* (1960).

Heinlein's credibility in many of his works comes from the technique of taking the future for granted. The characters are familiar with the world they live in and behave accordingly, but through their conversation, their actions, and the story's setting, the reader is adroitly filled in on the details which frequently are more fascinating than the plot. This eliminates the need for the creaking technique of bringing a man of the past into the future or somehow getting a message back to today's world.

Despite its positive factors and considering an elaborate rewriting which almost doubled its length when it appeared in book form as *Revolt of 2100* (Shasta Publishers, 1953), *"If This Goes On . . ."* is a poorly organized tale with the emphasis on action. Its badly mixed-up principal characters get nowhere in their private problems, and they play an inconsequential role in America's Second Revolution. The hero isn't even in a position to report well on a potentially fascinating event. Historically, *"If This Goes On . . ."* is a very important story. As a work of fiction it is lightweight entertainment.

It was *The Roads Must Roll* that convinced readers of ASTOUNDING SCIENCE-FICTION for June, 1940, that Heinlein had arrived as an important writer. Moving roads and walkways had been common fare in science fiction since Jules Verne, but Heinlein was the first to devote an entire story to a nation whose economy was geared to this form of transportation. The plot framework is simple and unimportant: what happens when the mechanics who operate these conveyor-belt roads strike. The picture outlined by Heinlein of the character of the civilization that would result from this type of transportation is ingeniously constructed and its every detail is engrossing.

Not everything Heinlein was writing at the time struck a responsive chord. *Let There Be Light,* probably rejected by ASTOUNDING SCIENCE-FICTION, found a home in a new magazine, SUPER SCIENCE STORIES (May, 1940), edited by Frederik Pohl. Because Pohl couldn't pay top rates, the story appeared under the pen name Lyle Monroe, the "Lyle" being the maiden name of Heinlein's mother. The plot deals with an inventor who discovers a new source of power and is blocked from marketing it by big power interests. He defeats them by making his secret available to the entire world at no charge. It was a passable sort of story, but aroused a predominantly unfavorable reader reaction because the attempt at naturalism through the use of slang and colloquialism, and the sex implications were misinterpreted.

With the publicity attendant upon *"If This Goes On . . . ,"* a sequel was not long in coming. *Coventry* appeared in ASTOUNDING SCIENCE-FICTION for July, 1940, and deals with the period after the Second American Revolution, when a special area, surrounded by an impassable electronic barrier, has been set up for people who will not conform to the rest of society. They have absolute "freedom" as long as they stay within physical bounds and can leave at any time they decide they don't like it. The theme was intriguing, but Heinlein failed to make effective use of all the idea's inherent possibilities. However, the story was revelatory insofar as it shed light on Heinlein's own thinking.

Once again we have the motif of the misfit, a recurrent major or minor plot device in a substantial portion of Heinlein's work. Not only is Heinlein obsessed with misfits, but in a surprising number of cases these characters are inherently noble and have a major contribution to make society. Frequently they are far superior to normal man.

In *The Misfit,* the youth taken for reorientation is a mathematical genius; the malcontents of "*If This Goes On . . .*" are the revolutionaries who will restore freedom to America; rebellious Venusian workers in *Logic Of Empire* form a community in every way more desirable than those of the rest of the planet; outcast "Muties" in *Universe,* despite their grotesqueness, possess the clarity of mind to lead man to the promised land; *Methuselah's Children*'s persecuted "Families" are a race of inherently longlived humans; *Waldo*'s protagonist must live apart from the human race, subsisting on brilliant invention; Thorby, a slave boy in *Citizen of the Galaxy,* turns out to be the heir of a great family business empire; and in many of Heinlein's juveniles we find emigrant families from earth, who can't make it on the home planet, ending up as courageous and fulfilled pioneers.

A very definite link to Heinlein's thinking is provided by Fader, a prime "misfit" in *Coventry* who really is a disguised military officer on a mission. Forced to retire from active duty with the armed services, Heinlein tried a variety of occupations, none of them permanent until he became a writer. A man with his sensitivity must have felt like a right hand being forced into a left-hand glove. Unable to use his military training effectively, it was easy for him to develop an empathy for others he met who were floundering or miscast.

A large percentage of Heinlein's misfits are eventually integrated into society, often through the aid of the military or through the adoption of military-like philosophies. Somehow, Heinlein has overlooked the fact that successful authors are not misfits in modern society. They may be different but they *are* accepted, frequently in a sickeningly lavish fashion. He is still not aware that he no longer needs to justify himself vicariously.

Heinlein's *Blowups Happen*, a novelette built around the tension of operating an atomic energy plant, seems more grimly prophetic in hindsight than it actually appeared to be when it was first published in ASTOUNDING SCIENCE-FICTION for September, 1940, considering that Campbell had been editorially pounding away at the proximity of atomic energy since 1938. Nevertheless, the story was effective when published, despite its conclusion that no atomic energy plant could safely be operated on the earth's surface and it would be found necessary to put such plants into orbit as earth satellites. This belief is said to have been held by Campbell during the period the story was published and it is quite possible it may have been a compromise to satisfy him. More positively, *Blowups Happen* was a model for *Nerves* by Lester del Rey.

Heinlein also tried his hand at a bit of good-natured buffoonery for UNKNOWN. *The Devil Makes the Law,* in the September, 1940, issue, is about an America where spells and incantations are part of everyday business, but despite its straight-faced approach it didn't quite come off.

Heinlein was so prolific now that it was essential that he adopt a pen name in order to be able to run more than one story an issue in ASTOUNDING SCIENCE-FICTION. Campbell, of Scotch descent, had a deep pride in his blood line. Two of his own pen names were Don A. Stuart and Arthur McCann. When Philadelphia science-fiction fan Milton A. Rothman sold his first story to him, Campbell christened him Lee Gregor. Isaac Asimov had successfully fought off a pseudonymous change of ancestry, but Heinlein compromised as Campbell took his middle name "Anson" and made him a member of the clan as Anson MacDonald.

The first story under that name, a novel called *Sixth Column,* ran for three installments beginning in the January, 1941, ASTOUNDING SCIENCE-FICTION. The plot outline was originally the basis of an unpublished novelette of Campbell's and dealt with an America of the near future, conquered by the Orientals, which forms a religion as a front for a revolutionary movement. The foundation of the United States' hopes is the invention of a device which can be set to kill Orientals discriminatingly while leaving other races untouched. The appearance of a scientifically produced thousand-foot-high black giant, dressed in the robes of the priesthood, is reminiscent of Campbell's *Cloak of Aesir.* Again, as in a large number of Heinlein stories, it is the military man who saves the day. Whatever Heinlein's other early impressions, his years as an officer in the Navy must have been most pleasant and psychologically rewarding, for he looks back at them with reverence and nostalgia.

The prose of *Sixth Column* was immaculate and the story well paced. The Anson MacDonald pen name was one of the poorest kept secrets in science fiction. Too many people knew it, yet, among the general readers, it must have understandably seemed that an important new talent had appeared on the science-fiction horizon.

Outside of one month's temporary employment, Heinlein was devoting full time to science-fiction writing during this period, and there was no question that he had now hit his stride. ". . . *And He Built a Crooked House,*" published in ASTOUNDING SCIENCE-FICTION for February, 1941, was a delightful fantasy and the first of his works to be anthologized (*The Pocket Book of Science Fiction,* 1943). An eight-sided house built in the form of a tessaract is shaken up in a California earthquake and its prospective buyers find it has cut catty-corner across the fourth dimension. Each side looks out on a different landscape and investigation of the paradox inspired Harry Walton to try to solve a postwar problem that way in *Housing Shortage* (ASTOUNDNG SCIENCE FICTION, January, 1947), a classic in its own right.

Logic of Empire (ASTOUNDING SCIENCE-FICTION, March, 1941) was an extremely well-done exposition on the possibility of a form of slavery reappearing when the planets are colonized (this theme is dealt with in considerably more detail in *Citizen of the Galaxy,* 1957). Here, a Heinlein weakness for hastily tying up the endings of his stories is particularly apparent. It is as though the exploration of the idea is all that interests him and its culmination proves a burdensome chore to be dispensed with as expediently as possible. With this story a footnote appeared to the effect that Heinlein's "stories are based on a common proposed history of the world, with emphasis on the history of America."

Readers were fascinated by an editorial, "History to Come," in the May, 1941, ASTOUNDING SCIENCE-FICTION, which called attention to a two-page chart outlining Heinlein's Future History from 1940 to 2140, with published and proposed stories fitted into the framework. Interest in his work mounted tremendously as a result, aided by the appearance of one of Heinlein's most inspired efforts, *Universe,* in the same number. The central idea of this story, a mammoth ship, a small world in itself, traveling toward the stars in a voyage that will take centuries, was first successfully used by Laurence Manning in *The Living Galaxy* (WONDER STORIES, September, 1934) but it was Heinlein whose example started a trend. His exposition of a human "crew" who had forgotten, through the centuries of traveling, the original purpose of the journey, of the formation of a religion to explain their strange, limited "universe," was brilliant. A revolt and the division of the ship's inhabitants into two camps, one composed largely of bizarre mutations resulting from radiation, offer elements of conflict. Excellent action and characterization set against one of the most unusual backgrounds in the history of science fiction up to that time made the story a pattern against which to match many other outstanding efforts of the type, including *Far Centaurus* by A. E. van Vogt, *The Voyage That Lasted 600 Years* by Don Wilcox, *One in Three Thousand* by J. T. McIntosh, and *Spacebred Generations* by Clifford D. Simak.

The same issue had Anson MacDonald's *Solution Unsatisfactory,* which, though it is dated today, was Heinlein's most prophetic effort. In it he predicted, before the United States entered the war, that we would develop atomic energy and produce a weapon from which there was "no place to hide." Heinlein envisioned radioactive dust, rather than a bomb, and was unable to offer any satisfactory solution for policing its use, hence the title.

With the exception of a below-par effort simulating the technique of L. Sprague de Camp, *Beyond Doubt,* written with Elma Wentz and published in ASTONISHING STORIES for

April, 1941, Heinlein showed himself to be a master of the short story. *They,* appearing in UNKNOWN the same month, was an incisively effective piece, reminiscent of Mark Twain's *The Mysterious Stranger,* that suggested the world was little more than façade, an aggregation of props, and only one intelligence, the central character, was a certainty. ". . . *We Also Walk Dogs"* under the MacDonald pseudonym (ASTOUNDING SCIENCE-FICTION, July, 1941) is a vastly entertaining, logical farce, about a company that will provide literally any service short of murder, from walking dogs to making other worldly aliens happy.

Heinlein began to gather the threads of his future history together in one of the unifying "masterworks" of the series, *Methuselah's Children,* a three-part novel which began in ASTOUNDING SCIENCE-FICTION for July, 1941. The powerful opening chapter owes a debt to A. E. von Vogt's *Slan,* a novel published less than a year previously. In *Methuselah's Children,* there are a widening group of "families" that have been inbreeding with individuals of exceptionally long life span until heredity has greatly increased their life expectancy. When the normal humans find out about this part of the population, a great wave of persecution proceeds, aimed at extracting the "secret." To save themselves, the "families" hijack a ship constructed for interstellar exploration to follow the voyage of the vessel in *Universe,* and start out on their own journey to the stars. Landing on a world of about earth's level of civilization, they leave in haste when they discover the "gods" these people worship are the true owners of the planet and far beyond the earthmen in mental power. The story almost breaks down into straight fantasy when they alight on a second world, whose friendly inhabitants can change the fruit of trees by thought impulses to taste like steak and potatoes or an ice cream soda, whatever the earthmen prefer. They leave to return to earth when they find these creatures have a community mind, similar to Olaf Stapledon's "cosmic mind," thus attaining a sort of immortality, and that some of the earthmen are deserting.

References to characters from previous Heinlein stories are frequent and the effect is like a joyous old home week with the abundance of ideas combining as an intoxicating "sense of wonder" party.

To many, Heinlein reached his peak in the October, 1941, issue of ASTOUNDING SCIENCE-FICTION, which featured *By His Bootstraps*. Without question, this is one of the greatest time-travel paradox stories of all time. A man comes back from the future to meet himself, fights himself, while himself stands by and watches. The man from 30,000 years hence is sent back to obtain certain items for a resident of the future who also turns out to be himself. The effect is like examining a Moebius strip or a Klein bottle from the other side. Of course, the story is a trick, but it virtually takes mathematics to disprove it, and Heinlein doesn't forget in the process to tell a good tale which has touches of the magic of H. G. Wells' *The Time Machine*.

Heinlein had made his point. Nineteen months after the appearance of his first story in August, 1939, a nationwide poll of science fiction fans, published in the February, 1942, issue of FANTASY FICTION FIELD, nominated Robert A. Heinlein as the most popular author.

Nine months earlier, almost as if in rehearsal of the event, Heinlein had been guest of honor at the Third Annual World Science Fiction Convention in Denver, Colorado, over the July 4, 1941, weekend. He said then: "I think that science fiction, even the corniest of it, even the most outlandish of it, no matter how badly it's written, has a distinct therapeutic value because *all* of it has as its primary postulate that the world *does* change." He appeared as guest of honor again at the 19th World Science Fiction Convention in 1961.

A dyed-in-the-wool military man, Heinlein found a way to serve his country after Pearl Harbor. As a mechanical engineer he put in long hours on highly secret radar and anti-kamikaze work. When he entered the service, science fiction lost three major authors: Robert A. Heinlein and Anson MacDonald for ASTOUNDING SCIENCE-FICTION and Lyle Monroe who was doing short novels for SUPER SCIENCE STORIES. Two other Heinlein alter-egos, Caleb Saunders and John Riverside, had a single story apiece published when the call came.

The most heralded "last" story of this first phase of Heinlein's writing was *Waldo,* which appeared under the Mac-Donald name in ASTOUNDING SCIENCE-FICTION for August, 1942. Depicted on the cover was a remote control device for manipulating objects, since built and utilized for handling radioactive materials in atomic energy plants and actually called "waldoes," in acknowledgment of the story in which they were conceived. This precise scientific prediction was one of a number in a wildly imaginative story with two precious characters: Waldo, a fat boy, born with a muscular weakness that made it possible for him to function properly only in the weightlessness of an orbiting earth satellite, who is forced to develop his abilities for survival and becomes a supreme mechanical genius; and Schneider, an ancient Amish-country hex doctor, who seems to be able to make metaphysics less "meta" and more "physics" under certain circumstances.

Waldo's struggle to gain normal muscular strength, utilizing the philosophy of the old hex doctor, is told in first-rank style with the superb science leavened by a touch of near witchcraft.

For almost a year after the end of World War II, nothing by Robert A. Heinlein appeared. Then, quite unexpectedly *The Green Hills of Earth,* a story in the Future History series, appeared in THE SATURDAY EVENING POST of February 8, 1947. It was followed the same year by *Space Jockey, It's Great To Be Back*, and *The Black Pits of Luna*. With the exception of *It's Great To Be Back*, a small masterpiece about the adjustment of long-term residents on the moon to the heavier gravitational pull of the earth, they were elementary primer science fiction in polished prose.

Heinlein, one of the most original of science-fiction writers, was now taking the most basic, near-to-the-present, space themes and proving that stylistically he was so adroit that he could write them for a general audience. THE SATURDAY EVENING POST was simply the first of the general magazines in which he appeared. He made ARGOSY with *Water Is for Washing* (November, 1947), in which an earthquake turns a portion of Southern California into an ocean, and again with *Gentlemen, Be Seated* (May, 1948), which involves the practical use of a man's padded rear end to stop a leak in a lunar excavation until help arrives. TOWN AND COUNTRY bought *Ordeal in Space* (May, 1948), telling how the rescue of a kitten from an apartment outside ledge helps overcome a spaceman's fear of falling; BLUE BOOK took *Delilah and the Space Rigger* (December, 1949), which dealt with the problem of a woman overcoming men's prejudice to help build a space station; THE AMERICAN LEGION MAGAZINE got *The Long Watch*, a story in which a moon-based member of the space patrol dies of radiation to prevent a military takeover of the earth, actually a variant of *The Green Hills of Earth,* in which the Blind Singer of the Spaceways, Rhysling, dies of radiation to save a spaceship from disaster.

In placing these stories, Heinlein broke down some of the barriers in the mass circulation magazines against the use of science fiction. THE SATURDAY EVENING POST, which had used only a few such stories in the 520 issues they published between 1930 and 1940, notably, *Mr. Murphy of New York,* by Thomas McMorrow (March 22, 1930) and *The Place of the Gods,* by Stephen Vincent Benèt (July 31, 1937), had a wide selection to choose from when they compiled an anthology of twenty such stories (all but one since Heinlein's appearance) in *The Post Reader of Fantasy and Science Fiction* (Doubleday, 1964). The pages—and the audiences— of COLLIER'S, ESQUIRE, PLAYBOY, as well as the POST, became more receptive to science fiction.

Perhaps the most significant sale he made was a juvenile to Scribner's, *Rocket Ship Galileo,* concerning three boys and a scientist who discover a base on the moon, established by Nazis whose purpose is to reverse the decision of World War II with atomic weapons they have readied. Though written with more competence than most, as teen-age volumes go, the book was nothing much out of the ordinary, but elements of it were adapted by Heinlein (in collaboration with Alfred van Ronkel and James O'Hanlon) as a screen play. The story interested Hollywood producer George Pal, who had received an Academy Award in 1944 for his specialty, the development of novel methods and techniques to attain unusual screen effects. Obtaining backing for the project, Pal retained Heinlein as Technical Advisor and, to prepare the sets, hired Chesley Bonestell, an industrial and science-fiction artist who could render imaginary astronomical landscapes with such detail and scientific authenticity that they were nearly indistinguishable from color photographs.

Destination Moon, the Technicolor production, was released in 1950 (a fiction version appeared in SHORT STORIES, September, 1950) to awed reviews of its unparalleled sets and special effects. The critics were not quite as kind to the story line, feeling that too much dependence had been placed on the natural sensationalism of the subject matter. Nevertheless, the release of the picture marked a movie milestone. A spate of above-average science-fiction motion pictures immediately followed, including two more by Pal from famous science-fiction novels, Balmer and Wylie's *When Worlds Collide* (1951) and Wells' *The War of the Worlds* (1953), and Fox's production of *The Day the Earth Stood Still* (1951), based on Harry Bates' novelette *Farewell to the Master* (ASTOUNDING SCIENCE-FICTION, October, 1940). Pal, who started the cycle, virtually killed it when he did an inferior job of fictionizing two factual books, *The Conquest of Space* by Willy Ley and Chesley Bonestell (for the title) and *Mars Project* by Wernher von Braun (for the subject matter), to produce *The Conquest of Space,* an inferior "documentary" of the future.

No one realized it at the time, but the science-fiction magazines had sent a missionary to the masses. Their top writer, Robert A. Heinlein, had begun a process of education of the general public to science fiction, beginning with the public's basic media of entertainment: mass-circulation slicks, the teen-age magazines (including serialization of his material in BOY'S LIFE), and, most influential of all, the motion picture screen, with all its attendant high-powered publicity and promotion.

The in-group of the science-fiction world was proud of Heinlein's achievements in the name of their literature, but they found it difficult to hide their disappointment that his success also meant an end to his pioneering taboo-breaking and mind-stimulating concepts, such as had marked *"If This Goes On . . . ,"* *Universe, Methuselah's Children, By His Bootstraps,* and *Waldo.* A resigned acceptance of Heinlein's new career began to become apparent in the ranks when his second juvenile, *Space Cadet* (1948), appeared. True, it was little more than a fictionalized approach to the training program of future spacemen, but there was such a wealth of fascinating science as well as a peek at a Venusian alien culture woven into the background that it seemed a bit more than "just a juvenile."

Each year another Heinlein teen-age book appeared, and each year the fabric became richer and the writing more adult. Only the characters and the situations remained on an elementary level. *The Red Planet* (1949) dealt with the problems of colonists on Mars; *Farmer in the Sky* (1951) involved an overpopulated, underfed earth cultivating the barren soil of Ganymede; *Between Planets* (1951) offered the space adventures of a "boy without a country" when a rebellion by Venusians breaks out against the Federation; *The Rolling Stones* (1952) told of a lunar family that wanted to move further "out," toward the asteroids; *Starman Jones* (1953) took the action out of the solar system; *The Star Beast* (1954) was an "alien pet" story; *Tunnel in the Sky* (1955) followed the training of a space "Robinson Crusoe"-to-order; *Time for the Stars* (1956) made a boy a key member of a project to discover new worlds to colonize; but buttressing those simple plots was an ingenious admixture of the elements of the everyday work, business, transportation, entertainment, and politics of the near and distant future so smoothly blended into the mix that reviewers cheered and serializations which started appropriately in BOY'S LIFE (1950), *Farmer in the Sky* as *Satellite Scout* moved into BLUEBOOK (September and October, 1951), *Between Planets* as *Planets in Combat* and then into the "adult" science-fiction magazines when THE MAGAZINE OF FANTASY AND SCIENCE FICTION ran *The Star Beast* as *The Star Lummox* (May to July, 1954).

The 1957 juvenile, *Citizen of the Galaxy,* appeared in ASTOUNDING SCIENCE FICTION as a four-part serial beginning in its September, 1957, number. When this tale of a sickly boy sold on the slave block of a planet in the far galaxy to a crippled beggar, who finally returns to earth to find himself heir to a mammoth interstellar commercial enterprise, won first place among the readers for each of its four installments, even Heinlein's book publishers, Scribner's, began to entertain doubts that he was still writing juveniles. *Have Space Suit—Will Travel,* his 1958 "teen-ager," ending with the burden placed on two children to convince a superior race that humanity must not be destroyed and should be permitted to follow its destiny, marked the last of the books published specifically for the juvenile market. When *Starship Troopers* was submitted, although it had an adolescent hero Scribner's refused to publish it, and a relationship terminated.

How did Heinlein succeed in retaining his influence and leadership in science fiction during the 12 years between 1947 and 1959, when, despite the excellent qualities contained in his parade of juveniles, he actually was writing in a straitjacket?

He had, of course, contributed an occasional original yarn to the science-fiction magazines. Outstanding among them was *Jerry Is a Man* (THRILLING WONDER STORIES, October, 1947), in which an intelligent talking ape must be proved "human" in court to save his life; *Gulf,* a two-part novel beginning in ASTOUNDING SCIENCE FICTION in November, 1949, dealing with a post-World War III world where an underground society, The New Men, seeks to restore progress to the world; *The Puppet Masters* (GALAXY SCIENCE FICTION,

September to November, 1951), an extremely well-written thriller on the old theme of "possession," in this case a race of slugs from out of space, each of whom takes complete physical and mental control of a human being; *Double Star* (ASTOUNDING SCIENCE FICTION, February to April, 1956), telling how an unemployed actor is required first to impersonate and then to become one of the most powerful men in the solar system (this won Heinlein a Hugo); and *The Door Into Summer,* (THE MAGAZINE OF FANTASY AND SCIENCE FICTION, October to December, 1956), in which money will buy you suspended animation in a deepfreeze and a new start in the future. This last novel, while it suffers from the Heinlein failing of a letdown at the end, has parts in which the prose style is of such engaging charm that "craftsmanship" becomes a totally inadequate term.

What actually sustained Heinlein's reputation was the rise of book publishing firms run by the science-fiction readers themselves, specializing only in science fiction and fantasy. This surge of free enterprise was made possible by the vacuum created when the major trade book publishers all but ignored science fiction. Even a Heinlein couldn't get his serious work into hardcovers first, though he had no trouble with juveniles. All this has something to do with library budgets and bookstore distribution, and the publishers' arguments are convincing, but the fact remains that the regular publishers felt that they were unable to make a profit in the science-fiction market, and demand for the books had to be satisfied by "specialty houses."

Fantasy Press, a firm run out of Reading, Pennsylvania, put *Beyond This Horizon* into cloth in 1948 and followed with four shorter Heinlein works (*Gulf, Elsewhen, Lost Legacy,* and *Jerry Is a Man* as *Jerry Was a Man*) as *Assignment in Eternity* in 1953. Gnome Press issued *Sixth Column* in 1949, and most effective was Shasta Publishers, which began reprinting the Future History stories in a series of collections: *The Man Who Sold the Moon* (1950), *The Green Hills of Earth* (1951), and *Revolt in 2100* (1953).

All of these were widely reviewed as hard-cover books and were reprinted as paperbacks, in many editions right through to the present, spreading Heinlein's work to literally millions of readers. The complete range of Heinlein, from his earliest to his current work, was constantly kept in print.

Beginning with *Starship Troopers,* Heinlein assumed the role of science fiction's maverick. The theories in that book and those in the books immediately to follow repelled many readers and inspired stormy controversy, but apparently did not keep them from reading Heinlein.

The book that followed, *Stranger in a Strange Land* (1961), was the major work of this phase, written, read, and reviewed as a serious book. The first half had been written years earlier and remained unfinished. Heinlein then picked it up, completed it (in a somewhat different style), and waited for response. Hopes of a critical success were dashed when the reviewer in THE NEW YORK TIMES excoriated the novel. The reaction and support of the in-group readers was the opposite. A philosophical work, in which a human being, born and raised on Mars, returns to earth to offer his pungent, outrageous, and shockingly original views on the sacred cows of our society, the early part of the novel was accepted pretty much as a story, but the latter portions, laden with sex and bizarre concepts of a different form of religion, left the readers shaking their heads, but still willing to vote it the best novel of the year.

It was now evident that though Heinlein would still come through periodically with a juvenile, such as *Podkayne of Mars* (1963), an engaging space adventure with a 16-year-old (earth reckoning) Martian girl as a protagonist, Heinlein otherwise was going to write what he wanted to in the manner in which he wanted to. Cases in point were *Glory Road* (1963), a departure from science fiction into fantasy and a spoof on a number of heroes and schools of escape fiction, and *Farnham's Freehold* (1964), a post-atomic-disaster story, with a difference, stressing the individual's obligation to society.

A master hand, Heinlein was proving that he knew enough about the rules to break them and still get away with it. He had established a separate status for himself, above and beyond the aspirations of most new writers.

However, decades earlier, because of his popularity in the science-fiction field and his later surehanded success with a wider audience, Heinlein had become the most imitated figure in science fiction. Authors by the dozen copied his matter-of-fact style, with major emphasis on the turn of the phrase. They seemed unaware of the flavor and substance contained in the background of the stories, or they were unable or unwilling to duplicate it. Heinlein was casual, but his work did not lack a sense of wonder. He was merely more sophisticated about the manner in which he introduced it. The readers were not cheated of the one thing that science fiction had to sell. What effectiveness would *The Roads Must Roll* have had without the carefully constructed picture of a society dependent on conveyors?

"Sense of wonder" was defined by Rollo May in his book *Man's Search for Himself*: "Wonder is the opposite of cynicism and boredom; it indicates that a person has a heightened aliveness, is interested, expectant, responsive. It is essentially an 'opening' attitude . . . an awareness that there is more to life than one has yet fathomed, an experience of new vistas of life to be explored as well as new profundities to be plumbed."

The newcomers and the imitators trying to emulate Heinlein misinterpreted style for substance, sliding their papier-mâché characters down well-grooved situations past improvised props, with an overall effect as unreal as a puppet show. "The art that concealed art" looked easier than it was. There were a great many imitators and they crowded the pages of the magazines until one by one the magazines disappeared.

Heinlein's legacy to his own field has therefore been a tragic one. Through no fault of his own, he played the role of a literary Pied Piper in the decline of science fiction that continued uninterrupted through the entire decade of the

1950's. One of his stories, published in 1941, in body and title was apropos. It was called *Lost Legions*; it told of a search for secreted powers, and it should have been dedicated to his imitators.

12

A. E. van VOGT

Men have become famous because they introduced a single new word to the language. A. E. van Vogt is a good example. His term "slan" as an appellation for a human being posessing genetically superior attributes has virtually supplanted "mutation" and "superman" in communication among science fictions readers. Like Karel Capek's *R.U.R.* which gave us the word "robot," van Vogt's term came from the title of a work of moving intensity. Its acceptance became an affirmation of its creator's narrative power.

"Slan! That's a nonsense word now—a meaningless syllable," announced editor John W. Campbell, Jr., in ASTOUNDING SCIENCE-FICTION. "Next month it will mean a story so powerful it's going to put a new word in the language! 'Superman' is a makeshift term—'slan' will be the designation you'll remember."

Slan first appeared in ASTOUNDING SCIENCE-FICTION, September, 1940, as a four-part novel. It justified every word of the preliminary press agentry. A highly original approach to the concept of the superman in science fiction, it was instantly apparent that it must be counted among the classics in its category.

Science fiction had enjoyed superman stories before: *Gladiator* by Philip Wylie; *Seeds of Life* by John Taine; *The Hampdenshire Wonder* by J. D. Beresford; and probably the best known, *Odd John* by Olaf Stapledon.

Van Vogt's story is a natural outgrowth of the last two. It deals with the development of a true mutation which will propogate its characteristics, but proceeds one step further than either novel. In *The Hampdenshire Wonder*, the superman is killed while still a boy by the villagers who are instinctively hostile to him. A colony of supermen in *Odd John*, about to be attacked by the fleets of the major nations, destroys itself rather than come into tragic conflict with the human race. Van Vogt seems to have been the first science-fiction author with the courage to explore the sociological implications of the superhuman race living in and among humans.

Slan is the story of a nine-year-old boy, Jommy Cross, who is a member of a superhuman race. His people possess both mental and physical superiority, being capable of reading minds through the aid of antenna-like tendrils in their hair; two hearts invest them with extrordinary stamina. His parents killed, Jommy Cross fights to survive in a society where organized hunts are conducted against slans by the humans and where tendrilless slans—born without the ability to read minds—are even more dangerous enemies.

The moving and dramatic detail with which van Vogt relates the perpetual persecutions of the slans by the "normal" people and the superb characterization of Granny, the drunken old woman who aligns herself with Jommy Cross, lift this novel a big step above ordinary action adventure. The story is convincingly told from the viewpoint of the superman or "slan," which helps to give an air of believability unmatched by its predecessors.

Beyond this, the pace of the novel is sustained and heightened by van Vogt's inventiveness in contriving a continuing series of taut situations. Even the scientific concepts contain much validity, particularly the great emphasis and detail on the use of atomic energy—in a story written five years before the explosion of the first atomic bomb.

Slan was van Vogt's most famous and perhaps his finest story, but it was by no means his first success in science fiction.

Alfred E. van Vogt was born of Dutch parentage in Winnipeg, Canada, April 26, 1912. His childhood was spent in a rural Saskatchewan community where his father was a lawyer.

Two childhood incidents, individually trivial, scarred van Vogt emotionally for the rest of his life. The first occurred when he was eight years old. "At that time I went to the rescue of my younger brother, who was being beaten up by a kid my size," van Vogt recalls. "Justice was on my side, but for once right did not triumph. The bully, who, as I have said, was no bigger than I, turned on me, and proceeded to give me the lambasting of my life. It was so unfair, so completely at variance with the moral teachings I had received, that I was devastated by the defeat. I who had been gregarious became a lone wolf. . . . Somewhere, at this time, I got hold of a fairy story book—and my reading began."

His reading preference was the cause of his second incident. "When I was twelve, and we had moved to a town in Manitoba," he vividly remembers, "one of my school teachers took a fairy book away from me, and ordered me out to play. 'You' she said, 'are to old for fairy stories.' I was profoundly sensitive to her implied criticism that I was backward. It was years before I looked at another fairy story. Childhood was a terrible period for me. I was like a ship without anchor being swept along through darkness in a storm. Again and again I sought shelter, only to be forced out of it by something new.

I have come to the conclusion that most people are like that. They arrive at adulthood battered, shaken by the countless misunderstood passions of their bodies, and they very seldom completely recover."

The family was living in Winnipeg when the depression struck in 1929. His father lost an excellent position as Western agent of the Holland-America Line, and as a result Alfred did not get to go to college. In the gaps between jobs as farm-hand, truck driver, and statistical clerk, he turned to writing.

It is strange that van Vogt did not immediately attempt science fiction, for he became a regular reader of AMAZING STORIES when he chanced upon the November, 1926, issue with the first installment of Garrett P. Serviss' epic novel, *The Second Deluge.* He secured most back issues and read the magazine regularly until 1930. But his initial literary success was with MacFadden Publications for a "true confession" story. During the next seven years he subsisted on sales of confessions, love stories, trade magazine articles, as well as occasional radio plays. When van Vogt turned to science fiction in 1939 his writing was already in every sense of the word professional.

He was inspired to write science fiction when he picked up a copy of the August, 1938, ASTOUNDING SCIENCE-FICTION containing John W. Campbell's *Who Goes There?* That story dealt with an alien creature capable of controlling the body of any living thing. The first science-fiction story van Vogt wrote was *Vault of the Beast,* concerning a shapeless metallic robot that can mold itself into the image of any life form. It is the agent of extradimensional intelligences who entrust it with the mission of inducing a master human mathematician to open the lock of an impenetrable vault on Mars in which one of their number is imprisoned. The story was sent back by Campbell for rewriting and he quickly received another one, *Black Destroyer,* also patterned after *Who Goes There?*

Black Destroyer won the cover position and first place in reader voting on stories in the July, 1939, ASTOUNDING

SCIENCE-FICTION, creating an overnight reputation for van Vogt. The "Black Destroyer" was Coeurl, an immensely powerful catlike creature who, unaided, almost conquers an earth spaceship which has landed on its planet. Possessed of advanced intelligence and the ability to change the vibrational pattern of metal so that it can dissolve walls, the beast proves a formidable foe.

In the early portions of this story, as in *Vault of the Beast,* van Vogt strives for mood as well as action by utilizing techniques he learned from reading Thomas Wolfe. It is noteworthy to point out that while stylistically van Vogt and other science-fiction writers of this period were influenced by the mainstream, their themes were derived from authors in their own fields.

Encouraged by the tremendous reception of *Black Destroyer,* van Vogt redid the story, substituting as a menace a six-limbed creature capable of walking through metal, who plagues the same ship that had so much trouble ridding itself of the super-cat. *Discord in Scarlet* (ASTOUNDING SCIENCE-FICTION, December, 1939) scored another hit.

But van Vogt was having trouble coming up with anything original. While there were no complaints about the skillfully done *Vault of the Beast* (ASTOUNDING SCIENCE-FICTION, August, 1940), it was becoming evident to readers that van Vogt was a one plot writer. He showed every evidence of repeating his monster bit as frequently as Ray Cummings had reworked *The Girl in the Golden Atom.*

No one was more aware of the situation than van Vogt. "I was in a very dangerous position for a writer," he admitted. "I had to break into a new type of story or go down into oblivion as many other science-fiction writers have done. . . . I had to have something. I thought to myself, what I need is all the alien attraction of the monster stories, but not about a monster. About this time I happened to glance through an old story for boys entitled *A Biography of a Grizzly* by Ernest Thompson Seton. That gave me the idea of what the story should be, and so the first chapters of *Slan* were written."

There was no ignoring *Slan*. By any standard it was a milestone in science fiction. One of the most striking features of the tale was the breathless pace at which it proceeded. Event followed event in a manner reminiscent of the old silent movie cliffhangers.

The method behind this compelling narrative flow was supplied by van Vogt in his essay *Complication in the Science Fiction Story* printed in *Of Worlds Beyond,* a symposium on "The Science of Science Fiction Writing," edited by Lloyd Arthur Eshbach and published by Fantasy Press in 1947. Van Vogt confided that he plotted his stories in terms of 800-word sequences, "Every scene has a purpose," he wrote, "which is stated near the beginning, usually by the third paragraph, and that purpose is either accomplished or not accomplished by the end of the scene."

By any reasonable standard, following the publication of *Slan* van Vogt should have instantly become the leading new author on the science-fiction horizon. He didn't, simply because 1941 turned out to be one of the most phenomenal years in author maturation the science-fiction field had ever seen. Robert A. Heinlein, Theodore Sturgeon, Isaac Asimov, L. Ron Hubbard, L. Sprague de Camp, Malcolm Jameson, Clifford D. Simak, Alfred Bester, Eric Frank Russell, Leigh Brackett, and Nelson S. Bond were all making their mark at this time.

During 1941 only two relatively minor short stories by van Vogt were published. *Not the First* (ASTOUNDING SCIENCE-FICTION, April, 1941) harkened back to that earlier period in the magazine's history when editor F. Orlin Tremaine established the magazine as leader in the field, through the device of featuring as "thought variants" startling new concepts and off-beat twists. In *Not the First,* a ship which has exceeded the speed of light is on a collision course with a star and unable to decelerate. It "saves" itself by backing up in time to the period just before it attained light's velocity. When time is permitted to flow normally, the same sequence of events repeats.

The second story, *The Seesaw* (ASTOUNDING SCIENCE-FIC-TION, July, 1941), tells the remarkable saga of a man who is sent back in time to before the creation of the universe. He has accumulated so much energy in transit that it is released in an immense explosion, which brings the universe into being. This story contains the earliest mention of the Weapon Shops, later to become the unifying element in one of van Vogt's most successful series.

The entry of the United States into World War II saw a siphoning of science-fiction writers from the field. Most of them were young men and many had a scientific education. Those who did not go into the army went into research and industry.

Van Vogt, living then in Toronto, had been turned down by his draft board because of poor vision. The year of his entry into science fiction, 1939, he had met and married Edna Mayne Hull, another professional writer, so his life revolved around the written word. Both of them began writing science fiction and fantasy with increased vigor and found the welcome sign out at ASTOUNDING SCIENCE-FICTION and UN-KNOWN.

The moment was opportune for van Vogt to return and he did it impressively. *Recruiting Station,* built around the theme of men from 20,000 years in the future discreetly enlisting men from the past, was the first of his "comeback" stories and appeared complete as a short novel in ASTOUNDING SCIENCE-FICTION, March, 1942. The concept was later much imitated.

The next issue of ASTOUNDING SCIENCE-FICTION contained *Cooperate—or Else,* an immensely readable action story held together by a philosophical debate between an earthman and an alien monstrosity of high intelligence on the need to pool resources for survival. Actually, the story was a switch on his old monster theme.

Asylum, a novelette in the May, 1942, ASTOUNDING SCI-ENCE-FICTION, was a superb improvisation on the vampire theme in future tense. By this time it was obvious that van

Vogt had developed a clear, sharp style of his own. It was virtually free of Thomas Wolfe, yet retaining emotional impact and employing astonishing adroitness. The paucity of ideas that seemed to limit him up until 1942 was now replaced by a seemingly endless stream of originality.

This was particularly noticeable in the novelette *The Weapon Shops*, December, 1942, ASTOUNDING SCIENCE-FICTION. Utilizing an idea first suggested in *The Seesaw*, he projected the most original retail chain store in fiction, shops appearing out of nowhere in dictatorial nations and selling advanced types of energy weapons. The slogan of the shops is: "The right to buy weapons is the right to be free." Operating interdimensionally and capable of moving in time, the shops are invulnerable to any force, and through thought-reading devices they screen out those inimical to their existence.

The enthusiasm which greeted this story resulted in a novellength sequel, *The Weapon Makers*, which ran in three installments beginning in the February, 1943, ASTOUNDING SCIENCE-FICTION. The complexity of time and spatial lore that van Vogt embroidered into the story was staggering to the imagination, but its long-range influence lay in the introduction of monarchies of the future, operating with a technology advanced enough to include spaceships.

The alacrity with which other authors seized upon this theme was at best disconcerting. Since the heyday of, first, Heinlein and then von Vogt, the bulk of modern science fiction has visualized governments of the future as outright dictatorships, religious dictatorships, military dictatorship, or unvarnished monarchies. There has been precious little utopianism, let alone liberalism.

There was no gainsaying van Vogt's emergence as an entertainer. There was a certain element of purity in his approach to writing. Above and beyond everything else the story was the thing. There rarely was any explicit propagandizing or moral message. His personal views and feelings he kept strictly in check. That he had his share of failures is an admission he has personally made, but in the worst of them he battled for reader interest in every line of the story, and where his motif became too cosmic to sustain the necessary sense of wonder, he substituted a note of mystery, which served nearly as well.

Through 1943 and 1944, van Vogt produced a steady stream of stories. It was apparent that he was adept in any length from short story to novel. The most acclaimed during this period was *Far Centaurus* in ASTOUNDING SCIENCE-FICTION, January, 1944, which embraced the notion (popularized by Robert A. Heinlein in *Universe*) of voyages to other star systems involving centuries of time. In this novelette, a group of men remain in suspended animation for 500 years in order to reach the nearest star Alpha Centauri. When they get there they learn that while they were in transit, faster-than-light ships were developed and a civilization hundreds of years old is waiting to welcome them.

His success as a writer prompted him to move to Los Angeles in 1944, a change that had pronounced repercussions. Los Angeles was the center of every conceivable form of scientific, religious, and naturalist cult. Van Vogt's inquiring mind was receptive to most of them.

The most profound effect upon his thinking resulted from the reading of *Science and Sanity*, "an introduction to non-Aristotelian systems and General Semantics" by Alfred Korzybski. A Polish-born engineer, Korzybski preached that the inability of men truly to interpret one another's words, really to communicate meaning, was a major cause of the world's woes. In *Science and Sanity* he attempted to show how one could evaluate words and facts sanely. He referred to his system as Null or $\bar{A}$, meaning non-Aristotelian. While there was some validity to Korzybski's theories, they were not original with him and the book was written in prose so ambiguous and involved that it virtually destroyed his premise. Van Vogt seized upon Korzybski's theories as a drowning man grasps at a floating spar. They became an obsession and swiftly appeared in his fiction.

His *World of $\bar{A}$,* a 100,000-word novel, began in the August, 1945, ASTOUNDING SCIENCE-FICTION. Bewildered Gilbert

Gosseyn, mutant with a double mind, doesn't know who he is and spends the entire novel trying to find out. This involves walking through walls, being killed twice, and several episodes on a Venus verdant with plant life but with no animal or insect life for cross-fertilization purposes. For these and many other mysteries van Vogt offers no explanation. A fascinating literary inspiration, a super computer, a "Games Machine," which selects the most advanced intellects on earth to be sent to Venus for Null A training, is scrapped early in the story. Though fast-paced, the novel is carelessly and choppily written with an alternate-chapter scene-transition technique lifted shamelessly out of Edgar Rice Burroughs.

Letters of plaintive puzzlement began to pour in. Readers didn't understand what the story was all about. Campbell advised them to wait a few days; it took that long, he suggested, for the implications to sink in. The days turned into months but clarification never came. Lured by the little quotes from *Science and Sanity* which led off various chapters in *World of Ā*, readers began to investigate semantics and Krozybski. Sales of *Science and Sanity* soared. This book, which then retailed at $9 a copy and had seen only two small editions since 1933, prepared its first large printing. A reading of *Science and Sanity* was enough to absolve van Vogt of deliberately aiming to confuse. His work was every bit as clear as its inspiration. Nevertheless, *World of Ā* created such a furore that the term "Null-A Man," like "slan," became another synonym for superman with science-fiction and fan publications adopting it.

General Semantics failed to supply all the answers for van Vogt. Suffering from extreme myopia, he decided to try the Bates' system of eye exercises, endorsed by Aldous Huxley among others. To many, among them van Vogt, the system offered the promise of disposing with glasses through a system of visual exercise and mental orientation.

"I took off my glasses, and started the long uphill fight of training my eyes back to the normal," A. E. van Vogt told an assembly at the Fourth World Science Fiction Convention in 1946. "This had a profound affect on my brain," he continued. "I could no longer write easily. In fact I could no longer write salable material. I determined to fight it through regardless of the cost. I reasoned that I had affected my vision centers, and that I must develop a new flow. I decided that it was a good time to take up other trainings. For thirteen years I had typed with two fingers, another bad habit."

He taught himself to type well with the touch system, "but my writing didn't improve. During the next seven months I did not produce a story that was worth anything as it stood. . . . Just before Christmas of 1945 I began to feel a difference. I sat down and wrote—in the shortest time in which I had ever turned out a story—*A Son Is Born*. Since then I have written approximately 160,000 words in spite of much sickness in the family."

A Son Is Born appeared in the May, 1946, ASTOUNDING SCIENCE-FICTION and was the first of a series based on a civilization of the future whose religion was worship of the atom with the scientists established as "priests." These stories were eventually published as a book, *Empire of the Atom,* by Shasta in 1956. The Empire parallels ancient Rome with a backdrop of interplanetary travel. The central character is a radiation-caused mutation of exceptional intelligence. Individually the stories were mediocre, but collectively they made an entertaining book, distinguished by truly superior characterization.

A two-part short novel which involved the use of the Bates system of eye exercises appeared as *The Chronicler* in ASTOUNDING SCIENCE-FICTION, October, 1946. This novel, woven about a man who had a third eye, is the most deliberately allegorical of all of van Vogt's works, with passages like: "I have got rid of all the astigmatism in my right or left eye, yet my center eye persists in being astigmatic, sometimes to the point of blindness." This followed the Bates theory, since discredited, that eye strain is due to "an abnormal condition of the mind."

New stories from van Vogt continued to appear with some

regularity through 1950. Whereas before they had been published predominantly in ASTOUNDING SCIENCE-FICTION, they now began to show up in other magazines. The quality of some, particularly the short stories, was exceptional. *The Monster*, published in ASTOUNDING SCIENCE FICTION, August, 1948, and *Enchanted Village*, in OTHER WORLDS, July, 1950, are regarded as among his very best. The first deals with beings who come to earth after all human life has ceased and resurrect four men of different eras, reconstructing them from the skeletal remains. The latter involves a space explorer stranded on Mars who survives by physically turning into a Martian.

Both of these were no more than fairy tales with scientific trimmings. The teacher who took the book of fairy tales from the hands of a twelve year old van Vogt never removed them from his heart and mind. In maturity, aided by a storyteller's sense of situation and drama and a clear, pleasing, stylistic talent, he escaped again and again into a dream-world of his own making. They could take the book of fairy tales from him, but not his ability to create more.

The 1947 Beowulf Poll conducted by Gerry de la Ree saw van Vogt edge out such formidable competitors as A. Merritt, H. P. Lovecraft, Robert A. Heinlein, and Henry Kuttner as science fiction's most popular author. When science fiction moved into its greatest boom at the end of 1949, van Vogt was still the leader and stood to profit the most. He might have, except for the appearance of an article which dramatically changed the course of his life.

That article was *Dianetics: The Modern Science of Mental Healing* by L. Ron Hubbard, which appeared in the May, 1950, issue of ASTOUNDING SCIENCE FICTION. Dianetics was a system of do-it-yourself psychoanalysis. All you needed was a copy of the book, which conveniently appeared one month after the article and swiftly rose to the top of the national best-seller list. Dianetics grew from Hubbard's personal experimental hypnotic treatment of psychosomatic illnesses. It offered the same hope as General

Semantics: a means of rationalizing one's self to complete "sanity." A person who accomplished this feat was called a "clear." On the way to being a "clear" a person could be cured, according to Hubbard, of ailments ranging from cancer to dementia praecox.

Within the science-fiction field this "science" found early adherents and, inevitably, A. E. van Vogt was among them. John W. Campbell, Jr., as treasurer of the Dianetics Research Foundation, enthusiastically encouraged such interest.

Hubbard had claimed that the first "clear" was his third wife, 25-year-old Sara Northrup Hubbard, who was therefore the only truly sane person on earth. Feature-article writers attributed the breakup of Dianetics to a disagreement in the ranks of the foundation, but it actually was shattered on April 24, 1951, when the United Press reported that Sara Northrup Hubbard, by her husband's admission the only "clear" and completely sane woman on the face of the earth, was asking for a divorce on the grounds that "competent medical advisers" had found her 40-year-old husband "hopelessly insane" and in need of "psychiatric observation."

This did not discourage van Vogt. He exuberantly set up a Los Angeles headquarters for Dianetics. Practically all of his writing ceased except for revisions of some of his earlier short works which he cobbled together for hardcover publication. In the years that have followed, van Vogt unflaggingly has dedicated all his energies to the teaching and promotion of a "science" that has been exposed as without foundation in a dozen or more periodicals, and which even Hubbard, its originator, has deserted for more "advanced concept" he terms "Scientology."

Why this search?

Perhaps the answer rests in the fact that A. E. van Vogt is a deeply religious man in the fullest sense of the phrase. As a child he sallied forth to protect his brother from an unfair beating by a bully and was himself beaten. The major religions of the world have taught that "right makes might." Right was on his side but might had triumphed. He could not, therefore, in all conscience accept orthodox religion, for did not this incident obviously prove that one of its basic tenets was false?

Yet, here is a man, fudamentally good, whose sincere belief holds that man has within himself Godlike powers if he will only work to discover and release them. His own life has been a dedicated, striving for self-improvement. General Semantics represented a means of cleansing himself of mental conflict through orderly thinking. The Bates system of eye exercises pointed to correction of a physical defect with the hope of concurrently clearing up negative thinking. With Dianetics he moved on to a promise of higher intelligence, elimination of mental conflict and freedom from disease.

In van Vogt's fiction, his characters follow the same course. They travel in a world of confusion sustained only by the knowledge that within them are undreamed-of powers they will eventually master. Jommy Cross, the mutation of *Slan,* struggles for survival in a world where all hands are turned against him, knowing that as he matures his mental and physical powers will give him the tools to attain supremacy; Gilbert Gosseyn, hero of *World of Ā,* undergoes incredible ordeals aimed at ultimately revealing to him that he is a superman with a double brain; Clare Linn, mutant of *Empire of the Atom,* who is almost condemned to death at birth, lives to discover and utilize the near-mystical powers within him; Drake, an amnesiac in *The Search* (ASTOUNDING SCIENCE-FICTION, January, 1943), solves the amazing riddle of his background after the baffling series of incidents which add up to the fact that he is a man from the future whose purpose is to alter history so that the unjust fates will not overtake the worthy.

Though van Vogt honestly adheres to his role as a storyteller, he writes in religious symbols. Jommy Cross, Gilbert Gosseyn, Clare Linn, and many others are Christ images with Christlike motives. His characters undergo symbolic crucifixion and resurrection so frequently as to make it possible clearly to discern a pattern. Gilbert Gosseyn in *World of Ā* twice is killed and comes to life in other bodies. Throughout the novel Gosseyn is aware that there is an Unknown Chessplayer involved in his destiny, and the destiny of all men. Eventually Gosseyn learns that he and the Unknown Chessplayer are one and the same; theosophically interpreted, he equates himself with "The Son of God."

The Monster, which, when anthologized in August Derleth's *The Other Side of the Moon*, was even retitled *Resurrection*, finds four earthmen brought back from the dead, each possessed of greater powers, until the last is able to revive long-extinct human life on the planet and preserve earthmen immortal forever.

It is in the book version of *Empire of the Atom* that we find a near-final religious coalescence of van Vogt's thinking. Religion in that novel is based on the worship of the atom and the scientists fill the role of priests. Clane Linn, the mutant born into royalty, becomes a figure of Christlike morality. Here van Vogt finally resolves the mysteries that confound him. A tiny floating ball appears at the end of the story which "contains the entire sidereal universe . . . it looked small but that was an illusion of man's senses."

Van Vogt had reduced the entire universe to a tiny, glowing, floating sphere. It was now something small enough to grasp. It also consciously or unconsciously suggested Spinoza's philosophy that the entire universe is God and everything that makes it up is part of Him. The story ends with the question: "Did this mean that . . . man controlled the universe, or that the universe controlled man?"

All his life van Vogt has sought for the positive in man and the good in himself. Bewildered and bemused though he has been, his stories usually speak affirmatively: man can attain anything if he really tries. His search for the powers within himself have led van Vogt on many false paths, and may have lost him the great power he always had: power he demonstrated every time he wrote a story like *Slan, The Weapon Makers, The Monster* or *Enchanted Village*.

Dianetics became the "religion" that van Vogt so urgently needed, one in which he could be a high priest and personally dispense knowledge for the betterment of mankind while providing a haven for himself. To a great extent, in so doing he sustained a nameless god of a formless belief at the sacrifice of his literary creativity, for nothing new came from his typewriter for almost the entire decade of the 1950's.

Then, in 1962, Farrar, Straus and Cudahy released *The Violent Man*, a novel of Communist China. The brain washings which had influenced so many young American prisoners of the Korean War to declare themselves for communism provided the inspiration of this work. Twenty-two mature adults of the West are captured by the Red Chinese, with the objective of determining whether they can be readily influenced to embrace the Marxist-Leninist philosophy and if the findings of this experiment can be employed against the free world. But one of the members of the group finds a flaw in the psychology of his instructor and turns the tables. The primary value of the book rests in its dialogues, which present the communist and western viewpoints. These have been exhaustively researched and lucidly presented. The creative stasis appeared to have been broken.

A year later the first new van Vogt science-fiction short story in fourteen years, *The Expendables*, a duel between a starship and an alien civilization to discover which is further advanced, appeared in IF for September, 1963, followed in the same magazine in 1964 by *The Silkie* and in 1965 by *The Replicators*. All three of the stories were to a degree a melange of elements van Vogt had used in his more successful stories as far as twenty-five years back. They showed a certain hesitancy in style and unsureness in plotting, but older readers hoped that the closing line of *The Replicators* would prove prophetic: ". . . the real *That* stirred, awakened and sat up."

13

THEODORE STURGEON

It walked in the woods.

It was never born. It existed. Under the pine needles the fires burn, deep and smokeless in the mold. In heat and in darkness and decay there is growth. It grew, but it was not alive. It walked unbreathing through the woods, and thought and saw and was hideous and strong, and it was not born and it did not live. It grew and moved about without living.

Those were the opening paragraphs of one of the most remarkable stories ever to appear in a science-fantasy magazine. *It* was the title of the story, and it appeared in the August, 1940, issue of UNKNOWN, a magazine dedicated to stories that were different from conventional weird science-fiction.

The intonations of the opening passage set the mood for the introduction of a monstrous life form, a mass of putrescence and slime coating the skeleton of a dead man that had spontaneously become instinct with life:

It had no mercy, no laughter, no beauty. It had strength and great intelligence.

And—perhaps it could not be destroyed.

Authors had created monsters before, many whose names became synonyms for terror, but none of them had been treated with such objectivity or presented with such incredible mastery of style.

"Styles" would have been the better term, for the author was a virtuoso, possessing an absolute pitch for the cadence of words, altering the mood and beat of his phraseology with the deliberateness of background music in a moving picture.

Theodore Sturgeon was not unknown to the science-fiction world. Four stories of his had appeared previously, the first, *The Ether Breather* in the September, 1939, issue of ASTOUNDING SCIENCE-FICTION, winning first place in readers' votes over all stories in that number. *The Ether Breather* was a clever spoof of the television industry, in a year when there was virtually no such industry, involving "etheric" intelligences that humorously altered television transmission. Lightly, almost frothily written, it invited examination of the style to no greater a degree than would a theatrical bedroom farce.

The same slick, lightweight prose and superficially bubbling good humor dominated *A God in the Garden*, which was published in the November, 1939, UNKNOWN, a fantasy in which a prehistoric "god" grants a man the handy attribute of having every word he utters come factually true, even if it were not so before he opened his mouth; *Derm Fool* (UNKNOWN, March, 1940) is built about the plight of several people who shed their skin every twenty-four hours as the result of a poisonous snake bite, and *He Shuttles* (UNKNOWN, April, 1940) is a variation of the old tale of a man granted three wishes which ends up with the wishes in such contradiction that the man must back up in time and perpetually repeat his actions. A. E. van Vogt picked up this idea in a spatial superscience story one year later with *Not the First.*

Sturgeon's first four stories had entertained but made no permanent impact. They were written, apparently by a lighthearted, pleasing young man with a facile style who intended to do no more than entertain. *It,* however, displayed that an extraordinary talent was at work, capable of producing serious work of a lasting nature. The twenty-two-year-old craftsman who had written *It,* handsome, sensitive, and whimsical of features, with a trim build and a captivating manner, was destined to become a giant of science fiction and fantasy.

Theodore Sturgeon was born Edward Hamilton Waldo, February 26, 1918, in St. George, Staten Island, New York. His father was in the retail paint business and was of Dutch-French ancestry, a line traced back to 1640 in the New World. His literary and artistic inclinations seem to root in his mother, a Canadian-English woman, a poetess, who taught literature in the schools and who, up to an advanced age, produced amateur plays.

A Protestant Episcopalian by birth, Sturgeon came from a background heavily weighted with the pressures of the clergy, with eight ministers on his father's side, one of them, the archbishop of the West Indies, a great-uncle; another, the Bishop of Quebec, a great-grandfather; an uncle, priest in Newfoundland—and his mother's sister had married a British minister. Young Edward and brother Peter, fifteen months older, attended church and Sunday School regularly until the age of 12. Since their parents liked to sleep late, the two boys made occasional exceptions to this routine, ducking church every time they could get their hands on a copy of BALLYHOO, a popular humor magazine of the early thirties. On completing their reading, they would return home with a vivid and detailed account of the religious services, which effectively reassured their parents.

While the boys' early home life was happy enough, all

was not well with the marriage. Sturgeon's father did not live at home after the boy was five years of age, showing up only once a week for Sunday dinner. The parents were divorced in 1927 when Edward had just turned nine, and his father remarried and went to live in Baltimore, having one daughter from that union, Joan.

Edward liked his first father, forgiving his rather strait-laced philosophy, but ran into trouble with his stepfather when his mother remarried in 1929. His stepfather, who had been an instructor of English in Scottish schools, was an accomplished scholar and revered anyone who took learning seriously. It was obvious that both his stepsons were highly intelligent, yet they were very poor students, attaching little importance to knowledge. Edward was more than lackadaisical; he was also perverse in high school, requiring constant discipline.

Though he liked the boys, the stepfather found himself psychologically incapable of excusing this attitude and, while he supported the youths and stood up for them in time of trouble, there were no monetary allowances or special kindnesses forthcoming.

He did, however, make possible Theodore Sturgeon's present name. The old Scotsman was named Sturgeon and young Edward had always wanted to be called "Ted," so when he was baptized his name officially became Theodore Hamilton Sturgeon and that is his legal name today.

Before high school, Theodore Sturgeon had gone to a private seminary in Staten Island up until the fourth grade, then to a boys' preparatory school in Pennsylvania. When he enrolled in high school, at the age of 12, his family was living in Philadelphia, and young Theodore was an emaciated weakling, a suitable subject for the "before" physical culture advertisements. High school proved a place of horror.

His mother forced him to wear short pants and he arrived for registration with golden, fuzzy hair, riding on a scooter. Most of the kids, then, wore knickers and he used to hide from them. Whenever he showed himself he was the target of bullies who pushed him around and hazed him unmercifully, despite his gallant attempts to fight back. To top it off he had virtually no interest in study.

Then, one day, he watched an exhibition of gymnastics on the school's parallel bars and the sport thrilled him. He begged for a chance to participate and when it was granted, he drilled with fanatical enthusiasm, getting up at five in the morning and leaving hours after the school day had ended. In twelve months he had gained sixty-five pounds and developed powerful arms and a heavy chest. Within that period his schoolmates' contempt turned to respect. The second year he became captain of the gym team and at the ages of 13 and 14 was permitted to instruct the class.

His consuming ambition, now, was to become a performer with Barnum & Bailey's circus and make gymnastics his career. This seemed close to realization when Temple University offered him a two-year athletic scholarship when he finished high school. Life now had a purpose.

One morning, when he was 15, he woke up sick. He tried to get out of going to school but his stepfather would have none of it. Two days later, he was unable to rise from bed; his case was diagnosed as rheumatic fever. Before he recovered there was a 16 percent enlargement of the heart.

That was the end of gymnastics, forever. His entire life came crashing down in ruin. He never was going to be a flyer for Barnum & Bailey. Now angry at the world, he began to give everyone trouble. He neglected his school subjects still further and began dressing in weird outfits just to be annoying.

To make things worse, his stepfather enforced seemingly harsh home conditions. Though they had a radio, the boys were not permitted to listen to it. Every evening, he and his brother were required to attend a one to one-and-one-half-hour reading in his father's library. The books, both fiction and nonfiction, covered an inspiring selection of subjects and the readings were sustained for many years. It was here that he first became acquainted with *The Time*

Machine by H. G. Wells and *Twenty Thousand Leagues Under the Sea* by Jules Verne, but Ted had no appreciation of the literary background he was getting. Exercising the prescribed right that the boys could ask any question they wished about what was read, Ted Sturgeon showed an unholy and recurring delight in innocently requesting the explanation of the word "orgy."

The father demanded that the boys earn their own spending money. Yet when he caught Ted selling newspapers on a corner one block away from Drexel University where he taught languages, he quickly put a stop to it. Bemused, Ted went out and got a job collecting garbage in an apartment house and failed completely to understand his stepfather's explosion regarding that.

When he finished high school he pleaded to be permitted to attend college, but his stepfather, suspecting that campus frivolity was Ted's motive, refused. This time Ted was sincere, but it did him no good.

He settled instead for Penn State Nautical School, which had a two-year course to obtain a third mate's papers. A $100 high school graduation present from his grandmother took care of most of the $125 tuition fee. In nautical school he encounted discipline and hazing on a scale he had not dreamed of. He stuck it out until the end of the term, then, at the age of 17, quit and went to sea as an engine-room wiper.

It was during his three years at sea that he began to write. He had thought of a "foolproof" way of cheating the American Railway Express Agency, but lacked the immoral courage to test it himself. Instead, he cast the mischief in the form of a short-short story which he sold to McClure's Syndicate in 1937. McClure's paid five dollars for the story and it was published in dozens of newspapers throughout the United States. During the next two years he sold them forty short stories, none of which were fantasy and all of which were published under his own name. These were not intended as hack work; Sturgeon did his best in each of them.

During this phase of his life he lived with an Italian ship-mate who had set up an apartment in the Hell's Kitchen section of New York. These years were punctuated by stints at sea and it was while trying to find a ship out of a Texas port that Sturgeon made a deal with a small-town politician who owned a general store to write his campaign speeches for him. In payment, Sturgeon received day-old cup cakes, literally all that stood between him and starvation at the time. The politician won the election. Sturgeon did write one science-fiction story at this time, *Helix the Cat,* about a scientist and his cat, but the story was never sold and the manuscript has been misplaced.

His decision to try to sell to the fantasy magazines came as the result of a friendship with a Brooklyn couple. The wife was a leading writer for "true confession" magazines. One day early in 1939, her husband slapped the first UNKNOWN down in front of Sturgeon and said: "This is the kind of thing you ought to try to write." Sturgeon was enchanted. This was not his first acquaintance with science fiction and fantasy. Though one of the taboos insisted upon by his stepfather was "No science fiction," since 1930 Sturgeon had intermittently read AMAZING STORIES, WONDER STORIES, ASTOUNDING STORIES, and WEIRD TALES.

In the line of pure fantasy he had been deeply impressed by *The Charwoman's Shadow* by Lord Dunsany, *Green Mansions* by W. H. Hudson, *Alice in Wonderland* and *Through the Looking-Glass* by Lewis Carroll. Before he seriously began writing fiction, Sturgeon had composed a good amount of poetry and an occasional bit of verse, of very high quality, appears in his short stories. His idols, here, were William Blake and William Morris. One poem by Sturgeon, *Look About You!* which appeared illustrated in the January, 1940, UNKNOWN, is exceptional enough to warrant consideration in any substantial anthology of modern poems by American authors. But he abandoned most serious atempts at verse after he began to sell fiction commercially.

With a copy of UNKNOWN before him, Sturgeon sat down and wrote a story minutely describing the feelings of a man about to be hit by a subway train. Editor John W. Campbell critically ripped the story apart on the ground that when the protagonist is the same at the end as he was at the beginning of the narrative, the result is not a story but an anecdote.

Fortified with this erudite dictum, Sturgeon went home and wrote *The God in the Garden,* the first story he sold to Campbell. This success caused him to quit the sea and settle down to work as a professional writer. While trying to write more stories for Campbell he found himself persistently distracted by a bizzare notion that kept creeping into his thoughts. Unable to continue with his regular work until he disposed of it, he interrupted the story he was working on and in four hours wrote *Bianca's Hands,* a horrifying tale of a man so enamored of the expressive hands of an idiot woman that he marries her to die in the ecstasy of having those superb hands choke the life from him. Sturgeon thrust the tale into the drawer with no immediate intention of selling it and continued with the story he was originally working on.

With sales being made regularly to UNKNOWN and ASTOUNDING SCIENCE-FICTION, Theodore Sturgeon decided to marry his school sweetheart, Dorothy Fillingame. Her parents violently objected to Sturgeon's occupation and background, but, a week after the girl turned 21, parental objections were defied and they married. In ten consecutive hours of inspiration, on their honeymoon, Sturgeon wrote the nightmarish masterpiece that created his first reputation, *It.*

He was now a fully accepted member of Campbell's "stable" of writers. As such he was sometimes given a chance at a special assignment. A crippled old man named James H. Beard had submitted several stories to Campbell which were strongly plotted but inadequately written. Beard's uncle was the Dan Beard who had founded the Boy Scouts of America, then 94 years old but still plying his profession as an illustrator. Old Dan Beard's claim to fame in the science-fiction world was a set of illustrations he had done for the best-selling interplanetary novel, *A Journey in Other Worlds* by none other than John Jacob Astor, published in 1894. Campbell asked Sturgeon if he would take Beard's plots and make them into stories. These appeared as *Hag Seleen,* a superbly written story of a Cajun girl child who turns a witch's magic against her (UNKNOWN WORLDS, December, 1942), and *The Bones,* a fantasy about a machine that permits the viewer to experience the last events that happened to fragments of matter placed in it (UNKNOWN WORLDS, August 1943). Both stories were written before June, 1940.

His wife pregnant, Sturgeon wrote steadily to support himself. *Butyl and the Breather* (ASTOUNDING SCIENCE-FICTION, October, 1940) was a light-hearted farce, a sequel to *The Ether Breather; Cargo* (UNKNOWN, November, 1940) told of all the brownies, fairies, and various other "little people" shipping out of Europe during World War II; *Shottle Bop* (UNKNOWN, February, 1941) proved to be very popular, a fantasy about the gnomelike owner of a shop who sold "bottles with things in them"; by this time Sturgeon was so prolific that *Ultimate Egoist* in the same issue appeared under the pen name of E. Hunter Waldo.

While it made no special impact at the time of publication, *Poker Face* (ASTOUNDING SCIENCE-FICTION, March, 1941) is historically important as one of the earliest science-fiction stories based on the notion that otherworldly aliens are living and working among us and at any moment may open the lid on that third eye or pull their extra hands from beneath their waistcoats.

Readers may not have grasped the significance of *Poker Face,* but *Microcosmic God* in the April, 1941, ASTOUNDING SCIENCE-FICTION had all the reaction of a bomb with a fast fuse. It was not that the idea was new; the concept of intelligent creatures in a microscopic world producing inventions at an accelerated rate relative to their own time span had been used in *Out of the Sub Universe* by

R. F. Starzl (AMAZING STORIES QUARTERLY, summer, 1928), had been defined in complete detail by Edmond Hamilton in *Fessenden's World* (WEIRD TALES, April, 1937), and had been recognized as a poignant classic in Calvin Peregoy's *Short-Wave Castle* (ASTOUNDING STORIES, February, 1934) —but Sturgeon did it best.

The modest fame as master of fantasy which Sturgeon had attained with *It* was far transcended by the acclaim brought to him by *Microcosmic God*. Far from being pleased, Sturgeon was first annoyed and then infuriated. The kindest thing he could say for *Microcosmic God* was that it was "fast paced." He deplored the fact that it did not have the "literary cadence" of many of his other less complimented works and he deeply resented the fact that readers didn't even seem to get the point: that a superman need not be a powerful, commanding person.

He failed to understand that he had struck the universal chord. Stories like *Shottle Bop,* where you got what you wanted by "wishing," were good fun but nobody in this modern technological age believed them. On the contrary, a story like *Microcosmic God,* where a man could get anything he wanted by logical scientific means, made possible the complete suspension of disbelief and utter absorption of the reader by the story. That was the story's appeal.

The Sturgeon name increasingly became a focus for readership, but one remarkably well-done story, *Nightmare Island,* under the pseudonym E. Waldo Hunter in the June, 1941, ASTOUNDING SCIENCE-FICTION, failed to achieve any special notice. Derived from a reference in a 1910 edition of the *Encyclopaedia Britannica,* concerning the "tube worm," it dealt with a kingdom of worms in which a castaway alcoholic was worshipped as a god.

Financial opportunity seemed to beckon in the form of an offer to run a luxury resort hotel in the British West Indies. This sounded like a heavenly way to make a living and seemed to provide a great deal more security than writing, so Sturgeon packed up his belongings, his wife, and his six-month-old baby girl, Patricia, and left the United States. He had barely settled himself comfortably in the hotel when Pearl Harbor was bombed and the United States entered the war. There went the tourist trade and the hotel job, so Sturgeon's wife took a secretarial job at Fort Symington and Sturgeon took to selling hosiery door to door. He finally got to run three mess halls and seventeen barracks buildings for the Army, then worked into operating a gas station and tractor lubrication center.

The powerful tractors, bulldozers, and cranes fascinated him, so he learned to operate them. He accepted a job in Puerto Rico as a Class-A bulldozer and just loved it, moving his wife and child to that island.

In 1944, with the European phase of the war drawing to a close, the base and the job folded and now there was a second child, Cynthia. He rented a house in St. Croix in the Virgin Islands and desperately tried to make ends meet. There had been no writing in two-and-one-half years. Campbell wasn't too helpful or encouraging, but spurred by necessity, Sturgeon applied himself and wrote *Killdozer,* a 37,000-word novelette, in just nine days. That story, about a primeval electronic intelligence that takes over a bulldozer clearing an airfield on a Pacific island, embodied the vivid impressions of a sensitive artist of the power, sound, smell, and mortal danger of those mechanical behemoths.

Campbell loved it and it became the cover story of the November, 1944, issue of ASTOUNDING SCIENCE-FICTION. The check that Sturgeon received, $545, was the largest single amount he had ever earned for his writing.

But the check didn't last long and Sturgeon went into a writing slump that he was unable to snap. He took advantage of a clause in his government contract which would pay for his plane fare back to the United States. He was to fly to a friend in Chicago, then go to New York, procure a literary agent, and make arrangements to get his family back to the States. The entire trip was to take but ten days.

Things didn't work out. He couldn't find an agent. He was unable to write. The ten days stretched into eight months. During certain periods his main source of sustenance was the three meals a week he ate at the home of his half-sister.

Finally a letter arrived from his wife. She wanted a divorce. For two months he couldn't make up his mind what to do, but finally a job he obtained as a copy editor for an advertising agency at $75 a week made it possible for him to raise enough money to return to St. Croix. He discussed the matter with his wife, but her confidence in him was shattered and they were divorced in a civil court in St. Thomas. In 1945 she married a mutual friend, retaining custody of the children.

Sturgeon returned to New York in 1946, moving into the bachelor apartment of L. Jerome Starton, then assistant editor of ASTOUNDING SCIENCE-FICTION. As far as finances were concerned, Sturgeon was able to contribute little. He was in a daze for months. Campbell befriended him, inviting him as a house guest for periods as prolonged as two weeks at a stretch.

Gradually, Campbell coaxed him out of his depression, until one day, in the basement of the editor's home, Sturgeon sat down at a typewriter and wrote the story *The Chromium Helmet*. Campbell read the first draft straight from the typewriter and accepted the story, which appeared in ASTOUNDING SCIENCE-FICTION for June, 1946. More like a television script than science fiction, this novelette of a hair dryer that fished one's most wished-for desires from the subconscious and made them appear to have happened only superficially disguised its artifices, yet it seemed to go over well with the readers.

Mewhu's Jet, a long novelette which appeared later that year in the November ASTOUNDING SCIENCE FICTION, was a much better story. Engrossingly, and with a style as clear as crystal, Sturgeon told of the landing of an alien in a spaceship, the attempts to communicate with it, and the final wry realization that the outsider was a lost child with a super toy who didn't know where he came from, let alone the workings of his mechanism.

During 1946, something else happened, Sturgeon had peddled dozens of products door to door in the past in an effort to make a living; now he decided to try his hand as a literary agent. In addition to handling his own efforts, he worked up a prominent group of clients, including A. Bertram Chandler, William Tenn, Judith Merril, Frederik Pohl, and Robert W. Lowndes. This profession lasted from January to December of 1946 and for years after that Sturgeon would not have an agent because "I wouldn't put my affairs in the hands of anyone in so much trouble."

Agenting was the open sesame to a new world. Up to now, Sturgeon had but a single market: John W. Campbell's magazines. Now, he found his old rejects from UNKNOWN and ASTOUNDING SCIENCE-FICTION welcome by editor Lamont Buchanan at WEIRD TALES. Within the next few years he would resurrect *Cellmate, Deadly Ratio, The Professor's Teddy Bear, Abreaction, The Perfect Host,* and *The Martian and the Moron* from the trunk and enjoy an enthusiastic reception and a new reputation at WEIRD TALES.

THRILLING WONDER STORIES, which for years had followed a juvenile policy, went adult in 1947 and they took Sturgeon's *The Sky Was Full of Ships,* a tale of a warning of interplanetary invasion told from so unusual an angle as to earn it a place on television and radio.

Through the years, Sturgeon had tried to sell the nightmarish *Bianca's Hands,* which he had written compulsively when he was 21. Agents, editors, friends were horrified by the concept. An editor told him he would never buy from an author whose mind could conceive notions like that. An agent told him he didn't want to be associated with an author whose bent carried him in such directions. Every magazine it was submitted to rejected it.

Impelled by his recent good fortune in selling to new markets, Sturgeon mailed the story to the British ARGOSY through which a prize of $1,000 was being offered for the best short story submitted before a certain date.

It won the prize—Graham Greene took second place—and was published in ARGOSY for May, 1947. More than just money was involved here. The various ups and downs of his literary career had severely shaken Sturgeon's estimate of himself. One of the most accomplished stylists in the field, he still doubted whether he could actually write well enough to be a sustained success at writing. The bull's-eye scored by this story, written at a very early stage in his career, convinced him that he had always possessed the qualifications to be a good writer. His work immediately began to reflect this new confidence.

Campbell had anticipated the advent of atomic power. Now he chronically egged his writers to explore the ramifications of this discovery. Sturgeon was scarcely immune from this insistence, but his first story of atomic doom, *Memorial* (ASTOUNDING SCIENCE-FICTION, April, 1946) was anything but memorable. Therefore, his second such story, *Thunder and Roses,* in the November, 1947, ASTOUNDING SCIENCE FICTION, routinely blurbed as an atomic energy story suggested nothing special. It wasn't until anthologist August Derleth picked it up for *Strange Ports of Call* in 1948 that it had a delayed-action effect on the science-fiction world. Sturgeon had taken the tritest of themes in science fiction, a United States nearly destroyed by an enemy nuclear attack debating the ethics of striking back, because the explosion of its retaliatory weapons would raise the radiation level in the atmosphere to the point where every higher organism would be eradicated, thus eliminating any hope for another creature to rise to a state of civilization. Yet, he pulled it off, magnificently, even including a poem in the story which was set to music and which Sturgeon played on a guitar, accompanying Mary Mair, a lovely showgirl with a pleasant voice, who sang it at the Fifth World Science Fiction Convention in Philadelphia, August 31, 1947.

Sturgeon was now ready for his first hard-cover anthology,

Without Sorcery, published by Prime Press in 1948, with an introduction by Ray Bradbury. That author was already gathering steam, building toward his present considerable reputation. He wrote: "Perhaps the best way I can tell you what I think of a Theodore Sturgeon story is to explain with what diligent interest, in the year 1940, I split every Sturgeon tale down the middle and fetched out its innards to see what made it function. At that time I had not sold one story, I was 20, I was feverish for the vast secrets of successful writers. I looked upon Sturgeon with a secret and gnawing jealousy."

Without Sorcery was dedicated to Mary Mair: "Who in spite of the envy of the angels will live forever." However, the 1949 marriage that resulted from their friendship did not last forever and dissolved in 1951. Accused of "lack of maturity," Sturgeon had previously defended his outlook in a story titled aptly enough, *Maturity,* originally published in ASTOUNDING SCIENCE FICTION for February, 1947, but rewritten for *Without Sorcery*. Robin English, hero of the story (Robin is the name of one of Sturgeon's sons), is an engaging but childlike man, whose sweetheart, an M.D., arranges to have him mentally raised to maturity by a series of chemical injections. Robin English becomes a literary superman with a series of phenominally successful plays, novels, and poems. The literary efforts eventually stop as the process of artificial maturity continues and Sturgeon pointedly offers the suggestion that the childlike outlook is necessary to the production of works of art. A completely mature man does not engage in that sort of occupation.

What is maturity? The closing lines of Sturgeon's story, when his "supermatureman" has willed himself to die, reveals it: "Enough is maturity."

Personal problems no longer brought Sturgeon to a standstill. Throughout his short and ill-fated marriage with Mary Mair, his production was regular, displaying constantly higher standards of originality and technique.

Through his friend L. Jerome Stanton he met his third

wife, Marion, a young girl with widely varied interests, ranging from dancing to literature. They were married in 1951 and 14 years and four children later, through a kaleidoscopic series of ups and downs, are still married; Sturgeon seems to have found a woman temperamentally suited to the inconsistencies of a full-time writer's life.

There appeared to be a change in Sturgeon's social outlook that contributed to stability. It all began when the October, 1952, issue of GALAXY carried a novelette by Sturgeon titled *Baby Is Three* about a 15-year-old youth who visits a psychiatrist to find out why he murdered a woman who befriended him and four other strange children, all gifted with one or more of the powers of telepathy, telekinesis, and teleportation. Sturgeon, basing his story on the Gestalt philosophy that "The whole is more than the sum of its parts," admirably made his point when he wrote a 30,000-word preface, *The Fabulous Idiot,* and a 30,000-word epilogue, *Morality,* the three appeared as *More Than Human* in simultaneous hard-cover and paperback editions in 1953.

One of the most original productions ever to appear on the theme of extrasensory powers, *More Than Human* won the International Fantasy Award for 1954, beating out even *The Demolished Man* by Alfred Bester. The International Fantasy Awards during the period they were given, 1951 to 1957, were without question the most distinguished and coveted honors in the fantasy world. *More Than Human* found itself in the company of such distinguished winners as *Earth Abides* by George Stewart, *Fancies and Goodnights* by John Collier, *City* by Clifford D. Simak, and *Lord of the Rings* by J. R. R. Tolkien.

It would be nice to be able to say that *More Than Human* marked an economic as well as a critical milestone in the career of Theodore Sturgeon, but that would be to ignore the facts. If ever an author eptomized the skittishness and sensitivity attributed to the "artist," it is Theodore Sturgeon. While he appreciated the need for money, his primary motivation was not the dollar. Despite the knowledge that he could sell *anything* of a fantastic nature he cared to write and with full awareness of a backlog of commitments (for some of which he had received an advance), it was typical of him to take a couple of months off to write a three-act play *free* for a small-town theater, with the review in a local weekly his sole reward.

Sturgeon was at the forefront of the taboo-breakers on themes involving sex, including homosexuality. Every time he wrote one of these stories he cut down the potential market. A most dramatic example was *Venus Plus X,* a full-length novel published first in a paperback by Pyramid in September, 1960, which reads like a leisurely tour of Utopia until it is discovered that the inhabitants of this idyllic civilization are all male and reproduce with the aid of grafted uteruses and surgery. The result of his writing on so off-beat a theme was that there were no first American serial rights, no original magazine appearance which might well have brought as much as or more than the amount he received for the paperback.

He also toyed with "disgusting" stories, prime examples of which were *The Girl Had Guts* (VENTURE SCIENCE FICTION, January, 1957), in which earthmen are infected by an alien virus that makes it possible for them during a momment of stress to disgorge their intestines, which attack a "danger" with digestive acids, and *Some of Your Blood* (Ballantine Books, 1961), a Freudian case history of a man who has a compulsion to drink blood, (preferably from a newly inflicted wound), but in one special relationship in a socially revolting fashion. These have helped foster a sad school of exploration of which Brian Aldiss' *The Dark-Light Years* (WORLDS OF TOMORROW, April, 1964), of a race that glorifies its feces is an example.

Sturgeon is eternally involved in something. One of his more fascinating projects was executed for the popular radio satirist Jean Shepherd, who for some years conducted a late program of berserk philosophical commentary on our civilization aimed at "The Night People." His audience has been usurped by Long John Nebel, The Amazing Randy, and other talk shows, but Shepherd first cultivated the all-night audience. In the course of his half-sage, half-zany observations, he frequently referred to and quoted from an imaginary book about the racy, colorful eighteenth-century Captain Lance Courtenay by one Frederick R. Ewing. The book, he stated, was the rage of England and the Continent.

Attempts by listeners to find this titillating volume resulted in frustration and angrily unkind implications that Shepherd and the truth were not on the best of terms. Shepherd arranged with Sturgeon to give birth to this imaginary book and it was published as having been written by Frederick R. Ewing by Ballantine in 1956, as *I, Libertine* (with a picture of Shepherd on the back posing as Ewing together with a fanciful biographical sketch of the "author").

When *Voyage to the Bottom of the Sea,* a motion picture by 20th Century-Fox, was ready for release, Sturgeon was induced by Pyramid Books to write a novel based on the original screenplay by Irwin Allen and Charles Bennett. The book was released as a paperback in June, 1961, to coincide with the general showing of the picture. When a weekly hour-long television series based on the title, was produced (1964) the book was reissued.

Sturgeon is fast becoming a living legend in the science-fiction world. He is likely to turn up any place at any time for the most whimsical reasons. The least likely place he was expected was as science-fiction book reviewer for the "conservative" NATIONAL REVIEW. He first appeared in their pages with the September 23, 1961, issue and has continued to contribute regularly. Since NATIONAL REVIEW is the only weekly that employs a specialist to review science-fiction books on a regular basis, it would appear that the genre is scarcely viewed any longer as radical in its notions.

Even more startling were the twelve pages that the December 21, 1964, issue of SPORTS ILLUSTRATED devoted to Theodore Sturgeon's fictionized exposition *How to Forget Baseball,* describing the national pastime of the far future (after the atomic war) called *quoit*. His success at incorporating believable slang and idiom of the far future and combining all these essentials of the game into a readable story rank second only to the remarkable circumstances of SPORTS ILLUSTRATED running it at all, even as a special feature of the issue called *The Future of Sport*.

As a tribute to his uniqueness, THE MAGAZINE OF FANTASY AND SCIENCE FICTION published a special Theodore Sturgeon issue in September, 1962, with a painting of the author by Ed Emsh on the cover, appreciations of him by Judith Merril and James Blish, and a biography of his works. They had an ulterior motive, a new Sturgeon novelette, *When You Care, When You Love,* really the first part of a projected novel in which a wealthy young woman sets out to incubate a replica of her dying husband from the cells of his own body. Her motivation is overpowering, unreasoning, complete love. The concept of love in all its meanings was to become Sturgeon's obsession.

As guest of honor at the 20th World Science Fiction Convention in Chicago, the point of his address of September 2, 1962, was love of self, self-esteem. "People who love have to love themselves first," he said. The key to Sturgeon's philosophy of love as well as the most complete expression of the growth and ramification of his faith appears to be contained in the development of *More Than Human*.

Admittedly, with a writer as superbly gifted as Sturgeon, who strives in *every* story to be as differently and bizarrely off-trail as he is able, whose adroitness at altering the rhythm of his writing to conform to the subject gives him as many styles as stories (an artistic facility that has cost him the accruing audience that familiarity brings), it is necessary to poise near to presumption in relating the subject matter of *More Than Human* to the personality of its author. Yet, the Gerard hero of *More Than Human* bears strong resemblance to his creator. The feeling in the story that individuals in the Gestalt relationship may be replaced without destroying the entity fits the pattern of Sturgeon's early marital changes;

just as does the final decision of Gerard to keep the unity intact, supplementing his abilities with responsibility.

All the children who make up the symbiotic power relationship in *More Than Human* have been sorely abused in their formative years, particularly the hero, who serves as the "ganglion" of the talented group. Though their lives are frequently far from comfortable, they gain courage from their mutuality. The dramatic finale arrives when, with the passing of years, the nerve center of the group learns the meaning of morality and the desirability of channeling his powers into constructive channels.

The literary production of Sturgeon ever since the appearance of *More Than Human,* with his obvious striving for achievement, lends strong credibility to the theory that, with his third wife and four children, Sturgeon finally has established a "Gestalt" arrangement that is emotionally harmonious without sacrificing that naive inquiry, best expressed in his poem *Look About You!,* which makes his literary creativity possible:

> We each live in a wonderland;
> A blue to you is a red to me,
> A shade is seen, and we call it green—
> I wonder what you see?

14

ISAAC ASIMOV

It has been said that the most difficult element to incorporate into science fiction—without destroying the integrity of both—is the deductive formula of the detective story. Acknowledgment that this literary feat has been accomplished on a number of occasions appears in the scholarly and very readable work, *The Development of the Detective Novel* by A. E. Murch, M.A. (Peter Owen, London, 1958), which states: "Two writers . . . have succeeded admirably in merging 'science fiction' with detective themes, Frederic Brown and Isaac Asimov, whose work has attracted attention on both sides of the Atlantic, and who may inspire a vogue for this specialized variation of the *genre*. Nothing of the same quality has yet appeared in England, though it is by no means improbable that the attempt will be made, and that English writers will continue to borrow or adapt American patterns in the future, as they have in the past."

It is no discredit to Frederic Brown, a master of the detective story in his own right and a gifted science-fiction writer, to state that when it comes to blending the two Isaac Asimov reigns supreme.

By every standard, *The Caves of Steel* and its sequel *The Naked Sun* are incontestably science fiction, yet they also fit every definition of the detective story, even if the "Dr. Watson" is a robot and "Inspector Lestrade" turns out to be the murderer. *The Caves of Steel* and *The Naked Sun* are the outstanding masterpieces in the delicate art of honestly solving a plausible crime within the framework of science fiction without succumbing to the temptation of permitting the killer to enter the locked room through the fourth dimension. Yet the techniques of this achievement represent but one of three major contributions Isaac Asimox has made to the development of science fiction in the past two decades.

That Isaac Asimov was permitted to make his contribution to science fiction at all is entirely due to an accident of heredity. He was born in the town of Petrovich, a suburb of the Russian city of Smolensk, in 1920. The name Asimov, in Russian, means "winter wheat grower," and his grandfather did own a mill under the czar, while his father worked at the mill as an accountant.

In their inhumanity toward Jews, the Russian government and people ranked only below Hitler's Germany and the Spanish Inquisition. Asimov's family was of the Jewish faith. Upon the establishment of the Communist regime after World War I traditional antisemitism was reinforced by Karl Marx's dogma, "Thus we recognize in Judaism generally an antisocial element" in league with the capitalists, since many Jews were owners of small shops. The great Russian famine of 1923 found the government more lenient toward emigration, and the Asimovs, with Isaac as a toddler and sister Marcia in arms, seized the opportunity to come to the United States.

Unable to obtain a position as an accountant because of

the language barrier, Asimov's father bought the first of what was to be a series of candy stores in Brooklyn. Grammar school education at P.S. 182 and P.S. 202 in Brooklyn helped Isaac get his citizenship papers in 1928, but 1929 was to be more memorable for him on two counts. First, a brother Stanley was born, offering long-range relief from the after-school chores at his father's candy store. Secondly, it was the year he read his first science-fiction magazine.

Though his father maintained strict censorship on his reading matter, the picture of two men being hypnotized by a ball of fire suspended over a test tube on the August, 1929, cover of AMAZING STORIES looked educational enough to pass muster. The story illustrated was *Barton's Island* by Harl Vincent, a tale of a young inventor exiled from a tyrannical United States, who returns to free his nation from bondage. Young Asimov was enthralled and decided to supplement his education with AMAZING STORIES from then on.

An astonishing recall of facts, verging on "photographic" memory, aided Isaac in completing grammar school at the age of 11½. At the age of 15½ he was out of high school. This facility for learning immensely pleased his parents but the boy had other characteristics that didn't please them as much. He was the despair of his sister Marcia, his verbal agility with barbed phrase, humorous aside, and left-handed compliment driving her nearly to distraction. On the street he was always preoccupied, brushing past people he knew with no sign of recognition. This upset his mother, whose ability to worry considerably transcended her four-foot-ten-inch height, and she had reason to worry since among the people whom Isaac so blithely snubbed were customers of her husband's candy store.

Isaac didn't care what anyone thought. He was, during those early years, extremely self-centered, introverted; the world revolved about him. His brother Stanley was a mixed blessing, for while he did assume the brunt of the work at the candy store, his early morning paper delivery service had to be taken over by Isaac every time he got sick. Unlike most young boys, Isaac had an aversion to any physical activity, particularly sports, which were second only to labor.

His entire youth spent in the city, Isaac grew to love the masses of concrete and steel vibrant with the eternal hum of traffic. He felt no particular affinity to nature, the closest thing to it being a fondness for cats, nor did he have any desire to travel outside the metropolis.

His first ambition and his family's desire was that he become a physician, but he had been unable to gain acceptance at any medical school. It proved a good thing, because Isaac had a tendency to grow faint at the sight of blood. Instead he settled on chemistry and his father scraped up the means to send him to Columbia University, which made Isaac happy because the school was within city limits.

While still at Columbia, Isaac took a flyer at writing science fiction and during that same period made the friendship of aspiring science-fiction writers and editors. Asimov participated in the formation of The Futurian Science Literary Society of New York on September 18, 1938, in Brooklyn, a group pledged to aid one another in climbing the ladder to literary success. Other charter members of the organization were Frederik Pohl, Donald A. Wollheim, Cyril Kornbluth, Walter Kubilius, and Robert W. Lowndes, each of them destined to become well known in the professional science fiction world.

Six weeks after that, on October 30, 1938, Orson Welles scared the United States out of a night's sleep with his adaptation of H. G. Wells' *War of the Worlds* on radio and The Futurian Society seized the opportunity to hold a debate on "Whether the Earth Should Voluntarily Give Up to a Superior Civilization or Whether They Should Put Up a Fight." Donald A. Wollheim debated for the Martains and Isaac Asimov, advocating terrestrial supremacy, took issue with him. November 13, 1938, was the science-fiction world's first exposure to the devastating barrage of extemporaneous shotgun humor, delivered with the expression of a stricken martyr in the tearful lament that was to become Asimov's trade-mark at open and closed meetings for the next twenty years.

It was Asimov's first talk before a science-fiction fan group but not as an amateur. Only weeks earlier he had made his first sale to AMAZING STORIES, *Marooned off Vesta* (March, 1939). The plot was directly derived from Asimov's chemistry studies. Survivors of a disabled space ship find themselves with three days' air and one year's supply of water. They save themselves by utilizing the principle that the boiling point of water is so low in a vacuum that the slightest heat will turn it into steam, which can be used for jet propulsion. This same principle is today commercially used in processing freeze-dried foods.

Marooned off Vesta was the third story Asimov had written. All had been submitted to John W. Campbell at ASTOUNDING SCIENCE-FICTION and rejected, yet, when announcement of the publication of *Marooned off Vesta* was made in the January 4, 1939, issue of FUTURIAN NEWS, official organ of The Futurian Society, it also carried the statement: "John W. Campbell remarked of Asimov that he expects him to go far as a writer. His works, as far as that editor has seen, being very, very good."

Campbell was as good as his word and took a story from Asimov titled *Ad Astra* which appeared in ASTOUNDING SCIENCE-FICTION for July, 1939, as *Trends*. While the story did not quite hit the target as entertainment, the theme was advanced for so young a writer in its premise that an anti-scientific attitude as a reaction to war might hold back space travel even when all the elements for its success were present. A few months earlier (May, 1939), Asimov's story *The Weapon Too Dreadful to Use* had appeared in AMAZING STORIES; it surmised that earthmen will tend to enslave inferior races they meet in their exploration of other planets. Extremely weak as a story, it nevertheless pointed up

Asimov's interest in the political and sociological aspects of interplanetary exploration, a vein he would eventually explore more fully.

ASTOUNDING SCIENCE-FICTION was the leading science-fiction magazine in 1939 and it would make exciting reading to learn that *Trends* proved the toast of the readership, but the fact is that Campbell featured in that issue the first story of a writer named A. E. van Vogt, *Black Destroyer,* as well as a novelette, *Greater Than Gods* by C. L. Moore. Asimov had to be satisfied with third place in "The Analytical Laboratory," the magazine's rating section, but he did have the ego-inflating satisfaction of beating out Nat Schachner, who, along with Edward E. Smith, was one of the two science-fiction writers he most admired.

While Asimov's parents barraged out-of-town relatives with letters urging them to buy the AMAZING STORIES issue with Isaac's first published story (and most people named Asimov in the United States are related, the name being relatively uncommon), they were discouraged from repeating it for other "successes." Many of the stories were misfiring. In 1938, Isaac had written to Clifford Simak, whose stories were beginning to appear again after a hiatus of some years, criticizing the ommision of transitions between scenes in that author's stories. New he began to wonder if Simak wasn't right, leaving out the dull parts to get to the point of the action. He decided to adopt that method.

Fred Pohl, who had been acting as his literary agent, secured a position with Popular Publications editing two new science fiction magazines, ASTONISHING STORIES and SUPER SCIENCE STORIES. ASTONISHING STORIES had the distinction of being the first 10-cent science-fiction magazine in history and its first issue (February, 1940), carried a novelette by Asimov, *Half-Breed*. The "Tweenies," children of Earth and Martian ancestry, identifiable by hair that grew straight up, are subjected to a mixture of the abuses which the Jews and Negroes have fallen heir to. The story of the Tweenies fight for equality and their eventual migration to Venus was skillfully told and was by far the most popular story in the magazine.

ASTONISHING STORIES carried in its April, 1940, issue, *Callistan Menace,* a tale of huge otherworldly worms that are able to kill at a distance by creating a deadly magnetic field. In terms of chronology, this was actually the second story written by Asimov. The first and six others written between late 1938 and 1940 were never sold and were later destroyed. Asimov eventually sold every story he wrote after 1940.

While making his literary mark, Asimov, with the aid of his trick memory, had obtained his B.A. in June, 1939, at the age of 19½; two years later he would have his M.A. The emphasis on physical sciences displayed in his earliest stories was to shift towards the sociological, but his technical education gave his stories an added touch of authenticity.

Normally a story as clever and entertaining as Isaac's next in ASTOUNDING SCIENCE-FICTION, *Homo Sol,* would have attracted considerable attention. Any hope of that was thwarted by the appearance in that same September, 1940, issue of A. E. van Vogt's *Slan* and Robert Heinlein's *Blow-ups Happen.* As it was, this satire of the positive and negative aspects of the human race as evaluated by members of a galactic federation considering whether to open commerce with the Earth, rated just below those two historic landmarks.

The first robot story attempted by Isaac Asimov, *Strange Play-fellow,* was submitted to and rejected by Campbell in June, 1939. Pohl published it in the September, 1940 SUPER SCIENCE STORIES. A pleasant tale of the affection of a little girl for her play robot, it caused no stir at the time of publication, though it did introduce the name "Robbie" for robot, which has since become as common a designation for a mechanical man as "Rover" used to be for dogs.

Undeservedly forgotten was a short story called *The Secret Sense,* a well-thought out and nicely written account of an Earthman whose cortex is stimulated by Martians to enable him to obtain a sensory experience common only to them. When he loses this ability after only ten minutes, he is overcome by anguish at the realization that he can never again know the beauty of that "secret sense."

This story was written free by Asimov for fellow Futurian Donald A. Wollheim, who had become editor of the low-budget COSMIC STORIES and STIRRING SCIENCE STORIES. When it appeared in the March, 1941, COSMIC STORIES, and word got to F. Orlin Tremaine, then editor of COMET, a magazine that *did* pay for its stories, he read the riot act to Asimov and insisted that he either show proof of payment or submit stories to him on the same generous basis. Asimov tearfully induced the powers at COSMIC STORIES to pay him, not because he feared Tremaine, but because the story had already gotten out and if Campbell at ASTOUNDING SCIENCE-FICTION were to take the same stand the results would be disastrous.

Had any ban been placed on Asimov, the loss would undoubtedly have been science fiction's, for at that very time he had submitted to Campbell a story about an intelligent robot assembled on a space station who refuses to believe either that there is an Earth or that robots were built by man. This story was to make history. *Reason,* published in ASTOUNDING SCIENCE-FICTION, April, 1941, laid the foundation for the now-famous Three Laws of Robotics.

The first time Asimov heard of those laws was when he walked into Campbell's office after the story was accepted and had them recited to him:

1. A robot may not injure a human being, or through inaction allow a human being to come to harm.
2. A robot must obey the orders given it by human beings except where such orders would conflict with the First Law.

3. A robot must protect its own existence as long as such protection does not conflict with the First or Second Law.

Asimov claims that Campbell invented the laws, but Campbell asserts they were implicit in the story, as indeed they were. The results were truly revolutionary. Not only did Asimov go on to write a tremendously successful series of robot stories (a selection of which were collected in *I, Robot,* Gnome Press, 1950), most of which were based on seeming breaches of the three laws, but these rules have come to be accepted by an ever-growing body of contemporary science-fiction writers. That robots, when they are eventually built, will be subject to the Three Laws of Robotics has become axiomatic in a large area of science fiction.

Ordinarily that story should have clinched Asimov's reputation. Unfortunately, Campbell was callous enough to include in the same issue as *Reason* Theodore Sturgeon's masterpiece *Microcosmic Gods* and a novel by L. Sprague de Camp at his satiric best, *The Stolen Dormouse.*

Asimov's ability was not lost on Campbell. At his next visit to Street & Smith's offices, Campbell read him the famous quotation from Ralph Waldo Emerson: *"If the stars should appear one night in a thousand years, how would men believe and adore, and preserve for many generations the remembrance of the city of God!"*

"What do *you* think would really happen if men saw stars only once in a thousand years?" Campbell asked.

Asimov shrugged.

"They would go mad!" Campbell shouted. "Now go home and write the story."

The realistic delineation of a world of six suns, where an eclipse causes darkness but once every two thousand years, and the account of the psychological doom that over-takes its inhabitants at that time, possessed such an impact that Campbell gave Asimov a financial bonus as well as the cover of the September, 1941, ASTOUNDING SCIENCE-FICTION. An acknowledged masterpiece, *Nightfall* was acclaimed at the time of printing but—again—the near-tragedy of including it in the same issue as the conclusion of Robert Heinlein's famed novel *Methuselah's Children* deprived it of a first-place rating. Nevertheless, it proved that Asimov had the stuff that makes front-rank science-fiction writers.

During the time Asimov was making his mark as a writer and adding a B.A. to his academic record he was not oblivious to the attractions of the opposite sex. Among the girls for whom he provided escort was Mary G. Byers, one of the few feminine science-fiction fans of that era, who was in New York on a visit from a Midwestern farm. She eventually was introduced to Cyril Kornbluth by Asimov, and she married him.

The girl who really "took," however, was Gertrude Bluger-man, a Toronto Miss whom Asimov met in Brooklyn on St. Valentine's Day in 1942 and married on July 26 that same year. Perhaps one secret of their marital success is, as Isaac put it: "As far as writing is concerned I am my own boss. She neither reads what I write nor offers advice nor in any way, directly or indirectly, guides my professional life. Around the house, it's another matter." Inordinately sensitive to even minor criticism, the last thing Asimov needed was a literary quarterback. Eventually there would be two children, David in 1951 and Robyn in 1955.

Only weeks before the wedding, Robert A. Heinlein was instrumental in helping Asimov obtain his first important job, at Naval Aircraft Lab in Philadelphia where Heinlein was then working, as was L. Sprague de Camp. Asimov spent 1942 to 1945 as a chemist in the experimental laboratories. But neither marriage nor the new position affected Asimov's devotion to writing. He came to Campbell with the plot suggestion for a story based on the raise of a second galactic empire after the fall of the first. Asimov had just read Edward Gibbon's *Decline and Fall of the Roman Empire* and was mightily impressed. He had initially intended but one story but Campbell suggested a series. The Foundation Stories, as they since become known, were based on the "science" of psychohistory, a means of accurately projecting trends, in a highly specialized manner, thousands of years into the future. The method was perfected by a man named Hari Sheldon who established two "Foundations" to speed the rebuilding of galactic civilization after its imminent collapse.

A related group of novelettes and novels, the series ran in ASTOUNDING SCIENCE-FICTION intermittently from 1942 through 1949. When they were concluded they were gathered into three volumes by Gnome Press: *Foundation* (1951), *Foundation and Empire* (1952), and *Second Foundation* (1953). The series, fundamentally, possesses the same appeal as Heinlein's "Future History." It adheres to a consistent pattern and a galactic frame of reference to which most of Asimov's major works, even those not part of the series, also conform.

The action is primarily cerebral. Everything that happens is the result of the machinations of a prime mover, shifting power elements like pieces on a chess board. In Asimov's own words: "It seems to me that the Conans are less apt to have permanent importance than the Richelieus. Even when a great conniver uses wars as a means to an end, they are only incidental and usually short." In this respect, physical action plays only a very minor role in most of Asimov's stories after 1942. There may be some relationship between this fact and the young Asimov who had no fondness for participation in sports.

The most important characteristic of the Foundation stories was not immediately obvious, possibly not even to Campbell and certainly not to the readers who ranked the first story in the series, *Foundation,* fourth in preference in the May, 1942, ASTOUNDING SCIENCE-FICTION in which it appeared, well behind Robert Heinlein's *Beyond This Horizon,* A. E. van Vogt's *Asylum,* and Alfred Bester's *The Improbable Man.* What the Foundation series contributed to science fiction was a concept. There had been galactic empires described in science fiction before. Olaf Stapledon outlined them magnificently in *The Star Marker* and they were inherent in the background of Edward E. Smith's *Galactic Patrol,* but this was the first time that any author had the effrontery to insist that *all* the myriad worlds of the vast galactic cluster would be colonized and dominated by a single species—man!

The psychological basis for this concept does not rest in imaginative inertia but may be found in Asimov's primer for his own "Future History," *The End of Eternity.* Rejected by the major magazines and finally published by Doubleday in 1955, it is the book that Asimov most enjoyed writing. Clearly inspired by John Russell Fearn's action epic *The Liners of Time* (AMAZING STORIES, May to August, 1935) and carrying echoes of A. E. van Vogt's *The Search,* it postulates a time traveling "foundation" whose members eventually change the past enabling human beings to conquer all the stars of our galaxy before alien intelligences can stop them. As the book nears its conclusion, Asimov, through one of his characters, states: "Without the interplay of human against human, the chief interest in life is gone; most of the intellectual values are gone; most of the reason for living is gone."

That is why aliens appear so infrequently in Asimov stories.

Drafted *after* World War II, Corporal Isaac Asimov was assigned to the Quartermaster Corps and ordered to a Pacific atoll where an atomic test was scheduled to be held. He got as far as Hawaii, where he was discharged after only six months. Asimov then returned to Columbia and worked toward his doctorate, which he received in 1949.

A faculty member of the Boston University School of Medicine who was an Asimov fan and correspondent urged him to establish himself at that New England institution. Asimov qualified for a post as instructor in biochemistry at Boston University in 1949.

The Asimov stories that appeared during his studies at Columbia were few but they were outstanding. Previously Asimov was rated in a secondary stratum of science-fiction writers. Every time a story of his appeared it would be over-shadowed by a still better one by a top-level writer. Beginning with the appearance of his Foundation story *Now You See It,* concerning the great mutant conqueror The Mule, in AS-TOUNDING SCIENCE FICTION for January, 1948, that wasn't going to happen so often any more. That one even beat out, in readers' estimation, the final installment of *Children of the Lens* by one of Asimov's old idols, E. E. Smith, Ph.D.

Yet, though growing swiftly in skill and maturity, Asimov still encountered sales problems. At the solicitation of Sam Merwin, Jr., who was in the process of publishing more mature material in his two magazines STARTLING STORIES and THRILLING WONDER STORIES, Asimov wrote a short novel which he titled *Grow Old Along with Me.* Merwin rejected it and so did Campbell. Two science-fiction fans, Paul Dennis O'Connor and Martin Greenberg, were ready to schedule it for a limited hardcover edition under the aegis of New Collector's Group, a fledgling company which had already published *The Fox Woman* and *The Black Wheel,* two unfinished novels by A. Merritt completed by Hannes Bok. Then word came through that Doubleday was looking for science fiction. Asimov sent it to Doubleday editor Walter Bradbury, who suggested the story be lengthened to full novel size. The result was *Pebble in the Sky,* a story inspired by lines from Robert Browning which Asimov had memorized in his youth:

Grow old along with me!
The best is yet to be,
The last of life, for which the first was made . . . .

Pebble in the Sky preached that the old-age of the planet Earth could be anything but beautiful. In the Galactic Era 827 Earth is radioactive, still inhabited, but by men who are pariahs to the rest of the galaxy. No one any longer remembers that Earth was the mother planet. Despite an over-burdening allegory against racial intolerance which weights down the book, the setting of a radioactive world and the society it breeds evoked some of the effectiveness of The Last Redoubt in William Hope Hodgson's imaginative *tour de force, The Night Land* (1912).

Joseph Schwartz, the older-than-middle-aged co-hero, is catapulted into the future from the twentieth century by an atomic mishap (he possesses a "trick" memory similar to Asimov's own). A device which temporarily stimulates the intelligence of mice, who usually die from the aftereffects, is tried on Schwartz, who has been as helpless as a moron in his strange situation. With his newly acquired advanced intelligence he is able to contribute toward saving himself and the entire galaxy. Daniel Keyes' Hugo-winning short story, *Flowers for Algernon,* could well have been inspired by *Pebble in the Sky;* it puts a different twist on the identical plot device.

This novel, more than any other single thing, was responsible for elevating Asimov into the top rank of science-fiction writers. Reviews of the book were excellent. It was reprinted in TWO COMPLETE SCIENCE ADVENTURE NOVELS, GALAXY NOVELS, in paperback, and abroad. Most significantly, it was made a Unicorn Mystery Book Club selection by Hans Stefan Santesson, who recognized classic mystery story technique in its plot structure.

Heartened by this success, Asimov decided to concentrate on novels. *Tyrann,* his first work deliberately written as a novel was serialized in the rapidly rising new science-fiction magazine GALAXY SCIENCE-FICTION beginning with the January, 1951, issue. Published in hard covers by Doubleday as *The Stars Like Dust,* it tells of a chase through the galaxy in search of a secret document which may be the key to the overthrow of tyranny.

Virtually the only redeeming feature of this novel is its denouement. In its early days, science fiction was thought of as a medium of utopian proclamation, most often constructive, democratic, and hopeful in tone. When dictatorships were projected, they were inevitably held up as a "warning." Since 1939, governments of the future based on democratic principles have been all-but-nonexistent in science fiction generally. Perhaps the pessimism created by World War II and the arrival of atomic explosives are responsible. But it is singularly notable that the "secret document," the object of the action in *The Stars Like Dust,* turns out to be a copy of the Constitution of the United States. When Asimov concludes, "The time for maturity has come as it once came on the planet Earth, and there will be a new kind of government, a kind that has never yet been tried in the Galaxy," he is, sadly enough, virtually the only science-fiction author in modern times to suggest it.

His next novel, *The Currents of Space* (ASTOUNDING SCIENCE FICTION, October-December, 1952), was a far better work. Especially memorable is Big Lona, the peasant girl of the planet Florina, who befriends Rik, a member of the galactographic corps. Scientific originality is displayed in describing the function of this corps, which measures the nature and movement of particles in space.

Asimov now felt up to attempting a full-length novel based on robots, broaching the idea to H. L. Gold, who suggested the incorporation of a robot detective and the Malthusian outlook on overpopulation. Serialized in GALAXY SCIENCE-FICTION, beginning in October, 1953, the novel, *Caves of Steel,* put Asimov in a class by himself. No one had previously succeeded so brilliantly in wedding the detective to science fiction and Asimov's carefully thought-out overpopulated metropolises of the future were drawn more with love than with loathing.

Science-fiction readers offered Isaac Asimov their greatest personal tribute. They made him Guest of Honor at the 13th World Science Fiction Convention, held in Cleveland, September 2-5, 1955.

The same year he was made Associate Professor at Boston University, pursuing research in nucleic acid. The exigencies of writing made it increasingly difficult for him to do justice to either vocation. A change in deans at the University resulted in pressure on Asimov for more research and less writing. Asimov, who had already had published several

books in a popular scientific vein, felt that he could be of
more benefit to the university in that manner than through
research. When Asimov took his post at the University the
rules of the institution permitted a faculty member with a
certain number of years of service to retain his title for life,
even if he resigned. Those rules had been changed in the
interim so that the title could be lost on departure. Asimov
took the matter to a vote of the full faculty and won out,
retiring to full-time writing in 1958 and holding his title of
Associate Professor by lecturing several times a year.

Science fiction was no longer a profitable market, so he
channeled his energies into scientific articles and books
written in popular language. His facility in expressing himself clearly and engagingly, which made him one of the finest
lecturers in the history of Boston University, coupled with
his extraordinarily retentive memory, added up to instant
success as a purveyor of popular education.

As many as six books a year flowed from his reference-
lined attic workshop: *The Chemicals of Life, The Wellsprings
of Life, The World of Nitrogen, The World of Carbon, Inside the Atom, Building Blocks of the Universe, The Clock
We Live On, The Realm of Numbers,* and many others. The
major opus in this area thus far is the critically acclaimed
The Intelligent Man's Guide to Science, a two-volume boxed
set, ambitiously aimed at familiarizing the layman with the
complete range of the physical and biological sciences.

The impact on the general public of Isaac Asimov's two-
pronged writing career is apparent to no one more than
brother Stanley Asimov, now night city editor of NEWSDAY,
the leading Long Island newspaper. "It's gotten so I avoid
telling anyone my name," he moans. "Co-workers, chance
acquaintances, people I meet in the course of business, all
follow the same pattern. 'Asimov? Asimov? Any relative to
the Isaac Asimov?'

"Why, when I was introduced to my wife Ruth, the first
words out of her mouth were: 'Asimov? Asimov? Any relative to *the* Isaac Asimov?' "

If Isaac Asimov has changed in any way in the past twenty years, it is in the gradual diminution of his mad exhibitions and the spontaneous explosions of humor which he employed to reduce his self-consciousness by making himself the center of attraction at any public function. Only the robot stories reflect this aspect of his nature and then satirically. At heart Isaac Asimov is and always has been a very serious man. Perhaps the accelerating acceptance by the public of his scientific expositions have convinced him that it is no longer necessary to guffaw and wiggle his ears to attract attention. It has been a long time since that was necessary in science fiction.

15

CLIFFORD D. SIMAK

It was Sunday afternoon, September 6th, 1959, in the banquet room of the Hotel Fort Shelby, Detroit, and Robert Bloch was reading the names of the winners of the Hugo awards to the audience as Isaac Asimov announced the categories. The revelation that Clifford D. Simak's novelette, *The Big Front Yard,* from the October, 1958, issue of ASTOUNDING SCIENCE FICTION had been voted the best story of its length during the previous year was lost in the gale of affectionate laughter precipitated by Bloch's expression as he opened the next envelope to find that his own story, *That Hill-Bound Train* (FANTASY AND SCIENCE FICTION, September, 1958), had won a Hugo as the best short science-fiction story of the year.

But by winning this Hugo, Clifford D. Simak had become the first science-fiction author in history to receive both of the major awards possible in the fantasy world. Earlier, he had taken the 1952 International Fantasy Award for the best novel of science fiction or fantasy published during 1952, *City*.

Had this point been emphasized, no one would have been surprised. Simak's *The Big Front Yard* was but one of dozens of his superbly wrought tales that endowed ordinary folk with the special qualities to cope with bizarre aberrations of space and time, as well as with technologies that would have baffled an Einstein.

In *The Big Front Yard*, Hiram Taine, repair man and antique dealer, in company with a handyman misfit who claims to be able to talk with animals, drives a hard bargain with the inhabitants of another world, who have warped his front yard through another dimension so that it faces out upon an alien planet in an unguessable corner of the cosmos. He was typical of scores of other Simak "heroes," who, whether dirt farmer, near-idiot, or love-struck robot, had a function, a reason for being in the universe, who could somehow fathom the unknowable and defeat the omnipotent.

Five years later, at the age of 60, Clifford D. Simak again received the Hugo at the 22nd World Science Fiction Convention at Oakland, California, September 6, 1964. This time it was for the best novel of the year and he was there to accept it. The novel was *Way Station* (Doubleday, 1963), originally serialized in GALAXY MAGAZINE as as *Here Gather the Stars* (June and August, 1963). It is the story of Enoch, who for one-hundred years, ever since the Civil War, has tended a way station in the Wisconsin hills for the intelligent races of the galaxy. Agelessly he carries on, with the macabre "good fellows" of a hundred worlds as his nocturnal companions, waiting for the day when circumstances will permit him to reveal his secret to the world—perhaps for its salvation. The Earth is on the verge of a cataclysmic war, but in the simple steadfastness of the rustic Enoch, there still rests hope.

Simak manages to accentuate the positive in the personalities of his diverse group of unlikely "supermen." He rarely dwells on the morbid, the horrifying, or the decadent. In his worlds and in the lives of his characters, there is room for hope, for kindness, for decency, and for a morality that would be obvious if the reader were not spellbound by the artistry of the storytelling. Regardless of their origins, his characters are more saints than sinners. Good predominates over evil and optimism over despair.

Simak's greatest love and affection is reserved for the farmer. Directly and indirectly, more farmers traipse through the science fiction of Clifford Simak than through the works of any author apart from COUNTRY GENTLEMAN's writers. Born on the farm of his grandfather Edward Wiseman on August 3, 1904, in the township of Millville, Grant County, Wisconsin, Simak has never sweated the sweet memory of rural life from his body. His grandfather's farm was on an inland promontory, from which the meeting of the Wisconsin and Mississippi rivers was clearly visible. It was a hill farm, with nearby woods filled with game and streams choked with obliging fish. Almost everything his grandfather's family ate came off that farm.

Clifford's father, John L. Simak, was born in Bohemia, in a town near Prague. Son of a butcher (though related to noblemen who had seen better days) he came to work as a hired hand on the Wiseman farm when he emigrated to America where he met and married Margaret Wiseman. A year later he secured some nearby acreage, used lumber from the land to build a log house, and gradually cleared a farm for himself.

Every fact seems to indicate that Clifford D. Simak was deprived by his family of all the elements needed to weave the tangled web of neuroses which are the birthright of many an author. "If you have read Bob Ruark's *The Old Man and the Boy*—well, that was my boyhood, too," Simak recalls. "We hunted and fished, we ran coons at night, we had a long string of noble squirrel and coon dogs. I sometimes think that despite the fact my boyhood spanned part of the first and second decades of the twentieth century that I actually lived in what amounted to the tail end of the pioneer days. I swam in the big hole in the creek, I rode toboggans down long hills, I went barefoot in the summer, I got out of bed at four o'clock in the morning during summer vacations to do the morning chores. For four years I rode a horse to high school —the orneriest old gray mare you ever saw, and yet I loved her and she, in her fashion, loved me. Which didn't mean she wouldn't kick me if she had a chance. And before high school, I walked a mile and a half to a country school (one of those schools where the teacher taught everything from first grade through eighth)."

Young Clifford had to toe the line when there was work to be done, but he was permitted to do all the romping he wanted when there wasn't any chore in the offing. Finances were generally tight, but despite problems the family, which included a younger brother, Carson (now in the insurance business), was closely knit and devoted.

Two very simple things set his mind toward journalism and writing. He recalls very vividly watching his mother read a newspaper when he was about five.

"Does the newspaper print all the news from all over the world?" he asked.

"It does," she replied.

"Does it print the truth?"

"It does."

"From that moment on I knew I wanted to be a newspaperman," Simak affirms. "And don't you, dammit, snicker."

A second contributing factor was the old family reading circle so popular years ago. The family would gather around while the mother or father read a book or newspaper. A magic and wonderful world came into view from those readings.

Though he got along well with other boys, Simak did not care for athletics. Academically he did well, standing second in his high school graduating class at Patch Grove, Wisconsin.

A series of diverse jobs followed high school, clustered about a two years' teacher training course, which found him an instructor for the next three years. An attempt to work his way through the University of Wisconsin failed and led to his first newspaper job on the IRON RIVER REPORTER, Iron River, Michigan.

During this period, several other events occurred which were to shape his entire life. An avid reader of Jules Verne, H. G. Wells, and Edgar Rice Burroughs, he picked up a copy of AMAZING STORIES in 1927 and became a regular reader.

A chance meeting with Agnes Kuchenberg at the motion picture theatre in Cassville, Wisconsin, while Simak was teaching there, blossomed into romance and they were married on April 13, 1929. Only weeks earlier Simak had accepted a staff position on the IRON RIVER REPORTER.

Like any newspaperman, he wanted to write and because he liked science fiction he decided that was his natural medium. His first effort, *The Cubes of Ganymede,* was completed and shipped to AMAZING STORIES in early 1931. The magazine's editor, T. O'Conor Sloane, then approaching his eightieth year openly confessing that "Old Man River" was his favorite song, didn't believe in rushing things. He never bothered to tell Simak whether he was going to use the story or not, but two years later the April, 1933, issue of SCIENCE FICTION DIGEST listed *The Cubes of Ganymede* as one of the "Stories Accepted by AMAZING STORIES for Publication." Finally, in 1935, Sloane returned the story as "a bit dated" in view of the changing trends in science fiction. Simak never quite recovered from the incident and the manuscript remains unpublished.

His next attempt was more successful. *World of the Red Sun* found acceptance at Hugo Gernsback's WONDER STORIES and appeared in the December, 1931, issue of that magazine. The time-travel story displayed a clear, stark writing technique. The adventurers into the future encounter a gigantic glass-encased brain which holds the degenerating remnants of mankind in slavery. They destroy it by employing the psychological weapon of derision. Beyond its obvious debt to H. G. Wells in its basic theme and in the concept of the ultimate degeneration of man as a species, *World of the Red Sun* was fundamentally a second derivative science-fiction story, whose framework and filling came from stories in the science-fiction magazines. It was the work of a man steeped in the still-fresh lore of the science-fiction world, who assumed that the reader was familiar enough with the medium to accept on faith imaginative notions that were destined to become literary dogma. It was so at the beginning as it would become more so as the years progressed that a Simak story would possess a background that was a distillation of the work in the medium.

World of the Red Sun was followed quickly by *Mutiny on Mercury* in WONDER STORIES for March, 1932, a minor action story of the revolt of Martian and Selenite workers on Mercury and their eventual defeat at the hands of an earthman wielding a sword dating from the Napoleonic wars.

Though badly overwritten and melodramatic, *The Voice in the Void,* which appeared about the same time in the Spring, 1932, WONDER STORIES QUARTERLY, showed considerable control in handling. The story concerns the desecration of a sacred Martian tomb containing the bones of the Messiah. The fact that the Martian tombs are constructed in the shape of a pyramid provide a clue to the fact that the sacred bones are those of an Earthman. As in *World of the Red Sun,* Simak's obvious familiarity with hundreds of science-fiction stories enabled him to avoid trite situations and close on a note of originality.

Simak experimented by sending his next story, *Hellhounds of the Cosmos,* to ASTOUNDING STORIES. That magazine, then part of the Clayton chain, one of the largest pulp groups in the world, paid 2 cents a word, four times what the other publications could afford, and they paid on acceptance. Published in the June, 1932, issue of ASTOUNDING STORIES, *Hellhounds of the Cosmos* told of a "black horror" out of the fourth dimension. To counter it, a scientist sends ninety-nine men into the fourth dimension, where they occupy a single grotesque body. They succeed in terminating the invasion at the price of remaining for the rest of their lives in the alien world. *Hellhounds of the Cosmos* is worth noting because it is the first story to betray the tendency toward mysticism that frequently sends Simak's science fiction over the ill-defined perimeter of science-fiction fantasy.

Simak's initial cycle of magazine publication ended with *The Asteroid of Gold* in the November, 1932, WONDER STORIES. A space pirate who takes the gold found on an asteroid from two explorers and leaves them there to die is doomed to live the rest of his life as an invalid, his back broken by his victims. Here, as in *Hellhounds of the Cosmos,* Simak draws a sharp line between black and white and brings about sure, grim retribution for the evildoer.

The temporary suspension of ASTOUNDING STORIES early in 1933 left Simak without a paying market for his work. Both WONDER STORIES and AMAZING STORIES, the only other magazines, were skipping months and it seemed likely that any issue might be their last.

Simak wrote one more piece of science fiction, literally for the love of it, since as far as he was concerned there was no market. "Had there been a market," he asserts, "the story would never have been written, for I would have slanted for that market." In that story, a time machine carries two earthmen to the laboratory of "a cone of light" that created our universe as an experiment. Three other otherwordly beings, by coincidence, also arrive on the scene. Together they act to prevent "The Creator" from destroying his achievement.

Shortly upon completing *The Creator,* Simak received from a science-fiction fan, William H. Crawford, notification of the publication of a "literary" science fiction magazine which solicited stories and offered a lifetime subscription as payment. Simak let Crawford have the story out of sheer admiration for any man with guts enough to try a new science-fiction magazine. *The Creator,* as published in the

March-April, 1935, MARVEL TALES was probably read by only a few hundred readers, yet, by letter, by word of mouth, and through comments in fan magazines, the word got around that Clifford D. Simak had written a "classic," a daring story that defied the taboos of newsstand magazines. While there are certainly crudities in *The Creator,* many polished modern writers would gladly exchange some of their stylistic sheen for the enthusiasm, excitement, and wonder of mysteries yet to be explored imparted by that early tale.

Simak still had the itch to write and tried a few things outside the science-fiction field, but felt they had come off too poorly to submit. Despite the economic pall of the depression years, he managed to keep working. His reporter's job on the IRON RIVER REPORTER grew into the editorship, but he left in August, 1932, to become editor of the SPENCER REPORTER in Spencer, Iowa. In July, 1934, he shifted again to the editorship of the DICKINSON PRESS, Dickinson, North Dakota.

The purchase of the SPENCER REPORTER by the McGiffin Newspaper Company of Kansas, a much larger organization, convinced him that it offered a better future and he returned there in April, 1935, in time to help convert the paper from a semiweekly to a daily. Pleased with his work, the company made him an editorial trouble-shooter, transferring him to Excelsior Springs, Missouri, where he worked on the EXCELSIOR STANDARD, then to the editorship of their Worthington, Minnesota, paper, and finally to the BRAINERD DISPATCH in Brainerd, Minnesota.

Though his outside writing activity had ceased, Simak continued intermittent reading of science fiction, without too much enthusiasm, until he learned that John W. Campbell, Jr., had been named editor of the revived ASTOUNDING STORIES in late 1937.

"I can write for Campbell," he told his wife, Kay. "He won't be satisfied with the kind of stuff that is being written. He'll want something new." There is the possibility, he now admits, that if Campbell had not been named editor of

ASTOUNDING STORIES, he might never have written science fiction again.

His first submission was *Rule 18,* a novelette of the annual football rivalry between Mars and Earth and how Earth goes back in time to assemble a team of all-time all stars to defeat the Martians: an off-beat story, certainly, in its use of scientific invention for influencing a sports event instead of the usual business of saving the world from disaster. Campbell enthusiastic, was sure he had discovered an outstanding new talent. He was a little chagrined to learn that Simak had written for ASTOUNDING STORIES almost six years earlier. *Rule 18,* which appeared in the July, 1938, issue, while popular, rated only fourth in the issue in the readers' estimate.

Nevertheless, Campbell gave prominent advance notice to Simak's *Hunger Death* in the October issue, a story dealing with the problems of Iowa farmers resettled on Venus, who have had that planet misrepresented to them but are saved from economic disaster when they discover growing on their land a plant which can cure an ancient Martian plague. This story is important, for it finds Simak writing of people he knows. Second only in frequency to the farmer in Simak tales is the heroic newspaper reporter.

Reunion on Ganymede, Simak's next, was featured on the cover of the November, 1938, number. Dealing with a planned anniversary get-together of veterans of a war between Earth and Mars, the story finds two members of opposing forces thrown into a situation where they reconcile their grievances. It was not an outstanding production, but it led the issue in reader approbation.

The themes of the three stories—a football game of the future, Iowa farmers on Venus, and an old war veteran going to a reunion on Ganymede—represented a major move in the direction of naturalness in science fiction. Simak was exploring territory that would eventually produce pay dirt.

The Loot of Time, published in THRILLING WONDER STORIES for December, 1938, was more traditional describing the sentimental attachment that springs up between a group of time travelers and a Neanderthal man who inadvertently gets caught up by future science.

In giving readers a new type of story, should an editor dispense with the old? Campbell felt that while change was inevitable, there was still room for what he called the "power" story and what has been termed by others the "superscience" or "thought variant" tale, something along the lines of Edward E. Smith's stories, in which entire universes are in the balance, where space and time are tools in the hands of advanced science.

At Campbell's request, Simak wrote *Cosmic Engineers,* which ran in three parts beginning in the February, 1939, issue of ASTOUNDING SCIENCE-FICTION. *Cosmic Engineers* employed epic ideas, including a civilization of robots who were guardians of the universe, a girl scientist in suspended animation for a thousand years (but improving her mind all the time), another universe in collision with ours, a council of great intellects of many worlds and dimensions brought together to cope with the problem and time travel: a novel with enough thrills for five sequels. Nevertheless, Simak considered the effort a failure. He had hoped to blend some of the ground-roots feel of ordinary people into the work but found that "you had to be grandiose in spite of yourself."

Read uncritically, *Cosmic Engineers* is a much more exciting reading experience than the author would lead one to believe. It does not bear close examination, however; there are too many loose ends, but it is reminiscent, in parts, of *The Creator,* even to a godlike manipulator who is senile and insane. This same "god" is the collective absorption of an entire race into a single mind, bearing some resemblance to Olaf Stapledon's "Cosmic Mind."

It is worthy of special note that, like Asimov, Simak acknowledges that an important influence on his work was Nat Schachner. Schachner, a lawyer and very prolific science-fiction writer of the 1930's, was a seemingly endless fount of ideas. His adept handling of the human element lifted him a cut above many of his contemporaries. He eventually became an outstanding writer of history, particularly acclaimed for his biographies of Alexander Hamilton and Thomas Jefferson.

Following *Cosmic Engineers,* Simak decided to embark on a new fictional project—a picture of each of the planets as science knows them today. The first in this series was *Hermit of Mars* (ASTOUNDING SCIENCE-FICTION, June, 1939), a cover story involving the efforts of an earth scientist to transform his flesh-and-blood body into one of pure force, like those possessed by the Martians, but the series was held in abeyance for the next nine months because Simak, feeling that he was at a dead end with the McGiffin Company, had resigned and gone to work on the copy desk of the MINNEAPOLIS STAR. As far as his newspaper career was concerned, he had found his niche. He soon would become chief of the copy desk.

His first story after the change of jobs was also one of his most successful. *Rim of the Deep* (ASTOUNDING SCIENCE-FICTION May, 1940) was an early attempt to deal with the exploitation of the sea bottom and the day when population pressures would force men to live beneath the waves. The novelty of the notion was not lost on readers but it has been infrequently picked up by other writers, the most notable subsequent works in this vein being *Fury* by Henry Kuttner and *The Deep Range* by Arthur C. Clarke.

Clerical Error (August, 1940, ASTOUNDING SCIENCE-FICTION) was the second in his "planets" series, dealing dramatically with conditions on Jupiter; *Masquerade* (ASTOUNDING SCIENCE-FICTION, March, 1941) was about a doctor who discovered crystals of immortality on Mercury. After *Tools* (ASTOUNDING SCIENCE-FICTION, July, 1942), concerning a radioactive gaseous life form on Venus, he dropped the series as a bad idea.

Simak wrote other solidly competent stories during this period, but the sad part about becoming a literary craftsman is that if a writer is really good people are seldom aware of his growing skill. In *Hunch,* in the July, 1943, ASTOUNDING SCIENCE-FICTION, he used his much-imitated technique of permitting the principal character to think to himself for the readers' benefit. *Hunch* brings into being "Sanctuary," an organization that helps rehabilitate or offer peace of mind to those who have mentally broken under the pressures of advanced civilization, offering a haven when all else fails.

> Sanctuary! Something the race had leaned upon, had counted upon, the assurance of a cure, a refuge from the mental mania that ranged up and down the worlds.
>
> Something that was almost God. Something that was the people's friend—a steadying hand in the darkness. It was something that was there, always would be there, a shining light in a troubled world, a comforter, something that would never change, something one could tie to.
>
> And now?
>
> Kemp shuddered at the thought.
>
> One word and he could bring all that structure tumbling down about their ears. With one blow he could take away their faith and their assurance. With one breath he could blow Sanctuary into a flimsy house of cards.

It was a newspaperman, armed with the tools of literary artistry and well versed in the problems of urban living, who took the very obvious theme of decentralization of cities and focused on its possible impact on the individual. It had been many years since David H. Keller, M.D., had dealt with the effect of then-current trends on the sociological and economic well-being of the average man. Looking back from the vantage of the present, the consensus rates *City* (AS-TOUNDING SCIENCE-FICTION, May, 1944) as a gem. But the theme sounded an unfamiliar note and opinion was divided.

It was the second story in the "City" series, *Huddling Place* (ASTOUNDING SCIENCE-FICTION, July, 1944), that solidified the positive reaction to Simak's effort. The story describes a decitified planet where personal contact had become increasingly abhorrent and culminates in the crushing horror of a man's realization that he is unable to leave his home, even to save the life of a good friend. *Huddling Place* is one of the masterpieces of science fiction, either as a part of the series or as a separate story. A decade later, Isaac Asimov would employ some of its elements in the creation of the remarkable science-fiction detective story, *The Naked Sun.*

Nathaniel, the talking dog of *Census* (ASTOUNDING SCIENCE-FICTION, September, 1944), took the name of Simak's own pet Scottie. When the "City" series was collected by Gnome Press in 1952, the book was dedicated to Nathaniel. From him also sprang the idea of presenting the tales as legends told by intelligent dogs of the future, long after man had disappeared from the planet. In this story, too, are introduced the mutants who bring technology to the ants.

Desertion (ASTOUNDING SCIENCE-FICTION, November, 1944) was written before the other stories and was not originally intended to be one of the series. Included as an afterthought when the book was assembled, to show the beginning of man's transference from human to Jovian bodies, it makes a natural prelude to *Paradise* (ASTOUNDING SCIENCE-FICTION, June, 1946), in which is made the political decision as to whether the bulk of the human race should migrate to Jupiter and convert to Jovian form.

In *Hobbies* (ASTOUNDING SCIENCE FICTION, November, 1946), the dogs and robots are given the opportunity to build a future for themselves without physical or psychological interference from the few remaining men. The Cobblies, strange creatures from another dimension, are introduced.

The near-primitive remnants of man show the robots how to dispose of the threat posed by the Cobblies in *Aesop* (December, 1947), a tale that teeters perilously close to fantasy and mysticism since the Cobblies allegorically assume the role of the ghosts and goblins (imaginary fears) that once plagued mankind.

The point of the entire series was delicately brought home

in *Trouble With Ants* (FANTASTIC ADVENTURES, January, 1951), when Jenkins, the robot guardian of the canine civilization, awakens a man from suspended animation to learn how to stop the ants, whose civilization threatens to end the dogs' reign on the planet. A simple way to end the menace, offered by the man, is rejected because it will mean killing. There has been no killing, even of fleas, for five thousand years, and the robots and dogs prefer to be dispossessed rather than resort to it again.

"The series was written in a revulsion against mass killing and as a protest against war," states Simak. "The series was also written as a sort of wish fulfillment. It was the creation of a world I thought there ought to be. It was filled with the gentleness and the kindness and the courage that I thought were needed in the world. And it was nostalgic because I was nostalgic for the old world we had lost and the world that would never be again—the world that had been wiped out on that day that a man with an umbrella came back to London and told the people there would be a thousand years of peace. I made the dogs and robots the kind of people I would like to live with. And the vital point is this: That they must be dogs or robots, because people were not that kind of folks."

From 1942 to 1945, science fiction was but a small part of Simak's fictional production. A larger portion of his spare-time efforts went into air war and western stories, particularly for Leo Margulies and Thrilling Publications. The tales were so formularized that Simak simply couldn't continue writing them and live with himself, so he dropped them and returned to science fiction.

Eighteen years after his marriage, in 1947, a first child, Scott, was born, and a second, Shelley, in 1951. Simak was promoted to news editor of the MINNEAPOLIS STAR in 1949, in which position he was responsible for the entire news content of that paper. When space and atomics became more important, he was put on special assignment, developing a science news program for the STAR and its companion paper, the TRIBUNE. In 1959 he began writing a weekly science column called "Tomorrow's World," which was received with enthusiasm.

Sitting as pivot man on the news desk of one of the nation's leading papers gave Simak a broad view of the world. The additions to his family added the humanity to temper his outlook on world events.

These elements combined in *Eternity Lost*, a novelette in the July, 1949, ASTOUNDING SCIENCE FICTION in which a senator of the future plays politics with the techniques of longevity. The story has a maturity of viewpoint and such consummate literary craftsmanship that it stands with the best, in or out of science fiction.

Horace L. Gold, then planning the new magazine GALAXY SCIENCE-FICTION, had written Simak asking to see something from him, just as the finishing touches were being put on the novel *Time Quarry*. Serialization began in the first issue, October, 1950, of GALAXY and played an important part in establishing the magazine.

The novel, an underrated masterpiece, crackles with a spectacular display of writing techniques that impel the reader through as imaginative a complex of events as ever has been presented in science fiction. Simak is as convincing as he is brilliant.

A man crashes on a world of formless intelligences, who restore him to life and invest in him the secret that they inhabit as hosts every creeping, crawling, flying life form that lives in the universe; as a race, theirs is the symbiotic destiny, to light the spark that eventually may lead to intelligence.

"Nothing walks alone" is the message they give him, which he includes in a book which becomes the bible of a new religion. It particularly fascinates the androids, who feel that this common denominator makes them the spiritual equals of men.

The efforts of future man to influence the writing of this book through altering events of the past carries the reader back to the farm where Simak was raised. The author's hob-

bies, his likes and dislikes, including touches from famous
science-fiction works, as well as a grizzled image of himself in old age, invest the work with a richness of content
that makes it completely satisfying.

Published as *Time and Again* by Simon & Schuster in
1951, the book did not receive the attention it deserved. This
relative neglect was compensated for by the granting of the
International Fantasy Award to *City* as the best fantasy
volume published during 1952.

After that Simak became the leading exponent of morality
among modern science-fiction writers, one of the rare few
who, while sensitive to the terrible pressures of the time, do
not succumb to despair.

His fantastic creations became symbols to illuminate
human problems. As far back as *Hunch,* the "sanctuary" al-
legorized the dependence of the masses on the crutch of
religion; *Eternity Lost,* in which a politician, making capital
of discoveries in longevity, literally loses his immortal soul,
makes its point figuratively; *Courtesy* (ASTOUNDING SCIENCE
FICTION, August, 1951) underscores the thin line between
dignity and arrogance; *How-2* (GALAXY SCIENCE FICTION,
November, 1954) had the dubious honor of being converted
into a gadgeted musical which didn't quite make it on Broadway, but its finale about the granting of civil rights to robots
could be taken as Simak's thoughtful approach to race
relations.

Like Olaf Stapledon, with whom he seems in philosophical
accord, Simak represents himself in his fiction as an agnostic,
searching the limits of imagination for an answer to the riddle of human life. His work reveals a tendency to depart into
mysticism, an indication of a fundamental religiosity which
Stapledon openly admitted at the very end of his life. The
difference is that Simak has not boxed himself in emotionally by raging at the inability of his imagination to answer
impossibilities.

Carefully exploring the richness of human behavior in
terms of the encounter with the alien and the unforeseen

classics of science fiction continue to come from Simak's typewriter. *A Death in the House,* published in GALAXY MAGAZINE (October, 1959), belongs in this category, delineating the kindness of an old farmer to a dying creature from another world; it is destined to be reprinted often.

One result has been that many new writers, notable among them Chad Oliver, have discovered and learned from the method of Clifford Simak. Yet the truth is that Clifford D. Simak, regardless of his age, works so hard both in technique and substance at the art of being a science-fiction writer that he represents a brighter prospect for the future than any newcomer in sight.

16

FRITZ LEIBER

The quotation from St. Matthew, "A prophet is not without honour, save in his own country, and in his own house," frequently is a truism when applied to a man of unusual ability or attainment. With Fritz Leiber, Jr., the reverse seems to be the truth. His unique talents have been recognized by the cognoscenti of the science-fiction and fantasy world but a wider renown has been painstakingly slow in coming.

From his fellow readers and authors, Fritz Leiber has the following to show:

Guest of Honor at the Ninth World Science Fiction Convention in New Orleans September 1-3, 1951.

A Hugo for the best science-fiction novel of 1958, *The Big Time,* serialized in the March and April, 1958, issues of GALAXY SCIENCE FICTION.

An entire issue of FANTASTIC SCIENCE FICTION STORIES, November, 1959, devoted to five new stories from his typewriter.

Over 40 short stories included in more than 50 anthologies.

As if this were not enough, Fritz Leiber, Jr., for decades now, has been regarded as the leading proponent and high priest of a movement to modernize, explain "logically" or "scientifically," all the dark forms and various accouterments of witchcraft and superstition that have so dishonorably been passed down by mankind from generation to generation and that now usually evoke laughter rather than horror in a world unsympathetic to their impotence. The antithesis of the late Pope John the Good, Leiber has sought to assemble a conclave of professional purveyors of literary evil to get them to update their paraphernalia and make it more palatable to the doubting body of disbelievers. Failing in that, he has advocated and demonstrated techniques for the symbiotic relationship of witches, familiars, devils, vampires, and haunted houses with science fiction.

"If you can't lick 'em, join 'em" has been his motto, and he demonstrated the techniques in *Gather, Darkness!* a novel serialized in the May, June, and July, 1943, issues of AS-TOUNDING SCIENCE-FICTION, in which the devil's advocates are the good guys and the priests and angels the bad guys in the fallen world of some postwar future.

What, if anything, the novel did for the declining prestige of the minions of blackness is open to discussion, but that Leiber's adroit and resourceful manipulation of these elements created his first major reputation is not open to debate.

Fritz Leiber, Jr.'s, very Germanic name, his fair hair, and his soaring height (in excess of 6 feet, 4 inches) frequently lead people meeting him for the first time to expect an accent. Actually, his father was born in Chicago and his grandfather, who left Germany after the revolutions of 1848, was a captain for the Union during the American Civil War and worked as a civil servant for the state of Illinois thereafter.

The years from Fritz Leiber, Jr.'s, birth, December 24, 1910, in Chicago, until he was old enough to enter school, were by no means normal ones. His father was an actor, destined to gain a national reputation as an interpreter of Shakespeare. His mother, Virginia Bronson, of British parentage, had studied acting and met the elder Fritz Leiber during a summer tour with Robert B. Mantell's Shakespearean Company, of which he was the leading man. His early years the child spent traveling with his mother and father, living at hotels and boarding houses, with "memories redolent of grease paint, spirit gum, curling colored gelatins of flood- and spot-lights; and of actors and actresses; wonder-world in reminiscence."

Fritz Leiber, Sr., set quite a reputation for Fritz, Jr., to live up to. A publicized athlete in high school, he won a citywide oratorical contest, which prompted him to try acting. He gained a local reputation with the People's Stock Company on Chicago's West Side and played Shakespeare for the first time with Britain's Ben Greet's Company when it toured the United States and Canada. Then he shifted to Mantell's for ten years. The boards were not his only medium, for he played Caesar opposite Theda Bara in the 1917 silent film production of *Cleopatra* and Solomon in *Queen of Sheba* starring Betty Blythe. He organized his own Shakespearean Repertory in 1920 and toured the country with it until 1935. From then until his death in 1949 he freelanced in motion pictures.

The closest thing to a permanent home that young Fritz enjoyed during his youthful years was the house his father built in Atlantic Highlands, New Jersey (because Robert Mantell lived there), where the family spent the three summer months together (providing there was no hot-months tour). During the school year, until the third grade, he lived with his maternal grandmother in Pontiac, Michigan, but then the death of her husband caused her to move to Chicago. There Fritz lived with his father's two sisters, Dora and Marie. Quiet and reserved, Fritz made few friends in school and those he did make were as lonely and introverted as himself. Though carefully protected during the school year by his aunts, Fritz was given carte blanche during the three months he spent with his parents. Discipline was actually unnecessary, since the boy rarely stepped out of line, and when he did a hurt look was all the admonishment required.

A literary leaning was induced in Fritz by his father, who, in addition to copious Shakespeare, read aloud liberally from Dickens and Conrad, as well as exercising his predilection for detective stories. Extraordinarily sensitive, Fritz was at times scared of his own shadow. A stage production of *The Cat and the Canary* shook him up badly: "I saw green hands coming out of the walls for months afterward." He was fearfully afraid of the dark and, during the formative years, the supernatural was a very real thing to him, a possible explanation of his later attempts to rationalize it in his fiction.

Taught chess by actor Alexander André of his father's company, Fritz became extremely proficient at it in high school, but engaged in no general sports except tennis. Eventually he was to win the Santa Monica open chess championship in 1958 and would use the game as the basis of at least three stories, most notable being *The 64-Square Madhouse* (IF, May, 1964), dealing with a computer entering a grandmaster tournament. Leiber considers chess a "dangerous game" because a preoccupation with it distinctly interfered with his literary creativity, and he regards it as a vice to be indulged in only with moderation.

His initial writing efforts in the weird and fantasy line were the result of a lack of confidence. He did not feel he could really fabricate a strong science-fiction effort and surmised that the fantasy field would be an easier area for the beginner, though he liked science fiction at least as much.

Beyond the classics of Jules Verne and H. G. Wells, and most especially Edgar Rice Burroughs, Fritz Leiber, Jr., was religiously devoted to AMAZING STORIES, which he began reading with its first (April, 1926) number, and stayed with for the next four years. He never read WEIRD TALES regularly, despite his admiration for a good supernatural story, rationalization always interfering.

During the years he was reading AMAZING STORIES, he entered the University of Chicago, majoring in psychology. He graduated in 1932 with honors, with the degree of Ph.B (Bachelor of Philosophy). At the back of his mind had always been the notion of continuing in the footsteps of his father as Fritz Leiber II. He had participated in dramatics in high school, and he both acted in and directed several plays for The University of Chicago Dramatic Association, including Ibsen's *Rosmersholm*. He also became a skillful fencer. More important, through a mutual friend he met Harry Otto Fischer of Louisville, who had aspirations as a writer, puppeteer, and ballet dancer, as well as a common interest in chess and fencing, science fiction and fantasy. Fischer would ultimately settle for the practical if unromantic job of designing corrugated cartons, but not until he had implanted the kernel of an idea which would eventually burgeon in Leiber's literary career.

In a lengthy correspondence, Fischer exchanged with Leiber essays, poems, and short stretches of fiction. The two vied with one another to present the most imaginative and original literary fare and one day Fritz received a letter containing a fragment which opened: "For all do fear the one known as the Grey Mouser. He walks with swagger 'mongst the bravos, though he's but the stature of a child. . . ." There, too, was the Grey Mouser's meeting with Fafhrd, the seven-foot giant from the north, as well as the background of a never-never era that somehow reminded the reader of familiar periods in medieval history. Of this, of course, more later.

Graduating from college in the depth of the Depression, Leiber was persuaded by the Rev. Ernest W. Mandeville, Episcopal minister of Middleton, New Jersey, that his oratorical and acting gifts might prove effective in saving souls. The Rev. Mandeville, who edited *The Churchman,* also ran an employment office for clergymen in New York. He enrolled Leiber in the General Theological Seminary, located between Greenwich Village and Hell's Kitchen in Manhattan, got him quickly christened and confirmed, and sent him out as lay reader and minister to churches in Atlantic Highlands and Highlands, New Jersey, which had no resident religious leader.

Lacking any deep conviction, Leiber thought he could rationalize his performance as "social service," but after five months found out that it didn't jibe with his conscience or temperament. He ended the experiment, but the experience was to shape his cynical attitude as well as provide background for *Gather, Darkness!*

Financed partly by a scholarship he had won during his last year at the University of Chicago, Leiber returned to that school for a graduate course in philosophy in the fall of 1933. He majored in speculative metaphysics and comparative religion. At the same time he took to hobnobbing with radicals, testing his capacity for drink, and generally unbottling his long-held repressions.

He joined his father's road company in 1934. From his mother's side of the family he assumed Francis Lathrop as a stage name and played Edgar in *King Lear* and Malcom in *Macbeth*. "This was depression nadir," Leiber recalls. "We played theaters that hadn't had their marquees lit up for years—there were bats in one, fine for *Macbeth*, not so hot for *The Merchant of Venice*." The tour closed for good in Tucson. Fritz Leiber, Sr.'s, days as a leading man were over. He took his wife to Los Angeles and reestablished himself, with moderate success, as a character actor in Hollywood.

While on tour Fritz, Jr., had sold some children's stories to THE CHURCHMAN, but he had not completely given up his idea of an acting career. Subsidized by his father, he half-heartedly attempted to make his way through the Hollywood jungle, obtaining one small part in *Camille*, which starred Robert Taylor and Greta Garbo, and a tiny bit in Errol Flynn's *The Great Garrick*, which "ended on the cutting room floor."

Disillusioned, he made an extended trip back to Chicago

and found among his former associates a strange assortment of party-line Communists, Trotskyites, and one lone Nazi. The manner in which these seemingly disparate extremists feuded in public and socialized in private made a lasting impression on him, causing him to look upon the motives of those who attempted to promulgate political ideologies with as jaundiced an eye as he turned on the "idealism" of clergymen.

While at the University of Chicago he had made the acquaintance of Jonquil Stephens, an English-born coed who possessed a common interest in weird and supernatural fiction, poetry, and English literature. There similarity ended, for Jonquil Stephens was under five feet in height and the contrast with the lofty elevation of Leiber verged on absurdity. But opposites, so the old saw goes, attract, and the two were married on January 16, 1936.

One more try at Hollywood, then they both returned despairingly to Chicago, where Fritz managed to obtain an editorial job with Consolidated Book Publishers, revising material for *The Standard American Encyclopedia* and *The University of Knowledge*. One son, Justin, born July 8, 1938, was eventually to achieve his father's initial objective of obtaining a Ph.D. and teaching philosophy.

Before his brief move to Hollywood, Leiber had made a do-or-die attempt at professional writing. A couple of short stories proved unsalable at the time (one of these may have been *Psychosis from Space,* published in "Department of Lost Stories," SATELLITE SCIENCE FICTION, April, 1959, based on Leiber's psychology courses). A "lost race" novel of Yucatan petered out before it had worked up a good head of steam. Finally, running across the first 10,000 words of a Grey Mouser and Fafhrd novel sent to him by Henry Otto Fischer in 1936 (which he completed as *Lords of Quarmall* in 1963, 34,000 words in all, with Fischer's portion intact, for publication in FANTASTIC, January and February, 1964), he decided to use those characters himself in a story titled *Adept's Gambit.*

The story, along with some poems, he submitted to H. P. Lovecraft for criticism, and the response was favorable. Lovecraft even sent the story on to Robert Bloch and Henry Kuttner. When Bloch visited Los Angeles in 1937, Henry Kuttner introduced him to Fritz Leiber, Jr., in what was the beginning of a lasting friendship.

Adept's Gambit did not sell then, yet this adult fairy tale, built around the characters of The Grey Mouser (personifying Harry Fischer) and the seven-food sword-wielding giant Fafhrd (the romantic incarnation of Fritz Leiber, Jr.), is beyond question not only the first but the best of the entire series Leiber was to write about these characters. It can be said of *Adept's Gambit,* as C. S. Lewis said of J. R. R. Tolkien's *The Fellowship of the Ring,* that here is a story ". . . good beyond hope." From the moment that the spell is cast upon Fahfrd that temporarily changes every woman into a pig the instant he kisses her; on to the Grey Mouser's consultation with the seven-eyed Ningauble, gossiper with the Gods, about what to do about it; through the supernatural sword battle with Anara; to the finale, in which the adept turned to a mouse contemplatively evaluates its chances of killing a bear cub, the story is a delight to read.

Leiber's sense of pace, rich background detail, taut battle scenes, fine characterization, fascinating supernatural elements, together with his extraordinary talent for weaving tasteful humor throughout the entire fabric of his story — a talent unsurpassed by any living fantasy writer today — make this a classic fantasy. Yet it did not see publication until Arkham House did a Fritz Leiber, Jr., collection, *Night's Black Agents,* in 1947 nearly ten years after it was written.

A subsequent Grey Mouser and Fafhrd story written in 1939 broke the professional barriers for Leiber. It was *Two Sought Adventure* (the title story of a collection of Grey Mouser tales issued by Gnome Press in 1957) and John Campbell bought it for his new magazine UNKNOWN, publishing it in the August, 1939, issue. The emphasis is on the physical prowess of the two protagonists as they defeat a small army to obtain jewels from a tower; the jewels turn out to be a catalyst for an unearthly "brain," which is capable of making the tower lay about it with the swiftness of a striking snake and the impact of a crashing plane.

This was followed by *Bleak Shore, The Howling Tower, The Sunken Land,* and *Thieves House* in the same magazine. While each contains the popular heroic elements of the sword-and-sorcery fantasy made so popular by Robert E. Howard's Conan stories, leavened with the masterful interplay of humor characteristic of Leiber, none of them is of the literary magnitude of *Adept's Gambit.*

Leiber had written all of the Grey Mouser stories for WEIRD TALES, which magazine had consistently rejected them. Campbell bought them for UNKNOWN, but always with the complaint: "These are better suited for WEIRD TALES."

Leiber had gotten into WEIRD TALES with *The Automatic Pistol* (May, 1940), about a gun that spontaneously did its own killing. A much more important story, *Smoke Ghost,* published in UNKNOWN for October, 1941, may well have been submitted to WEIRD TALES first. "Have you ever thought of what a ghost of our day would look like?" the main character asks. "I don't mean that traditional kind of ghost. I mean a ghost from the world today, with the soot of the factories in its face and the pounding of machinery in its soul . . . . It would grow out of the real world. It would reflect all the tangled, sordid, vicious things. All the loose ends. And it would be very grimy. I don't think it would seem white or wispy or favor graveyards. It wouldn't moan. But it would mutter unintelligibly, and twitch at your sleeve. Like a sick, surly ape."

The same thought was pursued in *The Hound* (WEIRD TALES, November, 1942): "The supernatural beings of a modern city? . . . Sure, they'd be different from the ghosts of yesterday. Each culture creates its own demons. Look, the Middle Ages built cathedrals, and pretty soon there were little gray shapes gliding around at night to talk with the gargoyles.

Same thing ought to happen to us, with our skyscrapers and factories." Leiber tried to give his idea of what a modern ghost would be like in each of these stories. His concepts were prosaic. In *Smoke Ghost,* it was essentially demoniac possession in black face; in *The Hound,* he resurrected the werewolf with but little change. Nevertheless, the idea was a good one.

Leiber abandoned this tack and, adopting traditional potions, spells, charms, incantations, attempted to show how they would be utilized in a modern setting. His background was drawn from the campus of Occidental College, Eagle Rock, Los Angeles, where his father had gotten him a job as instructor in speech, acting, and dramatics, beginning with the September, 1941, semester. Though moderately successful at teaching, he quit in the summer of 1942, got a house in Santa Monica Canyon, and sat down to freelance, first writing *Conjure Wife,* which appeared as a complete novel in April, 1943, UNKNOWN WORLDS. There was a much delayed reaction, but the novel would eventually prove a substantial success.

Dealing with a young wife who *knows* there is witchcraft being practiced on a university campus and employs elaborate supernatural precautions to protect her doubting husband, the story is great fun. Leiber's skill at dialogue is notable, his humorous notes polished and clever without descending to farce. His story is effective without recourse to any of the stock gothic devices. Ten years later, the novel went into hard covers under the aegis of Twayne Publishers. A television adaptation on "Moment of Fear" over NBC in 1960 was an artistic triumph, one of the finest fantasy hours ever shown on television. A film released by American International in 1963, using A. Merritt's old title *Burn Witch Burn,* starred Janet Blair and Peter Wyngarde and changed the setting to England, altered the characteristics of some of the lead characters, and proved to be much inferior to the television production.

Leiber had no way of knowing how successful that story

would eventually be. For the moment, its sale effectively but prosaically merely helped to pay the rent. He decided to abandon fantasy and make a more concerted effort to succeed in science fiction.

The only previously published science fiction of Leiber's was a long novelette titled *They Never Come Back* (FUTURE FICTION, August, 1941), whose major merit was in the notion that gravitational stresses as well as radio waves travel in circumscribed channels or "warps" and that all spaceships would have to route themselves accordingly, not only to utilize the concentrated power traveling along the "warp" but to maintain radio communication. Now Leiber sent Campbell several ideas for a science-fiction novel, including a variation on Robert Heinlein's *Sixth Column,* in which the military sets up a religion for the purpose of overthrowing America's Asiatic conquerors. "Oh, boy," Leiber said to himself, "let those scientists or military men set up a fine religion and seize power and they'll never let it go, they'll hang on to that power."

In the outline for *Gather, Darkness!* Leiber suggested an underground using witchcraft and holding up Satan as its idol to overthrow the despotic scientific religion. Campbell told him to go ahead with it. Leiber was far from the first to attempt to bend the supernatural to science fiction. H. P. Lovecraft had done it with singular effectiveness, inventing an entire new mythos in the process. In more recent science fiction, Jack Williamson attempted to explain the supernatural genetically in *Darker Than You Think* (UNKNOWN, December, 1940) and Heinlein used high-flying broomsticks in *Waldo* (ASTOUNDING SCIENCE-FICTION, August, 1942).

Perhaps Leiber was the better merchandiser of such ideas, possibly he was convincing where the others were not, but whatever the reason, and erroneously or not, in the minds of readers he came to be regarded as *the* transitional author who tied well-known elements of superstition to science in fiction.

Before the appearance of *Gather, Darkness!* Leiber was

regarded as an important writer. That one story placed him among the "big names." Yet, its techniques and stylistic flow are clearly devices taken from Edgar Rice Burroughs; the author keeps two or more situations going simultaneously, carrying them along in alternating chapters. The chase scene in which the hero, Jarles, is rescued from the mob by the old "witch" Mother Jujy is obviously indebted to A. E. van Vogt's treatment in *Slan,* where Jommy Cross is saved from the mob by Granny. The personality changer used on Jarles is reminiscent of Stanley G. Weinbaum's "attitudinizer" in *Point of View.* From Leiber's own acrobatic tower in *Two Sought Adventure* comes the notion of the flexible "haunted" house. But these were merely ingredients that Leiber obtained for the literary stew; the spice he added to flavor it no one could lend him. There is the satire, pitiless in its excoriation of religion, satire deriving from Leiber's own personal observations. There is the cynicism regarding the scientists' ability to do any better than the politicians. There is the humor, mature, not light, not raucous, blending into the story. And there is the gift for characterization, effectively evidenced in Brother Chulian, Jarles, Mother Jujy, and the Familiar.

This "triumph" was followed by a short story, *The Mutant's Brother,* which contains the seeds of a powerful emotional situation that no author has yet properly developed in science fiction. Two brothers, both mutants with special mental powers, come into conflict as one, a proponent of good, hunts down and then destroys the other, who is using his superior attributes for evil.

Pacifism obsessed Leiber following Pearl Harbor. The "witchcraft" movement in *Gather, Darkness!* reflected this, as did *Taboo* (ANALOG SCIENCE FACT & FICTION, February, 1963) in which pacifists maintain a sanctuary for involuntary expatriates of a warring world, as well as *Sanity* (ASTOUNDING SCIENCE-FICTION, April, 1944) where the entire population is manical and the "sane" leader is led off to the booby hatch because he does not conform to the norm, which is nonconformity. The preoccupation with pacifism so interfered with his writing that during the latter part of 1943 and early 1944 he decided he might as well take a job as an inspector at Douglas Aircraft in Santa Monica because it might help him "to stay out of the army."

After agonizing mental reappraisal, he gradually came to the conclusion that right and reason had been on the side of the anti-fascist forces. This mental reconciliation temporarily enabled him to write and the results were auspicious. *Wanted — An Enemy* (ASTOUNDING SCIENCE-FICTION, February, 1945) was a brilliant little story. A pacifist, with special scientific powers, exhorts the Martians to make a token attack on Earth so that humans will band together against the common menace and thereby end war. The Martians, who had their fill of war thousands of years earlier, had made a peace pact with the Venusians promising to confine themselves to their own planet. Convinced that the earthmen are potentially dangerous, the Martians vow to sterilize this planet. Appalled at his excessive success, the pacifist hies off to Venus to tell them the Martians are about to break their ancient pact. When the Venusian leader eyed him wonderingly and asked: "What are you?" a sudden surge of woeful honesty compelled Mr. Whitlow to reply. *"I suppose . . . I suppose you'd call me a warmonger."*

Only slightly less successful than *Gather, Darkness!* was *Destiny Times Three* (ASTOUNDING SCIENCE-FICTION, March-April, 1945) to which *Business of Killing* (ASTOUNDING SCIENCE-FICTION, September, 1944), a short story of the contemplated exploitation of simultaneous worlds, was a prelude. A machine built by an Olaf Stapledonian intelligence accidentally fragments the time stream of our planet into a number of "worlds of if," three of which, at least, have duplicated individuals on them leading different lives. One, an Orwellian world, decides to take over the original earth. The interplay of three alternate situations is again handled in the Edgar Rice Burroughs technique. Nightmares are explained as contacts with our duplicates on alternate worlds,

as are many of our superstitions. Influences of H. P. Lovecraft are stronger here than in any other major Leiber story.
Fundamentally, the novel is a fantastic allegory, splendidly
readable, with fast-moving action, and thoroughly polished.

When the war ended, Leiber returned to Chicago, where
he was tipped off that there would be an associate editor's
position on SCIENCE DIGEST by a friend, George Mann, whose
resignation was creating the opening. The magazine, published by the owners of POPULAR MECHANICS, required many
of the same skills that Leiber had employed in his encyclopedia work for Consolidated. The position led nowhere, but
Leiber was to retain it through to 1956, the longest stint
under a single employer of his lifetime. Writing ceased; the
first phase of his writing career had ended.

Early in 1949 Leiber began publishing an amateur mimeographed publication titled NEW PURPOSES as a creative out-
let. Among the contributors were his good friends Henry
Kuttner, Robert Bloch, and George Mann. The magazine
petered out after sixteen issues, but filling its pages had
started Leiber writing again. It contained chapters of what
eventually would become his book *The Green Millennium*
(Abelard Press, 1953). This novel was a discomfiting tale
of government in league with crime with the populace quieted
by sex diversions. Fred Pohl became his agent, sold a few
"dogs," and then was solicited by Campbell for *The Lion
and the Lamb* (ASTOUNDING SCIENCE FICTION, September, 1950). This was Leiber venturing out to the far reaches
of the galaxy, to the "Coalsack" where a group of runaway
colonists, after some hundreds of years, have set up a "primitive" culture, abhorring mechanical devices of all sorts.
Witchcraft and pacifism were strong elements of this smoothly
woven, completely modern novelette. The antimechanics aspect was new for Leiber, but the device of mentally projecting a frightening image was drawn from John W. Campbell's *Invaders of the Infinite* and the moving smoke images
parallel strongly the Dream Makers' illusions in A. Merritt's
The Snake Mother.

Leiber had felt a lifelong dissatisfaction with the sexual patterns of Western culture, holding that unhealthy frustrations contributed to the "sick" aspects of our culture. His personal preference rested with the social mores of The Last Men in Olaf Stapledon's *Last and First Men* (1930), in which men and women live in groups ". . . but in most groups all the members of the male sexes have intercourse with all the members of the female sexes. Thus sex with us is essentially social." He regarded with admiration John Humphrey Noyes' Oneida Community which flourished between 1840 and 1900 and practiced what Stapledon presented as fiction. These ideas were incorporated in a number of his stories beginning with *The Ship Sails at Midnight* (FANTASTIC ADVENTURES, September, 1950) which was derivative of William Sloane's *To Walk the Night;* they were implied in *The Green Millennium,* and most successfully presented in *Nice Girl with Five Husbands* (GALAXY SCIENCE FICTION, April, 1951), in which through a slip in time, a man wanders into an idyllic community of the year 2050 very similar to the Oneida Community.

Leiber's ideas on sex were presented in such impeccable good taste that there was little reaction to them. The opposite was true of *Coming Attraction* (GALAXY SCIENCE FICTION, November, 1951), which in every sense epitomized his second big successful period as a science-fiction writer. *Coming Attraction* introduces a British visitor to post-atomic-war life in New York City, where it is stylish for women to wear masks (since many of their faces were seared by atomic blasts) and where a warped culture has arisen which Leiber artistically unveils with magnificent indirection and almost psychiatric insight to produce one of the masterpieces of short science fiction.

Appointment in Tomorrow (GALAXY SCIENCE FICTION, July, 1952) is, in a sense, a sequel to *Coming Attraction.* Originally titled *Poor Superman,* it tells of a cult which regales a United States that *wants* to be hoodwinked with fraudulent claims for "Maizie," a "thinking machine" that is "solving" the world's difficult problems, and falsities of un-manned space probes which presumably have already made contact with civilized life on Mars. When the promotion man of the movement tries to convert all this humbug into reality, he is effectively stopped. It was just an ordinary sort of story, but *The Moon Is Green* (GALAXY SCIENCE FICTION, April, 1952) fell just a little short of greatness. In it, tender hopes and yearning for beauty of a woman closeted in the lead-lined radioactive world of tomorrow bring sorrow to her husband in a gamble, instinct with tragedy, based on illu-sionary hope.

That Leiber had become the poet of the world of post-atomic war was evident in *A Bad Day for Sales* (GALAXY SCIENCE FICTION, July, 1953) in which he keeps his focus on a vending robot that maintains its selling pitch and its built-in reflexes after the bomb has dropped, an effective variant on *There Will Come Soft Rains* by Ray Bradbury.

That he dropped his writing in 1953 before he solidified this second phase of his writing career was due to lack of psychological stamina. Working on SCIENCE DIGEST by day and writing in the evening and on weekends interfered with his creativity, he said. Instead of trying to reach an accom-modation, he took to drinking heavily, eventually leaving his job in 1956. Then as abruptly he quit drinking.

Some alcoholics have a lost weekend to worry about, but Leiber had nearly four years, irreplaceable years, of writing to account for. He made his comeback with *Time in the Round* (GALAXY SCIENCE FICTION, May, 1957). H. L. Gold, then editor of that magazine, exulted: "Leiber's back and GALAXY's got 'im!" The result was a pleasant story built around tomorrow's theater, which is capable of bringing into being images of the past and future. When some primitive men and dogs unprecedently solidify and threaten the audi-ence, they find themselves frustrated by a child with some mechanical pets.

The winner proved to be *The Big Time,* a two-part serial running in the March and April, 1958, issues of GALAXY

SCIENCE FICTION. This tale is of a war fought by changing the past and the future, and it is told in the vernacular of a party girl who is a hostess of The Place, a timeless night club suspended outside the cosmos. The philosophical upshot is the comprehension by mankind of a higher state of consciousness, and its evolution from time-binding (the unification of events through memory) to possibility binding (making all of what might be part of what is). It gained Fritz Leiber a Hugo as the best science-fiction novel of 1958 and catapulted him right back into the limelight, but then he decided that satire was being overdone and he would try farce. *The Silver Egg-Heads,* originally a novelette, was expanded to novel length for a Ballantine Books paperback. It was written in the broad, raucous tones of a Robert Bloch broadside, intending to spoof writers, agents, publishers, and their associates scientifictionally. It fell with a dull thud when submitted to Gold for GALAXY and eventually appeared in FANTASY AND SCIENCE FICTION, January, 1959. Leiber, a master at tasteful, subtle, balanced humor, was not suited to slapstick.

This seemed to break Leiber's stride. He had started his comeback so auspiciously, now he felt he had to search for other markets. He was welcomed with open arms at FANTASTIC, where an entire issue, November, 1959, was devoted to Leiber stories. The issue went over big and one short story, *The Mind Spider,* involving a danger that terminated the practice of telepathy, was used as the basis of his first short story science-fiction collection by Ace. More significant, the issue led off with his first new Grey Mouser novelette since 1951, *Lean Times in Lankhmar,* and it hit the jackpot of reader approbation. Clubs devoted to the science and sorcery school of fantasy had come into existence and Leiber, through the Grey Mouser, suddenly became the leading literary exponent of that literary form. So popular was he, in fact, that *Scylla's Daughter* (FANTASTIC, May, 1961) was nominated for, but did not win, a Hugo at the 1962 World Science Fiction Convention in Chicago; exactly the same thing happened to *The Unholy Grail* (FANTASTIC, November, 1962) in Washington, D.C., one year later.

Back in Hollywood again, Leiber found the going rough, with FANTASTIC his one steady magazine market, supplemented by Ballantine books, which helped to keep his name alive with a reissue of *Night's Black Agents* in paperback (sans *Adept's Gambit*) and following this with a horror collection, *Shadows with Eyes* (1962).

During 1960 and 1961, to keep food on the table Leiber did four three-month continuities for the Buck Rogers daily strip and Sunday page for the National Newspaper Syndicate. He found the effort of turning out sheer plot and dialogue no more profitable than writing pulp fiction.

When American International purchased *Conjure Wife* for a motion picture with a script written by accomplished fantasy craftsmen Richard Matheson and Charles Beaumont (this was the picture released as *Burn Witch Burn*), Leiber got a boost to his ego but no inflation of the pocketbook. He no longer controlled rights to the work.

Despite his precarious economic status, he decided to gamble the better part of a year on *The Wanderer,* a 120,000-word novel of a lacquered planet which abruptly appears in space alongside the moon, causing earthquakes and tidal disasters on Earth. This was intended to be the definitive world-doom story, told in alternating vignettes of various stratas of society.

Sticking close to grim "realism" has paid off richly in science fiction for Robert A. Heinlein, Arthur C. Clarke, John Wyndham, John Christopher, and various others, and it might have for Leiber, too, but he wouldn't follow the rules. Instead of settling for a single departure from the norm and then throwing the spotlight on human reaction, Leiber has connected the actions of his characters with bizarre extraterrestrial happenings.

The story builds with increasing fascination into a highly advanced epic, conceptually in the vanguard of modern science fiction and to that degree gratifying to the seasoned reader sated with predigested pabulum marketable to the masses by virtue of a self-imposed limit on imagination. The world-doom story, with the focus entirely on the fate and reactions of the "man in the street," has been told with high skill and extraordinary effectiveness for over 150 years. It is debatable if today's practitioners have added much that was not in *The Last Man* by Mary Wollstonecraft Shelley in 1826 or in *Deluge* by S. Fowler Wright nearly a century later (1929). Yet, it is quite possible that in *The Wanderer,* Fritz Leiber has shown that there are ways of writing science fiction so that it can hold both the basic and the advanced audience. In attempting to show the effect of the catastrophe on a dozen or more people concurrently, Leiber's effect becomes unartfully choppy. Nevertheless, though the reader moves bumpily along, he remains interested, never losing track of the disparate variety of characters and situations. As the invading planet is discovered to be a propelled world, inhabited by multitudinous diverse creatures working in harmony; with their revelation of the state of galactic civilization and travel through hyperspace, the story moves into superscience, but this is balanced and even made more acceptable by contrast with more ordinary events on earth and the reactions of the earthmen.

Interest grows as the inhabitants of the invading world attempt to rectify some of the harm they have done, prior to answering to a "police" world which is pursuing them, intent on preventing inadvertent damage to less advanced civilizations. Their makeshift efforts to right some of the wrongs they have done are rejected as insufficient by the pursuing globe and a clash of the two worlds moves them out of our space-time continuum.

The Wanderer is flawed but far from a failure. Had it first been published in hard covers and widely reviewed, it might have made a larger first impression. Amid a flood of paperbacks it was almost lost, but already laudatory bits and pieces are cropping up in science-fiction criticism. It may enjoy a delayed reaction, which could prove decisive in Leiber's career.

While Fritz Leiber has made his mark, his story is in every sense an unfinished one. The Grey Mouser series has established him as the greatest living writer in the sword and sorcery tradition. A pioneer in the attempt to modernize the ancient symbols of terror, he has also gained recognition for spearheading a movement to the lore of fantasy and witchcraft in the body of science fiction. As a stylist he ranks among the finest writers of fantasy today, one possessing rare gifts of characterization and humor. Even as an entertainer he has something to say, taking definite stands on social questions.

Throughout his writing career the "branches of time" theme has fascinated him. In three of his biggest novels, *Destiny Times Three, The Big Time,* and *The Wanderer,* as well as in many shorter works, he has speculated on what might happen if the reel of life could be rewound and played out again. *Destiny Times Three* is much more than the title of one of Leiber's finest stories; it is a symbol of the three separate starts he has made in his writing career, in search of he knows not what.

17

C. L. MOORE

E. Hoffman Price, pulp magazine writer of the 1930's, never tires of telling anecdotes about the remarkable Farnsworth Wright, editor of WEIRD TALES, who either discovered or helped develop a third of today's great names in fantasy fiction. Wright would invariably "dig into his desk, and thrust a manuscript at me," Price recalls. "The accompanying sales talk would have made the hypothetical Man from Mars mistake me for the prospective purchaser, and Farnsworth for the author's agent!

"But the highest peak was reached," Price says "in 1933, when he handed me a manuscript by one C. L. Moore.

"And that did take my breath. 'For Christ's sake, Plato (a nickname for Wright), who is C. L. Moore? He, she, or it is colossal!' This, of all times, was when my enthusiasm equaled Farnsworth's. He quit work and we declared a C. L. Moore Day."

Shambleau, the story responsible for the editorial holiday, appeared in the November, 1933, issue of WEIRD TALES. Wright led off the issue with the story and the impact on the readership was every bit as great as he anticipated. One of the most enthusiastic reactions came from the pen of the man Wright characterized as "the dean of weird fiction writers," H. P. Lovecraft, who wrote: *"Shambleau* is great stuff. It begins *magnificently,* on just the right note of terror, and with black intimations of the unknown. The subtle evil of the Entity, as suggested by the unexplained horror of the people, is extremely powerful—and the description of the Thing itself when unmasked is no letdown. It has real atmosphere and tension—rare things amidst the pulp traditions of brisk, cheerful, staccato prose and lifeless stock characters and images. The one major fault is the conventional interplanetary setting."

Shambleau was a triumph of imagination, but beyond that it was a "first" story of such storytelling skill as to place its author among the pulp fantasy leaders of the era, which included H. P. Lovecraft, Robert E. Howard, Clark Ashton Smith, and A. Merritt. It introduced Northwest Smith, a scarred space outlaw, as fast with the ray blaster as his prototypes in the old West had been with the six shooter. A man nearing 40, with steely no-color eyes, a streak of murder in his makeup, and a psychological hardness that has resisted the most soul-destroying horrors, Northwest Smith rescues a strange brown girl from a Martian mob and takes her to his lodgings. When she unloosens her turban, instead of hair a cascade of worm-like tendrils falls like a cloak almost to her feet. Despite his revulsion, he is seduced by her allure and, buried in her Medusan coils of loathsome horror, experiences a sensuality that threatens his life force. The intervention of his Venusian friend Yarol saves him from ecstatic oblivion.

The storyteller's sense of pace, the characterization, the richness of language and imagery, and the provocative sexual undertones, all superbly handled, indicated a talent of a very high order. Lovecraft was wrong when he said the interplanetary setting intruded. On the contrary, in *Shambleau,* as well as in the many Northwest Smith stories that followed, the setting on Mars and Venus made the extraordinary happenings far more believable than if they had occurred on Earth. Lovecraft himself, in his later years, leaned increasingly heavily upon the science-fiction format to give his horror themes reality.

Moore was at the forefront of a hybrid literature known as "science-fantasy," popularized in WEIRD TALES by Lovecraft, Clark Ashton Smith, Nictzin Dyhalis, and Frank Belknap Long, which made a slightly larger concession to science than to the supernatural in the presentation of what was otherwise unbridled fantasy. It required a rich, colorful style, which C. L. Moore possessed in common with the other masters of this genre of fantasy literature.

The fact that C. L. Moore was a woman was carefully kept from the readers of WEIRD TALES. Farnsworth Wright may or may not have been aware of it, since the story was submitted without comment. Her sex was revealed by fan columnists Julius Schwartz and Mort Weisinger, writing in the May, 1934, issue of THE FANTASY FAN. Since THE FANTASY FAN never topped sixty in circulation, the news was slow in being passed along the grapevine. But editors frequently used the term "the author" when they referred to C. L. Moore, which seems to indicate that they were aware of her sex but avoided revealing it.

While there had been many brilliant women writers of the supernatural previously—Mary E. Wilkins Freeman, May Sinclair, Gertrude Atherton, Elizabeth Bowen, and Edith Wharton among them—C. L. Moore was to become the most important member of her sex to contribute to science fiction since Mary Wollstonecraft Shelley wrote *Frankenstein.*

Born January 24, 1911, in Indianapolis, Catherine Lucille Moore claims to have been in training for a writing career ever since she could communicate. "As soon as I could talk," she recalls, "I began telling long, obscure tales to everyone

I could corner. When I learned to write I wrote them, and have been at it ever since. . . .

"I was reared on a diet of Greek mythology, Oz books and Edgar Rice Burroughs, so you see I never had a chance.

"Nothing used to daunt my infant ambition. I wrote about cowboys and kings, Robin Hoods and Lancelots and Tarzans thinly disguised under other names. This went on for years and years, until one rainy afternoon in 1931 when I succumbed to a lifelong temptation and bought a magazine called AMAZING STORIES whose cover portrayed six-armed men in a battle to the death [*Awlo of Ulm* by Capt. S. P. Meek, in the September, 1931, issue]. From that moment on I was a convert. A whole new field of literature opened out before my admiring gaze, and the urge to imitate it was irresistible."

Both her parents traced their families in this country back before the American Revolution and were of Scotch-Irish-Welsh extraction, with a flavoring of French added to the mixture in more recent generations. A Scottish-Gaelic background is given to James Douglas, hero of C. L. Moore's *There Shall Be Darkness* (ASTOUNDING SCIENCE-FICTION, February, 1942), as well as a penchant for Scottish ballads, played on a Martian harp, to Venusian melodies.

On her mother's side, her grandfather was a Methodist minister and on her father's side a medical practitioner. Her father was a designer and manufacturer of machine tools, a vocation still followed in Indianapolis by her only brother, who, in his trade has kept pace with the complexity of technological demands that seem to be science fiction come to life.

Illness plagued what would otherwise have been a very happy childhood, interrupting her schooling so drastically on several occasions that private tutoring was necessary. Poor health continued through her teen years, curtailing her social life and forcing her to turn to books for pleasure and to create her private dream worlds on paper.

A dramatically attractive brunette of average height, Catherine, with improved health, was entered at Indiana University and found herself popular with the men. Formal dances were her favorite type of date and a chow mein dinner the epitome of culinary delight. Boys of that period must have found her, as Forrest J. Ackerman, a frequent correspondent and one-time collaborator, expressed it: "Catherine the Great, toast of WEIRD TALES, is two persons! One, an austere, introspective, enigmatic woman; the other, charming, disarming, gay young girl."

The worsening economics of the depression forced her out of college after only a year and a half, and in 1930 she went to work as a secretary in an Indianapolis bank. After closing hours, she would sit on a balcony overlooking the main floor, undisturbed in the quiet solemnity of the institution, and write fiction. Her first professional try was aimed at AMAZING STORIES, according to a report in *Weird Whisperings* (a news column by Mort Weisinger and Julius Schwartz) in the September, 1934, issue of THE FANTASY FAN, and was rejected by editor T. O'Conor Sloane. They reported that she agreed the piece deserved to be turned down and went into her archives and was never seen again.

Northwest Smith, the famous character of *Shambleau,* first took form in her mind as a western gunman in a ranch called the Bar-Nothing. She reports that an epic poem about Northwest Smith as a space ranger was written even before the first story and it opened with the lines:

> Northwest Smith was a hard-boiled guy
> With an iron fist and a roving eye——

That, too, seems to have been filed in limbo, though there is a possibility that snatches of poetry that have appeared in Northwest Smith stories might be excerpts from that ballad.

The passing years have blurred Moore's recollections of the history of the first Northwest Smith story, *Shambleau.* However, there was an early report so precise in Mortimer

Weisinger's *The Ether Vibrates* column (FANTASY MAGAZINE, September, 1934) that it must be seriously considered. It read: "C. L. Moore first submitted her 'Northwest' Smith stories to Wonder [Stories] on June 8, 1933. They were rejected six days later — only because of their weird theme."

She was only 22 when Farnsworth Wright accepted and published *Shambleau*. The finished craftsmanship of that first story leaves little reason to doubt her claim that fifteen years of continuous writing for her own pleasure developed the artistry which made her an instantaneous scuccess.

Moore recalls that Farnsworth Wright rejected only one story of hers, the second submission. This may have been *Werewoman,* a Northwest Smith story that has never appeared in a professional magazine. It was published in the Winter, 1938-39, issue of LEAVES, a mimeographed fan magazine edited and stenciled by R. H. Barlow, a youthful poet best known as an acolyte of H. P. Lovecraft. Only sixty copies were run off by The Futile Press of Lakeport, California. Unlike the other Northwest Smith stories, it is neither science fiction or science-fantasy, but an outright weird-fantasy set in a never-never land. Here, a wounded Northwest Smith, on an unnamed world, fleeing from unspecified assailants, is surrounded by a pack of female werewolves. The wolf leader feels an affinity of spirit with him and saves him from death at the hands of her pack. In episodes of sheer dream fantasy they range timelessly through a valley where a forgotten civilization and people, bound by an ancient curse, still carry on a ghostlike existence. Northwest Smith destroys a gravestone from which emanate the vapors that hold the valley in thrall and returns to the real world, an enigma to a group of men who find him.

Actually the writing of the story is excellent, its weaknesses being in the inadequate plot and the fact that it is completely out of the pattern of the Northwest Smith series.

The second published Northwest Smith story, *Black Thirst,* appearing in the April, 1934, WEIRD TALES, delineated the special qualities of the lead character even more sharply than

Shambleau. His reactions to the menace of the Minga castle on Venus, where girls are selectively bred for their beauty, and his conviction that his ray blaster will take care of anything supernatural — a belief which is justified as he eventually succeeds in destroying Alendar, last of an ancient race that feeds on beauty — clearly illuminate his special qualities for the reader. A hint that the author might be a woman is dropped when Alendar turns to Northwest Smith and says: "I realized then how long it had been since I tasted the beauty of man. It is so rare, so different from female beauty, that I had all but forgotten it existed. And you have it, very subtly, in a raw, harsh way . . . behind your animal shell of self-preservation are depths of that force and strength which nourish the roots of male beauty."

Scarlet Dream, which followed (WEIRD TALES, May, 1934), is really a dream fantasy, but its tableau of a land where the grass sucks vampirelike at the feet of those who walk on it; where the only food is a liquid which tastes of blood, drunk from spigots in a temple; and the only purpose of the people is to wait for the interdimensional horror who controls the bizarre place to come and feed on them, make it one of the most memorable stories in the series.

Dust of Gods (August, 1934, WEIRD TALES) swings the pendulum back toward a purer form of science fiction as Northwest Smith and his Venusian friend Yarol search Martian labyrinths to uncover the secrets of ancient "gods," who fled to Mars when their world exploded.

All but the latter tale scored first place with the readers of WEIRD TALES in competition with superb works by Robert E. Howard, Clark Ashton Smith, E. Hoffman Price, Jack Williamson, Frank Belknap Long, and Edmond Hamilton, forcing Farnsworth Wright to raise his sights in his blurb for *The Black God's Kiss* (WEIRD TALES, October, 1934) and rank her with "Algernon Blackwood, Arthur Machen and H. P. Lovecraft."

The Black God's Kiss introduced Jirel of Joiry, a female warrior queen and spitfire of the fifteenth century, who, when captured and humbled by the conqueror Guillaume, enters a land of horror in another dimension to kiss a black image and, passing that kiss on to Guillaume, causes his death in revenge. As she views his body, she realizes that "the heady violence" that had possessed her every time she thought of him was inspired by love and not hate, and in exacting her revenge she has paid a bitter fee.

In its own way, the story is as effective as any one of the Northwest Smith stories. Moore's ability at characterization launched this new character in a parallel series with Northwest Smith and one almost as popular.

C. L. Moore's introduction to the science-fiction magazines was upon the invitation of the brilliant young editor, F. Orlin Tremaine, who had taken over ASTOUNDING STORIES and in a single year raised it to leadership in its field. He raided the other magazines for their best authors and had already borrowed from WEIRD TALES Frank Belknap Long, Clark Ashton Smith, Howard Wandrei, and Donald Wandrei. Eventually he would get H. P. Lovecraft, too, but for now the presentation of *Bright Illusion,* a novelette by C. L. Moore in the October, 1934, issue of his magazine was quite a coup.

In *Bright Illusion,* an earth man is whisked to another world by a powerful intelligence to overthrow a competing entity which has set itself up as a god. To permit the earthman to function, his mind is clouded by an illusion which makes the creatures and structures of this world appear in forms familiar to him. He falls in love with an alien counterpart of a female, which love is mutually sustained even when both are aware of their true forms. Eventually they choose death as the only way out of their hopeless situation. Science-fantasy, rather than science fiction, the story nonetheless appealed to the readership of ASTOUNDING STORIES strongly enough to establish a new reputation for the author in that magazine. In the next few years, *Greater Glories* and *Tryst in Time,* tales of a similar stripe, found high favor with the readers.

The literary triumphs also continued in WEIRD TALES as

C. L. Moore sent Northwest Smith to pit his courage and gun against the soul-challenging entities of the near planets, while Jirel of Joiry, with a spirit of unquenchable fire, jousted with the supernatural terrors of man's emergence from the dark ages. The procession of stories — *Black God's Shadow, Julhi, Jirel Meets Magic,* and *The Cold Gray God* — were wondrously woven literary tapestries, but there were also weaknesses. The climax of each story found Northwest Smith or Jirel of Joiry in the formless haze of spiritual battle with the unknown. The plot situations were rarely solved by a logical sequence of events, but instead by a burst of rhetorical hypnotism. A story that began as logical science fiction would be permitted to lapse into fantasy as an easy way out of a difficult situation. A story that began as an outright fantasy would be buttressed by science when the "willing suspension of disbelief" could no longer be sustained.

The battle was always against evil, but the standard of light was championed by a hero and a heroine who were themselves stained with the sins of humanity. For this honesty in characterization, a great deal could be forgiven.

One Jirel of Joiry story, *The Dark Land* (WEIRD TALES, January, 1936), was illustrated by C. L. Moore herself. Ostensibly showing Pav of Romne, prince of darkness who desires Jirel for his queen, the drawing actually was made many years previous to the writing of *The Dark Land* and once served as the inspiration for the gallant, dead Guillaume of *The Black God's Kiss.*

Romance came often to Northwest Smith and Jirel of Joiry, and it was always a very strange and unusual romance. Now, something of a storybook nature was to happen to C. L. Moore. The March, 1936, WEIRD TALES carried a shocker of a tale, *The Graveyard Rats* by a science-fiction fan named Henry Kuttner. Kuttner greatly admired the work of Moore but, shy by nature, did not possess the courage to strike up a correspondence. H. P. Lovecraft's request that he return some books to Moore after reading them gave him the excuse he needed, so he sent a letter to WEIRD TALES to be forwarded to *Mr.* C. L. Moore. The reply from *Miss* Catherine Moore was a tremendous surprise to him. A native of Los Angeles, Kuttner was then living in New York to further his ambition of becoming a full-time writer, but made frequent trips by car to the West Coast. They met for the first time in 1938, when Moore came to California on a vacation trip. In all they saw each other about five times in two years, as Henry Kuttner motored back and forth between New York and California, the rest of their courtship being conducted by mail. "His letters were a delight," Moore recalls, "and I still have all of them."

Out of one of these meetings sprang the idea for a collaboration, a story in which Northwest Smith and Jirel of Joiry would be brought together. C. L. Moore had collaborated once before, with Forrest J. Ackerman on *Nymph of Darkness,* a Northwest Smith Story published in FANTASY MAGAZINE for April, 1935, and a collector's item today, since it was also illustrated by Moore. In that previous collaboration, Ackerman had supplied the idea, of an invisible girl who enlists Smith's aid, and Moore had done the writing. In this new collaboration, Moore and Kuttner would share both the plotting and the writing.

The result appeared as *Quest of the Star Stone* in the November, 1937, WEIRD TALES. Though it won first place in the issue, it was not a very good story, possessing the previously mentioned flaws more glaringly than usual. Through necromancy, a magician brings Northwest Smith and his Venusian friend Yarol back through time to the fifteenth century, to wrest from Jirel a star stone which she wears around her neck. Memorable was the prelude to adventure in which Northwest Smith is a "surprisingly good baritone" expresses the homesickness of his exile by singing *The Green Hills of Earth,* which begins:

> Across the seas of darkness
> The good green Earth is bright—
> Oh, star that was my homeland
> Shine down on me tonight. . . .

and inconclusively ends:

> . . . and count the losses worth
> To see across the darkness
> The green hills of Earth. . . .

When Robert Heinlein read the story, he never forgot the phrase which became the title of one of his most famous short stories and of a collection, *The Green Hills of Earth*.

C. L. Moore and Henry Kuttner hit it off from the start, but it was anything but a whirlwind romance. Henry, in person, scarcely personified Northwest Smith. He was slight of build and ordinary in feature, with a retiring nature. Economically, things were anything but conducive to romance. Henry was only beginning as a writer and the country was in a state of acute depression.

Nevertheless, every time he traveled between Los Angeles and New York, Henry Kuttner stopped at Indianapolis. C. L. Moore eventually decided that "Northwest Smith would have been a very boring man to be married to. Henry Kuttner, as his writing must show and his friends could testify, was wonderfully resourceful, perceptive, fresh in his viewpoints and very, very funny. I think it's his humor that most of us remember most vividly. But he also had a quality of quiet strength and discipline that I have sensed in very few other people and for which I have enormous respect on the few occasions I do encounter it. In this area, I suppose, you could find a likeness between the real man and the fictional one."

They were married June 7, 1940, in New York and lived in that city about a year before they moved to Laguna Beach, California. When war came, Henry Kuttner, with a heart murmur that kept him from being assigned to overseas duty, entered the Medical Corps and was stationed at Fort Monmouth, New Jersey; Catherine lived at nearby Red Bank from 1942 to 1945.

Since their first meeting, new C. L. Moore stories had been few and far between. After the collaboration in *Quest of the Star Stone,* only one more Jirel story appeared, *Hells-garde* (WEIRD TALES, April, 1939); and a brief fragment, *Song in Minor Key,* in the fan magazine SCIENTI-SNAPS (February, 1940), about the return of Northwest Smith to earth, rang down the curtain on that character. An era was coming to a close for C. L. Moore. There would be some transition stories, but romance for the sake of romance was dead.

The turning point unquestionably came with *Greater than Gods,* in the July, 1939, ASTOUNDING SCIENCE-FICTION. Contact is made with a man by two probable future worlds, with powerful pleas that he take the course that will ensure their reality. The theme is mature and moving, the writing strong and direct. The vitality of the story rests in its emotional conflict, which is not diminished by the ending in which the protagonist takes a third course that wipes out the possibility of either of the two "worlds of if."

Whatever the reason for her lack of production between 1936 and 1940, the infrequency of the Moore name on stories after the turn of the decade rested in the writing relationship that sprang up between her and her husband. One story told of them most graphically illustrates the method. Henry Kuttner, who became somewhat of a recluse when on a writing binge, had fallen asleep from exhaustion without finishing a story he was working on. Catherine came into the room, read the manuscript, and by the time he awoke the story was completed and on his desk.

He was strong on beginnings, she was powerful on endings, and so a specialization grew up where each compensated for the weakness of the other. Some nineteen pen names were used, among them Lawrence O'Donnell, Lewis Padgett, C. H. Liddell, and Kelvin Kent. Collaborations were so involved that after a while both parties found it impossible to tell where one broke off and the other began.

Still, an occasional story appeared that was nearly 100 per cent C. L. Moore. *There Shall Be Darkness,* in ASTOUNDING SCIENCE-FICTION, February, 1942, was one such story, written in a style that was a throwback to the C. L. Moore of Northwest Smith. The potent Venusian drink *segir*-whiskey appears in this tale, which parallels the fall of the Roman empire, of Earth retreating from the last of her colonies to face the onslaught of interplanetary barbarians. Moore was an early comer to a trend that within a few months would find leading new writers A. E. van Vogt and Isaac Asimov popularizing the concept of interplanetary and interstellar empires.

The most dramatic and potent transition story by Moore was unquestionably the short novel *Judgement Night,* serialized in two parts in ASTOUNDING SCIENCE-FICTION beginning in the August, 1943, number. A galactic empire is beginning to crack up, and a princess of the controlling realm courts romance and death on an artificial pleasure satellite which circles her world. The description of the operation of the pleasure satellite Cyrille can only be termed inspired. The story is composed with a richness of imagery reminiscent of Jirel of Joiry and the plot is carried by action instead of cerebration, but it introduces an antiwar message of noble effectiveness and presents an alien creature, the Ilar, with the adroitness of a Weinbaum.

From here on there would be very few stories that would not have at least a trace of Henry Kuttner in their composition. Nevertheless, of those she could call her own, *Children's Hour,* published under the pen name Lawrence O'Donnell (ASTOUNDING SCIENCE-FICTION, March, 1944), concerning the man who discovers that the girl he is engaged to marry is the chaperoned child of some immeasurably superior race and he is but an educational playmate to be discarded when the time comes, is a masterpiece of sensitivity in its handling and memorable in its originality. Few stories in modern science fiction rank above it.

Shortly afterward, *No Woman Born,* the tale of the mental adjustment of a beautiful television star who has been nearly cremated by fire to the shiny metal machine which is now her body (ASTOUNDING SCIENCE-FICTION, December, 1944) was a most difficult attempt, which, despite the fact that it did not entirely succeed, is the most ambitious story written to date on that theme. Both *The Children's Hour* and *No Woman Born* eliminated physical action as the prime method for furthering the plot.

When the war ended, the Kuttners decided they wanted a very special house at Hastings-on-Hudson, New York. With only $50 between them, they knuckled down and made $1,000 in writing in one month to provide a down payment. It was at Hastings-on-Hudson that what many consider to be C. L. Moore's greatest story and one of the most brilliant stories in modern science fiction was written, *Vintage Season*.

When it was published under her pen name Lawrence O'Donnell in the September, 1946, ASTOUNDING SCIENCE-FICTION, acclaim was spontaneous. In *Vintage Season,* tourist observers from the future return incognito to periods in the past just before great events are to occur. They are strictly forbidden to interfere with events. One such group rents a house in the United States, and their purpose is discovered by the owner. Realizing that some tremendous event, possibly a tragedy, is about to occur, he does his best to get them to alter events, to no avail. One of the observers, Cenbe, is a creative genius of the future, who takes back to tomorrow the impressions for a great symphonia, blending pictures and sound. The fundamental plot line of this superb story has been copied repeatedly since its first appearance.

With stories like *The Children's Hour* and *Vintage Season* "Lawrence O'Donnell" was being classed among the hierarchy of new science-fiction giants, along with Robert A. Heinlein, A. E. van Vogt, Theodore Sturgeon, and Fritz Leiber. Rising with it was the name Lewis Padgett, whose work contained a preponderance of Kuttner. Revelation of the true identities behind these newly famous names elevated Henry Kuttner's name to the pantheon, because in effect he had proved himself, but that C. L. Moore could accomplish literary feats was taken for granted. Therefore, except among the cognoscenti, she suffered a net loss of incalculable extent. Through neglect of its use, the C. L. Moore name was known primarily to veteran readers. Lawrence O'Donnell had not been around long enough to establish a comparable reputation and, besides, it was a name only partly employed for her efforts.

A heart condition developed by Henry Kuttner forced them to move to the gentler climate of Laguna Beach, California, in 1948. In 1950, under the GI Bill of Rights, he decided to get the college degree he wanted. He began attendance at the University of Southern California in 1950 and managed to graduate in 3½ years. Not subsidized by the GI Bill of Rights, Catherine took a bit longer and obtained her B.A. in 1956. Henry was working for his M.A. and had everything completed but his thesis when his heart gave out on Feb. 4, 1958, and Catherine was left alone. They had both made Phi Beta Kappa and Catherine's degree had been *magna cum laude,* but the titles seemed rather empty now.

Toward the end, they had decided to label their stories correctly as individual efforts or collaborations. However, science fiction was already an unprofitable venture. In the late 1950's, they had turned out four novels about a psychoanalyst detective, with Henry writing the first draft and Catherine the final draft.

After Henry's death, C. L. Moore had published the already completed novel of the strange sociological tyranny of the America of the near future in *Doomsday Morning* (written in a semi-tough-guy style) as a Doubleday hardcover book, but her efforts were predominantly devoted to television. There were westerns and detectives as well as scripts for such famous shows as *Maverick* and 77 *Sunset Strip.* She took over a writing class which Henry had been teaching at the University of California and taught two mornings a week for four years.

Most of the students probably never realized the true stature of their instructor in the field she had so early chosen as her own. The young girl who blasted herself to fame overnight through the good right gun arm of Northwest Smith matured to become one of the most perceptive literary artists the science-fiction world has ever known. Perhaps because she brought to the field a rare feminine insight, her contributions were unique, enriching the field out of proportion to their numbers.

For herself, the 18 years of her marriage, though stranger than most fiction, had been rewarding and happy ones. Her ability in writing had carried her into a promising career. Commenting on the strange twists that life sometimes takes, she said: "No, I never really have meant to do full-time writing. I don't know quite what happened."

18

HENRY KUTTNER

Select in your mind any of today's science-fiction writers you consider third-rate, and imagine what the effect might be on you if he suddenly confessed to being the real genius behind the published efforts of Theodore Sturgeon and Clifford D. Simak, and, for good measure, coyly owned up to responsibility for the Mark Clifton, Cordwainer Smith, and Christopher Anvil stories, and you will approximate the impact when Henry Kuttner admitted for publication that he was Lewis Padgett and Lawrence O'Donnell, and was also willing to accept credit for Keith Hammond, Kelvin Kent, Paul Edmonds, and sundry other names that had been regarded as science-fiction writers to bear watching.

The identity of Lewis Padgett had been leaked by John W. Campbell, Jr., editor of ASTOUNDING SCIENCE-FICTION, back in the summer of 1943, and a single sentence reflecting that revelation had appeared in the August 11, 1943, issue

of FANTASY FICTION FIELD, a weekly news magazine devoted
to information about fantasy and science fiction, published
by an old-time fan and book dealer, Julius Unger; a more
complete story followed in the February 7, 1944, issue. This
information was picked up on faith by Arthur L. Widner,
then conducting a popularity poll on various aspects of
science fiction, and he lumped the Lewis Padgett votes for
the best author of the year in with those for Henry Kuttner.
Henry Kuttner, who had never even as much as "also ran"
on any previous reader survey, and who had been regarded
as a rather mediocre journeyman professional, abruptly
moved into 13th spot in the final tabulations published in the
September, 1943, LE ZOMBIE, a journal of news and commentary published by Wilson Tucker and E. Everett Evans
(both of whom would eventually become prominent professional authors).

Within two years, as the news traveled through the science-fiction world, Kuttner rose to first place in other sur-
veys over such competition as A. E. van Vogt, Isaac Asimov,
Murray Leinster, and Fritz Leiber, Jr. Many writers had
catapulted to overnight fame on the strength of a single outstanding story. Kuttner was the first in the science-fiction
world to rise to glory incognito.

Unlike his close friend, Ray Bradbury, who has bared
endless anecdotes concerning his tender years, Henry Kuttner in personal conversation and in print studiously by-
passed the subject. He was born in Los Angeles in 1914 of
parents who were of German, Jewish, English, Irish and
Polish extraction. He boasted of one grandfather who was
a rabbi. His father, who ran a book shop, died when he was
five. The early years were spent in San Francisco, where his
mother strove to support him and two older brothers, at one
period operating a boarding house. They moved back to
Los Angeles about the time Henry entered high school, and
upon his graduation he went to work in a literary agency
operated by a cousin through marriage.

His interest in fantasy followed traditional lines. He began with the Oz books, graduated to Edgar Rice Burroughs, and, at the age of 12, found himself "hooked" when the first AMAZING STORIES appeared in 1926.

As the years passed his interest shifted from science fiction toward weird-fantasy and as a devoted reader of WEIRD TALES he became a correspondent of H. P. Lovecraft and other members of the "Lovecraft Circle," particularly Robert Bloch.

Kuttner's first professional sale was a poem *Ballad of the Gods,* done in the pulsating rhythms of Robert E. Howard, published in the February, 1936, issue of WEIRD TALES. Kuttner is best remembered for his immense versatility, but in all evaluations his verse has been forgotten. True, most of it worshipped at the shrine of Robert E. Howard and some of it made obeisance to H. P. Lovecraft, but all of it is eminently readable and the acrostic titled *H. P. L.* and published in the September, 1937, WEIRD TALES, opening with the lines:

Here in the silent places, and the caverns beneath the world,
On the great black altars carven from the stones that the
gods have hurled,
Where the gray smoke coils and shudders through the eery
purple gleam
And the shadows of worlds beyond our worlds fall over
a dreamer's dream—

culminates with talented discipline in its tribute to Lovecraft's imagination:

Facing the gates of the universe, breasting the mighty stream
That bursts from the roots of Yggdrasil, in the splendor of
a dream.

Kuttner's fictional debut, *The Graveyard Rats,* in WEIRD TALES for March, 1936, marked the appearance of what is undoubtedly one of the half-dozen most truly *horrifying* short stories in the entire gamut of literature, *all* of literature. A ghoulish cemetery caretaker in New England's old Salem crawls after immense rats through underground tunnels to reclaim a newly buried body they have dragged from the coffin. His nightmarish struggle against the rats and an ancient cadaver still instinct with the reflexes of life build to a denouement of such revolting terror that the reader must almost drive himself physically to complete it.

In background, theme, buildup, style, and intent the story owes everything to H. P. Lovecraft. While no evidence has been uncovered to show that Lovecraft helped in the writing of the story, it would be hard to conceive that he had not read it and offered suggestions before publication. *The Graveyard Rats* is so powerful an exercise in fear, so basic in striking the chord of all that man holds abhorrent, and it rears so monstrously in effectiveness above any other weird tale that Henry Kuttner subsequently had published (indeed, when the final evaluation is made, it may be the best thing he ever wrote), that one finds it difficult to attribute it to a fledgling 21-year-old, his first time out.

For this reason the identity of the author was questioned. Replying to a reader in the May, 1936, issue of WEIRD TALES, editor Farnsworth Wright said: "No, Henry Kuttner is not a pen name. He is a young writer, for whom we predict real achievement; for he possesses genuine merit." It is ironic that a writer who would owe his reputation to his pseudonyms would initially be suspected of being one.

In later years, Kuttner grew literally to hate *The Graveyard Rats*. He resented requests for reprint rights and contemplated violence when an endless parade of readers kept telling him it was the best thing he had ever written. He regarded praise of the story as an insinuation that the decades had taught him nothing about the technique of storytelling. (Rachmaninoff felt the same way about his "Prelude in C# Minor.")

In *The Secret of Kralitz* (WEIRD TALES, October, 1936), a young baron becomes a member of the living dead; the theme of *It Walks By Night* (WEIRD TALES, December, 1936) involves the dead who feed on the bodies of the dead. Both of these tales were outright imitations of Lovecraft, and *The Eater of Souls* (WEIRD TALES, January, 1937) imitated Lovecraft's imitation of Lord Dunsany!

Early readers, judging Kuttner's personality by the catalogue of horrors he had printed in WEIRD TALES, were in for a shock when he joined the Los Angeles Chapter of The Science Fiction League late in 1936. A short, slight, dark-complexioned man, unhandsome and sporting a small, almost round moustache, he was timid and self-effacing, but from him flowed a seemingly inexhaustible stream of humor, dispensed in a dour, unsmiling fashion. His friends characterized him "as one of the funniest men alive." Of him as a person, descriptions like "the kindest, gentlest, most considerate human being it has been my pleasure to know" come from many of those who knew him closely.

Fritz Lieber, Jr., reporting on a 1937 meeting with Henry Kuttner in *Henry Kuttner: A Memorial Symposium,* published by Karen Anderson in August, 1958, said: "Hank (his favorite nickname) was already breaking sharply with the Lovecraft tradition."

This was evidenced by *I, the Vampire* (WEIRD TALES, February, 1937), where the vampire is portrayed sympathetically, a tragic victim of circumstance, capable of self-sacrifice. Hoffman Price, a close friend of Kuttner's, adopted the viewpoint several years later in writing *Spanish Vampire* (WEIRD TALES, September, 1939), a light and moving masterpiece.

In *We Are the Dead* (WEIRD TALES, April, 1937), the ghost of the Unknown Soldier deters a senator from promoting legislation that may lead to war. The young Kuttner wasn't up to the job, but polished veteran Seabury Quinn picked up the idea with elaborations and scored a hit with *Washington Nocturne* in WEIRD TALES for May, 1939.

But, there would, nevertheless, be other Lovecraft imitations, *The Salem Horror* (WEIRD TALES, May, 1937) and *The Jest of Droom Avista* (WEIRD TALES, August, 1937), for while Kuttner wanted to change he seemed unable to bring to bear any qualities that were fundamentally his own.

One of the most interesting and successful stories of this period was his collaboration with his close friend Robert

Bloch, *The Black Kiss* (WEIRD TALES, June, 1937). A tale of a sea creature that lures a man in his dreams to partake of its kisses, resulting in a transfer of bodies, this story employed a combination of the methods and styles of H. P. Lovecraft *and* C. L. Moore, the girl Kuttner was destined to marry. Another literary collaboration, in which Henry Kuttner and C. L. Moore united in one story her two famous characters Northwest Smith and Jirel of Joiry *(Quest of the Star Stone,* WEIRD TALES, November, 1937), symbolically anticipated their marriage some three years later.

During the thirties an outgrowth of the mystery magazines were publications like THRILLING MYSTERY, HORROR TALES, and TERROR TALES, which specialized in stories of sadism, torture, flagellation, and satanism, heavily flavored with sex. These stories were developed as though they related supernatural events, but it was the policy of the magazines to have normal, logical explanations for the erotic and sometimes debased content of the stories. Henry Kuttner sold regularly to THRILLING MYSTERY such tales as *Laughter of the Dead, The Dweller in the Tomb,* and *Lord of the Lions.* It is likely that he used pen names for stories in HORROR STORIES and TERROR TALES, for these publications were the most blatantly titillating of the group.

Julius Schwartz, his agent, convinced Kuttner that he should divert some of his energies toward science fiction. Kuttner was reluctant at first, because though he liked science fiction his scientific background was so skimpy that he felt inadequate to the job.

When the Earth Lived (THRILLING WONDER STORIES, Nov., 1937) is said by Schwartz to have been the first science fiction written by Kuttner, though *Raider of the Spaceways* (WEIRD TALES, July, 1937) was published before it. *When the Earth Lived* employed the fairly original idea of rays, projected by scientists in the macrocosmos, bombarding the earth and investing such unlikely objects as automobiles, boats, coffee pots, and jewelry with life, thereby raising hob. The treatment was corny, the writing amateurish, and the idea unbelievable, but Kutttner had launched his science-fiction career.

In *Raider of the Spaceways,* Kuttner used Stanley G. Weinbaum's *Lotus Eaters* as a model. In *The Lotus Eaters,* a male and female adventurer discover an intelligent talking plant in the twilight zone of Venus. In *Raider of the Spaceways,* a male and female adventurer discover an intelligent talking plant in the twilight zone of Venus. Kuttner gave it "his own" twist, however: Weinbaum's plant was friendly, Kuttner's wasn't.

For no apparent reason, the next Kuttner story appeared under the Standard Magazines house name Will Garth, *The Bloodless Peril* (THRILLING WONDER STORIES, December, 1937). It proposed as thesis that plant life, given the intelligence, would be as warlike and destructive as man.

Then Kuttner got his first big writing break in science fiction. THRILLING WONDER STORIES' editor, Mort Weisinger, asked him to write a series of novelettes based on the motion picture industry of the future. The first *Hollywood on the Moon,* appeared in the April, 1938, issue. Hollywood was something Kuttner knew, so he could write with some authenticity, but the stories were to be formularized Stanley G. Weinbaum. The principal characters, Tony Quade and Gerry Carlyle, were copied from Ham Hammond and Pat Burlingame of Weinbaum's *Parasite Planet, Lotus Eaters,* and *Planet of Doubt.* Each story featured strange, weird, lovable, or outré alien creatures of the type popularized by Weinbaum, and each story attempted to imitate the modern, swift dialogue characteristic of Weinbaum's writing.

In a magazine oriented toward the juvenile market, Kuttner's series on the Hollywood of the future had the virtue of being readable and mildly entertaining. No one realized it then, but the single element that enabled Kuttner to lift those yarns out of the cellar was that they required humor, an ingredient he had in abundance.

Almost simultaneously with *Hollywood on the Moon,* Henry Kuttner started another series for WEIRD TALES.

Robert E. Howard, a gifted storyteller, especially renowned for the creation of a character named Conan who fought and wenched in a mythical era called the Hyborian age, committed suicide in 1936. His popularity was such that Clifford Ball attempted to create a character similar to Conan, called Duar, but he dropped the idea after three stories. Kuttner now tried his hand at it with a heroic character titled Elak, brawling and loving in the manner of Conan (and in the style of Robert E. Howard), but with supernatural settings from H. P. Lovecraft and stylistic hyperbole *à la* C. L. Moore.

The first in the series was *Thunder in the Dawn,* a two-part novel beginning in the May, 1938, WEIRD TALES. It was good fun, but in Howard's stories the character of Conan was bigger than life. Elak, however, was overshadowed by the events of the story. The series terminated after four widely spaced stories.

When MARVEL SCIENCE STORIES' initial issue, dated August, appeared on the newsstands in May, 1938, it was the first new science-fiction magazine in seven years. Henry Kuttner had been writing sex-horror stories for its companion, MYSTERY TALES. The editor of MARVEL SCIENCE STORIES, Robert O. Erisman, had decided to experiment with a little sex in science fiction. Up until then, sex was taboo, probably unwanted by the readers. Even a thread of love interest was just about tolerated and most stories got along without acknowledging the existence of women. Since Henry Kuttner was experienced at both the writing of science fiction and the horror magazine concept of what constituted sex, he was a logical man for the task.

Kuttner took two unsold short novels, *Avengers of Space* and *Time Trap,* and inserted a few "racy" passages involving nude women and monsters with high libidos. The stories were fast-action science fiction and the "sex" by today's standards was rather tame, but they elicited a symphony of reader protest. Kuttner's never-high reputation skidded to a new low. Kuttner had two other decidedly second-rate stories in the first issue under pen names, *Dark Heritage* as Robert O. Kenyon and *Dictator of the Americas* as James Hall, the latter the most sex-laden story in the issue.

The only defender Kuttner had was Dr. Thomas S. Gardner, whose article *Sex in Science Fiction* appeared in the December, 1945, issue of FANTASY TIMES, seven years later. "A visitor to the Queens SFL in the winter of 1939 intimated that the author had a trashy mind because he enjoyed Kuttner's *Avengers of Space* in the first issue of MARVEL SCIENCE STORIES," Gardner wrote. "When men do not keep women clothed under such conditions, how can you expect alien minds to do so? The story of Kuttner's was real, men and creatures act like that in life."

Kuttner's best story of the year, *Hands Across the Void,* a poetic tale of the self-sacrifice of a Titanian to save Earthmen from destruction at the hands of their giant "servants," appeared in the December, 1938, THRILLING WONDER STORIES under the Will Garth name, so he received no credit for it.

His lack of popularity, combined with circumstance, forced Kuttner further and further into adopting pseudonyms as 1939 progressed. "Keith Hammond" originated as a device for running two stories in the same issues of STRANGE STORIES, a magazine similar to WEIRD TALES, published as a companion to THRILLING WONDER STORIES. Most of the stories under the Hammond name were imitations of Lovecraft and may even have been rejects from WEIRD TALES.

"Kelvin Kent" was used at first in collaboration, then alternately, with Arthur K. (for Kelvin) Barnes for a series of humorous stories in THRILLING WONDER STORIES. The stories revolved around Pete Manx, side-show concessionaire in an amusement park, whose consciousness is shunted back in time into the bodies of ancient Romans, Greeks, Egyptians, and other residents of historical and legendary lands, where through his crude but native cunning he cons his way to success. The first, *Roman Holiday,* in THRILLING WONDER STORIES for August, 1939, was the most popular story in the issue, ensuring a fairly long run for the series.

The name "Paul Edmonds" was first used in the May, 1939, issue of SCIENCE FICTION, a new magazine of that period edited by Charles D. Hornig, and was used to cover up the fact that Kuttner was selling his rejects at half the rate he received from THRILLING WONDER STORIES. Most of the stories under this name possess little merit.

Kuttner had visited New York occasionally on business and detested the city. On June 14, 1939, he had written to Julius Schwartz: "I don't intend to visit New York. I can get the same effect as I do in New York by crawling into the dirtiest corner of the garage and screaming at the top of my voice, blowing the auto horn, and energetically sniffing the exhaust. Once you visit California, me lad, you realize that New York is Satan's privy."

On December 3, 1939, Henry Kuttner showed up at a meeting of New York's Queens Science Fiction League in tow of Mort Weisinger, editor of THRILLING WONDER STORIES, and Julius Schwartz, his agent. He announced that though the city repelled him, the variety of markets he was selling to, including many in the adventure field, made it increasingly important that he live closer to his source of income. He had quit his job with a Los Angeles literary agency and was taking up residence in New York with his mother.

More than a year earlier, Henry Kuttner had made the acquaintance of Virgil Finlay, renowned WEIRD TALES artist, at a Times Square bar. They became fast friends and their frequent elbow bending was eventually enshrined in a short story Kuttner wrote around the cover of the May, 1943, issue of SUPER SCIENCE STORIES, *Reader, I Hate You,* with himself and Virgil Finlay as the main characters. Finlay had married his childhood sweetheart in 1938 and moved to New York at the invitation of A. Merritt, editor of THE AMERICAN WEEKLY, to accept a position on that magazine. He was visited at his one-room Brooklyn apartment during Easter, 1939, by Henry Kuttner and Jim Mooney, an aspiring Los Angeles artist who had illustrated a few of Kuttner's stories.

They brought with them, as a gift for Finlay's wife, a live rabbit. In return, Kuttner was served his favorite dish, fried chicken.

When Henry Kuttner brought Catherine Lucille Moore to New York, the only guests at the marriage ceremony at City Hall the morning of June 7, 1940, were Henry's mother and Mr. and Mrs. Virgil Finlay. Virgil paid the Justice of the Peace $10, bought the bride a dubonnet and soda, and the career of the most famous writing team in science-fiction history was launched.

Catherine then learned what every woman must, that you don't know a man until you've lived with him. Henry had his own little peculiarities. When he was cloistered in his room on an assignment, his closest buddy, returning from a three-year trip to Tanganyika, would not be admitted if his arrival was unexpected. An excellent driver, he hated to drive. He worked off nervous energy by pounding the piano insistently, horribly, and loudly. Shaving was a chore he indulged in as infrequently as possible, and the age and condition of the clothes he wore was enough to make the most jaundiced publisher compulsively reach for his checkbook.

It would be nice to say that Kuttner's transformation to a top-rank author began at the moment of matrimony, but the evidence indicates that his ability was growing immediately before that.

THRILLING WONDER STORIES, in its April, 1940, number, ran the memorable *Beauty and the Beast,* which tells of an intelligent creature from Venus who is killed because of his monstrous appearance, as he attempts to deliver a message that would have saved Earth from disaster from lovely but deadly alien plants.

The May-June, 1940, issue of FAMOUS FANTASTIC MYSTERIES carried his touching, well-told fantasy *Pegasus,* concerning a boy who catches and tames a flying horse. Though possibly inspired by Edmond Hamilton's masterpiece, *He That Hath Wings,* in the July, 1938, issue of WEIRD TALES, both stories dealing with attempts to earthbind the winged creature, Kuttner's story has sufficient difference and quality to stand on its own.

UNKNOWN for April, 1940, contained Kuttner's humorous fantasy *All Is Illusion*, whose subject is revealed by the title. In combining humor and fantasy Kuttner was in his element, but the speed at which he wrote divested this story, and a majority of his subsequent fantasies for UNKNOWN, of all believability. Even the flashes of cleverness and the author's increasing skill at turning a phrase failed to rescue them. Most of his science fiction, though based on tenuous premises, was momentarily believable. Virtually none of his deliberate fantasies possessed this essential.

After a year of New York, both Catherine and Henry Kuttner decided that they were not cut out to live in "Bagdad on the Hudson" and moved to Laguna Beach, California. More and more, writing became a symbiotic relationship. They frequently wrote in relays, one taking over sometimes in the middle of a sentence, helping the other past a writing block. Often one supplied the idea and the other wrote the story. Just as frequently Henry Kuttner would write the first draft and C. L. Moore would put it into final form. Kuttner was better than Moore at plotting, but Moore was a far more accomplished stylist.

Pearl Harbor played an unexpected role in their lives. For his magazines ASTOUNDING SCIENCE-FICTION and UN-KNOWN WORLDS, John W. Campbell, Jr., had developed a crack team of writers. Now, what with military service and war work, he lost Robert A. Heinlein, Isaac Asimov, Theodore Sturgeon, L. Sprague de Camp, and L. Ron Hubbard. He had to develop a new team of authors who would continue to produce the quality and style of fiction his readers had come to expect. His bright young men were in the Army. The only answer was to recruit and work with some of the second stringers.

Henry Kuttner was one of those approached, but because of his tarnished reputation a pen name was considered essential. He chose "Lewis Padgett." Lewis was Kuttner's mother's maiden name, and Padgett was Moore's grand-mother's maiden name.

The first story under the Padgett name, *Deadlock* (ASTOUNDING SCIENCE-FICTION, August, 1942), obviously was intended to emulate Asimov's highly popular series of amusing robot stories, but it barely passed muster. *The Twonky,* in the September issue, struck a highly original note; a radio which is really a robot censors reading matter, drinking habits, and other things possibly harmful to its owner, while obligingly pitching in to wash the dishes. The style, reading like something new to the science-fiction audience, was actually simulated John Collier. The result was widely praised. This story could have been the inspiration of *"With Folded Hands . . ."* and *". . . And of Searching Mind,"* the Jack Williamson stories about robots which never, under any circumstances, will permit humans to do anything that might be harmful to themselves.

The third story, *Piggy Bank,* in the December, 1942, issue of ASTOUNDING SCIENCE-FICTION, reverted to the Asimov robot formula, but the fourth, *Time Locker* (ASTOUNDING SCIENCE-FICTION, June, 1943) was not a robot story and was a small masterpiece involving a locker that emptied into the future, and the man who killed himself using it. It was slickly written with an adroit twist that could not have been anticipated by the readers. Kuttner's own name appeared on a second story in that issue, *". . . Nothing but Gingerbread Left,"* the title from a verse of Lewis Carroll. No one linked it with the Padgett story in the February issue carrying the Carrollian title, *Mimsy Were the Borogoves.* It dealt with toys from our future projected back in time to the present; they are found by youngsters who devise from them a formula for entering a non-Euclidean universe, disappearing forever from the sight of their parents. Immediately recognized as a classic in the field, it is quite obvious that this story served as the inspiration for *The Veldt* by Ray Bradbury, and possibly for his whole series of childhood-centered stories. At that time, Kuttner was personally helping Bradbury on his career, even to the extent of rewriting some of his stories. Later he would help Richard Matheson in the same way.

Shock, in the March, 1943, ASTOUNDING SCIENCE-FICTION, about a genius out of time who develops to be an escapee from a padded cell of the future, set the pattern for similar tales to come, including Gore Vidal's TV and stage play *Visit from a Small Planet.*

The same issue saw Lawrence O'Donnell's debut with *Clash by Night,* plot derived and expanded from Clifford D. Simak's *Rim of the Deep* dealing with a Venusian culture where all civilization survives in the "keeps," giant domes beneath the seas. This one Kuttner wrote on his own, but he had the help of Moore for the novel-length sequel *Fury* (1947), dramatizing the conflict between the long-lived and short-lived Venusians. Though primarily action stories, both proved very popular.

When the news eventually broke that Henry Kuttner was both Lewis Padgett *and* and to some degree Lawrence O'Donnell, all past transgressions were forgiven if not completely forgotten by the readers. Their enthusiasm was partially predicated on superior craftsmanship, partially on the desire to see the underdog come out on top, but predominantly because Kuttner usually reminded them of someone they liked. A superbly proficient literary mimic, Kuttner usually wrote like whoever was in demand at the time.

He left the Medical Corps in 1945 and for a while the Kuttners lived in Hastings-on-Hudson, New York. He moved back to Laguna Beach, California, and, in 1950, entered the University of Southern California as a freshman under the GI Bill of Rights. He felt acutely that he needed to find himself. Always weak in science, he included physics among his courses. His wife, too, went back to school. In 1954 he received his B.A. He had finished his thesis for his M.A., but died from an acute coronary on February 3, 1958.

In 1957 the Kuttners had been hired by Warner Bros.

to do a screenplay for Nathaniel Hawthorne's science-fiction masterpiece, *Rappaccini's Daughter.* Work had been started when a depression hit Hollywood and the idea was canceled. A month later they signed a contract to do a TV show and were in the midst of a revision when Henry died. As she had so often in the past, Catherine finished the script.

In the cold light of critical appraisal, detaching oneself from the man's likability as a human being, the introduction of the John Collier type of sophisticated fantasy into the science-fiction magazines was Kuttner's major contribution. *Presenting Moonshine* by Collier, published by Viking in 1941, comprising dozens of artistically superb fantastic ironies, had taken the literati by storm. Its popularity resulted in a Readers Club Edition in 1943 under the title of *A Touch of Nutmeg.* Like *Mimsy Were the Borogoves,* the almost-as-popular *Call Him Demon* (THRILLING WONDER STORIES, Fall, 1946, published under the pen name Keith Hammond), in which the children realize their "Uncle" is the physical manifestation of an extradimensional monster and sacrifice their grandmother to feed its appetite, is a variation of Collier's *Thus I Refute Beelzy.*

Kuttner felt, and many agree, that his best story in this vein was *Don't Look Now* (STARTLING STORIES, March, 1948), in which a man at a bar warns his drinking companion to be on the lookout for Martians, who can be recognized by a third eye in their forehead. As he walks away the listener opens his third eye and stares at him. The story has since been done frequently on television.

The Shock, The Twonky, and *Time Locker* (converted into a robot story to fill out the collection *Robots Have No Tails,* Gnome Press, 1952) are essentially in the same category with the addition of a diverting potpourri of fantastic elements, too rich for the blood of the uninitiate but grist for the mills of the science-fiction fans.

Kuttner's A. E. van Vogt kick, most obviously apparent in his well-done "Baldies" series, of which he wrote all but *Beggars in Velvet* (collectively published as *Mutant* by

Gnome Press in 1953), are variations on *Slan*. *The Fairy Chessman* and *Tomorrow and Tomorrow,* though creditable, are also attempts to duplicate the methods of van Vogt.

The Lancelot Hogben series which ran in THRILLING WONDER STORIES in 1947-49 (the last of which, *Cold War,* was completely written by Moore from a plot supplied by Kuttner), dealing with a family of hillbilly mutations, were ludicrously unbelievable comedies blatantly drawn from a series which Murray Leinster wrote under the name William Fitzgerald in the same magazine, about a character called Bud Gregory.

The popular A. Merritt imitations, beginning with *Earth's Last Citadel,* serialized in ARGOSY in 1943, reached a height of popularity with *Dark World* in the Summer, 1946, STARTLING STORIES, with its obvious echoes of *Dwellers in the Mirage*. The group obtained a note of authenticity from the contributions of Moore, whose colorful style at times was reminiscent of Merritt.

Who was the real Henry Kuttner? We will never know. The man had discipline, technical brilliance, immense versatility, and ingenuity, and these betrayed him. Lured by opportunism, suffering from an acute sense of inadequacy, he refused to stand alone, but leaned on others for support: H. P. Lovecraft, Robert E. Howard, Stanley G. Weinbaum, A. Merritt, John Collier, A. E. van Vogt, and, of course, C. L. Moore.

19

ROBERT BLOCH

Robert Bloch catapulted to public attention and accelerated success when Alfred Hitchcock's production of his novel *Psycho* not only shocked the nation and the critics, but boasted the second largest gross in the history of black-and-white motion pictures. This tale of the murder of a young girl in the shower of her motel room and the suspicion that focuses on a querulous old woman, who is heard but never seen, and her son, who appears to be covering for her, ends with an explosive impact that Hitchcock regarded as "technically the most satisfying" of any of his productions.

As those who have seen the picture know, the mother has been dead for years and the son has a split personality and talks to himself in a striking simulation of his mother's voice; he is in fact the actual murderer of the girl.

What, it might be asked, has all this to do with science fiction? The answer is: very little, except that Bloch has spent a good part of his lifetime as a fan and writer building a public image as a pillar of science fiction while scoring most of his successes outside of the field. He was guest of honor of the Sixth Annual World Science Fiction Convention in Toronto, Canada, July 3-5, 1948, and was anticipating the psychiatric punch line of *Psycho* when he prefaced his talk on "Fantasy and Psychology" by mimicking Peter Lorre in an animated stream-of-consciousness manner. Yet, for five years preceding the honor, science-fiction writing had made up a relatively minor portion of his work.

He received a Hugo for the best science-fiction short story of the year, *The Hell-Bound Train* (THE MAGAZINE OF FANTASY AND SCIENCE FICTION, September, 1958), a story built around a pact with the devil, a theme which does not belong in the science-fiction canon except allegorically.

It is obvious that Robert Bloch is a paradox, a special case, and a privileged character. How did he get that way?

He was born April 5, 1917, in Chicago, the first child of Raphael A. Bloch, a bank cashier, and Stella Loeb Bloch, a school teacher and social worker. Twenty-two months later a sister, Winifred, was born.

Though his parents were of German-Jewish extraction, most of the religious instruction he received was at the Methodist Church in Maywood, a suburb of Chicago. This was not due to any change in the family's religious persuasion, but resulted from the closeness with which his family's social activities were interwoven with those of the community.

Both parents had an abiding interest in the performing arts. His mother once turned down an offer to go into light opera, where she might have capitalized on an excellent singing voice. She was also a fine pianist and accompanist. The theater and vaudeville were his father's notion of grand entertainment. As a result, young Robert was introduced to the fabulous world of living players when it was still at its peak. At the same time he was privileged to watch the parade of stars of the silent screen: Lon Chaney, Douglas Fairbanks,

Charlie Chaplin, Harold Lloyd, Buster Keaton, Rudolph Valentino, and nostalgic scores of others.

Most children live a good part of the time in a make-believe world, but Robert Bloch rarely left it, recruiting the neighborhood youngsters for an endless series of "dramatic" plays, circuses, mock wars (with hundreds of lead soldiers), and "situation" games. The escapism was overdone, but it was largely accomplished in concert with other children, with Bloch showing signs of leadership.

His exceptional ability as a student quickly changed all that. Repeatedly skipping grades, he soon found himself lonely in the company of much older children who could not be commandeered to participate in his fun. Nor was he capable of physically matching them in sports. This forced a partial introversion and a dependence on the vicarious thrills and intellectual pleasures of books.

An economic turn for the worse in his parents' financial status in 1927 had the effect of socially cutting him off from the world. The bank where his father worked failed. So did a second at which he had procured another job. There were straws in the wind leading up to the 1929 Wall Street crash, but no one was properly interpreting them. His mother resumed social work to help support the family and they moved to another town. Now the ten-year-old boy knew no one. The necessity of taking care of his younger sister while his mother was at work hampered still further his making new friends.

Lon Chaney's motion picture *The Phantom of the Opera* scared the hell out of him, but it also converted him to the world of psychiatric terror and the supernatural. His introduction to the fantasy magazines came in August, 1927, when he was in a railroad station with his parents and his aunt. The aunt offered to buy him any magazine on the stands. To her consternation he gleefully selected the current issue of WEIRD TALES, featuring Otis Adelbert Kline's *The Bride of Osiris,* with a partially nude girl on the cover. Two issues later he really "flipped" when he read H. P. Lovecraft's *Pickman's Model,* a frightening tale of a painter who drew monsters from "real life."

His conversion to science-fiction magazines came with the February, 1928, AMAZING STORIES, featuring *The Revolt of the Pedestrians* by David H. Keller, M.D., a tale of city folk who gradually lose their ability to walk as a result of over-mechanization.

Gradually the effects of the Depression on his family caused the fantasy magazine purchases to cease. His father became afflicted with a strange malady that caused gradual paralysis of his lower limbs, was unable to obtain work as a bank teller, and was grateful to find employment as a night cashier in a restaurant. The family moved from place to place as the whims of economics dictated.

At Milwaukee's Lincoln High School, Bloch coasted in his studies but went full tilt into "dramatics." The stage appealed strongly to him, particularly comedy, and he not only acted but wrote skits as well. Bloch's scintillating wit and superb sense of pace, subsequently demonstrated in his numerous appearances as master of ceremonies at science-fiction affairs, had their origin here. He wanted to be a comic so bad he could taste it, vaudeville was disappearing and, with it, burlesque. The Depression was scarcely the time to begin a nightclub career. His activities on the school stage won him popularity, however, and he was five times elected head of the Student Council. As he grew older, the difference in age between him and the other students didn't matter as much. His circle of friends began to widen.

In 1932 he resumed buying WEIRD TALES, encountering Lovecraft's stories again. Strongly impressed, he wrote the author a fan letter. He was amazed to receive a friendly response and soon a correspondence ensued, during which time he sent Lovecraft trial literary efforts for criticism, some of which had been rejected by WEIRD TALES' editor Farnsworth Wright. Lovecraft suggested the science-fiction fan magazines and sent him copies of THE FANTASY FAN, containing his series of poems *Fungii From Yuggoth,* as well as recommending William Crawford's semiprofessional fantasy magazine, MARVEL TALES. It was there that Bloch first saw print with *Lilies,* a moving short-short story of an old lady who every Saturday night brings flowers from the country to her upstairs neighbors, reaching a climax when she brings the funeral lilies her son has left at her bier after her death. That issue was Winter, 1934, but a previously announced story by Bloch, *The Madness of Lucian Gray,* never appeared, possibly because it was patterned too closely after Lovecraft's *Pickman's Model,* the advance blurb reading: "a weird-fantasy story of an artist who was forced to paint a picture . . . and the frightful thing that came from it."

A second story accepted by Crawford appeared in UNUSUAL STORIES, a companion magazine, after Bloch had already made a number of sales nearly a year later. Titled *Black Lotus,* it dealt with a man who cut his own throat in a dream. The story was a minute stylistic recreation of a certain period in Lovecraft's writing when he was heavily influenced by the technique of Lord Dunsany. Readers were thus confronted, as they would be again when Henry Kuttner began to sell, with the ludicrous spectacle of a Lovecraft-struck acolyte imitating Lovecraft's imitation of Dunsany.

Another very early Bloch tale, *The Laughter of a Ghoul,* was a vignette concerning a man waiting for his wife to give birth to a child, only to find the mother dead and the newborn infant a chortling ghoul. This story, which appeared in the December, 1934, FANTASY FAN, was a literary failure, but nevertheless these test efforts of Robert Bloch's showed such definite ability that it was small surprise when in July, 1934, a month after his graduation from high school and two months after he turned 17, he sold a story to WEIRD TALES, *The Secret of the Tomb.* A second sale, a real shocker called *The Feast in the Abbey,* was published first. The story appeared in WEIRD TALES for January, 1935, and concerned a man who sits down to a feast with some "monks" in an old abbey, to discover in time the main meat course is his brother.

Despite the overpowering influence of Lovecraft, *The Feast in the Abbey* was a remarkably effective effort and tied for first place with three other stories in the same issue by Seabury Quinn, Clark Ashton Smith, and Laurence J. Cahill. The reader's department, "The Eyrie," was filled with begrudgingly favorable comment on Bloch's story, surprising since he had made the political error of venting his spleen on Robert E. Howard's *Conan* in a letter in the November, 1934, WEIRD TALES, and the readers were openly out to "get" him. The poorly timed letter had read: "I am awfully tired of poor old Conan the Cluck, who for the past 15 issues has every month slain a new wizard, tackled a new monster, come to a violent and sudden end that was averted (incredibly enough!) in just the nick of time and won a new girl friend, each of whose penchants for nudism won for her a place of honor, either on the cover or on the inner illustration. Such has been Conan's history, and from the realms of the Kushites to the lands of Quilenia, from the shores of the Shemites to the palaces of Dyme-Novell-Bolonia, I cry: 'Enough of this brute and his iron-thewed sword-thrusts — may he be sent to Valhalla to cut out paper dolls.' "

It was a close thing, for Howard was writing at his bloody best and his fans were legion, including even Bloch's newly acquired mentor H. P. Lovecraft, who must have taken small pleasure in the incident. Had Farnsworth Wright, editor of WEIRD TALES, printed first the story Bloch had sold him, *The Secret in the Tomb* (which eventually appeared in the May, 1935, issue), there would have been a literary massacre. *The Secret in the Tomb* was a pathetically weak mood piece of a man who discovers his ancestor is a ghoul.

Equally inadequate was *Suicide in the Study* (WEIRD TALES, June, 1935), in which a scientist splits his good and evil personalities into two physical bodies and is destroyed in the act. If the tale has any significance, it is that it was the first in which Bloch made the slightest gesture in the direction of scientific explanation for the strange events he relates.

The Howard incident was an important lesson learned early. Rarely again did Bloch ever pervert his brilliant wit to vitriolic ends. Instead, he became a master of the art of making people feel important as he ribbed them, of investing his literary or verbal lampoon with an implied compliment. As a result, his friends were to become legion and his detractors negligible.

During this early period of his writing, Bloch was held completely in thrall by Lovecraft. Virtually nothing of his own showed through. Such popularity as he enjoyed was obtained by basking in the reflection of the master. *The Shambler from the Stars* (WEIRD TALES, September, 1935) was not only dedicated to H. P. Lovecraft but made him the central character, who unwisely utters an incantation that draws a monster from the unknown, to break him up like kindling wood and suck the blood from his body. Lovecraft employed a "famous" book as a literary device in his stories, *The Necronomicon;* Clark Ashton Smith was fond of *The Book of Eibon;* and August Derleth coveted the *Cultes des Goules,* so why couldn't Bloch invent his own book? He did: *De Vermis Mysteriis* (Mysteries of the Worm), by Ludvig Prinn, a man allegedly burned at the stake in Brussels as the result of his activities as an alchemist and necromancer.

"Robert Bloch deserves plenty of praise for *Shambler of the Stars.* Now why doesn't Mr. Lovecraft return the compliment, and dedicate a story to the author?" suggested reader B. M. Reynolds of North Adams, Mass., in WEIRD TALES' *Eyrie* for November, 1935. His suggestion became reality when H. P. Lovecraft wrote *The Haunter of the Dark* (WEIRD TALES, December, 1936) as a sequel to *Shambler of the Stars* and dedicated it to Robert Bloch. In this story he returns the compliment, and Robert "Blake" is killed by a loathsome monstrosity which breaks out of an abandoned church tower in Providence, Rhode Island, under the cover of darkness caused by an electrical breakdown.

A resident of Milwaukee during 1935, Bloch received a write-up in the local papers underscoring his success as a weird-fiction writer. Soon there came an invitation to join a unique literary group called The Milwaukee Fictioneers, some of its members writers working in the fantasy field. The group met once every two weeks, barred all women, and confined its membership to professionals only. It had a rule against reading manuscripts at meetings but worked extremely hard, together, on story plotting. Meetings were held alternately at members' homes and the size of the group rarely exceeded twelve. The result was writing discipline that paid off for all and gave Bloch a feeling of professional acceptance.

Among its members was Stanley G. Weinbaum, whose influence on writers who followed was more far-reaching than even that of Lovecraft; Ralph Milne Farley (Senator Roger Sherman Hoar), who had built up a considerable reputation for his "Radio Man" novels in ARGOSY, and Raymond A. Palmer, who was to become the editor of AMAZING STORIES. Earl Pierce, Jr., a contributor to WEIRD TALES, was also a resident of Milwaukee whom Bloch met at the time.

Bloch became a frequent visitor to Weinbaum's home; they had in common a strong interest in James Branch Cabell. Bloch remembers Weinbaum as a soft-spoken Southerner (originally from Louisville), a good-looking, unassuming man, living quietly and modestly with his wife. Among the "secrets" that Bloch confessed to Weinbaum and other Milwaukee Fictioneers was the fact that he still yearned to be a comic. His adulation of Lovecraft was light years removed from this ambition, but he recalls, "I did submit gags to F. Chase Taylor, of the then-popular comedy team Stoopnagle and Budd, whom I admired, and got a couple of small checks. When Roy Atwell, then appearing with Fred Allen, came to town in vaudeville, I appeared on an amateur show at the theater. Atwell was not only interested in my impersonation, he also bought the monologue material I used for myself. For a short time I did nitery stints as M. C. or monologist, but the money was poor even by Depression standards, the hours were terrible, and the whole *milieu* seemed seedy and seamy. I wasn't hip enough to thrive at the trade."

The death of Lovecraft on March 15, 1937, affected Robert Bloch much harder than he admitted in his eulogy, which appeared in the June, 1937, WEIRD TALES. "Of course there ought to be a memorial volume, with stories chosen by the readers," he wrote. "That's the smallest tribute we can pay." (A few years later August W. Derleth and Donald Wandrei accomplished that objective and the beginning of a new fame for Lovecraft.)

"But there's an end of the world," Bloch continued, "the world of Cthulhu, Yog-Sothoth, Nyarlathotep, and Abdul Alhazred; the finest world of fantasy I know."

During the past year Bloch's stories in the Lovecraft vein had been growing in effectiveness, predominantly a result of greater care in building the backgrounds of his stories. Their popularity became undeniable, but equally undeniable was the fact that the endings were forced and unbelievable. Stories like *The Druidic Doom, The Faceless God, The Grinning Ghoul, The Opener of the Way, The Dark Demon,* and *Brood of Bubastis* were cast in the same mold. The author seemed unaware that in the majority of his later writings Lovecraft had abandoned the supernatural in explaining his horrors and had leaned with increasing weight on science. Bloch was actually writing pastiches of early Lovecraft.

In this respect he had company. Henry Kuttner, as fervid a Lovecraft enthusiast and imitator as Bloch, had broken into the professional ranks by the same road. They had been correspondents for years, and when Lovecraft died, sensing Bloch's bereavement, Kuttner's mother suggested to Henry that Bloch be invited as a guest to their Beverly Hills home. C. L. Moore was in town visiting at the time, and Bloch was also introduced to another aspiring author who would eventually make his reputation in fantasy ranks, Fritz Leiber, Jr. They were as curious about Bloch as he was about them, and what they saw was a tall, angular young man, not yet turned 21, with features as sharp as his wit (largely expressed in the science-fiction fan magazines) and rimless glasses that imparted an intellectual appearance. In person they found Bloch was soft spoken, quiet, almost gentle.

Kuttner was barely getting under way as a writer. Besides WEIRD TALES he was selling to THRILLING MYSTERY and was evaluating other markets. It would be years before Bloch would seriously try for any magazine other than WEIRD TALES, and then only by accident.

On the recommendation of Ralph Milne Farley, Ray Palmer had been given the job as editor of AMAZING STORIES by Ziff-Davis Publications, a Chicago firm that had purchased the magazine from Teck Publications in the spring of 1938. Palmer was desperately casting about for Chicago-area writers he could shape into a dependable team and he urged Bloch to try his hand at writing science fiction.

Bloch's first attempt, *The Secret of the Observatory* in the August, 1938, AMAZING STORIES, was a potboiler about a camera that could photograph through walls, but it did force Bloch to write dialogue. Lovecraft couldn't write dialogue, so precious little appeared in any story by writers influenced by him. In his nearly four years of fantasy writing, Bloch probably hadn't written 1,000 words of dialogue in his fantasy, though of course he did some for comedy routines.

In his second attempt at science fiction, Bloch hit the bull's-eye. No one knew it at the time, but Bloch had found the thing he was best at and that would eventually lead to the writing of *Psycho*. Authors had detailed every conceivable aspect of the physical side of space flight, but in *The Strange Flight of Richard Clayton* in AMAZING STORIES for March, 1939, Bloch explored its psychological aspects.

A man is sent to Mars in a windowless space ship on a journey that will take ten years. His instrument board is smashed on take-off so he has no way of estimating distance or duration. Time passes and his hair whitens, his skin shrivels, and he begins to grow old. Finally the ship stops vibrating and he emerges to learn that the ship never left Earth, that he was sealed inside for only one week.

New space developments may possibly date the story, but at the time of its appearance it was a masterpiece based on excellent scientific knowledge (atomic energy engines) with a finale that figuratively tore the reader's head off.

It was in the same magazine that Bloch was first able to express a broad note of humor, accomplishing this in *The Man Who Walked Through Mirrors,* a tale that was a spoof on AMAZING STORIES' cover slogan of that period: "Every Story Scientifically Accurate."

In science fiction he felt uninhibited, under no obligation to be anything but himself. In weird fiction, the ghost of H. P. Lovecraft bound him in a literary straitjacket that he would be years in completely extricating himself from, though there were a few early indications that this was coming. One was in *Slave of the Flames* (WEIRD TALES, June, 1938), in which he briefly and superbly explored the psychology of a pyromaniac. Another was in *The Cloak* (UNKNOWN, May, 1939), which departed from the Lovecraft style, showing instead heavy dependence on dialogue, a faint implication of humor, and even a note of romance before the traditional horrific denouement.

Branching out into AMAZING STORIES, STRANGE STORIES, UNKNOWN, as well as into the mystery-horror magazines, gave Bloch enough income in 1939 to consider marriage seriously. In addition, he was doing political ghost writing, something he would continue through 1941. He met Marion Ruth Holcombe in 1939 and they were married in October, 1940. As a child she had suffered from tuberculosis of the hip, and symptoms of this began to recur in 1941, forcing Bloch to look around seriously for a steady job and temporarily at least to give up thought of making magazine and free-lance writing his main source of income.

He took a job with the Gustav Marx Advertising Agency

as a copywriter in 1942, feeling it was just a temporary expedient, but in 1943 a daughter, Sally Ann, was born and his wife's illness became almost chronic, at one point necessitating nine months' treatment in a sanitarium. As a result, Bloch stayed with the Gustav Marx Agency for the next ten years, writing in his spare time.

Despite his problems, he began a series of humorous stories in the Damon Runyon manner for FANTASTIC ADVENTURES, built around the character of Lefty Feep. Some were science fiction, others fantasy, and still others straight weirdies, but one and all they were the most insane melange of cockeyed humor the fantasy magazines had ever seen. From the first, whose title has since become an American axiom, *Time Wounds All Heels* (FANTASTIC ADVENTURES, April, 1942), through the last, appropriately labeled *The End of Your Rope* (FANTASTIC ADVENTURES, July, 1950), the stories were little more than a blend of situation comedy and vaudeville done narrative-style, replete with puns, mixed metaphors, rhyming phrases, alliteration, phonetic dialogue, and anything else that could be thrown into the pot. This madhouse concoction ran to twenty-two stories, most of them novelette length.

Bloch was also proving he could do some effective work in straight science fiction with *The Fear Planet* in the February, 1943, SUPER SCIENCE STORIES, relating the fate of space explorers who turn into carnivorous plants, and *Almost Human* in the July, 1943, FANTASTIC ADVENTURES, about a robot whose outlook on life is conditioned by gangsters.

The most unexpected result came from what Bloch considered a routine horror story titled *Yours Truly, Jack the Ripper* which appeared in WEIRD TALES for July, 1943. It told of the son of one of the women Jack the Ripper had slain in England, still searching for him in today's United States, convinced that he is alive and that his killings are necromantic sacrifices that sustain his youth. What makes a story catch on? No one knows. But on January 7, 1944, *Yours Truly, Jack the Ripper* was adopted for Kate Smith's radio show on

CBS when radio was still king. The Mollé Mystery Theatre on NBC dramatized it again on March 6, 1945. It was done again for *Stay Tuned for Terror,* and still again for *Murder by Experts.* Anthologies began to pick it up, including *The Mystery Companion, The Harlot Killer,* and *The Unexpected,* but most important it was included in *The Fireside Book of Suspense Stories,* edited by Alfred Hitchcock, in 1947, bringing Bloch to his attention and ultimately to the production of *Psycho.*

The Kate Smith rendition of *Yours Truly, Jack the Ripper* may have helped Bloch get an assignment in 1944 to adapt thirty-nine of his own tales, science fiction as well as weirds, for radio for a program called *Stay Tuned for Terror.* Though the show enjoyed moderate popularity, being broadcast in Canada and Hawaii as well as the United States, it folded when its Chicago producer, John Neblett, died in an airplane crash at the same time that a major backer, Berle Adams, came down with a serious illness.

Helping to take the edge off the loss of *Stay Tuned for Terror* was the prestige publication of the first collection of Robert Bloch's short stories by Arkham House in 1945. Arkham was a publishing firm founded by August Derleth and Donald Wandrei to publish a memorial volume to Lovecraft. They quite literally made Lovecraft famous with *The Outsider* and *Beyond the Wall of Sleep,* two omnibus volumes containing the best of that writer's works. They had followed with collections by Clark Ashton Smith, Henry S. Whitehead, Derleth himself, Donald Wandrei, J. Sheridan Le Fanu, Frank Belknap Long, and other similar fantasists. Their books were handsomely produced, coveted by collectors, and prominently reviewed.

The Opener of the Way contained an excellent cross-section of the best of Bloch's work to date, including *The Strange Flight of Richard Clayton; Yours Truly, Jack the Ripper; The Feast in the Abbey; Slave of the Flames;* and a sampling of his stories in the Lovecraft vein. To fill out the volume, Bloch wrote a new story, *One Way to Mars,* a psychiatric fantasy about the antics of a man trying to avoid being sold a one-way ticket to Mars. It had a polish and finesse which Bloch, writing after hours and at full tilt, rarely bothered to give his work, and betrayed no trace of the Lovecraft "monkey on his back."

As early as 1943, Bloch had switched a major part of his writing to magazines such as MAMMOTH DETECTIVE, NEW DETECTIVE, THRILLING MYSTERY, and DIME MYSTERY. In 1947 he tried his hand at a full-length mystery, *The Scarf,* published by Dial. Here he wrote in the manner of Raymond Chandler, short, jolting, hard sentences carrying events relentlessly forward. This was the first of seven mystery novels, his own personal favorite, outside of *Psycho,* being *The Kidnapper,* an orginal paperback published by Lion Books in 1954. "Nobody, but nobody, liked this little effort, which is a matter-of-fact, straightforward account of a vicious psychopathic kidnapper, told in the first person," he complained. "I think it is my most honest book; there are no 'tricks' and there's no overt 'Look, Ma—I'm writing!' touches. I believe it was disliked just because it *was* realistic, and hence unpleasant."

Bloch had educated himself out of the Lovecraft style, but he would never lose the Lovecraft method. True, now his themes were conveyed with merciless, naked realism, where before the language of a more genteel school of rhetoric partially softened his meaning. But his practice was still the same. To tell all. To hold nothing back. To build toward the ultimate horror with every device at hand and then spring it on the reader in its "hideous totality." The terrors he described had slowly converted from virtually unbelievable mythos to all-too-frightening aberrations of the human mind. But the public wasn't ready for his brand of brutal directness, regardless of its authenticity.

Writing a biographical sketch in THE FANSCIENT for Summer, 1949, Bloch, at the age of 32, was optimistic. The past decade, despite personal problems, had seemed all of one growth. His stories had appeared regularly on radio, a collection of his works had been published, his detective novels were clicking, anthologies were including his efforts as a regular thing, and the booming science-fiction and fantasy field was wide open to him.

Ten years later, at the age of 42, this attitude had become one of depression bordering on despair. Not even winning a Hugo for his short story *The Hell-Bound Train* could temper his pessimism, which he kept no secret. There had been some good things, most important of which were the new tuberculosis drugs which had rescued his wife from semi-invalidism by 1954. The same year he severed association with the Gustav Marx Agency to engage in full-time writing. The rest had been somewhat of a nightmare.

Story writing went on endlessly till there was no joy in it. Occasionally there was a radio adaptation. Periodically a mystery novel appeared. He frequently made sales to better men's magazines like PLAYBOY, but just as many yarns were still going for little better than a cent a word. He was on an endless treadmill. He wasn't going anywhere. There was no better-liked man in the entire science-fiction world, but popularity didn't seem to be paying off in dollars.

Among the countless friends that Bloch had made was a science-fiction enthusiast with the unlikely name of Samuel Anthony Peeples. They had met at the 12th Annual World Science Fiction Convention at San Francisco in 1954. Peeples' major claim to fame in science fiction was the writing of a preface for the hard-cover anthology, *Travelers in Space,* published by Gnome Press in 1951. However, the field of the western novel was another matter. Frank Gruber, famed detective story writer, was so impressed by his ability that he brought Peeples to Hollywood in 1957 where he became a "solid sender" in TV.

Peeples was just as sold on Bloch's ability and determined to pull a "Gruber" on him. Before attending the 17th World Science Fiction Convention at Detroit in 1959, Bloch was feeling so low that he poured the accumulated disillusionment into a dark piece called *Funnel of God* (FANTASTIC

SCIENCE FICTION, January, 1960), which reminded readers of the defiant negativism of Mark Twain's despairing *The Mysterious Stranger*. Upon his return from the convention, he received a long-distance phone call from Peeples, who dangled before him the carrot of a guaranteed assignment to do one script for the TV show *Lock-Up*, a series built around the career of a wealthy lawyer who takes on worthy "hopeless" cases without fee.

The thirty-nine adaptations he had done for *Stay Tuned for Terror* now stood him in good stead. The producer liked his first script and asked for more. Bloch took up temporary residence in Hollywood and picked up an assignment to write for the Alfred Hitchcock Show, from "The Master of Suspense" who had already purchased the film rights to Bloch's novel *Psycho*. No one, least of all Bloch, expected anything special from it. When it connected Bloch was not only successful but *famous* as well. Public taste had finally caught up with Bloch.

With his wife well enough to travel and his daughter having just completed a school semester, he moved his family out to Hollywood in July, 1960. For television he expanded his writing to include *Thriller*, the hour-length Alfred Hitchcock Shows, *Whispering Smith*, as well as work on Jack Webb's *True* series. Motion pictures credited to him included *The Couch, The Cabinet of Caligari,* and *Merry-Go-Round,* based on a story by Ray Bradbury. It was only the beginning, for Bloch carried with him to Hollywood the disciplined capacity for work that had characterized his twenty-five years of ceaseless self-training. Writing scared, writing hungry, with the tools of his craft sharpened to a razor's edge, he had brilliance to spare when the opportunity was offered.

Evaluating most writers in the fantasy field, one concludes by asking: What did he contribute to the development of science fiction? In this case the question should be reversed to read: What part did science fiction play in the development of Robert Bloch? The answer is that it provided the catalyst which made it possible for him to emerge as one of the nation's greatest writers of psychological terror. Therein lies the solution of the puzzling and paradoxical "love affair" that has so long existed between Robert Bloch and the science-fiction world.

20

RAY BRADBURY

Beyond cavil, the most widely and enthusiastically accepted author to vault out of the perishable pulp paper obscurity of the science-fiction magazines in the present generation has been Ray Bradbury. Product of a field where outstanding literary achievement is rewarded only by the adulation of a coterie of devotees and a few cents a word from the publications, his achievements, notable by any standards, are unparalleled.

In 1954 The National Institute of Arts and Letters presented him with the $1,000 annual award "for his contributions to American Literature in *The Martian Chronicles* and *The Illustrated Man*," two integrated collections of short stories, most of them culled from the science-fiction magazines. The same year The Commonwealth Club of California gave him their Second Annual Gold Medal for *Fahrenheit 451*, the book title of *The Fireman*, a short novel which first appeared in GALAXY SCIENCE FICTION.

Those were merely two of dozens of special honors heaped upon him since 1946, as the special quality of his work was recognized by a wider audience. Awards were not the only satisfaction Bradbury received. Following an almost continuous stream of sales to top-paying markets like SATURDAY EVENING POST, COLLIER'S, ESQUIRE, NEW YORKER, MCCALL'S, SEVENTEEN, and MCLEAN'S MAGAZINE, he received a contract to write the screenplay of John Huston's *Moby Dick*, starring Gregory Peck. Reprints and anthology appearances of his stories have mounted into the hundreds and the presentations of his stories on radio and television is rapidly approaching the 100 mark.

When a new Ray Bradbury book appears it gets serious attention from the newspapers and periodicals that count. No one any longer debates his qualifications for the big time. The question now is how fine will his skills develop and how far will they carry him.

Usually an evaluation of an author will at least lightly touch upon his childhood, even if events there do not directly appear to influence his writings. In Bradbury's case, his childhood and teen years are a major consideration in his motivation.

Ray Douglas Bradbury shares with comedian Jack Benny the distinction of having been born in Waukegan, Illinois. The date was August 22, 1920. His father was descended from an English family who settled in America in 1630. His mother was of Swedish origin. A brother and sister died during infancy and he grew up with one older brother. Bradbury's infrequent references to his mother display considerable affection. He rarely mentions his father "who had a job with a power company," and when he finally pulls back the curtain in his dedication to *A Medicine for Melancholy*, published in 1959: "For Dad, whose love, very late in life, surprised his son," it is most revealing.

There are implications of a non-too-happy childhood in his autobiographical sketch in WEIRD TALES for November, 1943, where he states: "Some of my first memories concern going upstairs at night and finding an unpleasant beast waiting at the next to the last step. Screaming, I'd run back down to mother. Then, together, we'd climb the stairs. Invariably, the monster would be gone. Mother never saw it. Sometimes I was irritated at her lack of imagination.

"I imagine I should be thankful for my fear of the dark, though. You have to know fear and apprehension in some form before you can write about it thoroughly, and God knows my first ten years were full of the usual paraphernalia of ghosts and skeletons and dead men tumbling down the twisting interior of my mind. What a morbid little brat I must have been to have around."

He also refers to his problems with youthful bullies and most pointedly, in his essay *Where Do You Get Your Ideas* in the 1950 issue of the amateur publication ETAON SHRDLU, says: "One is not very old before one realizes how alone one is in the world."

Many of the tales of the weird, horrifying, and supernatural written by Bradbury are derived from his childhood fears and are set in midwestern Waukegan. The same background is provided for *Dandelion Wine*, a connected series of short stories issued in 1957, which recreates with nostalgia the Waukegan of 1928. In the 1950's it is a plusher, more contented Bradbury assembling this book, with a wife and three daughters, a fine reputation, a bank account, and a pleasant home. Therefore, the painful is subdued and the pleasant highlighted. Nevertheless, the youthful hero, Douglas (and Douglas is Ray Bradbury's middle name), has woven a few of his horror tales into the fabric, most notably *The Night*.

Bradbury's autobiographical sketches reveal an almost uninterrupted indoctrination in fantasy, starting before he could read. His mother read him the Oz series and his aunt let him have Edgar Allan Poe straight.

Bradbury's introduction to magazine science fiction is recorded with preciseness. It was the Fall, 1928, issue of AMAZING STORIES QUARTERLY, featuring A. Hyatt Verrill's intriguing novel *The World of the Giant Ants*, illustrated by the fascinating imaginings of Frank R. Paul, which were more than enough to evoke a sense of wonder in any normal child. The issue was passed on to the eight-year-old by a teen-age girl boarding with the family.

The Depression hitting bottom in 1932 may have been one factor in the Bradburys' moving from Waukegan to Arizona. There, he struck up a friendship with a youth who had a boxful of old AMAZING STORIES and WONDER STORIES, and he borrowed and read them all. Bradbury also never tires of telling of his fixation on Edgar Rice Burroughs' tales of Tarzan and Mars at the age of 12, and how, lacking money, he pounded out his own sequels on a toy typewriter with all capital letters.

Two years later, in 1934, his family made its final move, to Los Angeles. Richard Donovan, in his article *Morals from Mars* in THE REPORTER for June 26, 1951, refers to the Bradbury of this period as "a fat boy who wore spectacles and could not play football satisfactorily. Humiliated, he turned to writing."

A turning point in his life came in early September, 1937, when while poring through the books and magazines in Shep's Shop, a Los Angeles book store that catered to science-fiction readers, he received an invitation from a member to visit the Los Angeles Chapter of the Science Fiction League. At the September 5, 1937, meeting, held at the home of one of the members, he was handed the first issue of a club magazine titled IMAGINATION! The possibility that he might actually get something published in that amateur effort was the convincer. He joined at the following, October, meeting.

Bradbury's first published story, *Hollerbochen's Dilemma*, appeared in the fourth (January, 1938) issue of IMAGINATION! It was scarcely a distinguished literary work, but its plot of a man who generates a tremendous amount of energy by "standing still in time" and blows himself and the city off the map when he resumes his normal place, is repeated so closely in A. E. van Vogt's first Weapon Shops story, *The Seesaw,* published in ASTOUNDING SCIENCE-FICTION for July, 1941, as to raise a question.

This story was almost out of character for Bradbury at the time, who apparently played the role of the club clown. One of the members described him as "the funny man of the Los Angeles League. In other words, he is the Big Joke." Most of his published works of that period were pathetically inept attempts at humor, both in fiction and nonfiction. Today, they are the despair of the collector trying to put together all of Bradbury's writings, having been published in obscure amateur mimeographed journals with titles like D'JOURNAL, FANTASCIENCE DIGEST, NOVA, MIKROS, FANTASY DIGEST, POLARIS, and SWEETNESS AND LIGHT.

An amusing and surprisingly accurate account of Bradbury's physical appearance at that time was supplied by himself in the June-July, 1939, FANTASY DIGEST: "That horrid thing in the mirror has toddled through life wearing glasses, blue eyes, a frowsy hank of blondish hair, twin ears, hot and cold running drool, and a nose that would pass for a cabbage in a dim light. He has white teeth, his very own, and a reddish complexion (weaned on catsup, you know). He stands (or rather leans) to five feet and ten inches not counting the green familiar that rides around on his eyebrows on cool days and sings 'Frankie and Johnnie.' "

Virtually every early description of teen-age Ray Bradbury by a personal acquaintance speaks of unfailing affability, puncture-proof good nature, constant buffoonery, and self-effacement. He appeared to be a man without a tart opinion on any subject. The stark contrast with the fear-haunted, angry, sensitive, and hurt Bradbury revealed in his later writings suggests a deliberate early façade.

A possible confirmation of this surmise rests in the appraisal of Bradbury made by one of his closest early friends, T. Bruce Yerke, in a booklet entitled *Memoirs of a Superfluous Fan,* published in December, 1943. "The feature which marked him among the members of the group was his mad, insane, hackneyed humor," wrote Yerke, "but underneath his ribald and uncontrollable Bacchus . . . was a deep understanding of people and signs of the times."

The Los Angeles club was a very good thing for Bradbury. Among the members at the time were selling fantasy authors like Henry Kuttner and Arthur K. Barnes, and later, Robert A. Heinlein and Leigh Brackett. When Bradbury graduated from high school in 1938 he shed his theatrical ambitions and even his dreams of becoming an artist. A few of his attempts at stenciled illustrations were published. Now he seriously gave priority to the notion of becoming a writer, and the local writing members and frequent visiting professional authors found Bradbury a veritable leech, insatiable in his quest for the formula to successful professional writing.

However, not only did sales elude the youthful Bradbury, but even among the amateur science-fiction fan magazines, which then rarely rejected anything, he received a surprisingly negative response. There was only one thing to do. In the early Summer of 1939, Ray Bradbury mimeographed his *own* periodical, FUTURIA FANTASIA. The first issue featured a cover by Hannes Bok, who was then virtually unknown, and a story by Ray Bradbury under the pen name Ron Reynolds.

More significantly, most of the issue was devoted to promoting a movement known as Technocracy, Inc. Under the direction of Howard Scott, Technocracy briefly gained ground during the depths of the Depression. Hugo Gernsback turned out two issues of a magazine titled TECHNOCRACY REVIEW (February and March, 1933); wrote an editorial *Wonders of Technocracy* in the March, 1933, WONDER STORIES, and in the same issue published a story *The Robot Technocrat* by Nat Schachner. He presented the idea objectively and then dropped it, made uncomfortable by the company he was keeping.

The technocratic masterminds had a theory that the American economic system would collapse by 1945. They were prepared to step in with an appointive hierarchy of scientists, who would run the country with complete scientific preciseness and infallibility. They estimated that under their system there would be the equivalent of $20,000 annually for every individual in the country, redeemable in energy certificates. People would work four hours a day, five days a week. The country would be split into one hundred zones and an industrial complex allocated to take care of the needs of each zone.

Bradbury said then: "I think Technocracy combines all of the hopes and dreams of science fiction. We've been dreaming about it for years—now, in a short time it may become a reality."

Bradbury today is excoriated for his antiscientific attitude. His fear of science misused is real and evident. This attitude was *not* present in 1939 when he idealistically forecast that a country run completely according to the dictates of a scientific technate was a good thing. The fact that there were no provisions for elections in this system did not bother him because he felt, at that time, that a "limited dictatorship" was desirable.

Within weeks after publishing the first issue of FUTURIA FANTASIA, Ray Bradbury attended the First World Science Fiction Convention, held in New York over the July 4th weekend in 1930. On July 7th he went up to see Farnsworth Wright, the editor of WEIRD TALES, with a dual purpose. First, to examine possibilities of selling stories to that magazine and, second, to show Wright samples of the artwork of Hannes Bok, whose specialty was a baroque style ideally suited for the weird tale. The latter mission was a complete success. Wright enthusiastically purchased Bok's work and Bradbury was the instrument of that artist's appearing on the professional scene.

From the long-range viewpoint, the most important thing Bradbury accomplished during his New York visit was to meet Julius Schwartz for the first time. Schwartz was then the leading literary agent specializing in science fiction and fantasy. The Fall, 1939, issue of FUTURIA FANTASIA contained Ray Bradbury's story *Pendulum,* published anonymously. Bradbury induced Henry Hasse, an enthusiast who had previously sold a number of science fiction stories on his own, to help him rewrite it. This Schwartz dutifully attempted to market as a collaboration, hoping Hasse's reputation would ring up a sale, but nothing happened.

In the summer of 1941, Julius Schwartz and writer Edmond Hamilton decided to rent an apartment together in Los Angeles for the months of July and August. Schwartz would vacation and Hamilton would pound the typewriter. The first afternoon, Schwartz strolled fifty yards from the apartment on Norton Street to the corner of Olympic, to be stopped by the call: "Paper, Mister?" He turned to discover that the newsboy was Ray Bradbury. Bradbury sold newspapers every afternoon on that corner, his main source of income between the years 1938 and 1942.

Bradbury was relentless. Before and after his newspaper stint he was everlastingly underfoot at the Schwartz-Hamilton apartment. The situation became all but impossible when on July 18, 1941, news arrived that *Pendulum* had been purchased for $27.50 by SUPER SCIENCE STORIES. This story, which appeared in the November issue of that magazine, told of a scientist of the future, who in demonstrating a new discovery, accidentally kills two dozen of the world's leading savants. As punishment, he is imprisoned in a giant swinging pendulum. The motion renders him almost immortal and he watches the centuries pass, ultimately to dissolve into dust when invaders from outer space stop the action of the pendulum. In both writing and plotting, the story was below the minimum level of acceptability, even for that period.

Credit for the discovery of Bradbury (despite the fact that he published, without pay, a short nonfiction bit in SCRIPT seven months earlier) belongs to Alden H. Norton, who had taken over the editorship of SUPER SCIENCE STORIES only a week previously from Fred Pohl. Norton went on to become associate publisher of Popular Publications.

Another collaboration with Henry Hasse, *Gabriel's Horn*, was going the rounds and would eventually sell to CAPTAIN FUTURE, but at the moment Bradbury's chief consideration was how to accomplish sale number two. He dug back into the files of FUTURIA FANTASIA and in its fourth and final issue found *The Piper* under his pen name Ron Reynolds. Back he was on the doorstep of Schwartz's apartment. It was a hot day and both of them sat down on the curb, revising *The Piper* according to Schwartz's instruction. Whenever they took a break, Bradbury would have a hamburger and a malted milk, the staples of his diet in those days.

The Piper was the first sale Bradbury made on his own and his first tale of Mars. Well written, it appeared in THRILLING WONDER STORIES for February, 1943, and told of the last civilized Martian who lures a primitive race out of the hills through music to destroy the Jovians who are exploiting the planet.

The original version in FUTURIA FANTASIA, while inferior, was much closer to the style Bradbury would eventually adopt. Instead of Jovians, the exploiters of Mars were Earthmen. The description of their cities is very close to *The Martian Chronicles*. The history of this story reveals that in attempting to ape the methods of the selling writers Bradbury made a mistake. He would have made it quicker and better on his own.

Bradbury had no one to tell him this. He rented an office with a typewriter and a desk, and for eight hours a day ground out stories, none of which sold. He eventually burned three million words of manuscript and in desperation sheered away from science fiction and tried to get into the pages of WEIRD TALES. To this end he enlisted the help of Henry Kuttner, who actually wrote the last two hundred words of *The Candle*. This very weak tale of death wish and retribution was bought by WEIRD STORIES for $25 and published in its November, 1942, issue.

Promotion to Satellite, a short story of an Italian who dies in space saving members of the crew of his ship and whose body is permitted to become a satellite circling Earth as a monument to his heroism, was the next sale and this appeared in THRILLING WONDER STORIES for Fall, 1943. This story almost came off and showed early traces of the later, more successful, Bradbury.

Up to now, Bradbury had been trying to imitate other science-fiction writers. In *The Wind* in WEIRD TALES, March, 1943, he chose as his model Ernest Hemingway and the bulk of a longish short story of a man threatened and finally absorbed by the wind is related in trim dialogue so characteristic of the master. Hemingway remained a major stylistic influence on Bradbury thereafter.

The following, May, 1943, issue of WEIRD TALES contained his short story *The Crowd*, clearly a variant of Edgar Allan Poe's *Man of the Crowd*, dealing with those people who seem to spring from nowhere when an accident occurs.

The Scythe, appearing in WEIRD TALES for July, 1943, was a chilling allegory of the Grim Reaper, but Bradbury really rang the bell with *The Ducker* in the November, 1943, issue. The story of Johnny Choir, who thought that real war was a children's game and came through unscathed, was Bradbury's first tapping of the rich mine of childhood memories that was to make him famous. Reader response was so immense that a sequel featuring the same character, *Bang! You're Dead*, appeared in the September, 1944, WEIRD TALES. The magazine requested and ran his biography, and Bradbury was off to his first big reputation.

The slow, discouraging progress in selling science fiction forced him to redouble his efforts on fantasy. The top market in the science fiction world of 1942 was ASTOUNDING SCIENCE-FICTION, and its editor consistently got first look at every Bradbury story and just as consistently turned it down. He finally invested $45 in a near-fantasy submitted as *Everything Instead of Something* which was published in the September, 1943, ASTOUNDING SCIENCE-FICTION as *Doodad*. The story, a transparent take-off on van Vogt's Weapon Shops idea, concerned a store that sold gadgets from other time periods capable of doing virtually anything. The hero uses them to defeat a gangster in as pitiful a piece of fantasy as ever appeared in ASTOUNDING.

ASTOUNDING SCIENCE-FICTION's companion magazine, UN-KNOWN FANTASY FICTION, next bought one of Bradbury's weird tales. Ironically, the publication collapsed before the story could be published, and *The Emissary* eventually appeared in Bradbury's first hard-cover collection, *Dark Carnival*, published by Arkham House in 1947. The contrast in quality to *Doodad* is incredible. In *The Emissary*, the story of an invalided boy whose dog regularly brings a kindly young woman to visit and who finds the animal has succeeded one last time in his mission, after she is dead and buried, Bradbury created a minor classic in terror.

So, Bradbury reluctantly poured most of his energies into the weird, horrible, and terrifying. Drawing primarily on memories of childhood, he sold a continuous stream of outré, grotesque, bizarre tales with titles like *The Sea Shell, Reunion, The Lake, The Jar, The Poems, The Tombstone,* and, probably most memorable of all, *The Night,* a realistic portrayal of the gradually rising tension and fear engendered by the waiting and then the searching for a child out too late and overdue.

One such story, *The Long Night,* fell into the detective story category, and Julius Schwartz submitted it to Popular Publications' NEW DETECTIVE. On buying it, editor W. Ryerson Johnson told Schwartz: "This Bradbury is beyond question the most promising writer I have ever read. He's going places and let me see more." Schwartz passed the message on to Bradbury, who began alternating weird tales with detective stories, eventually selling nearly a score of them to DETECTIVE TALES, DETECTIVE FICTION, DETECTIVE BOOK MAGAZINE, DIME MYSTERY, and NEW DETECTIVE. One, *Wake for the Dead,* in the September, 1947, DIME MYSTERY, was science fiction, built around the concept of a completely automatic coffin. Another, *The Small Assassin,* has become a Bradbury classic, concerning a baby that murders both of its parents.

Occasional Bradbury science fiction appeared. *I, Rocket* in the May, 1944, AMAZING STORIES was an effective interplanetary adventure told from the viewpoint of the rocket ship. A little earlier, *King of the Grey Spaces* in the December, 1943, FAMOUS FANTASTIC MYSTERIES, was a sensitive story of a young boy trained and finally selected from among many to go to space.

The most dependable market for Bradbury's science fiction was the action-adventure pulp PLANET STORIES. At first he conformed to adventure formula, even doing a revival of Robert E. Howard's Conan-style adventure in *Lorelei of the Red Mist*, (Summer, 1946), in collaboration with Leigh Brackett. The notion of a morgue spaceship, to pick up bodies after interplanetary wars, was unique, but his use of the theme in two stories, *Morgue Ship* (Summer, 1944), and *Lazarus, Come Forth* (Winter, 1944), was undistinguished.

Then it happened. A story submitted to PLANET STORIES as *The Family Outing* appeared in the Summer, 1946, issue of that magazine as *The Million Year Picnic*. In cash it was worth only $32, but in reader reaction incalculably more. This story of the last family from earth, sailing down a river on Mars to become the first of a new race of Martians, was not only the first of his Martian Chronicle stories to see print, but also one of the best.

Far more remarkable, but almost forgotten until reprinted as *Frost and Fire* in his Doubleday Collection *R is for Rocket* (1962), was *The Creatures That Time Forgot* (PLANET STORIES Fall, 1946). This was Bradbury's second longest story, nearly 22,000 words in length, and had all the earmarks of an epic. Somewhere, somehow, the 26-year-old Ray Bradbury had been confronted by the "realization of mortality." In this story, which he originally called *Eight Day World*, he envisaged a group of humans stranded on a radioactive planet, where the entire process of human growth and life were speeded up to only eight days. "Birth was quick as a knife," wrote Bradbury. "Childhood was over in a flash. Adolescence was a sheet of lightning. Manhood was a dream, maturity a myth, old age an inescapably quick reality, death a swift certainty."

Bradbury's friend Edmond Hamilton based a short story, *The Ephemerae* (ASTOUNDING SCIENCE-FICTION, December, 1938), on a human race whose life-span was but seventy days, but even if this was the spark that ignited *The Creatures That Time Forgot,* no apologies were in order. At times, the efforts of the proponents to fight their way to a spaceship that offers escape and a normal life before they die of old age descends to the action level of the pulps, but the allegory is so powerful that the overall effect is memorable.

The year previous, Bradbury's hopes had been raised by the sale of a nonfantasy, *The Big Black and White Game,* to the AMERICAN MERCURY (August, 1945). Then published by Lawrence Spivak, the AMERICAN MERCURY was a prestige magazine and, though its rates were very low compared to most other general magazines, they were the highest Bradbury had ever received. Again, drawing from childhood, Bradbury attempted a mainstream theme of interracial tension at a ball game. The story was selected for inclusion in Martha Foley's *The Best Short Stories of 1946.*

This, together with the power displayed in Bradbury's science fiction, was an augury. The April 13, 1946, issue of COLLIER'S carried his short story, *One Timeless Spring,* and the April, 1946, issue of CHARM, *The Miracles of Jamie.*

MADEMOISELLE published *The Invisible Boy,* a touching tale of a witch woman trying to conquer loneliness with spells that never work, in its November, 1945, issue. The same magazine rang all bells with *Homecoming* in its October, 1946, number, a story selected for inclusion in the O. Henry Memorial Award Prize Stories for 1947. *Homecoming* tells of the gathering of a family of witches, vampires, and dybbuks, and the teen-age boy among them who has been born human and its patronized by his more "fortunate" relatives. Here is expressed the yearning of children for some of the magical attributes of the creatures of superstition and fancy, brilliantly defined, with the hint that Bradbury's intimation of mortality was derived in his early youth from folklore.

An underrated story is *Defense Mech* in PLANET STORIES

for Spring, 1946, which really is an early try, and a nearly successful one, at the theme made famous in *Mars Is Heaven,* except that here a single mentally disturbed space traveler suffers from the hallucination that he is viewing Earth scenes on Mars. *Zero Hour,* in PLANET STORIES for Fall, 1947, was billed by the editors as "one of the best science fiction stories we have ever seen. Perhaps you will think it the *best!"* It is another classic in the tradition of *Sredni Vashtar* by Saki, *Thus I Refute Beelzy* by John Collier; and *Mimsy Were The Borogoves* by Henry Kuttner, reflecting the gulf in understanding between parents and children and the resultant antagonism.

Up to then, Bradbury had rarely received more than a cent a word for his stories, but now the rate on the science fiction climbed to two cents a word. PLANET STORIES paid that for *Pillar of Fire,* a total of $250 for one of Bradbury's strangest tales. A zombie climbs from its coffin, the last cadaver in a world that burns all its dead. Here we learn of the Mars of *The Martian Chronicles.* Here, too, the books have been burned and the burning of this "living dead man" will obliterate the last memories of Edgar Allan Poe, Ambrose Bierce, H. P. Lovecraft, Nathaniel Hawthorne, and other masters of fantasy. When the authorities finally apprehend and burn this last dead man, *Pillar of Fire* becomes an enthralling prelude to *The Exiles* (THE MAGAZINE OF FANTASY AND SCIENCE FICTION, Winter-Spring, 1950), in which ghosts of great writers of the past, hiding on Mars, are expunged when the last memory of them is gone.

Mars Is Heaven followed in PLANET STORIES for Fall, 1948. A possible influence on Bradbury here was Stanley G. Weinbaum's *Martian Odyssey,* in which a predatory plant conjures up visions of the most desired objects of its prey in order to lure them to their deaths. Earthmen land on Mars to find everything just like a midwestern town, complete to brass band. They find their dead relatives waiting to welcome them and then, while asleep in their memories of childhood, they are killed. It is certainly one of the most original methods of repulsing an interplanetary invasion ever conceived.

In May, 1947, Ray Bradbury's first hard-covered collection, *Dark Carnival*, made up primarily of his weird tales, was published by Arkham House. Bradbury sent a copy to Julius Schwartz with an inscription which read: "For Julie, in fond remembrances of Norton Street—'The Piper'—The Moon Festival in Chinatown—Lil Abner—'Are You Kidding?'— That old song, circa 1941: 'Daddy'—The beach—The burlesque—And then New York and George Brunis—God, what a beautiful night!—and because you sold almost every story in this book for me—With luff, from Ray Bradbury."

Six months later, when Schwartz sold *The Black Ferris* to WEIRD TALES on January 2, 1948, their business relationship was ended. Schwartz was a specialist in science fiction. He wrote to Bradbury and candidly told him that as an agent he had taken him as far as he was able. From this point on he would be retarding, not helping to advance his client.

On his own, Bradbury was already clicking with THE NEW YORKER and HARPER'S. A few years later CORONET would condense *Mars Is Heaven* and ESQUIRE would reprint it in full. ESQUIRE would also reprint *The Earth Men, The Spring Night,* and *Usher II,* all from the science-fiction pulps. Bradbury had long been selling below his market. Bradbury could no longer be ignored. Newspaper and magazine critics were generous, but in the fantasy and science-fiction field opinion was mixed.

It was common for critics of Bradbury to state that all he had to sell was emotion. This is considerably removed from the truth, which reveals a substantial Bradbury influence on science fiction. Richard Matheson was unquestionably indebted in style, mood, and approach to Bradbury. His most famous story, *Born of Man and Woman,* is a variant on Bradbury's use of childhood horror. Charles E. Fritch closely imitated Bradbury in a series of stories in the early 1950's. Judith Merril, who established her reputation with *That Only Mother,* a story of a mother who can see nothing wrong with her mutated, limbless child, published in ASTOUNDING SCI-

ENCE FICTION for June, 1948, certainly owes some inspiration to Bradbury, whose touching vignette, *The Shape of Things,* in THRILLING WONDER STORIES for February, 1948, deals with a woman who can see nothing wrong in her child, born in the shape of a triangle. James Blish, who went on to win a Hugo in 1959 with *A Case of Conscience,* a novel of the dilemma of a priest on a planet where creatures exist without original sin, should bow respectfully in the direction of Bradbury's *In This Sign* (*The Fire Balloons*), published originally in IMAGINATION, April, 1951, which tells of priests who go to Mars and discover Martians without original sin.

Bradbury has won several lawsuits—including one directed against *Playhouse 90,* for its *A Sound of Different Drummers* because of its similarity to *Fahrenheit 451*—for appropriating ideas from his works. Obviously, there must have been something more substantial than emotion and mood borrowed.

Most significant of all, ASTOUNDING SCIENCE-FICTION, which got first look at most Bradbury stories, including *Mars Is Heaven, Zero Hour, Pillar of Fire, The Million Year Picnic,* and *The Earth Men,* and rejected them all as not being the right type, now sometimes runs precisely that sort of story. See, for example, *The First One* by Herbert D. Kastle in its July, 1961, number, dealing with the aloneness of the first man back from Mars and the gap he finds between his family and himself.

The Martian Chronicles (1950) and the collection *The Illustrated Man* (1951) gave Bradbury acceptance among general readers for his science fiction. The question has frequently been raised as to why the highly original and skillful weird tales in *Dark Carnival* and later, most of them reprinted in *The October Country,* failed to gain similar acclaim. The answer seems to be that there are many extraordinarily brilliant practitioners in the field of the off-trail, horror, and supernatural: men and women with superb command of the language and remarkable originality—John Collier, Roald Dahl, Edgar Allan Poe, Ambrose Bierce, A. E. Coppard, Algernon Blackwood, Theodore Sturgeon, Walter de la Mare,

Saki, M. R. James, W. F. Harvey, E. F. Benson, May Sinclair, and Lord Dunsany, to name a portion. Bradbury can stand above a few of them, with most of them, and below some of them, but in that kind of competition he cannot lead.

The reverse is true in science fiction. There, his ideas appear strikingly original and his style is scintillating. In style, few match him, and the uniqueness of a story of Mars or Venus told in the contrasting literary rhythms of Hemingway and Thomas Wolfe is enough to fascinate any critic. Mainstream themes and mainstream writing in a science-fiction setting are Bradbury's contributions to fiction. In this he is singularly original and magazines like COLLIER'S have not hesitated to run such stories as *There Will Come Soft Rains* (May 6, 1950), graphically depicting atomic disaster by indirection, or *To the Future* (May 13, 1950), on the attempt of a couple to escape from a 1984-type future to the relative freedom of modern Mexico City. So, too, THE SATURDAY EVENING POST featured *The World the Children Made* (September 23, 1950), concerning a playroom in three-dimensional TV whose pictures resolve into fourth-dimensional reality, or *The Beast from 20,000 Fathoms* (June 23, 1951), in which a prehistoric monster rises from his sleep in the muck of the Atlantic to respond to the notes of a foghorn.

One charge brought against Bradbury is true, that his stories raise issue on purely emotional levels and offer no logic to support the stand he takes. It is often difficult to determine which issues he artificially adopts for the sake of the story and on which he is sincere.

The problem was resolved by the publication in book form of *Fahrenheit 451* (Ballantine Books, 1953), the closest Bradbury has ever come to writing a novel. A lengthened version of *The Fireman,* which ran in GALAXY SCIENCE FICTION for February, 1951, this story presents, in some detail, the basis of Bradbury's grievances. Because of this, this story of a future America where the job of a fireman is not to put out fires but to burn books, reads a bit more slowly than

Bradbury's shorter works, but it is by all odds one of his best and most revealing.

Between the lines, it tells us that Bradbury's use of racial prejudice in *Way in the Middle of the Air* (OTHER WORLDS, July, 1950), and its sequel, *The Other Foot* (NEW STORY, March, 1951), is merely contrived and not heartfelt and, moreover, in *Fahrenheit 451* he displays his adamant opposition to non-ethnic minority groups that in his view are a major factor in censorship of newspapers, books, magazines, motion pictures, radio, and television, a subject upon which he is most vehement. It offers scarcely a word on religion which was the core of *In This Sign* and *The Man* (THRILLING WONDER STORIES, February, 1949), so we may reasonably conclude that his use of this material was for impact value and not through conviction.

It tells us *why* he fears science, but does not tell us *when* he came to fear science. A good theory is that it happened this way. Few things affected Ray Bradbury as traumatically as the Nazi book burnings. His wrath and indignation at this action, his conviction that civilization is today "burning" books; if not literally, then through neglect, recurs constantly in *Fahrenheit 451*. A psychologist might say that since writing offered Bradbury his one hope of immortality, the destruction or loss of public interest in the vehicles necessary to convey his thoughts virtually threatens his soul. The very idea is the theme of *The Exiles,* where the spirits of great authors of the past vanish one by one as the final copies of their books are burned as the last person who remembers them dies.

In 1942, Technocracy, Inc., placed advertisements in 100 American newspapers demanding an end to U. S. aid to the allies fighting Nazi Germany. This was the signal for a number of exposés of Technocracy, a number of which were summarized by FANTASY REPORTER, June 1942 (an early title of SCIENCE FICTION TIMES), calling the fans to task for supporting the movement.

Among the points FANTASY REPORTER underlined were the following:

1. Fascist dictator of Italy, Mussolini had publicly "adopted" the aims of technocracy previously and was applauded for it by technocrats.
2. Alfred Rosenberg, Hitler's early edition of Adolph Eichman, was quoted as saying that "condemnation of technocracy is simultaneously condemnation of German genius of invention."

The technocracy which Ray Bradbury had so idealistically supported was now allied with the burner of books. Science was after all merely the instrument, not the savior, of mankind. In the wrong hands it could destroy the world. Atomic bombs and German rockets a few years later added the terror to this view which we later find reflected in his works.

By any standards, *Fahrenheit 451* is only a short novel, surpassing in length Henry James' *Turn of the Screw,* one of the longer classic short stories by only 10 pages. Even in so short a compass, Bradbury could not sustain the same poetic tempo that characterized his short stories, but lapsed into long periods of straight narrative, competent but undistinguished. His inability to sustain his style over length had evidenced itself previously in the novelette *The Creatures That Time Forgot.*

He thought he could fake it by assembling a group of predominantly nonfantasy short stories from THE SATURDAY EVENING POST, CHARM, MCCALL'S, COSMOPOLITAN, and EVERYWOMAN, seed a single character through them, connect the pieces with interim chapters, and call it in big letters on the jacket "a novel." This was *Dandelion Wine* (Doubleday, 1957), and while it contained some extremely well written, perceptive, and sensitive short stories, it wasn't a novel.

Bradbury wasn't a quitter. The next try, *Something Wicked This Way Comes* (Simon and Schuster, 1962), tried another approach—expanding the short story *Nightmare Carousel* (MADEMOISELLE, January, 1962), to novel length. Combining elements of boyhood memories and carnival nostalgia, Bradbury uncovered the sinister side of this small-town entertainment, focused upon a merry-go-round that made its riders younger when it was reversed and older when it moved forward. Here he succeeded in writing the entire book at a high level of craftsmanship, but he forgot that a novel is more than words and finished with an absurdly drawn-out short story.

Several times there had been talk of putting *Fahrenheit 451* on Broadway as a legitimate play but each time the idea had fallen through. A few of Bradbury's stories had been adapted as one-act plays. *A Scent of Sarsaparilla* was set to music by Charles Hamm, with narration by Anthony Boucher, as a feature of The 12th World Science Fiction Convention in September, 1954, in San Francisco: the story of a henpecked husband who finds such comfort in the objects of a happier past in his attic that he vanishes into that simpler period. Extremely effective were a number of Bradbury stories adapted for television.

At the threshold of his writing career, Bradbury made the choice to sidetrack his theatrical aspirations. A stay in Ireland writing the script for *Moby Dick* renewed his interest. Several years after the completion of *Moby Dick* he began to include playwriting as part of his work itinerary. The fruit of this was *The Anthem Sprinters and Other Antics,* a collection of four one-act plays about Ireland published by Dial in 1963.

Frustrated in earlier attempts to get his plays produced, Bradbury obtained nationwide publicity when three of his plays, possibly with his own financing, under the heading of "The World of Ray Bradbury," opened October 8, 1964, at the Coronet Theatre, Los Angeles. The plays were all futuristic fantasies: *The Veldt* (originally *The World the Children Made,* SATURDAY EVENING POST, September 23, 1950), about the three-dimensional play room that proves real; *The Pedestrian* (THE REPORTER, August 7, 1951), of an era when a man walking the streets at night will be regarded as an eccentric who should be arrested; and *To the Chicago Abyss,* depicting the attitudes of after-the-atomic-war society. The intent was to expand the number of plays and take them around the country in repertory. To get them produced Bradbury, had to organize The Pandemonium Theater Company himself. Reaction was unexpectedly good, with especially strong support from columnist Cecil Smith writing in the October 26, 1964, LOS ANGELES TIMES, who said: "Unquestionably, the most exciting theatrical event of the year here was the opening a couple of weeks ago of three short fantastic plays by Ray Bradbury under the collective title 'The World of Ray Bradbury,' which are fascinating and horrifying capacity audiences nightly at the Coronet Theater."

At almost the same time, he was reported working on the film script of *The Martian Chronicles* for what was said to be a ten-million-dollar production by the producing-acting team of Alan Pakula and Bob Mulligan for Universal Films.

It was significant that achieving a critical theatre success with three of his science-fiction plays, even if it proved limited, and in connecting with the single biggest motion picture offer of his career for one of his own stories, it was Bradbury's science fiction that turned the trick. Bradbury is today an important writer on the American scene but his emphasis on science fiction seems to be a thing of the past. His stories in that genre are usually created for a special event, such as the special Ray Bradbury issue of THE MAGAZINE OF FANTASY AND SCIENCE FICTION (May, 1963), for which he wrote *To the Chicago Abyss,* and not as a regular part of his writing schedule. In the period between 1955 and 1965, he had fewer stories included in science-fiction anthologies than any other major figure in the field, according to *A Checklist of Science-Fiction Anthologies,* compiled by Walter R. Cole (1964). His literary output during that time was not even mainstream, it was conformist, whether written for PLAYBOY or a literary journal. It was good, skillful work, but like his weird material, it was bracketed by legions of other good, skillful writers.

When a new book of his is reviewed, all too frequently the few items of science fiction are singled out and most of the rest given a polite nod. The only books of Bradbury's that the future is not likely to "burn" are those that follow closest to the style of *The Martian Chronicles*. His "messages" get across only when clothed in the vestments of science. H. G. Wells and Jules Verne both had to learn that lesson. It is now Bradbury's turn.

21

ARTHUR C. CLARKE

Among science-fiction writers who have gained their eminence since 1940, possibly Ray Bradbury is the only one as
familiar to the general public as Arthur C. Clarke. This is a
popularity that has been rewarded in terms of economics as
well as prestige. Clarke's suspenseful novel, *A Fall of Moondust,* published in 1961, achieved the unprecedented distinction of being the first interplanetary story ever used by
Reader's Digest Condensed Book Library. The hundreds of
thousands of subscribers to that immensely successful book
club chewed their fingernails as they read of the scientifically
tense battle to save the occupants of a moon ship buried deep
in the treacherous sands of a lunar crater.

A Fall of Moondust was a good book, certainly one of the
better science-fiction novels of the year, and it deserved the
book club selection, yet it is doubtful if it would ever have
been considered were it not for the fact that Clarke had nine

years previously enjoyed a Book-of-the-Month-Club choice (July, 1952) for his exposition of popular science, *The Exploration of Space.*

The always substantial publicity attendant on a Book-of-the-Month-Club nod gave Clarke literary status. Book publishers who had ignored his fiction previously now were delighted to feature it on their lists. Not only did Clarke's science-fiction books receive principal reviews, but they were evaluated as serious efforts. *A Fall of Moondust* was possibly the most profitable of all Clarke's works of fiction, but his standing as an important writer was established when THE NEW YORK TIMES and other highly regarded sources of literary criticism gave lead and praise-saturated reviews to his Stapledonian concepts in *Childhood's End,* published by Ballantine Books in 1953.

Almost as far back as the family tree can be traced, all of the Clarke family had been farmers. When Arthur was born, December 16, 1917, in his grandmother's boarding house, in Minehead, Somerset, England, it was reasonable to suppose he would follow in the tradition.

That this would not prove to be the case began to evidence itself as early as the age of 10 when his father presented him with a series of cigarette cards of prehistoric animals and the boy became deeply interested in the subject of paleontology, collecting fossils at a furious rate. Before Arthur was 12 his father had died and his mother had to struggle to keep the farm going and her son in school. She received small help from the boy, whose interest had shifted from paleontology to astronomy. To implement this switch he constructed his own telescopes out of old Meccano parts.

Alexander Graham Bell, inventor of the telephone, had also patented the photophone, a device by which sound waves vibrated a beam of reflected sunlight and the receiver changed the varying light intensity back into sound. Clarke had built his own photophone transmitter from a bicycle headlight, and also played with audio modulation of sunlight by mechanical means by the time he was 13.

In 1927, Clarke discovered AMAZING STORIES, which served as a literary hypodermic, injecting him with an imaginative drug that required increasingly larger dosage as he grew older, until the day that he received an entire crate of WONDER STORIES for 5 cents a copy stood out with such memorableness that it was to be recorded unfailing in each autobiographical sketch he wrote.

He must have seemed a strange teen-ager to fellow students of Huish's Grammar School in Taunton, but by his fifteenth birthday he had adjusted to the point where he was writing fantasies for the school paper and making his mark as an assistant editor. As early as that it was obvious that all his life he would be torn between the fascinating realities of science and the siren call of imaginative literary day dreams.

Today, with the American Rocket Society and the British Interplanetary Society, respected scientific institutions, recognized as factors in the advancement of research through their handsome journals, it has been forgotten they were both launched by science-fiction editors, writers, and readers. The American society was pioneered by David Lasser, editor of WONDER STORIES, in New York on March 21, 1930. The British Interplanetary Society was founded by P. E. Cleator, a science-fiction enthusiast, in October, 1933, in Liverpool, England. Clarke discovered the existence of the English organization through science-fiction correspondents and joined it during the summer of 1934 as an associate member. This seemingly simple act of enthusiasm was to turn out to be the most profound and far-reaching decision of his life.

Without the money for higher education, Clarke found himself with the urgent necessity of earning a livelihood. He took a civil service examination for a position as auditor in His Majesty's Exchequer and Audit Department. It was the Depression and openings were scarce. Over 1,500 people competed for the available positions, and Clarke, who came out twenty-sixth in ratings, managed to secure a post in London.

He moved to London in 1936 and rented a room in a house that was so tiny that it became the standing joke of his acquaintances. When he entertained a visitor, he had to open the window and sit partly outside the room, otherwise there wasn't any space for the two of them and the bed. The other alternative was to leave the door open and have one sit in the hall.

A London branch of the British Interplanetary Society was formed on October 27, 1936, at the offices of Professor A. M. Low, 8 Waterloo Place, Piccadilly. Low was a respected inventor and the editor of ARMCHAIR SCIENCE, as well as the author of a number of books of popular science and juvenile fantasies. Behind this was a desire to move BIS headquarters to London. Cleator resigned in protest as president of the organization and Low ascended to his position. Arthur Clarke was made treasurer of the society and began to work actively for the group.

Earlier, he had begun writing for the British science-fiction fan magazine NOVAE TERRAE, a mimeographed, quarto-sized publication which was the official organ of the Science Fiction Association. In his article *Science Fiction—Past, Present and Future* (June, 1937), he stressed the importance of accurate science about rocketry in science-fiction magazines, since most of the BIS membership was recruited from the ranks of their readers. In the same magazine he advocated excellent science with good writing in a literary debate with C. S. Youd, who was to become well known as John Christopher, author of *No Blade of Grass.*

Clarke joined forces with Maurice K. Hanson, editor of NOVAE TERRAE, and William F. Temple, eventually to become a prominent science-fiction author, and rented an apartment at 88 Gray's Inn Road. NOVAE TERRAE was mimeographed there and the science-fiction club used the apartment as a weekly informal meeting place. Club activities both in rocketry and science fiction helped Clarke come in contact with people who could help in a writing career.

The first money he received from writing was from Eric

Frank Russell. Russell, a fellow member of the British Interplanetary Society, used some ideas supplied to him by Clarke in a science-fiction story he sold and turned part of the proceeds over to the young aspirant.

Even more important was Clarke's association with Walter Gillings, the leading science-fiction fan in Britain during the thirties and publisher of SCIENTIFICTION, a very professional-appearing fan magazine. Gillings had been driving hard to convince British publishers to issue a science-fiction periodical and after many failures had convinced Worlds Work (1913) Ltd. to try a one-shot, TALES OF WONDER. Worlds Work had a uniform series of 128-page pulp-magazine-sized titles which they called the "Master Thriller Series." Among them were TALES OF THE SEVEN SEAS, TALES OF THE AIR, and TALES OF TERROR. If TALES OF WONDER proved profitable they would publish a second collection under that title. In June, 1937, they set down on the news stalls, with Gillings as editor, the first issue of TALES OF WONDER. It did well enough to warrant quarterly publication.

Because of relatively low rates per word and the paucity of English authors in the field, Gillings relied heavily on reprints, but he also published original material. He purchased from Arthur C. Clarke two articles. The first, *Man's Empire of Tomorrow* (Winter, 1938), was a smoothly written rehash of what was known about the planets of the solar system. The second, *We Can Rocket to the Moon—Now!* (Summer, 1939), championed the practicality of space flight. Clarke was now a professional writer.

Secretly Clarke was working on a novel, which would eventually solidify in 1946 as *Against the Fall of Night,* but during this period his only ventures into fiction were three minor efforts, *Travel by Wire, How We Went to Mars,* and *Retreat from Earth,* the last two appearing in the March, 1938 issue of AMATEUR SCIENCE STORIES, a legal-sized mimeographed fan magazine edited by Douglas W. F. Mayer and published under the auspices of The Science Fiction Association to encourage budding British writers. *Retreat from Earth* was the longest and the best of these, quite read-able in its story of termite science saving Earth from Mar-tian invasion.

Important to the direction of his future was the appearance of his first technical article in THE JOURNAL OF THE BRITISH INTERPLANETARY SOCIETY for January, 1939, *An Elementary Mathematical Approach to Astronautics,* dealing with the problems of determining ratios of combustion of fuel to mass of the rocket as related to velocity.

Actually a heavy percentage of Clarke's time had been devoted to science-fiction fan activities, including reviews of the current science-fiction magazines and a biographical skit of his roommate William F. Temple (now an author ap-pearing in TALES OF WONDER) for NOVAE TERRAE. When that periodical suspended with its January, 1939, issue he switched his activities to other similar hobbyist journals.

Time was running short for careers as far as science fiction was concerned. England was fighting World War II by the fall of 1939. No one realized the seriousness of the Nazi challenge and for a while draft calls were slow. For another year some semblance of normality was retained. As far as Clarke was concerned it was a good time for a frolic.

C. S. Youd's publication, THE FANTAST, in its inaugural (April, 1939) issue, featured on the cover a long poem by Clarke, *The Twilight of the Sun,* which ended with the lines:

The Intellect, pure, unalloyed, on courage
    eternally buoyed.
Will span the vast gulfs of the void and win
    a new planet's fair face.
For one day our vessels will ply to the uttermost
    depths of the sky,
And in them at last we shall fly, ere the darkness
    sweeps over our race.

The poem was serious, but much of Clarke's other material was zany, including a fictional extrapolation involving science-fiction fans, *A Short History of Fantocracy, 1948-1960,* (De-cember, 1941), or gambols like *At the Mountains of Mirki-*

ness or Lovecraft-into-Leacock, a spoof in the Lovecraft tradition for an undated (1940) issue of a journal named SATELLITE published by John F. Burke (later to become a prolific science-fiction author).

Modesty was not one of Clarke's youthful virtues and his nickname, everywhere in the amateur publications, was "Ego." After a while it became so much a part of him that he began to byline his articles Arthur Ego Clarke.

Conscription cut short the period of his science-fiction play and Clarke entered the Royal Air Force in 1941 and would remain until 1946. He started as a radio technician and rose to flight lieutenant. His scientific interests and aptitudes now stood him in good stead, since he was involved as a technical officer on the first experimental trials of Ground Controlled Approach Radar. The units were built in the United States and shipped to Britain complete with the scientists who had worked on its development. Once Clarke had mastered the unit, he spent two years teaching others how to operate it and to tend its 400 vacuum tubes. Another two years was spent in service electronics.

While in the RAF he began writing again. A technical paper on time-basis circuits appeared in WIRELESS ENGINEER, but more important was *Extra-Terrestrial Relays* in WIRELESS WORLD for October, 1945, in which he proposed three earth satellites in orbit for global television. This may have been the first serious suggestion of the concept and Clarke indulged in self-recriminations for not attempting to patent the idea at profitable length in an article he did for ROGUE magazine, November, 1962, *How I Lost a Billion Dollars in My Spare Time by Inventing Telstar.*

At the end of the war he won first prize in RAF QUARTERLY for his essay *The Rocket and the Future of Warfare,* involving the wedding of atomic warheads and rockets.

Major credit for reviving The British Interplanetary Society after World War II belongs to Clarke. He strenuously set about drawing other rocket societies under the aegis of the BIS. Early in 1946 the BIS resumed operations and the same year Clarke was elected chairman of the society in recognition of his services. These services transcended the mere organizational when he enrolled George Bernard Shaw as an enthusiastic member. Shaw voluntarily sent in his membership when he received Clarke's article *The Challenge of the Spaceship,* published in the December, 1946, issue of THE JOURNAL OF THE BRITISH INTERPLANETARY SOCIETY. The article superbly explained the scientific and philosophical reasons for space travel and was the title essay of a book of related articles published by Ballantine in 1961.

With the end of the war, the British publishing industry struggled to return to normal. Edward John Carnell, a leading scientifictionist who had been guest editor of the December, 1937, issue of the JOURNAL of the BIS, talked Pendulum Publications into issuing a new science-fiction magazine, NEW WORLDS (the title of a fan magazine previously published by Carnell and the English translation of NOVAE TERRAE). At the same time, Walter Gillings whose magazine TALES OF WONDER was forced to suspend because of the paper shortage in 1942, convinced The Temple Bar Publishing Co., London, to try a similar venture, FANTASY.

Learning that Gillings was recruiting British authors, Clarke, still in uniform, began spending some time on science fiction. Gillings accepted several stories, including one titled *Earthlight.* Delays continued to plague the first issue of the magazine so he suggested that Clarke try elsewhere, returning among other stories *Rescue Party.*

Clark began submitting to ASTOUNDING SCIENCE-FICTION in the United States, impressing its editor, John W. Campbell, with a short story titled *Loophole,* which appeared in the April, 1946, issue. Martian attempts to prevent earth from using space ships are counteracted by the invention of matter merit publication.

Much stronger, *Rescue Party,* published in the following (May, 1946) number provided taut, fascinating, imaginative suspense as an alien spaceship attempts to explore earth's vacated cities eight hours before the sun will explode into a nova. In this short story, two of the major influences on Clarke are instantly apparent: John W. Campbell, in the Don A. Stuart vein creating a mood of sympathy and admiration for the creations of man and the faithful machines that have served him, and Olaf Stapledon, whose intellectual grandeur sent the imagination racing to the limits of time and space.

Suspense in *Rescue Party* is created by the intellectual presentation of the problems and not by its stylistic rendition. In method, Clarke acted in this story and in most of his future stories as the observer or historian and never as the participant. The reward for concentration in reading is a surprise ending. *Rescue Party* proved to be a matter for chagrin to Clarke because its popularity and frequent reprintings implied that he had improved little over the years. This attitude toward any unusual popularity of early stories is often found among successful writers.

Gillings finally cleared postwar paper-shortage hurdles and got the first issue of FANTASY out with the date line December, 1946, carrying Clarke's story *Technical Error*. The plot concerned a powerhouse accident in which a technician's body is reversed like a mirror image and he is unable to absorb nutrition from his food as a result. In an attempt to restore him to normalcy by repetition of the accident, the entire installation is destroyed. The story required concentration for impact because of the heavy-handedness of its telling, but it won first place in reader approval in the issue and four years later was reprinted in the United States by THRILLING WONDER STORIES (June, 1950) as *The Reversed Man*.

FANTASY ran only two more issues and Clarke had a story in each under a pen name, "because I want only my choice pieces to appear under my own name." He used Charles Willis for *Castaway* in the April, 1947, issue, a mood piece in which navigators on an airliner obtain a glimpse of a strange and awesome life form that has been blasted free of the sun and is dying in the "frigid" clutch of the earth. Nothing else happens, but Clarke successfully conveys the wonder and the tragedy of that brief encounter. *The Fires Within,* published under the name E. G. O'Brien in the August, 1947, and final issue of FANTASY (printed in the United States in the September, 1949, STARTLING STORIES) was one of Clarke's most successful short stories. The discovery and emergence of a high-density race of creatures from underground inadvertently destroys all surface life, leaving the subterranean race conscience-stricken.

Through the auspices of a Member of Parliament, Clarke as a war veteran was subsidized by the government at King's College, London, where in two years he obtained a First Class Honors B.Sc. in physics as well as in pure and applied mathematics. He entered school in October, 1946, and graduated in 1948. Little of his writing appeared during these two years but he finally saw published *Against the Fall of Night* in the November, 1948, STARTLING STORIES, a novel regarded as one of his key works.

Against the Fall of Night was begun in 1937 and after five revisions was completed in 1946. It had been turned down for ASTOUNDING SCIENCE-FICTION by Campbell, who probably was instantly aware that this novel had been intended as a prelude to his own stories *Twilight* and *Night,* published in 1934 and 1935.

In *Twilight,* a man is transferred to the future and finds a curiously decadent people served by efficient, almost immortal machinery. Transcendental cities function automatically for "masters" who no longer understand how they run. This is the situation in the city of Diaspar, when young Alvin begins searching for answers as to what lies beyond the city.

The smoothly functioning underground transport, which so fascinates Clarke in both *Against the Fall of Night* and *Rescue Party,* is derived from Warner Van Lorne's two popular stories, *Strange City* (ASTOUNDING STORIES, January,

1936) and its sequel, *World of Purple Light* (ASTOUNDING STORIES, December, 1936.)* The poetic passages in *Against the Fall of Night* reflect the method of Clark Ashton Smith in capturing a mood but with a shallower rhetorical depth. A bow should also be made here in the direction of Lord Dunsany, who also was one of the shapers of Smith. The final chapters with all their far-flung implications acknowledge the direction of Olaf Stapledon.

What Clarke has done in his novel of a determined boy who frees a moribund civilization of its ennui and gives it back the stars is to explore in additional detail the implications of the intriguing cities of Campbell's *Twilight*, with the utilization of the fascinating automatic transportation of Warner Van Lorne, creating a mood in the fashion of Clark Ashton Smith, and zeroing in to a climax on the ideas of Olaf Stapledon. Clarke essentially changed nothing when he expanded the novel to *The City and the Stars* in 1956.

Knowledge of the early genesis of this particular story buttresses a generalization that Clarke is one and apart from today's body of science fiction. It is as if Robert Heinlein, A. E. van Vogt, Theodore Sturgeon, Isaac Asimov, Ray Bradbury, and the entire crew of "moderns" had never existed. He owes nothing to them and has derived nothing from them. His roots lie back before 1938 and his method has evolved from the older body of science fiction.

After emerging from college, he got a job in 1949 on the staff of the Institution of Electrical Engineers as assistant

---

* An all-but-forgotten name today, Warner Van Lorne was a controversial author who appeared in ASTOUNDING STORIES and ASTOUNDING SCIENCE-FICTION from 1935 to 1939. For 25 years his true identity was speculated upon. People close to the magazine felt he was a pen name for F. Orlin Tremaine, one-time editor of ASTOUNDING STORIES. It eventually developed that while Tremaine had written one Van Lorne story, *The Upper Level Road*, the rest were the work of his brother Nelson Tremaine, now a resident of Glen Rock, New Jersey. Warner Van Lorne's last story to be published was *Wanted: Seven Fearless Engineers*, a distinctly superior bit of science fiction which ran in the February, 1939, AMAZING STORIES.

editor of SCIENCE ABSTRACTS. This kept him abreast of the latest developments in science and gave him time to step up his writing schedule.

History Lesson, published in the May, 1949, STARTLING STORIES, evolved from the same basic idea as *Rescue Party* but took a different direction. Here, Venusians land on earth after human life has been destroyed by a new ice age and they judge the life and inhabitants of the planet solely by an old Donald Duck cartoon they find.

The Wall of Darkness, which appeared in the July, 1949, SUPER SCIENCE STORIES, is beyond doubt one of Clarke's finest short stories. Related in the manner of Lord Dunsany, it tells of a far-off world at the edge of the universe, completely "separated" by a gigantic wall, a wall with only *one* side like a Moebius strip. It is a highly original and beautifully written story which deserves far more attention than it has received.

Of particular significance was *Hide and Seek*, which appeared in the September, 1949, ASTOUNDING SCIENCE FICTION. This short story is built around the problem of a man in a space suit on the Martian moon Phobos who must keep alive and out of sight of an armed space cruiser until help arrives. How he does it is the story. This type of story is known as the "scientific problem" yarn: put the character into a difficult situation that can be solved only by legitimate scientific reasoning.

Ross Rocklynne popularized this type of story in a series concerning an interplanetary criminal, Deveral, pursued by an interplanetary cop, Colbie. The rogue Deveral always got away by figuring out a tricky scientific puzzle. A typical situation is the one in *The Men and the Mirror* (ASTOUNDING SCIENCE-FICTION, July, 1938) in which criminal and cop have to decide how to stop sliding eternally back and forth across a frictionless concave surface on another world. This approach eventually led to Clarke's *A Fall of Moon Dust* where the problem of finding a ship in a sea of sand and bringing its occupants to the surface makes the puzzle.

In 1950, Clarke slightly changed direction. He secured a commission to do a short book, *Interplanetary Flight, an Introduction to Astronautics*, for Temple, London. Though it was mildly technical, it sold well enough to warrant distribution in the United States by Harper. This led to the suggestion that he try a longer, more ambitious work, and he began research on *The Exploration of Space*.

A novelette written during this period, *Guardian Angel*, was considered strong enough by his American agent to aim at a higher-paying market. His agent was told by the editor of one of the better general fiction magazines that he might be interested if the story were trimmed from 15,000 to 10,000 words. James Blish, who was working for the agency at the time, cut the story and added an additional twist concerning an impending Armageddon that he felt would strengthen it. The yarn was nevertheless rejected, but eventually it was sold in its full length to FAMOUS FANTASTIC MYSTERIES (April, 1950), with Blish's addition intact. The original version appeared the same year in England in the Winter, 1950, NEW WORLDS.

The story concerned omnipotent creatures from out of space who stop all war on earth and get mankind to behave. The big mystery is what they look like, since no one has ever seen them. The punch line comes when they appear, replicas of the Devil. With and without changes the story was a fine job, but the kernel of the idea was taken from John Campbell's *The Mightiest Machine* (ASTOUNDING STORIES, December, 1934, to April, 1935), in which a race of devillike creatures who first lived on earth migrate to another planet and once again constitute a danger to the mother world.

Prelude to Space, an ambling novel of the preparation for the first trip to the moon, written the summer of 1947, appeared in GALAXY SCIENCE FICTION NOVELS in 1951 and proved to be unexpectedly popular. The science was good and the motives of the characters involved were effectively portrayed, but the book was too close to the present and has already become outdated. We now know that that's not how the first trip to the moon is going to take place at all.

Another novel, *Sands of Mars*, published in hardcover by Sidgwick Jackson, London, in 1951, was documentary in approach, possibly inspired by *Wreck of the Asteroid* by Laurence Manning (WONDER STORIES, December, 1932) and it concerned a science-fiction writer's trip to Mars and his efforts to win the confidence of the pioneers there. Except for the inclusion of several very adult inferences, the book, all protestations to the contrary, should be classed as a juvenile.

Superiority, a short story published in the August, 1951, issue of THE MAGAZINE OF FANTASY AND SCIENCE FICTION, brought Clarke prestige when it was made required reading for certain classes at the Massachusetts Institute of Technology. The story had a moral for those scientists so determined to increase the sophistication of their work that they lose out to those aggressively using conventional methods.

The same month, THRILLING WONDER STORIES carried *Earthlight*, the novelette originally written for Gillings' short-lived FANTASY. This story of a power struggle between the planets to gain control of the mineral resources of the moon contains one of the most vivid and thrilling space battles ever to appear in science fiction, not excepting the interstellar extravaganzas of E. E. Smith and John W. Campbell which it deliberately set out to top. The story was expanded into a full-length novel, published by Ballantine Books in 1955.

By far the most important event of 1951 for Clarke was the publication of *The Exploration of Space* by Temple Press Ltd., London. A feature of this book was four full-color paintings by Leslie Carr, derived from drawings by R. A. Smith (who also had some black-and-white astronomical drawings in the volume). Harper's distributed the book in the United States, where it was submitted to the Book-of-the-Month Club for consideration. Basil Davenport, a science-fiction enthusiast and literary critic, was then a reader for the organization. He understood the scope of Clarke's book and highly recommended it to the judges. It happened to be a month when no "important" work appeared, so after some debate the judges decided on a joint selection for the month of July, 1952, one of them *The Exploration of Space*.

A report written by Arthur Jean Cox in the first April, 1952, issue of FANTASY TIMES stated that Clarke had received a $20,000 advance for *The Exploration of Space*. This was disputed by The Scott Meredith Literary Agency in the second (May, 1952) issue of that magazine as "an understatement." Whatever the amount, Clarke triumphantly sailed to America to pick up his check personally. A hero in the science-fiction world, he was feted at the May 4, 1952, meeting of the Eastern Science Fiction Association in Newark, N. J., and featured at The Third Annual Midwestern Science Fiction Conference in Sharonville, Ohio, on May 12. At these meetings members of the science-fiction community attempted to put their finger on the quality that had caused Clarke's book to become the success it was. There had been other books on space travel before, some more definitive, embodying much more of the discoveries of research and even more fascinatingly written. Clarke's, they finally decided, was the first to define the "reasons why." He presented the case for space travel not only in terms of mechanics and economics but *philosophically*, and no one had done that as well before.

To write *Childhood's End*, Clarke used *Guardian Angel* (his own version) as the foundation of the early part of the story and then built from there to a Stapledonian finale in which all mankind unifies into a single intelligence and ascends the next step in the ladder of evolution—which is to be sent to a spatial heaven in a mystical parallel to religion. Does this then make Clarke a subconscious religionist? As if to anticipate that question, on the copyright page of the book, Clarke prints in lieu of a dedication the disclaimer: "The opinions expressed in this book are not those of the author."

Childhood's End (Ballantine Books, 1952) received the

major review in THE NEW YORK TIMES for August 27, 1952. Admitting that the ingredients of the novel were science fiction, the reviewer, William Du Bois, acknowledged: "Mr. Clarke has mixed them with a master hand." He termed the book "a first-rate tour de force that is well worth the attention of every thoughtful citizen in this age of anxiety." In conclusion he stated: "The review can only hint at the stimulation Mr. Clarke's novel offers." If a science-fiction novel had ever received a more favorable review in a publication of major influence it is well hidden. *Childhood's End* was certainly Clarke's most important and effective work of fiction and was generally recognized as such by a majority of the reviewers.

Clarke toured the United States. Finally decided he liked Florida and spent some time there skin diving. He married an American girl he had met and known for only a few weeks in 1954, but a separation occurred after a relatively short time.

Interest in skin diving brought him together with Mike Wilson, a crack photographer who had done work for LIFE magazine in the Orient. They went into partnership engaging in underwater photography along the Great Barrier Reef of Australia and off the coast of Ceylon. Mike Wilson married a Ceylonese girl and settled down in Colombo; Clarke became a citizen of Ceylon and moved in with the Wilsons.

He wrote a number of books on skin diving, but his science-fiction novel *The Deep Range* (Harcourt, Brace & Co., New York, 1957), which was dedicated to Mike Wilson, is one of the finest and most absorbing expositions on future farming of the seas ever done. Impressed by the potentialities, THE WALL STREET JOURNAL reviewed the book as of interest to the business community (April 2, 1957).

The highest honors in the science-fiction world were both presented to Clarke at the 14th World Science Fiction Convention in New York in 1956, where he was guest of honor and also was given the Hugo for the best short science-fiction story of the previous year, *The Star* (INFINITY SCIENCE FIC-

TION, November, 1955). This story, dealing with the discovery of the remains of the star that became a nova at the time of Christ's birth and thus destroyed a noble race, poses a moral dilemma intended to strike the reader with considerable impact. Despite almost a clumsy telegraphing of the punch line by the author, it still had the desired effect on its readers.

A far greater honor for Clarke was the receipt of the 1962 Kalinga Prize, awarded by UNESCO for the popularization of science. The honor carries with it $2,800 in cash, but from the prestige standpoint it placed Clarke in company with such past winners as Julian Huxley, Bertrand Russell, and George Gamow. The prize was given in acknowledgment of the fact that Clarke's writings in fiction and nonfiction, educating the masses in science, have resulted in sales of over two million books in fifteen languages as well as more than three hundred articles and stories in publications as distinguished as READER'S DIGEST, THE NEW YORK TIMES, HORIZON, HOLIDAY, HARPER'S, PLAYBOY, VOGUE, and SATURDAY REVIEW.

Though there was admittedly an element of good fortune in Clarke's BOOK-OF-THE-MONTH-CLUB selection, augmented by his own shrewdness in making capital of it, the momentum of his progress, particularly as a writer of fiction, could be sustained only by performance.

His "failings" as a writer are many in the realm of science fiction. For the most part he was not an innovator. As a literary technician he was outclassed by a number of contemporaries. His style, by current standards, was not "modern." Yet, people in many countries bought and read him with enthusiasm and hard-headed critics applauded his efforts.

What is the answer to this seeming paradox?

In an age fraught with horror and despair he was optimistic. Mankind, in his stories, is essentially noble and aspires and triumphs despite all difficulties.

Behind each of his stories is a thought-provoking concept or philosophy. Whether these are or are not original with him is beside the point; some nugget of thought is always present and they read new to this generation. The ideas are never introduced obliquely or discussed in a blasé, over-sophisticated, or matter-of-fact manner, a method indigenous in too much of modern science fiction. Instead, he vests them with all the poetry, wonder, awe, mystery, and adventure that he is capable of conjuring up. Even if it is only the preparation of the first space rocket, he attempts to communicate the richness and implication of an overwhelming experience.

His science is thorough, authentic, yet easily followed.

These factors, together with his obvious sincerity, entranced the reader and won over the critics.

For Arthur C. Clarke, the direction his science-fiction writing was to take was decided at the end of World War II. Consciously or not, he went against the trend. For him, a paraphrase of Robert Frost's famous lines certainly applies: He took the road least traveled by and that made all the difference.

22

PHILIP JOSÉ FARMER

One of the most extraordinary and significant things about science fiction is its almost total lack of sex, even of fake sex —except, of course, in the 'mad scientist's' operating-chambers particularly prominent in the movie versions," states G. Legman (called "without any reservations whatever—the principal living specialist in erotic folklore") in *The Horn Book, Studies in Erotic Folklore and Bibliography* (University Books, 1964).

As a generality, Legman's point was valid, except that his investigations into science fiction prior to taking up residence on the French Riviera in 1949 were superficial and he apparently has lost contact with it altogether since that time. If he had not, he could scarcely have remained oblivious to the impact of a midwesterner with the regionally appropriate name of Farmer on the field of science fiction with a short novel, *The Lovers* (STARTLING STORIES, August, 1952), which fathered a brief but traumatic revolution contributing toward the maturation of science fiction.

An introductory blurb, "Entrance Cue," by Samuel Mines, editor of STARTLING STORIES, said of *The Lovers*: "We think this story is a delicate and beautiful, yet powerful and shocking piece of work. . . . We think that Philip José Farmer is the find of the year." To his readers, in the department "The Ether Vibrates," he made a further telling point: ". . . we think *The Lovers* is an important story. Important not necessarily because it is great literature but because it will make a lot of fine writers sit up and be quoted as blurting: 'My gosh, I didn't know we could do anything like that in science fiction!' or words to that effect."

He was, from the vantage of hindsight, 100 per cent right.

The revolutionary approach in *The Lovers* grew from the following story line. An earth ship lands on a planet where the manlike dominating species has evolved from insect forms. A "human" race once lived there, too, infiltrated by a parasitic form of insect that grew into the precise form of a woman. These parasites, the lalitha, were all female and could breed only by mating with a human male. After pregnancy, the mother would die and the larvae would feed off her flesh until mature enough to emerge. It was discovered by the lalitha that the heavy drinking of a foul-smelling liquor made from beetle juice, prevented pregnancy. When an earthman, Yarrow, unaware of the true nature of the lalitha, enters into an affair with one named Jeannette he becomes so fond of her that he waters her beetle juice, to cure her of what he thinks is a leaning toward alcoholism. The result is conception and her death.

This love story was clothed in unparallelled richness of background and related with a fascinating, absorbing literary technique. The old saw, "If you borrow from one author it's plagiarism, but if you borrow from many it's research," has an application here. Farmer owes a debt to easily a score of writers, but what he does with the elements he utilizes becomes singularly and uniquely his own.

The smoothly handled incorporation of sex in the story he may have picked up from L. Sprague de Camp, whose work he admired and whose *Rogue Queen*, describing the methods of procreation and social mores in a humanoid society patterned after the bees, had appeared in a Doubleday book in the spring of 1951. Many of the characteristics of the Wogs, the dominant insect race of the alien planet, were taken from L. Frank Baum's *The Marvelous Land of Oz*, which had a famed character named The Woggle Bug. Further evidence of the Baum influence is apparent in the planet's name: Ozagen. The treatment of the alien creatures owes much to Stanley G. Weinbaum. The stylistic modernity and the careful build-up of future civilizations is reminiscent of Robert A. Heinlein. To say all this is no more disparaging than to say that Bradbury exhibits a paradoxical blend of the styles of Ernest Hemingway and Thomas Wolfe, for what Bradbury has done with his method is distinctly his own, and what Farmer has homogenized from his sources represents a personal achievement.

Not unexpectedly, it was not the end result that other science-fiction writers admired in Farmer, but merely the sensationalism of his using biological sex as his central theme. This represented to them the breaking of a barrier and their reaction was immediate.

A California author, Sherwood Springer, reading *The Lovers*, rushed a story he had written over a year previously to editor Mines. It was published as *No Land of Nod* in the December, 1952, THRILLING WONDER STORIES and concerned the problem of the continuation of the race when the last man and woman on earth are father and daughter. The decision is eventually made by the daughter as it was by Lot's offspring in Genesis.

The reverse situation appears when the last woman on earth, pregnant, realizes she must have a boy if the race is to continue, in a story by Wallace West, appropriately titled *Eddie for Short* (AMAZING STORIES, December, 1953).

From that point on, science-fiction writers decided to become really daring. At the forefront was Theodore Sturgeon, with *The World Well Lost* (UNIVERSE SCIENCE FICTION, June, 1953) in which two lovebirds from another planet turn out to be homosexuals; and, for good measure, he contributed *The Wages of Synergy* (STARTLING STORIES, August, 1953) which starts with the shocked reaction of a woman whose lover dies while they are amatorily involved. Some years later he would write *Affair with a Green Monkey* (VENTURE SCIENCE FICTION, May, 1957) which was little more than an adroitly phrased dirty joke.

It is possible that the field was moving in that direction anyway, and that *The Lovers* merely was the first of an inevitable trend. Alfred Bester's *The Demolished Man* (GALAXY SCIENCE FICTION, January-February-March, 1951) had made it very clear that the world of tomorrow would know what sex was all about, and Richard Matheson, in his novelette *Lover When You're Near Me* (GALAXY SCIENCE FICTION, May, 1952), had centered his story around the telepathic seduction of an earthman by an alien female physically abhorrent to him.

Yet, despite this, science fiction is surpassed in prudery only by the Frank Merriwell stories. Even in hard cover books, where a higher price made an adult audience certain, sex has not been too common in science fiction. It does appear as a prime motivator in S. Fowler Wright's novel *Deluge* (1928), where surviving males, after a worldwide inundation, battle for the possession of females. It probably contributed as much to the sale of *Brave New World* (1932) by Aldous Huxley as the author's philosophy, what with the encouragement of erotic play in children, the feelies replacing talking pictures and the popular pastime of Orgy Porgy. Even the philosophy of the novel was deeply concerned with sex as related to reproduction. Far more serious and philosophical, Olaf Stapledon's *Last and First Men* (1931) projected the history of mankind's future for hundreds of millions of years to come, and made a point of detailing the sexual changes and mores in the evolving race. Later, in *Sirius* (1944), Stapledon uses a tragic relationship, between a mutated dog of human-level intelligence and a girl, as a moving allegory.

However, even as early as 1930, hardcover books no longer represented the mainstream of science fiction, but were already on the fringe. The body of science fiction, the real area of development, was in such magazines as AMAZING STORIES, WONDER STORIES, and ASTOUNDING STORIES, in which everything was rigidly puritanical. The female of the species, when present at all, was usually a professor's daughter whose prime function was to be captured by and be rescued from some bug-eyed monster. Some psychologists have tried to read sexual implications into that plot device, but it is probable the readers were more correct than naive when they assumed that the beast was hungry.

Among the rare and "racy" moments that diligent research might uncover was an episode in *Via the Hewitt Ray* by a woman author, M. F. Rupert, published in the spring, 1930, SCIENCE WONDER QUARTERLY. A ray takes Lucille Hewitt, daughter of its inventor, into the fourth dimension. There, the dominant civilization is entirely female, except for a few males permitted to live for breeding purposes. A little questioning, however, reveals to Miss Hewitt the scandalous fact that "the males whose intelligence average was below our mental standard but who had physical beauty were made sterile by a special process and housed on the thirteenth tier."

"But you don't need these sterile men," Lucille Hewitt points out. "Why do you keep them?"

"We changed a lot of things," she is candidly told, "but we were unable, without danger to the future of our race, to change the fundamentals of natural instincts. When we women have borne two children to the race we are not allowed to reproduce a third time. Nevertheless the old biological urge returns and then we find use for the sterile male."

"But that is downright immoral," Lucille objects.

Her guide refuses to be trapped in a discussion on morality and finally puts her down with the reply: "Well, to you, with your present standard of morals it isn't right, but to us it is a highly efficient manner of settling our difficulties."

There were no repercussions from SCIENCE WONDER QUARTERLY readers to that "salacious" exchange, possibly because it comprised only a few paragraphs in an issue that otherwise lived up to the highest standards of Fred Fearnot.

The renamed WONDER STORIES QUARTERLY didn't get away with a "zippy" approach a second time, when it published a gay satiric frolic by Don M. Lemon, *The Scarlet Planet*, in the Winter, 1931, number. Thousands of girls inhabit a scarlet planet on which an earth ship lands, and thousands more rest in underground vaults in suspended animation. Some of them are blood-sucking vampires, others half-snake and half-women manufacturing a narcotic gas from the evaporation of their tears. The earthmen don't care; they romp around the world with a leer in their eyes and some very obvious banter on their lips. Despite the fact that they make honest women out of two of the girls at the end of the novel, the readers didn't take to men who *thought* that way. Don M. Lemon had contributed fantasies to periodicals like ALL-STORY MAGAZINE since 1905, but this was to be his first and last appearance in a science-fiction publication.

Apart from a few test-tube babies, the magazines steered remarkably clear of sex until the entrance of MARVEL SCIENCE STORIES, with its first number dated August, 1938. The editor, Robert O. Erisman, gave the field one of the finest underground civilization novels of all time, *Survival* by Arthur J. Burks, but he also had decided that the opportunity was present for a bit of titillation. Henry Kuttner, who was eventually to become a major modern shaper of science fiction, had submitted several action potboilers. Erisman told him he would take them if some risque passages, in the manner of HORROR TALES and TERROR TALES, which mixed sex and sadism, were interpolated. Kuttner revised to this formula four stories under his own and pen names in the first two issues. The howls of protest were such that all sex was dropped with the third issue of the magazine and the name of Henry Kuttner was so discredited in science fiction that it took him five years to reestablish his standing, and then under pen names.

When the competition of a flood of new science-fiction magazines in 1939 put MARVEL SCIENCE STORIES into financial trouble, it changed its name to MARVEL TALES with the December, 1939, issue and switched to a straight formula of sadism and sex. Again the policy lasted only two issues, published six months apart, and the magazine altered its title to MARVEL STORIES and a "no funny business" policy with its November, 1940, issue.

There were those who felt that the ban on sex was wrong. Writing in the December, 1945, FANTASY TIMES, Thomas S. Gardner, Ph.D., said: "Sex should be incorporated into science fiction as a standard life pattern and treated from all phases just as political systems are discussed. . . . But just mention sex and one has not only a figurative fight but a literal fight on his hands. Sex is very, very tabu, and can cause the most violent disagreements possible. Just why that is so is hard to understand."

G. Legman, erotica authority, presented his theory. "The reason for this (omission of sex from science fiction) is neither due to oversight nor external censorship, but the fact that the largest percentage of the audience for the *echt*-pulp science-fiction literature is composed of adolescent boys (who continue reading it even after they are grown up), who are terrified of women, sex, and pubic hair."

The foregoing might explain the policy that kept sex out of science fiction, but it fails to explain the absolute rejection of such material until Philip José Farmer's *The Lovers*. The answer most probably is that science fiction is a literature of ideas. The people who read it are entertained and even find escape through mental stimulation. Sex, vulgar or artistic, is available to them in countless forms if they wish it, but the type of intellectual speculation they enjoy is presented only in science fiction.

Farmer's stories were scientifically based on biology which happened to involve sex. The stories could not have been written without the sexual elements. Not only was the sex integral to the story, but the concepts were entirely new. Because the presentation of thought-provoking speculation, sex or otherwise, is a legitimate function of science fiction, Farmer succeeded. In doing so, he established a precedent and thereby became one of the prime movers of modern science fiction.

The author of *The Lovers* was christened Philip José Farmer after his birth, January 26, 1918, in North Terre Haute, Indiana. The "Jose" was the first name of his father's mother and the change to "José" was made by Philip himself, who resented being labeled for a woman and correctly decided it would lend color to the drabness of his last name, Farmer. Actually, his father was born George Park, but he adopted the last name of a relative who raised him. The father was an electrical power engineer by profession, a practicing Christian Scientist of Irish, English, and Dutch extraction. The mother, Lucille Theodora Jackson, was of German, Cherokee, Scotch and English background and became a Christian Scientist after marriage.

One of five children, Philip had a happy and normal childhood. Even during the Depression, the family was adequately fed, clothed, and housed. His problem was that, despite participation in high school dramatics and the fact that he was outstanding at football, track, and the broad jump, Philip suffered from a distinct inferiority complex and an extrarigid puritanical streak.

His spare time was heavily occupied with reading. Already Edgar Rice Burroughs, H. Rider Haggard, A. Conan Doyle, Jules Verne, and Carl H. Claudy were at the top of his list, and when he spotted the first (June, 1929) issue of SCIENCE WONDER STORIES it was as if Diogenes had found a reason to blow out his lamp.

His first job, in 1935 and 1936, was summer work as a ground man for Illinois Central Power and Light, Peoria, where his father was employed as engineer and supervisor.

He tried attending Bradley College during 1936-37 and then dropped out for full-time work as a ground man. He re-entered Bradley in 1940, and there he met Bette Virginia Andre, then a freshman. They were married the spring of 1941. A first child, Philip Laird, was born in 1942 and a second, Kristen, in 1945. To support his family, he worked eleven straight years from mid-1940 as a laborer, billet-chopper, and inspector for Keystone Steel & Wire, Barton-ville, Illinois. It took him until 1950, attending nights, to secure his B.A. in English from Bradley.

Farmer had written imaginatively and at length since the fifth grade. His early efforts were in the heroic tradition, placed in the eras of the Romans and the Vikings with an occasional venture in the African and Malayan Jungles. Farmer wrote and had rejected by ASTOUNDING SCIENCE-FICTION two short stories highly imitative of Stanley G. Weinbaum. A science-fiction novel had been returned from ARGOSY with a polite letter. Controversial stories submitted to the SATURDAY EVENING POST and GOOD HOUSEKEEPING were "hurled back."

Nevertheless, the first tale was a good one. He had written a story called *O'Brien and Obrenov*, in which American and Russian soldiers jointly occupy a German town. They draw a chalk mark through the center of it separating zones of influence. A Nazi war criminal they flush out, when subdued, is flat on his back across the division line. He is held supine for days while O'Brien and Obrenov, the American and Russian commanders, negotiate over who is to claim him. The matter is solved when a statue of Goethe, with a sword in his hand, is pushed over, splitting the prisoner's head open.

The SATURDAY EVENING POST offered to buy the story if a drunk scene were excised. Farmer refused and sent it to ARGOSY. They didn't want it, but passed it on to their companion magazine, ADVENTURE, where it was purchased by editor Kenneth White and run in the March, 1946, number. Two more tries at ADVENTURE were refused. Farmer decided he just didn't have it and went back to working hard in the steel mill days and reading omnivorously nights.

One evening in 1951, something in a book on biology he was going through reminded him of another volume he had recently read on ant parasites. He vividly recalled the use of the subject matter in Bob Olsen's *The Ant with a Human Soul* (in AMAZING STORIES QUARTERLY for Spring-Summer, 1932). He began to amplify possibilities and the next he knew he was immersed in writing the first draft of *The Lovers*. The final version was turned down by John Campbell at ASTOUNDING SCIENCE-FICTION as "nauseating." H. L. Gold of GALAXY SCIENCE FICTION sent it back and later offered divers justifications, including the fear that the story supposition of the rise of Israel to world power and the springing up of a new religion led by a half-Jewish character might be misunderstood. He also felt the story should have been rewritten in the present with the lalitha as historical influences on earth.

When the story was sent to STARTLING STORIES, it was first read by assistant editor Jerome Bixby, a well known author in his own right, who enthusiastically recommended it to Sam Mines, the editor, and science-fiction history was in the making.

A man with a T-bone steak on his mind is not likely to be distracted by the offer of crepes suzettes, no matter how tasty. So it was that Farmer's next story, a short titled *Sail On! Sail On!*, was dismissed by readers as an appetizer rather than heartier fare.

That was a mistake.

Sail On! Sail On! is a story of parallel worlds, where Ptolemy is right. Where Roger Bacon is encouraged by the Church and begins an age of invention including electricity, radio, and the electric light. Where Columbus is turned down by Queen Isabella of Spain and sent out by the Church instead. Where frantic messages from outer space are decoded too late to prevent the ships from sailing off the edge of the earth.

Sail On! Sail On! is a classic, not merely because of its clever ending, but because in plan and execution it is no less than brilliant. Few who have read the story are likely to forget the punch line: "They had run out of horizon."

The lack of response did not discourage Farmer. The readers' columns of STARTLING STORIES were still full of letters of comment on *The Lovers,* most of them highly laudatory. Shasta Publishers, a Chicago firm specializing in science fiction, had contracted to put *The Lovers* out in book form. Hugo Gernsback, who had returned to science-fiction publishing with SCIENCE-FICTION PLUS, a slick-paper, large-size magazine, solicited stories from the new sensation. Farmer was feeling no pain.

On rush order Farmer turned out a novelette for SCIENCE-FICTION PLUS called *The Bite of the Asp,* in which the protagonist is injected with a protein molecule which causes his body to expel matter that arouses an unreasoning fear in any living creature approaching too closely. Hastily written, the story required rewriting. When finally published as *The Biological Revolt* in the first issue of SCIENCE-FICTION PLUS, March, 1953, the work was badly mangled editorially. Despite this, it won an overwhelming first place in readers' preference from a return of 2,000 return-postage cards bound into the magazine.

The anger Farmer felt at the published version of *The Biological Revolt* was quickly dissipated by the reader reaction to his novelette, *Mother,* which appeared at almost the same time in the April, 1953, THRILLING WONDER STORIES. In many ways this story was even better than *The Lovers.* From reading a criticism of Freud, Farmer had conceived of a plot involving a literal return to the womb. The "womb," in this case, is a tremendous otherworldly female, outwardly resembling a rock-encrusted hill, forever stationary, and able to reproduce only by attracting roving beasts with blasts of appropriate mating scents. Any moving creature that gets close is seized and dragged into a gigantic womb. When the trapped animal attempts to claw its way out of a prison of flesh and muscle, the irritation it produces on the walls provides the stimulus for conception. Having performed its function, it is then digested.

Mother is the story of an earthman, always dependent on his mother, who is thus trapped by one of the organisms, communicates with the organism that has captured him, and then makes the gigantic womb his permanent home.

The announcement that *Moth and Rust,* a sequel to *The Lovers,* would appear in the June, 1953, STARTLING STORIES was big news in the science-fiction world. The story, however, substantially longer than *The Lovers,* received only a lukewarm reception. It was not a sequel at all. The only points of similarity were that it took place in the earth culture that had made contact with the Wogs and the lalitha. Actually, it is a fast-moving cloak-and-dagger novel of the future, comparable in theme to *1984.* Isolating and outlining the nature of the sex in the story would suggest pornography, but in context it must have proved rather disappointing to those who read the novel for kicks. Religion rather than sex is the major story ingredient. Farmer explores the rise and nature of hypothetical new religions of the future with the same scientific objectivity with which he previously outlined the sex life of aliens. His sex stories are no more off-color than his religious prognostications are blasphemous, which is not at all. This was particularly true of his handling of *Strange Compulsion* (SCIENCE-FICTION PLUS, October, 1953) in which the theme of possible involuntary incest brought about through parasite infestation was handled so clinically that it almost slowed the story to a stop.

By the time of the 11th Annual World Science Fiction Convention in Philadelphia, September 6, 1953, Philip José Farmer seemed to be riding on the crest of a wave. He was presented with the first of the series of awards later to become known as Hugos as the best new science-fiction author of 1952. Appropriately enough, the subject of his talk that day was "Science Fiction and the Kinsey Report."

STARTLING STORIES had announced that it was going to

run its first serial novel ever, an 80,000-worder by Farmer entitled *A Beast of the Fields*. The story was paid for but never published, because STARTLING STORIES had become a bi-monthly. The action takes place fifty years hence on a planet around a nearby star. "The hero is a descendant of one of the members of the so-called Lost Colony of Roanoke, Virginia, having been forcibly removed from North America, along with the baby Virginia Dare, and transplanted to the far-off planet," according to the author's summary.

The most dramatic event of the year for Farmer proved to be a contest sponsored by Shasta Publishers, offering $1,000 for the best new novel submitted, plus $3,000 for paperback rights from Pocket Books, Inc. Farmer spent every working hour for thirty days producing a 100,000-word novel, *I Owe for the Flesh*. The plot dealt with all of humanity being resurrected along the banks of a river ten million miles long on a faraway planet, with Sir Richard Francis Burton brought to life as the major character.

Sent in just under the wire, *I Owe for the Flesh* won the contest, beating out, among others, *The Power* by Frank M. Robinson, which since has become, financially, one of the most successful contemporary science-fiction novels. Ecstatic, Farmer left Peoria for Chicago to be photographed with the top men of Shasta and the vice president of Pocket Books, Inc.

In the early flush of accomplishment, he threw up his job at Keystone Steel & Wire for full-time writing. He secured an agent to help him sell to the big-time markets, and when he sold *Queen of the Deep* to ARGOSY (March, 1954), concerning a robot Russian submarine which captures an American and then is outdone in a game of wits, man against machine, it appeared that he was really on his way. This story is better known as *Son*, under which title it appeared in the 1960 Ballantine Books collection of Farmer's stories, *Strange Relations*.

Undeterred by a number of rejections, he made the pages of THE MAGAZINE OF FANTASY AND SCIENCE FICTION with

Attitudes, the first of a series of tales about a space priest named Father John Carmody, who was to become a popular character.

But then Shasta asserted Pocket Books was not satisfied with *I Owe for the Flesh* and had requested a revision. This done, a second rewriting was asked for. Because of the novel's length, months passed by and no money came in. Payments on the mortgage fell in arrears. Finally, Farmer had his agent get in touch with Pocket Books to find out just what it was they wanted. He learned that they had never asked for any rewriting, that they had sent their $3,000 through some time back and were waiting for hard-cover publication. Full payment never came through and the book was never published because Shasta foundered. Farmer lost his house, his wife became ill, and, in desperation, he secured a job with a local dairy. His literary career seemed to have blown up in his face. Depressed, he ceased writing. Stories continued to appear through 1954, but they had been previously written.

Of special interest was a long novelette, *Rastignac the Devil,* which was published in the May, 1954, issue of Leo Margulies' new magazine, FANTASTIC UNIVERSE. Actually this story was related to *The Lovers*, for the protagonist, Rastignac, will eventually become the sire of Jeannette, the unfortunate lalitha who died for the love of earthman Yarrow. Like *More Than Human*, by Theodore Sturgeon, it explores the area of gestalt relationships, in this case made possible by "skins," living organisms voluntarily worn by the inhabitants of the planet New Gaul which keep them attuned to other wearers and prick them like a physical conscience when they do wrong.

There is a wealth of fine ideas in this story, including a philosophical justification for a cult of violence (as opposed to Gandhian nonviolence) to counter the conditioning leading to the enslavement by the "skins." Here, Farmer's omnipresent sense of humor, which grimaces in even the most solemn of his efforts, plays him false. *Rastignac the Devil* degenerates into a satiric farce where the "ancient secret" of using alcohol to get drunk renders the "skins" ineffective, and the obvious parody of Seabury Quinn's popular occult detective Jules de Grandin, with exclamations of *"Sacré Bleu!"* by clergyman Father Jules, makes it impossible to take the story seriously.

This same wild sense of humor came close to blasting Farmer's reputation in *Daughter* (THRILLING WONDER STORIES, Winter, 1945), a sequel to *Mother*. Expecting something equally fascinating and thought-provoking, readers were given a spoof of *Mother*, told in the vein of *The Three Little Pigs*. Actually, *Daughter* is extremely clever and good fun, but to readers approaching it without warning soon after reading *Mother* it was devastatingly disappointing.

Only a single story by Philip José Farmer appeared during 1955 and 1956 when he all but abandoned writing to nurse his economic wounds and regain the will to try again. That story was a not altogether successful novelette, *Father* (FANTASY AND SCIENCE FICTION, July, 1955), with a plot so ambitious that it must have been a prime factor in provoking Alfred Bester to comment: "Mr. Farmer has too much engine for his rear axle." The story concerned one gigantic "Man" who has fathered an entire planet's life forms and offers a Bishop, a friend of Father Carmody's, a chance to play temporary god while he is on a leave of absence. It is in this story that Father Carmody takes on character as a rather pious incarnation of Jack Williamson's Giles Habibula. How he got that way was revealed two years later in *The Night of the Light* (FANTASY AND SCIENCE FICTION, June, 1957).

A minor success was scored with the novel *The Green Odyssey*, published as an original paperback by Ballantine Books in June, 1957. The very humor which frequently misfired in Farmer's other works engagingly redeems the saga of an earthman, stranded on a far planet in a medieval stage of development, endeavoring to reach a space ship he learns has landed in a far country.

Perhaps it was L. Sprague de Camp's special wit that made Farmer so fond of that author for not only does *The Green*

Odyssey bear some relationship to the Krishna stories but *The Alley Man* (FANTASY AND SCIENCE FICTION, June, 1959) was unquestionably a different approach to de Camp's ideas in *The Gnarly Man*. It attempted a prolonged slice-of-life character sketch of a Neanderthal man who has survived to the present day. Basing the personality of his Neanderthal man on that of someone he actually knew, Farmer managed to write a successful character sketch, but it almost failed as a science-fiction story, predominantly because the fantasy element was so slight.

More positively, a short novel written under the title of *My Sister's Brother* and published as *Open to Me, My Sister* ranks with *The Lovers* and *Mother* as one of Farmer's best. It was rejected by Campbell with a comment to the effect that the physical descriptions and implications made him feel ill. Farmer's outline of the method of reproduction of a race of very humanlike Martians was enough to unsettle even unsqueamish stomachs. Still, unpleasantly or not, Farmer had something to say, and the rich, imaginative fabric he brocaded in presenting the Martian culture was the work of a master craftsman.

Robert Mills, editor of FANTASY AND SCIENCE FICTION, had first rejected the story. It was accepted by Leo Margulies and under the title of *The Strange Birth* was actually set in type for the June, 1959, SATELLITE SCIENCE FICTION, with three illustrations by John Giunta. The magazine was killed before any copies came from the presses, but several sets of page proofs were run off and exist as collector's items. Mills changed his mind about the story and summoned the courage to publish it as *Open to Me, My Sister* in the May, 1960, FANTASY AND SCIENCE FICTION.

Beyond its story quality, *Open to Me, My Sister* was the indication of Philip José Farmer's psychological recovery from his bitter disappointments. His unique talent was not to be lost to the field.

Not that smooth sailing lay ahead. FANTASY AND SCIENCE FICTION promptly rejected a novelette titled *The Screaming*

Goddess. Horace L. Gold, editor of GALAXY MAGAZINE, asked Farmer to expand the story into a novel for Beacon Books, who, in 1960, were publishing "Galaxy Novels," a series with a sexy slant. *Flesh,* the enlarged story, had the dubious distinction of being the only novel that Beacon cut because it was too hot to publish as written.

The hero of *Flesh* is a significantly altered man, capable of prodigious virile prowess, who is utilized as a religious sex symbol in a procession from Washington, D.C., to Poughkeepsie, New York, where he is ultimately to be ceremonially slaughtered. Though Farmer's tongue was in his cheek, *Flesh,* accepted in the frame of its publisher's special requirements, must be recommended as a fine effort.

A seduction scene was written as an introduction to *Moth and Rust,* and it, too, enjoyed the special privilege of appearing in 1960 as a Galaxy/Beacon effort under the provocative title of *A Woman a Day.*

A try at a "mainstream" novel in *Fire and the Night* was issued as an original paperback by Regency Books, Chicago, in 1962. The story, concerning an affair between a married Negro woman and a white man, is a thoroughly professional and competent job.

At his worst, he can be undisciplined, verbose, in bad taste, and indiscriminate in his blend of literary influences. There are times when he works so hard at character development that he slows the story. When it comes to ideas he lacks a sense of proportion. On the one hand, he will nurse a pet notion through 20,000 precisely developed words as though it were the last note of originality he would ever strike. On the other hand, he will throw ideas like a boxer whose every punch is a haymaker.

At his best, he ranks at the very top of the writers to emerge in science fiction during the decade of the fifties. No single new author of that era approaches him in strength, originality, and fecundity of ideas. Few authors in the history of the field match his ability to exploit the implications of imaginative concepts. His immense respect for logical extrapolation dates back to Hugo Gernsback, and because of this most of his stories breathe the "sense of wonder." When not rushed, he is topped only by Theodore Sturgeon and Richard Matheson in adaptability of style or word pattern to fit a special situation. Lack of racial bias in his work extends to his writing techniques, which incorporate much of what is good from both new and old science fiction and from the literary world outside.

Despite the spontaneous acclaim accorded some of his works, Philip José Farmer is still underrated. This is the result of a tendency to credit his reputation to sensationalism and from the appearance of a sizable portion of his fiction in secondary and lightly held markets.

Farmer is much more than a taboo breaker. Sex is not his only topic. As much, if not more, of his writing centers around religion. In a field as sensitive to sex and as careful of avoiding religious offense as science fiction, the merchandising potential of his subject matter is self-limiting. This should not be permitted to disguise the fact that he is a storyteller of high artistry, and at least a few of his works have an air of permanence about them.

23

STARBURST

There is no substitute for hindsight in literary appraisal. Most of the authors evaluated in this book are still in active production. Time may bring either greater stature or diminution of popularity, and there is much to be said for both the inaugurators and the popularizers. Edgar Allan Poe crystallized the notion of the extraordinary deductive sleuth with C. Auguste Dupin, but Sherlock Holmes is no less a classic because A. Conan Doyle built upon an established formula.

There are several writers who have made contributions to the art of science fiction notable enough to be acknowledged, but who, with one outstanding exception, have not as yet influenced or had time to influence the direction of the literature. The exception is the Englishman Clive Staples Lewis. Until the age of 31 an acknowledged atheist, Lewis swung to the extreme of Christian fundamentalism, believing that every reference in the Bible was literal truth; he was undeniably evangelistic thereafter in proclaiming the faith.

He was a master stylist and so skilled a literary debater that he was frequently accused of bringing to an argument for religious belief as much guile, cunning, and adroitness as the devil's disciples brought into play against it. His acceptance as an important *modern* voice on theology is all the more surprising since he argued not just for the living God, but for the existence of the angelic hosts and the physical reality of the devil, and he proclaimed a fervent belief in the reality of the visions of Milton and Dante.

Those very notions he incorporated into science fiction with *Out of the Silent Planet* (The Bodley Head, London, 1938), a novel of the planet Mars, where live three alien races who have never fallen from grace, ruled over by an angel. Each of the planets has such an angel as its spiritual leader, all in communion with God, except Earth, which is the "occupied territory" of the Dark Angel and has not been heard from since the fall of man.

Earlier evangelistic interplanetary tales were usually such contrived absurdities as to relegate them to the limbo of curiosa. Lewis' avid affection for science fiction helped give the background of his novel a ring of authenticity, which, teamed with a superior literary style, brought his work serious attention.

Perelandra (Macmillan, 1944) possessed more inherent drama than *Out of the Silent Planet*, to which it was a sequel. This time Venus is the locale, and an earth scientist acts as a minion of Satan to compromise the Eve of this emerging world. The struggle between the scientist who would bring about her downfall and the philologist who would save her is on both an intellectual and a physical level.

The third novel of the trilogy, *That Hideous Strength* (John Lane, London, 1945), tells of the efforts of the Devil, through the auspices of The National Institute of Co-Ordinated Experiments, to regiment and reshape man to his own evil designs.

During a period when space travel was emerging as a

scientific and engineering probability, Lewis contributed to making science-fiction writers conscious of the story possibilities of the confrontation of the more rigid precepts of religion with the realities of the space age. Robert A. Heinlein showed very clearly the dangers to human progress of theocratic dictatorship, as did Fritz Leiber and Isaac Asimov. However, it was Ray Bradbury who, in *The Man* and *In This Sign,* provided the bridge between C. S. Lewis and the main body of science fiction in the magazines.

Religious themes have given two other authors special recognition in science fiction.

The first is James Blish, a workmanlike writer previously best known for his Oakies series, about independent self-propelled cities of the future which voyage from world to world in search of life-prolonging drugs (*Earthman, Come Home,* Putnam, 1955).

Possibly inspired by reading Bradbury's *In This Sign,* Blish had published (in IF, September, 1953) *A Case of Conscience,* telling of Lithia, a world fifty light years from Earth, where a Catholic priest encounters a race of intelligent reptiles who are apparently without original sin. His suspicion of a satanic trap of cosmic scope ends in irony when one of the idyllic monstrosities gives him, as a parting gift, a fertilized egg to take back to earth, with implications that it may be a new "Christ" in a scaly, grotesque guise.

The original short novel was extended for the paperback version of *A Case of Conscience* (Ballantine Books, 1958). The hatched reptile grows to maturity on Earth, where it acts dangerously against established moral precepts. When word is received that the alien is on his way back to his world of origin, the priest contemplates with horror that conceivably it will prove to be the proverbial "snake" which will bring about the "fall" of the Lithians. Desperately he resorts to exorcism via long-range television focused on Lithia to test its reality. When that world disolves in space, he is convinced that it was all a snare of the Devil from which he has saved mankind, even though the more logical explanation of the explosion of a fusion plant under construction is diagnosed as the actual cause.

A Case of Conscience won the Hugo as the best science-fiction novel of 1958. A short story on a religious theme by Arthur C. Clarke, *The Star* (INFINITY SCIENCE FICTION, November, 1955), had previously received a Hugo as the best short story of 1955.

Further confirming the interest of science-fiction readers in the adjustments of religion to events of the future was the award of a Hugo to Walter M. Miller, Jr., for *Canticle for Leibowitz* as the best novel of 1960. It was the second such honor he had received; the first was for the novelette *The Darfsteller,* published in 1954, an angry expostulation against the slow usurpation of man by machine. The awards had not been unexpected, for Miller had displayed exceptional promise ever since his first story appeared in the AMERICAN MERCURY in 1950. He remained the perennially promising author until three novelettes from THE MAGAZINE OF FANTASY AND SCIENCE FICTION were expanded into *A Canticle for Leibowitz* and published by Lippincott in 1959.

The critical reviews in and out of the science-fiction world were enthusiastic. The story revolved about the Albertian Order of St. Leibowitz, a flickering light in a world dissolved in darkness after atomic holocaust. St. Leibowitz, was an atomic scientist who had been canonized (after hanging) as the spiritual inspiration of a Catholic order. *A Canticle for Leibowitz* is very much an answer to Robert Heinlein's warning, *". . . If This Goes On,"* against the tyranny of religious dominance. The Church of *A Canticle for Leibowitz,* in every aspect of its dogma and ritual, is bent upon restoring through its rigmarole, the human race. Sense slowly crystallizing from the nonsense, the story proceeds with such high humor and fine characterization from era to era, that it is a joy to read. The ending fails to do justice to the superb narrative line. Perhaps it would have been enough if only, as the final spaceship of monks escapes from a war-blasted earth, the tottering figure of The Wandering Jew, who threads like the conscience of mankind through the entire history, made one final appearance to wave his basket hat in farewell. Despite this, *A Canticle for Leibowitz* remains the high point of those stories which may be designated as religious novels to appear in the science-fiction magazines.

One author who today might be rated with the giants of modern science fiction—with Heinlein, Sturgeon, Van Vogt, and Asimov—if only he had continued to write, is L. Ron Hubbard. Recruited from the adventure pulps where he had been a superior stylist capable of touches of human interest that evoked comparison with the great pulp air story writer George Bruce, he ably carried this talent into science fiction when recruited by John W. Campbell. His three-part novel *Final Blackout,* which began in the April, 1940, ASTOUNDING SCIENCE-FICTION, was a stunning achievement, certainly the most powerful and readable "warning" story that had appeared in science fiction to that date.

The progress of today's events has made much of *Final Blackout* prophetic—and just as much of it outdated. Hubbard, in his introduction to the hard cover edition (Hadley Pub. Co., Providence, Rhode Island, 1948), played down the story and stressed the prophecy. Time has highlighted the story and downgraded the prophecy. There have been many incisive predictions cast in fiction form in the past. *Final Blackout's* real strength rests in Hubbard's characterization of the superhuman leadership qualities of The Lieutenant, making it a masterpiece in a literature where good characterization is rare. As a story it grips the reader from the first sentence and will not release him until the author is through.

The readers waited for Hubbard to come back from the war. When he did his red hair had become pure white from suffering caused by injuries, and it was some years before its normal color began to return; it was years more before his writing seemed to assume its old magic. For a flash, in *To the Stars* (ASTOUNDING SCIENCE FICTION, March-April, 1950), in which a still youthful spaceman returns to earth and searches for the young girl he left behind, to find her, finally, an aged crone, he came near to writing the most effective human drama based upon the time dilatation effect.

One month later, ASTOUNDING SCIENCE FICTION, May, 1950, published his article *Dianetics, the Evolution of a Science,* and L. Ron Hubbard was launched on a new career which marked a point of no return as far as his science-fiction writing was concerned.

A major landmark in science fiction may be credited to Hal Clement, pen name of Harry Clement Stubbs, a New England science teacher who reflects his specialty in his writing. In *Mission of Gravity* (ASTOUNDING SCIENCE FICTION, April to July, 1953), a novel dealing with the problems or recovering recorded information from a rocket probe grounded on a planet with nearly 700 times the gravitational pull of the earth, he wrote what is generally regarded as the epic of the scientific problem story in science fiction.

As a solution for his problem he worked out the biological attributes for an alien race capable of living on this world and involved them in supplying the muscle for the recovery problem. To add to the interest, a good portion of the story is told from the viewpoint of the aliens.

Previously Clement had distinguished himself with a cleverly fabricated interplanetary detective story, *Needle,* with both the hunted and the hunter aliens, serialized in ASTOUNDING SCIENCE FICTION, May and June, 1949.

There is a tendency to regard the format of *Mission of Gravity* and the style of its author, Hal Clement, as a throwback to the earlier days of science fiction, when Hugo Gernsback set policy and heavy science was more in the vogue. The implication is present that if the old science fiction had consistently produced material as provocative as *Mission of Gravity,* modern readers and critics would display more tolerance toward science fiction's pioneers. Actually this type of story is a manifestation of science fiction's modern development.

In truth, the popularizer of the scientific problem story was actually Ross Rocklynne in a series of stories about an interplanetary policeman, Lt. Jack Colbie, who pursues criminal Edward Deverel in and out of a number of cosmic traps, beginning with the problem of getting out of the interior of a hollow planet in *At the Center of Gravity* (AS-TOUNDING STORIES, June, 1936), and ending with the problem of escaping from the frictionless concave mirror on a newly discovered planet in *The Men and the Mirror* (AS-TOUNDING SCIENCE-FICTION, July, 1939).

Ross Rocklynne was also a successful exponent of telling the story from the viewpoint of the alien, as in his fantasy masterpiece of the intelligent spiral nebula "Darkness" who began his cosmic career in *Into the Darkness* (ASTOUNDING SCIENCE-FICTION, June, 1940).

Editor Campbell of ASTOUNDING SCIENCE-FICTION favored the scientific problem story, encouraging the radio engineer George O. Smith to present and solve a number of technical dilemmas in interplanetary communications with a group of stories beginning with *QRM—Interplanetary* (ASTOUNDING SCIENCE-FICTION, October, 1942), which were later collected as *Venus Equilateral* (Prime Press, 1947). Jack Williamson's contraterrene matter series, written under the pen name Will Stewart, were basically scientific problem stories.

An extremely capable author whose versatility has acted to minimize his reputation is Poul Anderson. He began writing in 1947 as an alternative to entering industry as a physicist. With the expanding science-fiction market he found little difficulty in selling all he could write, for he could write whatever the market demanded, and moreover he was able to do considerable work outside the field, in nonfiction, mystery, and historical sagas.

As the years passed and his skills sharpened, there were probably few authors in the field who did better financially.

There were many outstanding stories, scattered among a large body of work, but it was not until the appearance of *The High Crusade,* a novel serialized in ASTOUNDING SCIENCE FICTION*, July to September, 1960, that he began to come into his own. This novel tends to contradict the thesis advanced by Mark Twain in *A Connecticut Yankee in King Arthur's Court,* that a man possessed of modern science would necessarily have been at an advantage in an encounter with the ancients. Poul Anderson's view is that the noblemen and knights of fourteenth-century England may have been ignorant but they were not stupid. How they cope with the crew of a spaceship that lands in England during their period makes for a highly original and outstanding novel.

The year of *The High Crusade*'s appearance Anderson was beaten out for the Hugo by *A Canticle for Leibowitz,* but received the award for the best short story of the year for *The Longest Voyage* (ANALOG SCIENCE FACT & FICTION, December, 1960). For this, Anderson hypothesized a seafaring civilization, developed along the lines of the Norsemen, and their proposal to reactivate an old spaceship and their reasons for changing their minds. He again won the Hugo for a shorter work for *No Truce with Kings* (THE MAGAZINE OF FANTASY AND SCIENCE FICTION, June, 1963), a story that also incorporated elements of the action and philosophies of past cultures in the hackneyed setting of a post-nuclear-war America, reemerging and reuniting. Anderson's interest in using historical cultures as the background for his science fiction has given him the stature in the field that his previous diversity of effort did not bring him.

One of the most renowned teams in literary history was that of Erckmann-Chatrian, French authors of the past century, noted for an impressive list of novels and plays, as well as their excellent short science-fiction stories, including *The Inventor* and *Hans Schnap's Spy-Glass.* Few collaborations have proved as successful as that team, for, in most

---

* Later known as ANALOG SCIENCE FACT & FICTION.

partnerships, dissident elements tend to creep in and disrupt the harmony. In recent times, one noteworthy short-term collaboration was that of Frederik Pohl and Cyril Kornbluth in science fiction. Both had significant literary accomplishments to their credit, but their united effort in *Gravy Planet* (GALAXY SCIENCE FICTION, June to August, 1952), representing the America of the future as completely dominated by the advertising agencies, seemed to strike a responsive chord in readers and critics alike. It was in part due to the times, when "Madison Avenue" had become both a symbol and a theme on the American scene. The science-fiction format, an excellent medium for satire, was especially well adapted to exaggerating the long-range effects of advertising's influence. Elements of the baronial business arrangement of the future presented in *Gravy Planet* (published in hard cover and paperback as *The Space Merchants*), particularly the legalization of feuds, owes some debt to L. Sprague de Camp's *The Stolen Dormouse*.

It is claimed that the story was jointly plotted and then written in relays by Pohl and Kornbluth. At the time of the collaboration Kornbluth was by far the more prominent literary personality. He was born talent, displaying an advanced stylistic and storytelling instinct even in his early teens. With Frederik Pohl and Donald A. Wollheim, he was a member of The Futurian Literary Society in the late thirties, a group that had as one of its major tenets that its members assist one another to literary advancement. When both Wollheim and Pohl became editors of low-budget magazines, Kornbluth became one of their mainstays, contributing scores of stories under a variety of pen names to their various publications.

After active service as a machine gunner in Europe in World War II, Kornbluth did not return to science fiction until 1949, although he wrote and sold many detective stories. When he resumed writing for the science-fiction magazines, his short stories showed a snideness, an irreverence, a trace of a sneer, and a hint of blackness that clearly labeled them as coming from his typewriter. Blackness had frequently been Kornbluth's mood even as a teenager, though the cause of his bitterness was not readily apparent. It intensified when both of his children were born mentally retarded.

Collaborations with Judith Merril under the pen name Cyril Judd resulted in the novels *Mars Child* and *Gunner Cade,* which appeared in GALAXY SCIENCE FICTION (May to July, 1951) and ASTOUNDING SCIENCE FICTION (March to May, 1952) then quickly as books. When he teamed up with Fred Pohl, *Gravy Planet* followed quickly and reestablished him solidly.

Fred Pohl had collaborated with Kornbluth twelve years earlier when the two of them wrote stories for STIRRING SCIENCE STORIES and ASTONISHING STORIES, both now defunct, under the pen name S. D. Gottesman. Pohl was the first editor of the latter magazine, beginning in February, 1940, and also of a companion, SUPER SCIENCE STORIES from its first issue March, 1940. He contributed stories to the magazine under the pseudonym James MacCreigh.

Suave and urbane, Pohl was an effective businessman and he entered a literary agency after World War II, building an impressive roster of leading science-fiction authors whose careers he guided into the early fifties. The success of *Gravy Planet* encouraged him to continue in a series of further joint efforts with Kornbluth, which, while well-starred, did not again score as strongly as with *Gravy Planet.*

Most readers had credited Kornbluth as the big talent in the collaboration and presumed that Pohl would be ineffective on his own. Pohl had been in advertising agency work and had shown outstanding competence in putting together a number of science-fiction anthologies, the most impressive being a series of collections of original stories for Ballantine Books called *Star Science Fiction Stories.* Solo novelettes and short stories, predominantly for GALAXY SCIENCE FICTION, began to appear. The most revealing was *Tunnel Under the World* (GALAXY SCIENCE FICTION, January, 1955), in which researchers for advertising agencies have reproduced the brain patterns of an entire town of 21,000 people to market-research their techniques. Pohl's style in that story alternated between slick "savvy" and unabashed forthrightness. He wrote like a man who knew just what should be done and how to go about doing it. *Tunnel Under the World* strongly suggests that if Fred Pohl, with his own advertising background, did not indeed provide the plot framework for *Gravy Planet,* he certainly could have done so.

Cyril Kornbluth, in his other major books *Takeoff* (Doubleday, 1952), *Syndic* (Doubleday, 1953), and *Not This August* (Doubleday, 1955), employs overdone, even trite themes for his frameworks, and while he, like the Danes, may serve mashed potatoes with fringed edges, they remain mashed potatoes with no steak in sight. His novels tell of getting the first space rocket up; of a bizarre "utopian" future menaced by a gangster-operated culture; and of conquered Americans who overthrow the yoke of the conquering Russians.

Pohl was well on his way to greater recognition as a writer, especially of novels, when he was seduced by the challenge of editing GALAXY SCIENCE FICTION and its proliferation of companions (IF, WORLDS OF TOMORROW, and MAGABOOK) after H. L. Gold suffered an illness which made him unable to continue. This was something he had always wanted to do, and he did it well. It became rapidly apparent that he soon would have to make a choice between continuing as an editor or returning to writing, in either of which pursuits he could be a success.

There comes a time when a magazine's policy and an author's direction seem to coalesce, when a writer is discovered who in style and subject matter epitomizes everything a publication stands for. That happy situation occurred when H. L. Gold finally coaxed Alfred Bester into writing a novel published as *The Demolished Man,* which Gold triumphantly ran in GALAXY SCIENCE FICTION (January-

March, 1953). Bester was in no way a Gold discovery, having first appeared as the winner of an amateur story contest in THRILLING WONDER STORIES (April, 1939), with *The Broken Axiom,* but he had previously never rated even as high as an "also ran" in the roster. His climb from the ranks of pulp writers had led him into the anonymous oblivion but better-paid role of comic-strip continuity writer, then into radio, and finally into television. In television he did well enough so that science fiction was to him, at best, an avocation.

The world of *The Demolished Man* is run by a new elite, a guild of ESPers (telepathic mind readers, practitioners of Extra-Sensory Perception), whose involvement in business, psychiatry, crime detection, and other pursuits revolutionized society. The difficulties of planning, committing, and keeping secret a murder in such a world provide the essence of the plot. There is a great amount of ingenuity displayed in describing a semitelepathic society, but the wholly unfair advantage of a detective who can read minds inveighs against the effectiveness of *The Demolished Man* as a mystery story. Its impact rests principally upon the dazzling narrative technique of the author, whose ability to convey sight and sound, and to create special effects with words on the printed page, far transcends that of virtually all of his contemporaries. Laced through the entire fabric of the novel is an insight into the employment of psychoanalysis which gave the partially deserved designation to GALAXY SCIENCE FICTION as "the magazine of psychiatric fiction."

While Alfred Bester stylistically awed most of his fellow science-fiction writers, his view of himself was not as elevated. When *The Demolished Man* was issued in hardcover by Shasta Publishers, Chicago, in 1953, the biographical sketch on the book jacket stated: "Alfred Bester, the author of *The Demolished Man,* is a successful writer for radio and television. . . . He is married to a well-known radio and television actress." The same year, the early paragraphs of his book *"Who He?"* (Dial) seemed frankly autobiographical, reading: "I'm a scriptwriter by trade, specializing in mystery shows. I'm married to an actress. We're both of us second-raters in the entertainment business . . . mostly anonymous to the public, fairly well-known to our colleagues. Between us we make from ten to twenty thousand dollars a year, depending on the breaks. This is only fair money in our business.

"It seems like a fortune to our families, and we dazzle them with our glamour. . . . We realize that people want their friends to be glamorous, so we've stopped trying to avoid undeserved admiration."

The science-fiction world has, since 1953, understandably expected Bester at any moment to become the frontrunner of the field. One other novel, and a scattering of short stories that followed, neither advanced his standing nor diminished his promise. But to become the leading science-fiction writer is not a prize to which Bester can economically afford to aspire; he probably will remain an admired dilettante.

Before the Hugos became part of the science-fiction scene, the most respected presentations in the field were The International Fantasy Awards, originated by a group of British science-fiction fans in 1951 and presented annually (except for 1956) through 1957. The selections were made by a committee of science-fiction book reviewers for the leading magazines and newspapers and so excellent were their choices that there was rarely a murmur of protest. When Edgar Pangborn's *A Mirror for Observers* was selected as the best fantasy novel of 1954, it did raise questions because it had appeared only in book form (Doubleday), and few had read it. It beat out so illustrious a contender as *Mission of Gravity* by Hal Clement, but its choice was deserved. Two segments of a Martian culture who have lived secretly on earth for many centuries wage a battle for the mind of the youthful genius, Angelo Pontevecchio. In the process, the author carries on a running commentary concerning mankind and civilization, which, despite its pedestrian pace, proves utterly fascinating. This book, which could not enjoy wide appeal, reads like something written by a leisurely Olaf Stapledon with limited ambitions. It is, nevertheless, extremely rewarding.

Pangborn first came to the attention of the science-fiction world when his short story *Angel's Egg* appeared in the June, 1951, issue of GALAXY SCIENCE FICTION. His 1964 novel, *Davy,* received so widespread a positive reaction from science-fiction readers that it may eventually eclipse *A Mirror for Observers* as his chef-d'oeuvre. Here with more stress on adventure and less on philosophy, in a story of a post-atomic-war world, the elements of realism combine with fine characterization to redeem an overworked plot.

The original concept of the American paperback book was to offer the public a volume (for only 25 cents) that in hard covers might cost up to $5. For some time, paperback publishers would have little to do with originals, feeling, among other things, that this would destroy the bargain-basement image and put them in the class with the dime novels. As the years progressed, certain paperback publishers occasionally subsidized a very limited hard-cover edition and used the same plates for a paperback. Kurt Vonnegut, Jr., author of *The Sirens of Titan,* an original paperback published by Dell in 1959, helped break precedent by selling that novel for a subsequent hardcover edition.

Houghton Mifflin Co., Boston, picked up *The Sirens of Titan,* originally sold for 35 cents by Dell, and issued it in cloth binding at $3.50 in 1961. The novel rated it. A wildly imaginative extravaganza of the future, involving many of the planets of the solar system, it was in every sense an avant-garde fantasy. It may seem tiresome to the reader to have everything compared to something by Olaf Stapledon, but he is clearly the source of the plot embellishments of *The Sirens of Titan.* What belongs to Vonnegut is an air of flippancy, cynicism and irreverence, enough to give him an edge in novelty over many other hard-working writers.

Vonnegut possesses a better scientific background than most science-fiction authors, particularly in the areas of biochemistry and anthropology. His science fiction began to appear frequently in ʿCOLLIER'S in 1950 and was sometimes inept—as typified by *Thanasphere* (September 2, 1950), in which a rocket test pilot, 2,000 miles above the earth, finds the spirits of the dead revolving around like a legion of satellites—or strictly cornball—like *Epicac* (November 25, 1950), in which a computer falls in love with a girl. A first novel, *Player Piano* (1953), an anti Electronic Age Utopia was well received despite a lack of originality.

Vonnegut is excellent raw material unfortunate enough to get started in the better magazines instead of learning his trade in the pulps. He needs discipline, practice, and considerably less smugness. He increasingly strikes notes of freshness which promise much, but he doesn't often deliver. It would help him to know not only what concepts have been done to death, but also what it was that finished them off.

The great boom in science-fiction magazines that started in 1949, reaching its peak in 1953, provided a golden opportunity for new talent. A score of young science-fiction writers found they could sell almost everything they wrote as fast as they could write it. Some of them had little difficulty in selling forty or fifty stories a year. Among such recruits was Philip K. Dick, who prolifically filled the pages of science-fiction magazines, gaining more positive than negative reaction but no special recognition. That was the way it continued through 1962, when his novel *The Man in the High Castle* was issued by Putnam. It hypothesized a world in which the Berlin-Tokyo axis had won World War II, partitioned the United States and the world between them.

The idea had been done before by no less distinguished an author than William L. Shirer; LOOK (December 19, 1961) devoted 13 illustrated pages to his feature, *If Hitler Had Won World War II*. Shirer's effort was the framework upon which *The Man in the High Castle* was built, and Dick did a great deal with what he borrowed. Most of the story is set in the western United States, dominated by the Japanese through a white puppet government. The Japanese are humane, decent, and to a degree democratic. The Japanese craze for collecting such Americana as old comic books, election posters, and bottle caps lends a note of originality and authenticity to the work. The "Man" in the High Castle is an author who has written a book telling what would have happened if the United States had won the war. All these elements gave the novel a difference which helped win the Hugo as the best novel of 1962 and lifted Dick a substantial notch upward in general regard.

The "Worlds of If" theme had long been a popular one in science fiction and Dick's novel proved that it could produce fiction good enough to outrank the entire year's production. Working on what would have happened if the South had won the Civil War, an all-but-unknown author, Ward Moore, sprang to prominence with a single short novel, *Bring the Jubilee* (THE MAGAZINE OF FANTASY AND SCIENCE FICTION, November, 1952). Moore's previous novel, published by William Sloane Associates in 1947, told of a chemical that causes a special variety of grass to grow with such uncontrolled vigor that it crowds out the crops of the world. Told with broad catastrophic sweep, Moore's *Greener Than You Think* went all but unnoticed.

The resourceful inventiveness of *Bring the Jubilee,* projecting the possible difference in technology as well as politics of today's world if the South had won the war, helped win it recognition. A man living in that hypothetical world goes back in time to a pivotal action at the battle of Gettysburg, to deliberately swing the battle in favor of the North to secure what he feels must inevitably be a better future. To appreciate how exceptionally difficult was Moore's job and how fine his achievement, one need only compare it with a similar attempt made by MacKinlay Kantor in LOOK, November 22, 1960, called *If the South Had Won the Civil War.* Kantor, author of the Pulitzer Prize-winning novel *Andersonville,* displayed a lack of imagination and a paucity of convincing detail which stand in sharp contrast to the achievement that is *Bring the Jubilee.*

"The Worlds of If" theme was in vogue in the early sixties, for John Hersey, who used science fiction in 1960 in *The Child Buyer,* used it again in White Lotus (1965) to present a world in which atomic energy has never been invented, but in which elements of the American civilization of the 1930's still exist. Hersey is a reporter who writes directly and extremely well. Yet, in this "tale of an old shoe on a new foot," his parallel between the hypothetical world in which Occidentals are the inferior race in a world ruled by Orientals and the situation of the whites and Negroes of today is so exaggeratedly obvious and his situations so deliberately contrived that the book becomes an affront to the intelligence.

"The Story That Shocked the Editors" was what THE SATURDAY EVENING POST called *No Blade of Grass* by John Christopher as they began its serialization in their April 27, 1957, issue. "This, as my colleagues had warned me, was no mere adventure story," Ben Hibbs, the POST editor, wrote, "no epic with a happy ending, no pleasant escape to the world of let's pretend. This was a book unlike any THE SATURDAY EVENING POST had ever published—a story that for violence of deed, for horrible fascination, was unknown to our columns."

A virus attacks the basic sources of food supplies: the rices and grains. Once they are depleted, the entire structure of civilization collapses and the "law of the jungle" prevails. John Christopher tells the story of the shocking breakdown in morality of a small group in England, seeking to survive on their way to a valley haven. In the process, the meek become remorseless killers and these conscienceless killers almost emerge as heroes in the fight for survival.

On the strength of the POST's buildup, motion picture rights were sold for a figure alleged to be $80,000 and the author, John Christopher, was catapulted overnight into a position of literary prominence.

Untold was the fact that *No Blade of Grass* had been rejected by one-cent-a-word markets only weeks before it was taken by the POST. The theme was far too elementary for the regular science-fiction magazines.

Christopher Samuel Youd, the Englishman behind the pen name John Christopher, had gone through life with a position in the diamond-cutting industry, only infrequently selling a short story to some low-paying market. His major influence in style and method was another British author, John Wyndham, who had come to renown a few years earlier when COLLIER'S made a similar fuss over *The Day of the Triffids*. If anything, Christopher was even more conservative than Wyndham as he continued to try for that one big novel by taking elementary science-fiction themes to create an abnormal situation and throwing the weight of his narrative onto the reaction of human beings under stress. Among the novels that followed were *The Long Winter* (1962), in which a new ice age drives the whites into Africa for survival and they become the subservient race; *The Possessors* (1964), in which alien wills assume control of members of a Swiss chalet cut off by a snowslide; and *Sweeney's Island* (1964), built on the much-abused theme of civilized people reverting to their true natures on a deserted island, but this time on an island in which an atomic experiment has mutated the local vegetation and animals.

A single novel elevated ex-newspaperman and professional photographer Frank Herbert to a position of distinction among science-fiction writers and it was a novel placed in the world just beyond tomorrow. Science fiction had anticipated atomic submarines by employing the precise terminology as far back as Stanton A. Coblentz's *The Sunken World* (AMAZING STORIES QUARTERLY, Summer, 1928). Frank Herbert in his novel *Under Pressure* (ASTOUNDING SCIENCE FICTION, November, 1955 to January, 1956) extrapolates only modestly from the atomic fleet that we know today.

A four-man crew on an atomic submarine of the future, one of them a saboteur and another a psychologist intent upon ensuring the mental stability of the captain, set out to capture an undersea oil supply as part of the twenty-first-century war. The tensions and strains of their prolonged living cooped up together, accentuated by a number of brushes with death, lend a realism to the proposed situation that scored impressively with the readers.

Anyone who produces a truly outstanding literary work in any specific field is watched with care to see if he can do it again. Herbert made another bid with *Dune World* (ANALOG SCIENCE FACT & FICTION, December, 1963, to February, 1964), a novel graphically bringing to life the ecology of a world that was virtually bereft of moisture, of the precious spice melange that represents its major source of wealth, and of the structure of the society which rules it. This was followed by a massive sequel, *The Prophet of Dune* (ANALOG SCIENCE FACT & FICTION, January, to May, 1965) portraying the struggle for survival and dominance in this grim land. It may be said that, in the sense that the battle for intelligence over alien environment serves as a backdrop, the dune stories bear an affinity to Hal Clement's *Mission of Gravity*. However, the incorporation of the atmosphere of earth's medieval political and moral climate make the plot development almost traditional by modern standards. Further, the prominent use of psi phenomenon adds a note of conformity, which combined with the political climate, robs the effort of realism and transforms it into little more than a well-done adventurous romance.

EPILOGUE

Science fiction of the past quarter century has had a greater impact on world thinking than even most of its enthusiastic devotees claim. People of every nation with a high order of technology, particularly those behind the Iron Curtain, have read it with an intellectual avidity that goes far beyond the relative importance in the literary scene of its leading writers.

The bulk of this science fiction is the work of American writers, the contributors of the next largest segment being British. Science fiction is not carried abroad as part of a cultural exchange program. Officialdom usually does not even consider it in that light. Instead, it is imported by popular demand into Russia, Czechoslovakia, Poland, West Germany, France, Holland, Sweden, Denmark, Italy, Argentina, Mexico, and Japan. In all of these countries, and others besides, publishers turn out a stream of books and magazines containing science fiction, most of it reprints or translations of stories published in the United States and Great Britain.

Modern science fiction is a relatively sophisticated product, whose techniques have been polished continually in the United States for over fifty years. During that period we have had a number of specialized publications printing it in substantial quantity. British writers, because they share the same language, have been able to find a ready market in the United States and have been thus enabled to perfect their skills. Countries not having English as their national language developed no such pool of writers and when, after World War II, interest in science fiction began to grow, publishers found it easier and cheaper to buy and translate American authors than to encourage their own. Science-fiction magazines published abroad are usually franchised counterparts of American periodicals or sometimes are independent publications containing American stories bought separately and shuffled into a individual selection. So popular are American writers abroad that in Western Germany and Spain native science-fiction writers tend to adopt American pen names to gain readier acceptance.

The Russian's have been the one nation earnestly trying to upgrade their native science fiction. They have put back into print everything worthwhile from Konstantin Eduardovich Tsiolkovsky's 1895 anticipation of an earth satellite, *Dreams of Earth and Sky,* through party-line-oriented Professor Ivan Yefremov's *The Heart of the Serpent* (1959), an ideological reply to American writer Murray Leinster's *First Contact,* which describes the initial meeting of an earth space ship with that of an alien civilization. Soviet Russia, aware that American science fiction, for the most part aimed at a pulp market, is rarely written with political motivation, has been liberal in permitting a wide spectrum of it to be read and reprinted, because "science fiction helps one peep into the thought and life of Americans."

A recent anthology of American science fiction printed in the USSR was *Science Fiction Stories by American Writers,* edited by Alexander Kazantsev, a leading contemporary Soviet science-fiction writer. Among the selections were works of Robert A. Heinlein, Ray Bradbury, Murray Leinster, H. Beam Piper, and Tom Godwin.

A surprise speaker at the September 6, 1964, session of The 22nd World Science Fiction Convention in Oakland, California, was Josef Nesvadba, a Czechoslovakian psychiatrist, who is also the leading science-fiction writer of the country. Several of his stories have appeared in America in THE MAGAZINE OF FANTASY AND SCIENCE FICTION, and eleven of them have been collected under the title of *Vampires Ltd.* and printed in English in Prague. In his talk, he confirmed that American science-fiction authors were the most popular not only in Russia, but in Czechoslovakia and Poland as well. He brought with him a copy of a handsomely elaborate science-fiction anthology published in Czechoslovakia titled *Labyrint.* Of the twelve stories in the book, eleven are by modern American authors, among them Ray Bradbury, A. E. van Vogt, Robert A. Heinlein, Lewis Padgett (Henry Kuttner), Clifford D. Simak, Frank M. Robinson, and Robert Abernathy. The Iron Curtain countries do not have copyright agreements with the United States, and this anthology stands unique as the first from that part of the world actually to send American authors payment for republished stories.

Within recent years The Foreign Languages Publishing House in Moscow has translated many Russian science-fiction stories into English and made them available in the West. These include works by Konstantin Tsiolkovsky, Count Alexei Tolstoi, Alexander Belyaev, Ivan Yefremov, Alexander Kazantsev, Vladimir Obruchev, and Arkady and Boris Strugatsky, among others. Discounting stylistic inadequacies which are possibly attributable to translation, they are, by American standards, elementary in theme and overweighted with infusions of pro-Soviet propaganda.

One explanation of the simple concepts in Russian science fiction was offered by a Russian editor (who preferred to remain anonymous) interviewed at the Frankfort, Germany, Book Fair in 1963. *Gamma* (No. 3, 1964) reported that he said that Russians preferred the adventurous aspect of science fiction to its psychological and sociological manifestations. He spoke with nostalgia of Edgar Rice Burroughs to underscore his point. In response to the direct question: "Is American science fiction popular in the Soviet Union?" he replied, "Very popular. But even there the stories we like best are the ones that avoid political or sociological considerations."

Western Germany, where American science fiction has been received with especial enthusiasm (where today fan conventions are held), has seen scholarly approval of the trend in *Die Entdeckung Amerikas und die Sache der Weltraumliteratur* by G. Gunther (1952) and undisguised admiration in Dr. Martin Schwonke's *Vom Staatsroman zur Science Fiction* (1957).

The most telling proof of the acceptance of American science fiction is that the term "science fiction" has supplanted all other labels for the genre, not only in Germany but in all other foreign countries so well. So American-oriented are the world's science-fiction lovers that special editions of their fan magazines in German, French, Swedish, Japanese, and Spanish are translated by their *publishers* and sent to American enthusiasts, who thereby can stay in touch with world thinking on the subject. Interest in science fiction is rapidly becoming a more important link to friendship with the United States in many nations than elaborately planned intergovernmental cultural programs.

This mutual affinity resulting from science fiction was expressed most poetically by Takumi Shibano, editor of the International Edition of UCHUJIN, official organ of the Science Fiction Club of Tokyo: "We find innumerable particles of cosmic dust floating in the nothingness, when we turn our eyes to the universe. Some of them may be attracted by gravity to planets or stars and burn up to meteors; others may keep floating indefinitely. And some 'fortunate' ones among them may pull to each other and join together to be concentrated into a large heavenly body. Then it starts to shine brilliantly by itself in the darkness. . . . This is the process that symbolizes 'Uchujin' and its fandom."

The direction of science fiction remains indeterminate. The final chapter of this book must remain an open end. It is impossible to state that the era that we now regard as "modern" in science fiction, which came into full flower under the aegis of John W. Campbell in 1939 and the years that followed, has ended. If so, that something else which is gradually taking its place has not hardened into a definite form. The authors dealt with in this book are uncontestably the great names of today, but we do find that certain of the "run-of-the-mill" writers who broke in a decade or more ago are developing into late bloomers and are just now beginning to make their mark. New names are appearing regularly and rising to popularity. More chapters remain to be written. The fiction whose main concern has always been the shape of the future incontestably still has a future.

INDEX

Principal entries throughout are under the best-known name of an author, whether real or assumed, even though occasionally this requires referring a pseudonym to another pseudonym. Cross-references to the principal entries are in SMALL CAPITALS.